Alexander the Great

Alexander the Great

The Unique History of Quintus Curtius

Elizabeth Baynham

Ann Arbor
THE UNIVERSITY OF MICHIGAN PRESS

First paperback edition 2004
Copyright © by the University of Michigan 1998
All rights reserved
Published in the United States of America by
The University of Michigan Press
Manufactured in the United States of America
♾ Printed on acid-free paper

2007   2006   2005   2004   5   4   3

No part of this publication may be reproduced, stored in a retrieval system, or transmitted in any form or by any means, electronic, mechanical, or otherwise, without the written permission of the publisher.

A CIP catalog record for this book is available from the British Library.

Library of Congress Cataloging-in-Publication Data

Baynham, Elizabeth, 1958–
    Alexander the Great : the unique history of Quintus Curtius / Elizabeth Baynham.
      p.   cm.
    Includes bibliographical references (p.   ) and index.
    ISBN 0-472-10858-1 (acid-free paper)
    1. Alexander, the Great, 356–323 B.C.   2. Curtius Rufus, Quintus. Historia Alexandri Magni.   3. Greece—History—Macedonian Expansion, 359–323 B.C.—Historiography.   4. Generals—Greece—Biography.   5. Greece—Kings and rulers—Biography—History and criticism.   I. Title.
DF234   .B356   1998
938'.07'092—dc21
[B]   98-19713
                                                                                                        CIP

ISBN 0-472-03081-7

Collegae optimo atque amico

Acknowledgments

As a general principle, a book is not written completely in isolation, and there are many people, including other scholars, friends, and family, to whom I owe a special gratitude. This monograph on Quintus Curtius' *Historiae* is based on my doctoral dissertation, which was submitted to Victoria University of Wellington, New Zealand. Its evolution into a book has resulted in considerable development and rethinking of much of the original dissertation. However, I would like to thank Professor Godfrey Tanner and Mr. Terence Ryan of the University of Newcastle and my former supervisor Dr. Arthur Pomeroy of Wellington. Much of their guidance still remains within the current study.

A note of thanks belongs with Ray, who helped me during the earlier stages of the book's composition. My colleague Mr. Hugh Lindsay gave me a considerable amount of useful advice and allowed me to plunder his library at will; I am also grateful for the informed opinions of Dr. Tim Parkin, whom I have had occasion to consult on aspects of Greco-Roman social history. Dr. Edward Miller provided valuable assistance, and the Auchmuty Library's Interloans staff consistently answered my requests with professionalism and good humor. The University of Newcastle's Classics Department's secretary, Miss Donna Statham, deserves my heartiest expression of appreciation for her help and cheery support.

I am very grateful to Professors Nicholas Hammond and James Hamilton, both of whom read earlier drafts in toto and kindly offered many helpful comments. Recently, the ease of communication brought by the electronic post has allowed me to correspond with other well-known scholars. Professors John Yardley and John Atkinson generously supplied references and publications (sometimes advance copies). Within the same context, I especially thank Professor Waldemar Heckel, whose constructive advice, criticisms, and incisive observations helped clarify much of my argument in this book.

I am also glad to acknowledge the inspiration I have received from the multiple studies of Professor Brian Bosworth. His interest in my work has been a great stimulus, and his careful reading of my entire manuscript saved me from numerous errors. Moreover, his comments and suggestions have enriched this book's content: if I have not always accepted his advice, I am the poorer for it. As always, any remaining infelicities or flaws are my responsibility.

I have very much appreciated the courtesy of Dr. Ellen Bauerle and Christina Milton of the University of Michigan Press and their staff. Finally, and most importantly, my warmest appreciation is offered to those who, at various times and in different ways, helped bring this book to completion—especially to my parents, Derek and Lorna Miles, for giving me quiet but consistent encouragement.

Contents

Abbreviations xi

Chapter 1. Introduction 1

Chapter 2. "Roman" Curtius 15

Chapter 3. Quintus Curtius' Sources and
His Historical Methods 57

Chapter 4. *Fortuna* 101

Chapter 5. *Regnum* in the First Pentad:
Alexander and Darius 132

Chapter 6. *Regnum* in the Second Pentad:
Alexander, King, General, and Tyrant 165

Appendix: The Problem of Curtius'
Date and Identity 201

Bibliography 221

Index 227

Abbreviations

These abbreviations of the following authors and titles, which are frequently cited, have been adopted.

ALEXANDER HISTORIANS

Arrian — *Anabasis Alexandri* (unless otherwise stated). Trans. P.A. Brunt. In *History of Alexander and Indica*, vols. 1 and 2. Cambridge, Mass., 1976–83.

Curt. — Quintus Curtius
- Bardon — *Quinte-Curce, histoires.* Trans. H. Bardon. Paris, 1976.
- Mützell, Q. — *Curtii Rufi de Gestis Alexandri Magni Regis Macedonum.* Ed. J. Mützell. Berlin, 1841. Reprint, Hildesheim, 1976.
- Rolfe — *Quintus Curtius* Trans. J.C. Rolfe. 2 vols. Cambridge, Mass., 1946.

Diod. — Diodorus Siculus
- Welles — *Diodorus of Sicily.* Vol. 8. Trans. C.B. Welles. Cambridge, Mass., 1963.
- Goukowsky — *Diodore de Sicile: Livre XVII.* Trans. P. Goukowsky. Paris, 1976.

J. Justin. — *Epitoma Historiarum Phippicarum.* Ed. O. Seel. 2d ed. Stuttgart, 1972.

Metz Epit. — *Metz Epitome, Incerti Auctoris Epitoma Rerum Gestarum Alexandri Magni.* Ed. P.H. Thomas. Leipzig, 1965.

Plut. *Alex.* *Plutarch's Lives.* Trans. B. Perrin. Vol. 7. Cambridge, Mass., 1919.

MODERN STUDIES

Atkinson, *Curtius* i J.E. Atkinson. *A Commentary On Q. Curtius Rufus' Historiae Alexandri Magni Books 3 and 4.* Amsterdam, 1980.

Atkinson, *Curtius* ii J.E. Atkinson. *A Commentary On Q. Curtius Rufus' Historiae Alexandri Magni Books 5 to 7.2.* Amsterdam, 1994.

Berve H. Berve. *Das Alexanderreich auf prosopographischer Grundlage.* 2 vols. Munich, 1926.

Brunt, *Arrian* P.A. Brunt. *Arrian, History of Alexander, and Indica.* Vols. 1 and 2. Cambridge, Mass., 1976–83.

Bosworth, *CE* A.B. Bosworth. *Conquest and Empire.* Cambridge, 1988.

Bosworth, *FAA* A.B. Bosworth. *From Arrian to Alexander.* Oxford, 1988.

Bosworth, *HCA* A.B. Bosworth. *A Historical Commentary On Arrian's History of Alexander.* Vols. 1 and 2. Oxford, 1980–95.

Dosson S. Dosson. *Étude sur Quinte-Curce.* Paris, 1886.

Duff, *Silver Age* J.W. Duff. *A Literary History of Rome in the Silver Age.* London, 1927.

FGrH F. Jacoby. *Die Fragmente der griechischen Historiker.* Berlin and Leiden, 1923–.

Hamilton, *Plutarch* J.R. Hamilton. *Plutarch "Alexander": A Commentary.* Oxford, 1968.

Hammond, *Sources* N.G.L. Hammond. *Sources for Alexander the Great: An Analysis of*

	Plutarch's Life and Arrian's Anabasis Alexandrou. Cambridge, 1993.
Hammond, *THA*	N.G.L. Hammond. *Three Historians of Alexander the Great.* Cambridge, 1983.
Heckel, *Marshals*	Waldemar Heckel. *The Marshals of Alexander's Empire.* London, 1992.
Heckel and Yardley, *Justin*	Waldemar Heckel and J.C. Yardley. *Justin Epitome of the Philippic History of Pompeius Trogus Books 11–12: Alexander the Great.* Oxford, 1996.
McQueen	E.I. McQueen. "Quintus Curtius Rufus." In *Latin Biography*, ed. T.A. Dorey. London, 1967.
Norden, *Kunstprosa*	E. Norden. *Die Antike Kunstprosa.* 2 vols. Leipzig, 1915.
OLD	Oxford Latin Dictionary.
Pearson, *LHA*	L. Pearson. *The Lost Histories of Alexander the Great.* New York, 1960.
Pédech, *Historiens*	P. Pédech. *Historiens compagnons d'Alexandre.* Paris, 1984.
Pomeroy, *Appropriate Comment*	Arthur J. Pomeroy. *The Appropriate Comment: Death Notices in the Ancient Historians.* Frankfurt am Main, 1991.
Porod	Robert Porod. "Der Literat Curtius: Tradition und Neugestaltung: zur Frage der Eigenständigkeit des Schriftstellers Curtius." Diss. der Karl-Franzens-Universität Graz, 1987.
RE	*Realencyclopädie der Classischen Altertumswissenschaft.* Ed. A. Pauly, G. Wissowa, W. Kroll, K. Mittelhaus, and K. Ziegler. Stuttgart, 1893–1980.

Rodriguez, *Aspectos de Q. Curtius Rufus* — J. Costas Rodriguez. "Aspectos de Q. Curtius Rufus estudio semantico-lexicologico una contribucion al problema de su datacion." Diss. Salamanca, 1975.

Rutz — Werner v. Rutz. "Zur Erzählungskunst des Q. Curtius Rufus." *Aufstieg und Niedergang der Romischen Welt* 32, no. 4 (1986): 2329–57.

Seibert — J. Seibert. *Alexander der Grosse.* Erträge der Forschung, no. 10. Darmstadt, 1972.

Walsh, *Livy* — P.G. Walsh. *Livy, His Historical Aims and Methods.* Cambridge, 1961.

Woodman, *Rhetoric* — A.J. Woodman. *Rhetoric in Classical Historiography.* London, 1989.

All translations are by the author unless otherwise stated.

Chapter 1

Introduction

As the author of a work in Latin usually known as the *Historiae Alexandri Magni Macedonis,* Quintus Curtius Rufus presents a number of unique and perplexing issues. The first two books of ten have been lost and with them perhaps a preface, in which the historian may have stated any autobiographical details as well as indications of his method and purpose. We simply do not know who Quintus Curtius was or when he wrote his history, although these questions have received a considerable amount of scholarly attention. To add to the problems, the work as a whole is frequently beset by textual uncertainties that occasionally cause great difficulties in interpreting the author's emphasis.[1]

Textual cruxes in Curtius (as with other ancient authors) generate a separate field of study, with proposed emendations often causing a clash of interests between text critics and historians.[2] Moreover, books 5, 6, and 10 are marred by substantial lacunae. These breaks in the text not only result in the loss of historical information but also undermine the author's literary continuity.

No ancient commentator, critic, or historian refers to Curtius' work; in contrast, the accounts of Trogus, Plutarch, Arrian, and Diodorus Siculus, fellow extant authors on Alexander, were quoted by other writers in antiquity.[3] The career and works of Arrian provide a pointed contrast

---

1. For example, see Curt. 6.11.9–11, 6.11.40; see also A.B. Bosworth, *CPh* 78 (1983): 150.
2. See J.E. Atkinson, *ANRW* II.34.4 (1997): 3447–83 section 2. I am grateful to Professor Atkinson for sending me an advance draft of his submission.
3. On Curtius' lack of impact in antiquity, see E. Schwartz, *RE* 4 (1901): 1891. On Trogus' reputation, see J. praef. 1–6; O. Seel attempted a reconstruction of Trogus based on Justin's *Epitome* and what he determined were echoes, in *Pompei Trogi Fragmenta* (Leipzig, 1956). See esp. 1–3 for his collection of *testimonia*. R. Syme, *Historia* 37 (1988): 364–65, argues Trogus' history had fallen into obscurity by the fourth century A.D. Arrian was commended by Lucian and Photius; see Bosworth, *HCA,* 1:36–38; *FAA,* 24 ff. On Diodorus' fame, see Pliny *NH* praef. 25; see also Jane Hornblower, *Hieronymus of Cardia,* 18 f.

with the unknown Curtius. The former was a senator, active and successful in the imperial service, who during his life was both suffect consul at Rome and eponymous archon at Athens. He was also a prolific author, with much of his work extant today.[4] Indeed, in the so-called second preface (1.12.5) of his *Anabasis,* Arrian claims that his established expertise as a man of letters makes him more worthy than other authors to write the definitive history of Alexander.[5] We know a lot about Arrian; Curtius is a far more obscure figure to retrieve.

Given the apparent silence in both the imperial period and late antiquity on Curtius' history, the survival of the text is a mystery. Yet its famous topic would have continued to offer undeniable appeal in later eras. For example, the Alexander romances were enormously popular in the Middle Ages, and Alexander the Great remained a favorite subject for the court artists of powerful Italian and French aristocratic and royal families during the Renaissance and in the sixteenth and seventeenth centuries.[6]

The sixteenth-century Italian artist Paolo Veronese was possibly inspired by various historical traditions, including that of Curtius, to paint the encounter between the victorious Alexander and Darius' captive family after the Battle of Issus. The same scene was also painted by Charles Le Brun, court painter and interior decorator of Versailles during the reign of Louis XIV. Le Brun also depicted Alexander's entry into Babylon, and Curtius is the only historian who describes this episode in any detail.[7]

There are other probable reasons for the history's durability. Curtius' *Historiae* has been preserved in a considerable number of codices—in all, some 123, which derive from an incomplete archetype dating from the ninth century A.D. In modern times, about five manuscripts have been

---

4. Arrian's career and works have received considerable treatment in recent years; see chap. 3, 67–68.

5. Cf. Arrian praef. 3. See Bosworth, *FAA,* 34 n. 89; for other bibliographical references on Arrian's prefaces, see my chap. 3.

6. On the distribution of the Alexander romance in the Middle Ages, see Cary, *The Medieval Alexander,* and my chap. 3. For Curtius' influence on the medieval epics, see Cary, loc. cit., 16 f.; H. Bardon, *LEC* 15 (1947): 11 f.

7. For Paolo Veronese, see B. Berenson, *The Italian Painters of the Renaissance* (London, 1968). On Charles Le Brun, see M. Gareau, *Charles Le Brun* (New York, 1992); R. Hartle, "The Image of Alexander the Great in Seventeenth-Century France," in *Ancient Macedonia* (Thessaloníki, 1970), 387–406, and "Le Brun's *Histoire d'Alexandre* and Racine's *Alexandre le Grand,*" *Romantic Review* 48 (1957): 90–103.

considered the best; Edmund Hedicke's original (1867) text of Curtius, perhaps one of the most influential in terms of shaping twentieth-century editions, was based on this selection of five manuscripts, which includes the Bernensis (B), Florentinus (F), Leidensis (L), Parisinus (P), and Vossianus (V) codices. In turn, these codices were divided into two classes: the Parisinus codex, 5716, which features some significant differences, forms a valuable balance to the four other codices in the group.[8]

Over the last millennium, Curtius' reputation has oscillated sharply. He appears to have been greatly admired during the Middle Ages and in the Renaissance. Between 1184 and 1187, Gautier de Chatillon composed a popular Latin epic, *Alexandreis,* based on Curtius, which told the story of Alexander in the spirit of the *Aeneid.* In 1230 Rudolf von Ems presented an attempt at a historical portrait of Alexander, again cast in the form of a poem. In 1250 Bishop Philip Walter also wrote an *Alexandreis* that drew on Curtius.[9] In the fourteenth century, the ancient historian was used by various Italian humanists, such as Benzo of Alessandria, Lombardy, an encyclopedist and historian who regularly mentioned Curtius. Guglielmo da Pastrengo, a scholarly lawyer of Verona in the mid–fourteenth century, praised Curtius' style.[10]

Alfonso V of Aragon, in the fifteenth century, was supposedly cured of an illness, perhaps melancholy, by reading the *Historiae.*[11] Curtius was also popular with the North Italian princes, who were the patrons of scholars and humanists. In 1438 Pier Candido Decembrio translated Curtius into Italian, evidently for the use of these soldier princes. He compared Tacitus unfavorably to Curtius. A little earlier in the same age, eager humanist book hunters had searched for a surviving, complete copy of Curtius' text. In 1426 Cardinal Nicholas of Cuse (1401–64), philosopher, canon lawyer, diplomat, and scholarly enthusiast, believed he had found a Curtius with a complete first book. Unfortunately, as it turned out, he had only found an ordinary Curtius, with a

---

8. For manuscripts, titles, and traditional book divisions of the work, see Dosson's full inventory in his app. 1, pp. 315 f., and p. 2 n.2. On the codices and modern editions, see Rolfe, 1:x f.; Bardon, 1:x f. On the value of Codex P, see Atkinson, *ANRW* II.34.4 (1997): section 1.

9. On Bishop Walter, see Rolfe (supra n. 8), xiv.

10. See Remigio Sabbadini, *Le scoperte dei codoci latin e greci ne' secoli xix e xv* (Florence, 1914), 2:142. For Guglielmo da Pastrengo, see ibid., 1:12. I am very grateful to Ms. A. Holcroft, University of Canterbury, New Zealand, for these references.

11. See Duff, *Silver Age,* 81.

page from an unrelated book bound into it at the beginning.[12] Curtius' text was sought by the literati of the Middle Ages and early Renaissance, not only for its subject, Alexander, but also for its moral tone and excellent style; in about 1470 or 1471, Vindelinus Spirensis published in Venice what is acknowledged as the editio princeps—or first printed edition—of Curtius.[13]

The *Historiae* continued to generate interest; other texts appeared in 1472, 1475, and 1481, and the editio princeps was modified by Bartolemo Merula in 1494.[14] Important texts with further corrections were published in the sixteenth century by Franciscus Asulanus (Aldus, 1525) Hadrianus Junius (1546), and Franciscus Modius in Cologne (1579, 1591). Even more influential in popularizing Curtius as an author was the edition of Johannes Caspar Freinsheim (Strasbourg, 1648). Freinsheim's book was widely used in the scholarly world, not only for his commentary, but also for his reconstructions of Curtius' lost, first two books, which he based on the other principal Alexander traditions, and for his supplements to the lacunae throughout the text. These restorations were frequently repeated by later editors, including Hedicke, with often very little change in the wording.[15]

H. Snakenberg's text (Delft and Leiden) appeared in 1724. According to C.G. Zumpt, this editor left Freinsheim's text unaltered out of a sense of reverence for him.[16] However, Curtian scholarship expanded in the nineteenth century, with the 1822–24 editions of N.E. Lemaire and with Julius Mützell's substantial edition with commentary, which was published in 1841. One should also note the editorial work of Zumpt, who claimed in his first edition (Berlin, 1826) that he was more thorough than his predecessors and had used more manuscripts. Zumpt frankly admired Curtius' rhetorical qualities, but his extravagant praise of the historian drew a negative response from other scholars, and Zumpt's own text (revised in 1849 and 1864) met with criticism because of its dismissal of Codex P.[17]

---

12. See Sabbadini, *Storia et critica di testi latini* (Padua, 1971), 171, 323. For Nicholas of Cruse, see Sabbadini (supra, n. 10), 1:111.

13. See Rolfe, 1:xxxii; Bardon, 1:xviii.

14. See Rolfe, 1:xxxii.

15. Freinsheim's reconstructions were considered superior to earlier attempts; he also produced restorations of sixty books of Livy. See J.E. Sandys, *A History of Classical Scholarship* (Cambridge, 1908), 2:367.

16. C.G. Zumpt, *Q. Curtii Rufi, De Gestis Alexandri Magni* (Edinburgh, 1849), iv.

17. On Zumpt, see Rolfe, xxi; Atkinson, *ANRW* II.34.4 (1997): section 1.

According to J.E. Atkinson, Edmund Hedicke's book influenced T. Vogel's Teubner edition (Leipzig, 1889–1903) and the (1954) text of K. Müller and H. Schönfeld; J.C. Rolfe also claimed that he based his (1946) Loeb edition on a later (1908) Teubner edition of Hedicke. Müller and Schönfeld produced what is considered by some to be the best edition of the modern texts, with a translation into German and a critical appendix; however, Rolfe's text and translation remain readily accessible today, along with H. Bardon's version for the Budé series.[18] The (1984) Penguin translation of Curtius by John Yardley with notes by Waldemar Heckel was based on the latter.

Editions aside, in 1886 the French scholar S. Dosson published a substantial and broad-ranging discussion on Curtius, and the competence of Dosson's work was acknowledged by the great E. Norden in his monumental *Antike Kunstprosa*.[19] Perhaps not surprisingly, Dosson's *Étude sur Quinte-Curce* and E. Schwartz' article in *RE* remained, for some time, the most significant overviews on any large scale.

However, in the twentieth century, Curtian study has sometimes been characterized by not only apathy but, on the odd occasion, downright hostility. An explanation for these attitudes is not hard to find. Apart from issues in textual criticism, most scholarship has addressed the problems of identity, date, and sources. Also, many of those scholars who read Curtius were historians, interested chiefly in his subject, and for a long time Curtius' choice of sources and his methodology were unfavorably compared with Arrian.

For instance, in this century, Curtius has been criticized for being careless, overblown, flowery, and unhistorical. Sir William Tarn called him a "gifted amateur" and said that he lacked "historical principle" and "advertised it."[20] Other eminent scholars have reinforced Tarn's impression, with descriptions of Curtius as a "hasty and irresponsible rhetorician" (Charles Edson) and an "accomplished dilettante" (F.R.D. Goodyear). Sir Ronald Syme condescendingly wrote that Curtius was "little better than a superior journalist."[21]

Something of Tarn's branding of Curtius as a careless, brilliant dab-

---

18. See Atkinson's comments on Müller and Schönfeld, as well as his criticism of Bardon, in *ANRW* II.34.3 (1997): section 1.
19. Norden, *Kunstprosa*, 1:305.
20. W.W. Tarn, *Alexander the Great*, 2:91–92.
21. C. Edson, review of *Pompei Trogi Fragmenta*, by O. Seel, *CPh* 61 (1961): 200; F.R.D. Goodyear, *Cambridge History of Classical Literature* (Cambridge, 1982), 641–42; Syme, *Historia* 37 (1988): 370.

bler who recklessly used his sources to suit his own literary pretensions filtered down to the late Mary Renault, a well-known historical novelist, who wrote,

> Muddled sensationalism is typical of Curtius, an unbearably silly man with access to priceless sources now lost to us, which he frittered away in the course of a tedious literary concept about the goddess Fortuna and many florid exercises in Roman rhetoric.[22]

Since Renault undoubtedly based her fictitious Alexander on Tarn's works (despite his vehement denial of the existence of her protagonist, the eunuch Bagoas), her views are not surprising.

The nature and genre of Curtius' *Historiae* have once again possibly increased certain unfavorable responses to it. Curtius' history has been labeled as sensationalist, deliberately written for popular appeal—in fact, almost a work of "historical fiction," or, as Harry MacL. Currie would describe it, within "the didactic novel tradition."[23] This view ignores Curtius' own stated opinion at *Historiae* 5.1, namely, that he is writing a serious account and has given heed to literary and historical considerations.[24] In fact, he comments elsewhere in the *Historiae* on historiographical technique (8.9.37), which one would hardly expect in an account that had been carelessly thrown together for the sake of thrilling an audience. Perhaps the advocates of Curtius' work as fiction could still suggest that, in a parody of the conventions, he may have incorporated hoax methodological comments as a deliberate measure to create an impression of verisimilitude, as occurs in Seneca's beginning of the *Apocolocyntosis* (1–3) or in Lucian's *Verae historiae* (1.2–4). Yet the supporters of this line of argument must produce evidence that Curtius has indeed falsified his comments; until a prima facie case can be created, Curtius' statements of principle have to be taken at face value as typical of the historiographical genre. One should also stress that Curtius appears to have been an author who read widely, for he displays consid-

---

22. Mary Renault, *The Persian Boy* (Penguin, 1972), 412.
23. H. MacL. Currie, "Quintus Curtius Rufus: The Historian as Novelist?" places Curtius in the same tradition of romantic biography as Xenophon's *Cyropaedia*. Cf. B. Perrin, "The Genesis and Growth of an Alexander Myth," *TAPhA* 26 (1895): 56–68.
24. See C.A. Robinson, review of "Die Zeit des Quintus Curtius Rufus," by Dietmar Korzeniewski, *AJPh* 82 (1961): 316–19.

erable knowledge of Persian and Macedonian customs.²⁵ On occasion, Curtius also evaluates his sources, if the caustic comments he passes on Ptolemy, Cleitarchus, and Timagenes (as noted in chapter 3) may be taken as evidence. If he draws on his authorities to produce a composite version of an event or freely adapts his material for the sake of literary theme and to suit his own characterization of Alexander, the ultimate result is still the same for him as for his fellow ancient historians. Every Alexander historian, including modern historians, exercises selectivity. Wilcken's perceptive comment has become something of a truism; every Alexander historian creates his or her own Alexander.²⁶

In his choice of Alexander the Great as a subject for a full-scale history, Curtius is unique among Latin authors, and he has thus been placed outside Roman mainstream historiography. Yet in many ways he is also a product of his times. Naturally, an immediate question is raised: what was Curtius' epoch?

It is certain from a panegyric in book 10 that Curtius wrote during the imperial period, and it is probable, because of his references to the Parthian Empire as a contemporary, that he wrote before 228 A.D. Within this period, the nature of the digression in book 10 that praises a *princeps* for either stopping or averting civil war suggests several emperors: Augustus, Claudius, Vespasian, and Septimius Severus. Other less likely candidates have been put forward, including Nero, Galba, Trajan, Hadrian, and Severus Alexander, while J.R. Fears has argued consistently for a date after the fall of the Parthian Empire.²⁷

However, that no modern scholar from the fifteenth century to the present day has been able either to date precisely Curtius' work or to identify its author in an entirely satisfactory and conclusive manner suggests a certain insuperability or futility about these problems. A survey of modern scholarship on Curtius' date from, for example, 1959 to 1995 leaves one with an impression comparable to viewing an Escher drawing. The same internal evidence is assessed and reworked, and the same problems are approached from angles ranging from close linguistic analysis of the text to examination of the external evidence offered by the legends of imperial coins.

---

25. See Tarn, *Alexander the Great,* 2:106–8; J.M. Cook, *The Persian Empire* (London, 1983), 23, 104–5, 133, 137–38, 253; my chap. 3, 80, 99.

26. See U. Wilcken, *Alexander the Great,* with preface, notes, and bibliography by E.N. Borza (New York, 1967), 29.

27. J.R. Fears, *Hermes* 102 (1974): 623–25 and *CPh* 71 (1976): 214–23.

Some ingenious solutions have been proposed in all of these areas. The exercise is not an idle one, since an understanding of the historian's motive is sharper if one can establish a date and identity at least, with a reasonable degree of probability: hence I offer in the appendix a discussion of the problem of Curtius' date and identity. From the problematic evidence available, many modern scholars now accept a date in the middle to late part of the first century A.D. as a likely floruit for Curtius. The only emperors who fit the ambiguous excursus in 10.5.1–6 are Claudius or Vespasian. It is also logical that the identity of the historian should be suggested using what evidence is known of Curtii Rufi from within this period. The candidates most favored by scholars are a Curtius Rufus, proconsul of Africa, who is mentioned by Pliny (*Ep.* 8.27) and Tacitus (*Ann.* 11.20–21), and a rhetorician, Q. Curtius Rufus, who is cited in Suetonius' index to *De rhetoribus et grammaticus*.[28] However, the historian need not necessarily have been either of these men; it is just as plausible that he was a relative of one or both of them.

The primary objective of this book is an analysis of Curtius' historiographical methods and arrangement of his material and an evaluation of his chief themes. Paradoxically, although the study will explore issues like Curtius' persona, literary techniques, style, and attitude toward "historical truth," the problems of his identity and date are important but not crucial. For the moment, if one accepts the consensus view that Curtius belongs to the first century A.D., the literary and historical influences on his style and method of composition become clear. As Syme noted, with the exception of Velleius Paterculus, Curtius is the only Latin historian we possess between Livy and Tacitus; and as will be demonstrated (in chapter 2), Curtius has features in common with both these writers.[29]

E.I. McQueen noted that there are strong biographical elements in the *Historiae* and that the work may be seen as a "fusion of both genres," history and biography.[30] McQueen also suggested that along with the biographical elements in framework, such as Curtius' choice of a great individual, rather than a history of a people, as his subject, one can detect aspects of the composition of an encomium, where a subject's life is treated chronologically, including his or her youth, education, deeds, and

---

28. Suetonius, *De Gram*, trans. J.C. Rolfe (Cambridge, Mass., 1979), 2:395.
29. Syme, *Historia* 37 (1988): 367.
30. See McQueen, 20.

sayings.[31] Some qualifications must be added to his point. The biographical aspects of the work, particularly in relation to its interest in character and motive are undeniable, but these aspects often occur in Greco-Roman historiography in general and indeed are a major focus of Sallust and Tacitus.[32] Moreover, the loss of the first two books of Curtius' history makes any comment on youth and education very problematic, and other indications suggest that the historian did not examine Alexander's early life.[33]

In the first century A.D., because of the rhetorical training undergone by most writers in their youth, it was inevitable that Latin poetry and prose should show the influence of rhetorical schools. We know from Seneca the Elder, Quintilian, and Valerius Maximus that Alexander was a topic for declamation. It is true that Curtius' episodic narrative has common elements with the rhetoricians' use of topoi, but it is equally important to consider his history as a cohesive structure; these issues are considered in chapter 2, together with the possible nature and expectations of the historian's audience.

Curtius' rhetorical training is evident in his use of paired speeches that give opposing points of view and are equally skillfully composed, as well as in his careful attention to both the beginning and ending of each book, his moral sententiae, and his use of epitaphs on both individuals and cities. The latter are a feature of Greco-Roman historiography as a whole: however, in Curtius they are highly rhetorical pieces, a fact that perhaps adds to the conclusion that, in Curtius, as in so many Roman historians, rhetoric and historiography should not be separated.[34] The rhetorical nature of the work is intrinsic and should be accepted before passing judgment. Only a detailed evaluation of the history's structure and composition, themes, and insight into what is essentially a study of power can furnish an appreciation of Curtius' interests and his literary merit.

In his consistent skepticism—if not occasional outright contempt—

---

31. On the encomium aspect in Curtius, see McQueen, 19–20. Cf. Quint. *Inst.* 3.7.10–17. Curtius may have also been influenced by the same school of thought.

32. See R. Syme, *Tacitus,* 2:526 f. On Curtius' interest in character and motive, see Atkinson, *Curtius* i, 70 f.

33. See chap. 2, 39.

34. See McQueen, 31–32; Duff, *Silver Age,* 90–91. For historiography as a branch of oratory, see Cic. *De. or.* 2.15.62–64; cf. *Ad fam.* 5.12. See also the remarks of Quintilian at 10.1.31–34 and my chap. 2.

about omens, oracles, portents, and magical practices, Curtius seems in tune with a certain attitude expressed by other writers of the first century A.D. Also, again as McQueen has pointed out, Curtius' philosophical views are hard to determine, as he displays a mixture of Stoic, Epicurean, and Academic attitudes, without appearing to adhere to any one.[35] The belief he most consistently emphasizes is the concept of personalized *fortuna* and destiny or *fata*. The significance of these ideas and the aforementioned issues are discussed in chapter 4.

The *Historiae* also contains a vast amount of geographical, zoological, and ethnographical detail, the result of both the historian's sources and Greco-Roman literary conventions. The most detailed of these excurses is the digression on India (8.9.2–37), although, as Curtius notes himself (8.9.37), he is careful not to let these digressions detract from his main historical narrative or his characterization of Alexander.[36]

It remains to introduce Curtius' major literary themes and purpose. Why did Curtius choose Alexander the Great? As the conqueror of a vast extent of territory, Alexander held an innate fascination for the Romans, themselves a warlike and imperialistic people. This fascination is amply illustrated not only by Alexander's popularity as a rhetorical topos but by several Roman generals' apparent *aemulatio* and *imitatio* of the Macedonian and even by emperors' outright admiration for him. However, mixed with admiration, the Romans also expressed ambivalence and hostility.[37]

---

35. Cf. Curt. 7.7.8. See McQueen, 32 f. Cf. Tacitus' skepticism (*Hist.* 1.10; *Ann.* 14.12) and attitude toward astrologers (*Hist.* 1.22), but note the eclectic digression in *Ann.* 6.22, where he expresses a favorable view of astrology when it is practiced properly and not perverted by ignorant practitioners or quacks; see H. Furneaux, *The Annals of Tacitus*, 1: ad loc. and introduction, 30 f.; cf. Syme, *Tacitus*, 2:525 f.

36. Cf. Arrian 5.4–6; see my chap. 6. On the ethnographical tradition in general, see T.F. Thomas, *Lands and Peoples in Roman Poetry*.

37. Traditionally, Scipio Africanus, Pompey, Julius Caesar, and Octavian were the Roman republican figures most famous for their *imitatio* and *aemulatio* of Alexander; see O. Weippert, "Alexander-Imitatio und Römische Politik in Republikanischer Zeit" (Diss. Julius-Maximilians-Universität zu Würzburg, 1972). In particular, P. Green, "Caesar and Alexander: Aemulatio, Imitatio, Comparatio," in *Classical Bearings: Interpreting Ancient History* (New York, 1989), 193–209, argues that such behavior was based only on the need to amplify Roman achievement and thus that Alexander was a foil, rather than a model. However, during the early imperial period, the traditions record the *imitatio* of a number of emperors: of the Julio-Claudians, Caligula wore Alexander's breastplate (Suet. *Gaius* 52), while Nero named a legion the "phalanx of Alexander" (Suet. *Nero* 19.2). Trajan "esteemed Alexander happy" [τόν τε Ἀλέξανδρον ἐμακάριζε] but also declared that he had advanced further than the Macedonian (Dio Cass. 68.29.2). On Roman attitudes toward Alexander (a vast topic), see J.R. Fears, *Philologus* 118 (1974):

As a subject for rhetorical declamation, Alexander, owing to his well-known excesses documented in sources like Cleitarchus, provided a convenient yardstick for *virtus* and *vitia* alike. Among Roman authors of the early imperial period, Livy's patriotic, lengthy digression in 9.17–19 explains just how and why Rome would have beaten Alexander had he ventured westward.[38] Seneca the Younger is one of the most eloquent and poisonous of Alexander's Roman critics.[39] Lucan (*De bell. civ.* 10.20–35) describes Alexander as *proles vaesana Philippi* [the mad offspring of Philip] and a *sidus iniquum* [adverse star]. Tacitus (*Ann.* 2.73) compares Alexander unfavorably to Germanicus. While Alexander remained the epitome of the military commander *(dux)*, he was also the undeniable favorite of *fortuna;* Plutarch's expositions *De Alexandri fortuna* immediately suggest that there was a corpus of literature that attributed Alexander's success to his *tyche*.[40]

Another reason for Roman curiosity about Alexander was undoubtedly because he was a king. Naturally, interest in kings and kingship was not confined to the Romans: Greek authors had already written a considerable amount on the subject.[41] The Romans hated but were fascinated by kingship. *Regnum* is featured widely as a theme in Roman literature, from Cicero, Sallust, and Livy to Seneca and Tacitus.[42] Trogus' substantial work, the *Historiae Philippicae,* in forty-four books, was in essence a history of kings and kingship. However, that historian's attitude is anti-autocratic, and his portrayal of individual kings is mostly

---

113–30; G. Wirth, "Alexander und Rom," in *Alexandre le Grand, image et réalité,* Fondation Hardt, *Entretiens* 22 (Geneva, 1976), 181–210.

38. See F.W. Walbank, "Livy, Macedonia, and Alexander," in *Ancient Macedonian Studies in Honour of Charles F. Edson* (Thessaloníki, 1981), 335–56.

39. Seneca reflects a considerable amount of rhetorical hostility toward Alexander, often picturing him ruled by excessive behavior: see *De ira* 3.17.1, 3.23.1; *Ep.* 83.19–20, 94.62; *Clem.* 1.25.1; *QNat.* 6.23.2., etc.; but cf. *De ira* 2.23.1. See also Fears, *Philologus* 118 (1974):113–30.

40. See S. Schroeder, *MH* 48 (1991): 151–57. Schroeder's article explores the structure of Plutarch's discourses and suggests that the extant texts are part of a wider scenario; Plutarch himself may have written a treatise on Alexander's debt to fortune (now lost) and may have answered it in our extant works.

41. The subject is too broad to document: in particular, see Hdt. 3.79 f.; Plato *Repub.* 8.4–9; Aristotle *Pol.* 5.10–11; Polybius 6.6–7. See also K.W. Welwei, "Könige und Königtum in Urteil des Polybios" (Diss. Cologne, 1963).

42. The theme of *regnum* in Roman literature, like kingship in Greek thought, is also too complex to supply a full list of references. However, see Cic. *Repub.* 1:26 f., and see *Pro Marc.*, where Cicero advises an autocrat (Caesar) on how to deal with friends and subjects. On the "tyrant" figure, see my chap. 5, 134–35.

negative. It is possible, for instance, that for the Alexander books, Trogus may have deliberately avoided sources that were overly pro-Macedonian, such as Ptolemy or Aristobulus.[43]

To the Romans, Alexander's appeal would have been twofold: he was world-famous and a king. This last aspect underlines one of Curtius' major themes of the *Historiae—regnum*. To Curtius, the life of Alexander apparently offered a supreme opportunity for a study on politics and power. Alexander began his career as a king of Macedon and died the lord of Asia. His position changed from that of a *primus inter pares* to that of a king whose power was absolute; ironically, in some ways, Curtius' interpretation is not dissimilar to the "Titanic" Alexander of the famous German scholar Fritz Schachermeyr.[44]

Given the parallels between the political conflict Alexander's power brought and the principate of Curtius' day, it is not surprising that the *Historiae* should be colored with contemporary overtones. Scholars have often commented on this aspect of Curtius, but it is erroneous to see the work as a simple allegory—or to see Alexander as a "whipping boy" (A.M. Devine's term)—for any one *princeps*.[45]

Standard elements of the Greco-Roman view of Alexander, particularly as the consummate *dux,* the *fortunatus rex,* and the *tyrannus* corrupted by his own great *fortuna,* are present in Curtius, but as this study will argue, they are molded and composed in the author's own, highly independent way. Structurally, he seems to have divided the ten books of the *Historiae* into two pentads that are linked by the themes of *fortuna* and *regnum;* the argument for such an arrangement is elaborated in chapter 2.

The extant books of Curtius' first pentad depict Alexander and his antithesis, the Persian king Darius, as well as how *fortuna* affects the careers and personalities of each. The second pentad focuses on the figure of Alexander as *dux, rex,* and *tyrannus* as the scale of his power matches the scale of his *virtus* and *vitia.* The political conflict between *regnum* and *libertas* is prominent. The historian is aware of the enormous potential of *regnum* for glory and evil alike, but perhaps his ultimate judgment is reflected in book 10; kingship is necessary, for it is better than civil war.

Within each book Curtius adopts an episodic structure, apparently

---

43. See Hammond, *THA,* 114.
44. On Schachermeyr, see chap. 3, 65–66.
45. See Devine, *Phoenix* 33 (1979): 157. See also Atkinson's comments on what he terms the "sub-text" in Curtius, in *ANRW* II.34.4 (1997): section 10.

based around subsidiary motifs, such as *contumacia, fides, libertas, virtus, pietas, clementia, licentia, crudelitas, ira,* and *superbia,* which are linked to the dominant themes of *regnum* and *fortuna.* Certain scholarly opinion has suggested that Curtius' history was based around a series of interesting pictures, with only a dull or loose narrative to bind the structure. Such a view was recently reinforced by R. Porod, whose main thesis was that Curtius did not aim at homogeneous composition or a consistent narrative.[46] But this book argues that Curtius' literary sophistication and political insight are most evident in his careful placement and balance of his episodes, his manipulation of theme, and the inherent cohesiveness of his composition.

As with chapter 2, the purpose of chapter 3 is also preliminary; it offers a survey of the traditions available to Curtius and the problems associated with them, as well as an outline of the basic principles of Curtius' own methodology. In chapters 4–6, these principles are elaborated through selected exempla from each pentad. Finally, cross-referencing to the other extant Alexander historians, especially the other representatives of the so-called Alexander vulgate tradition, remains a necessary exercise to continually elucidate Curtius' interests and approach.

As a historian of Alexander, Quintus Curtius has his faults. He is commonly accused of sensationalism, carelessness, and confusion of sources, names, and military and geographical details, as well as bias; and examples of these flaws can be readily found in the text.[47] However, recent scholarship has also queried the sources and methods of Arrian, who for so long has been regarded as unequivocally the "best" of the extant Alexander sources.[48] Under close scrutiny, each of the Alexander historians reveals biases, distortions, and inaccuracies. Given the complexity of the Alexander tradition, as well as the prejudices of any age or individual, no single Alexander historian can be completely satisfactory. At the very least, Curtius has provided depictions of Alexander that are valuable for their insight into power, as well as for their author's rhetorical skill.

---

46. See Bosworth, *CPh* 78 (1983): 158; W.E. Heitland, *A Portion of the History of Quintus Curtius* (Cambridge, 1905), 10. But see N. Holzberg, *WJA* 14 (1988): 185–201, and in general the commentaries of Atkinson (*Curtius* i and ii), who also proposes a careful structure in the *Historiae*.

47. See Duff, *Silver Age,* 85; J. Roisman, *CQ* 34 (1984): 377; my chap. 5. But for a more favorable view of Curtius' accuracy, especially in terms of geographical detail, see D.W. Engels, *Alexander the Great and the Logistics of the Macedonian Army,* 7, 84, 101.

48. See R.D. Milns, "Alexander's Pursuit of Darius through Iran," *Historia* 15 (1966): 256. For further discussion of Arrian's methodology and for bibliography, see my chap. 3, 67–68.

Over one hundred years have passed since Dosson's book appeared, and post–World War II Alexander historiographical criticism and technological advances have revived interest in Curtius. For example, the application of computerized analysis techniques to Curtius' vocabulary in relation to the perennial question of his date has led to such studies as the 1975 doctoral dissertation of J. Costas Rodriguez.[49] There has also been renewed discussion of Curtius' historiographical and narrative techniques; a selection of recent, pertinent studies includes E.I. McQueen's entry on Curtius in T.A. Dorey's *Latin Biography* (1967), the 1983 monograph of Francesca Minissale, Werner v. Rutz' important 1986 article in *Aufstieg* (32, no. 4), R. Porod's 1987 book on literary aspects of Curtius, and H. MacL. Currie's 1990 contribution in the *Groningen Colloquia on the Novel*. In addition to his discussion of the historian's methodology, J.E. Atkinson's 1980 commentary on books 3 and 4 and his 1994 commentary on book 5 through 7.2 continue to offer authoritative comment on the historical content of Curtius, while his *Forschungsbericht* in *ANRW* provides a worthwhile update of Rutz' earlier study.[50]

As we saw earlier, the mutilated nature of Curtius' extant text creates serious problems for the modern student. Even more serious is the complete lack of surviving, ancient response to him. Not only would contemporary or postcontemporary comment have helped solve the question of Curtius' date, but it would have put us in a better position to judge the literary qualities of the work itself and the audience for whom it was intended. However, to make a plausible case for treating Curtius Rufus with a little more respect as a representative of the Greco-Roman historiographical tradition, we need to examine just how he fits into that genre.

---

49. See Rodriguez, *Aspectos de Q. Curtius Rufus,* who examined Curtius' affinities with pre-Augustan, Augustan, and Silver Age authors; his date for the digression in 10.9 was Vespasianic, and he concluded (371) that Curtius should be put close to Frontinus but before Tacitus.

50. For Currie, see supra, n. 23. Some discussion of Curtius' methods with particular emphasis on personalities is provided by L.L. Gunderson, "Quintus Curtius Rufus: On His Historical Methods," in *Philip II, Alexander the Great, and the Macedonian Heritage,* ed. W.L. Adams and E.N. Borza (Washington, 1982), 177–96. Francesca Minissale, in *Curzio Rufo: Un romanziere della storia,* concurred with Rodriguez (and others) in that the history was published in the aftermath of 68–69 A.D.; however, she also suggested that the work was heavily influenced by Nero's eastern policy and the campaigns of Corbulo. She likewise put Curtius as post-Livy but pre-Tacitus; her discussion also contained an exposition of the historian's prose style and his figures of speech. Cf. F. Minissale, "Tra storiografia ed epica: Modelli e techniche imitative in Q. Curzio Rufo," in *Poesica epica greci e latina,* ed. C. Salvatore (Sileno, 1988), 135–78. For earlier bibliographical data on the problems of Curtius' date, sources, and historical reliability, see Seibert, 30–34; Rutz, 2329 f.

Chapter 2
"Roman" Curtius

This chapter considers Curtius' place in Greco-Roman literature, the most important historiographical influences on him, and his rhetorical heritage. In particular, the discussion explores aspects of Curtius' literary structure, including his possible imitation of Livy and his similarity to Tacitus in his political concerns.

The search for Curtius' date has resulted in some comprehensive linguistic analysis of the historian as well as examination of his affinities with a range of Augustan and post-Augustan authors, including in the latter category Velleius Paterculus, Valerius Maximus, Seneca the Elder, Seneca the Younger, Lucan, Silius Italicus, Statius, Tacitus, Pliny the Younger, and the late imperial historian Ammianus Marcellinus.[1] However, it is not the purpose of the chapter or indeed the book as a whole to offer a critique of this scholarship or even to elaborate on these issues to any large degree. It also seems hardly necessary to offer an exposition of the development of Greco-Roman historiography and related genres.[2] Rather, my aim is more general—simply to demonstrate Curtius' literary context and to establish a background for an appreciation of the historian's arrangement of his material and the development of his main themes.

Curtius' Literary Background

Curtius, as Dosson noted, was a "Roman who wrote for Romans."[3] Although this statement is largely true, it needs qualification. Who were

---

1. See Rutz, 2336 f.; Atkinson, *Curtius* i, 39 f. See also Atkinson, *ANRW* II.34.4 (1997): section 7, on the literary borrowings and influences in the text.

2. For a selection of treatments, see Norden, *Kunstprosa;* T.A. Dorey, ed., *Latin Historians* (London, 1966); C.W. Fornara, *The Nature of History in Ancient Greece and Rome.* Walsh's discussion (*Livy*, 20–45) is a good survey. See most recently Simon Hornblower's excellent introduction in *Greek Historiography*, 1–72.

3. Dosson, 218.

the Romans who comprised Curtius' audience, and how did he accommodate their presumed wishes? Undoubtedly the audience came from the well-to-do strata of Roman society, but it can hardly be seen as uniform. There would be considerable variations in taste and very different standards of literary criticism.

Curtius' subject matter had undeniable appeal, yet the appeal did not lie only in the novelty of the facts presented. If Curtius' readers wanted information, they could profitably look elsewhere. Any serious scholar presumably would have been able to consult the same first-generation sources that Curtius used himself. Ptolemy and Aristobulus may have been comparatively difficult to obtain (given the frustrations inherent in the ancient book trade),[4] but Cleitarchus was well known and seems to have been quite widely read.[5] There were also general, universal histories available, such as Timagenes, Diodorus Siculus, or the Latin *Historiae Philippicae* of Pompeius Trogus.

The availability of universal histories is not an insignificant point; many of Curtius' readers may well have looked for a specialized authority in their own language. But what mattered was not the content or the historical reconstruction of Alexander's reign. Literary composition was the primary goal, and Roman sources from the time of Cicero and Sallust increasingly emphasize the popularity of prose and poetry as avocations of cultured leisure. In that context, history enjoyed a high reputation as a genre, a kind of poetry in prose *(carmen solutum)*, as Quintilian (*Inst.* 10.1.31) termed it. The canons of the genre were stylistic, and popularity depended on style. Even a specialist history like Curtius' would rely on its presentation and its rhetorical sententiae for its appeal.[6]

In the fourth century B.C., Isocrates' rhetorical and poetic devices apparently had a profound influence on two historians (albeit not extant today), namely, Ephorus and Theopompus, who were also allegedly his pupils in popular traditions.[7] The latter's rhetorical debt to Isocrates is

---

4. On the book trade and its difficulties in antiquity, see E. Kenney, *Cambridge History of Classical Literature* (Cambridge, 1982), 20; R. Thomas, *Literacy and Orality in Ancient Greece* (Cambridge, 1992), 1; Hornblower, *Greek Historiography,* 62 n.156.

5. On the (relative) obscurity of Ptolemy and Aristobulus and the popularity of Cleitarchus, see chap. 3, 69, 76, 79.

6. Cf. A. Wallace-Hadrill's remarks in *Suetonius* (London, 1983), 10 f.; he defines the ancients' criteria for historiography as "structure, subject matter and style."

7. See Cic. *De or.* 2.13.57; Quint. *Inst.* 10.1.74; *FGrH* 115.T.20; Gellius *NA* 10.18.6. Cf. *FGrH* 70.T.28a, 115.T.28. According to the Suda, Isocrates allegedly remarked on each pupil's style that Theopompus needed a curb and Ephorus a spur; cf. Quint. *Inst.* 10.1.74. A similar remark is also told of Aristotle and Xenocrates; see Diog. Laert. 4.2.6.

acknowledged by Dionysius of Halicarnassus in his lengthy exposition of the historian's style.[8] Polybius (12.28) admired Ephorus' composition and considered him to be his predecessor in writing universal history (5.33.2); however, although Theopompus' work was evidently well known, it was also judged inconsistent and extravagant by ancient critics.[9]

It is probably true that historiographical interest in character and motive originated with Herodotus and was developed further by Xenophon in his quasi-historical *Cyropaedia* and encomiastic *Agesilaus*. One could also suggest that Theopompus' *Philippica,* a history based on the rise of Macedon under Philip II, not only continued the psychological aspect but made the study of an individual central to a world context. This interest continued to pervade historiography from the early Hellenistic historians—including first-generation Alexander authors like Cleitarchus—down to Roman times and the advent of Sallust and Livy; "biography" developed as a related genre.[10]

By the late first century B.C. and into the early imperial period, Roman historiography was a sophisticated literary form, the product of centuries of refined thought on style, rhetoric, and historical narrative, although this thought was not necessarily homogeneous. A.D. Leeman noted that historiography could be loosely divided into several forms, each with its own ancestry: the propagandist, quasi-Xenophontean format, represented by Caesar's *Commentaries;* the imitators of Thucydidean style in Sallust and Asinius Pollio; and a Herodotean concept of history embodied in Livy's epic narrative of Rome's past.[11]

Leeman's distinctions are helpful up to a point. Livy and Herodotus are indeed grouped together by Quintilian (*Inst.* 10.1.101), but most likely on their mutual stylistic appeal. The aims of each historian appear somewhat different. Herodotus' emphasis in his understanding of ἱστορίη was inquiry; he explained that he was going to investigate the

---

8. *FGrH* 115.T.20 = Dion. Hal. ad Cn. Pomp. 6. On Theopompus' rhetorical characteristics, see Norden, *Kunstprosa,* 1:121 f.

9. See, for instance, Polybius' diatribe against Theopompus (8.9 f.), but cf. Duris of Samos (*FGrH* 115.T.34), who censures Theopompus and Ephorus for their lack of emotional treatment. See F.W. Walbank, *A Historical Commentary on Polybius,* 2:80. On Theopompus in general, see G.S. Shrimpton, *Theopompus the Historian;* M. Flower, *Theopompus of Chios.*

10. On the problems of differentiation between history and biography, see A. Momigliano, *The Development of Greek Biography* (Cambridge, Mass., 1971).

11. A.D. Leeman, *Orationis Ratio,* 1:243.

achievements of the Greeks and the barbarians and demonstrate how these peoples came into conflict. The main theme of his study was a great war and was, from that perspective, consistent with Homeric tradition.[12] Livy claimed his objective to be a didactic exposition of Rome's glorious past by way of highlighting its present moral decline (praef. 9).

Despite the pervasive and considerable fame of Sallust (cf. Quint. *Inst.* 10.1.102), it seems clear that in the Augustan Age, one historian who achieved considerable impact in terms of both literary style and popular appeal was Livy. Among the literati, Livy had his critics—Asinius Pollio's problematic epithet *Pativinitas* may allude to either Livy's Latinity or his naive, provincial approach to history.[13] The emperor Caligula, who is credited with some pithy literary remarks in Suetonius, described Livy as *verbosus* (verbose) and *neglegens* (careless).[14] In a similar fashion, within its context, Quintilian's favorable description of Livy's style as *lactea ubertas* is not complimentary in terms of the author's historicity.[15]

Certainly by Polybius' expressed criteria on what a historian should do (12.25e), Livy would fall short of the ideal. Admittedly, Livy did not always consult the earliest authorities, but Polybius likewise used secondary historians like Fabius Pictor and Philistus for the period before the Second Punic War; moreover, Livy used Polybius—a choice that the latter would have only applauded. However, Livy did not bother with accuracy in relation to topographical or geographical detail, and he did not have personal military or political experience.[16] Yet, although Polybius' "pragmatic" approach to historiography may have influenced historians like Sempronius Asellio,[17] Polybius himself remained in the

---

12. See Hornblower, *Greek Historiography*, 18.

13. See Walsh, *Livy*, 167 f.; but see R. Syme, *The Roman Revolution*, 485.

14. Suet. *Gaius* 34.2. See P.G. Walsh, "The Negligent Historian: 'Howlers' in Livy," *G&R* 5 (1958): 83–88; H. Lindsay, *Suetonius, Caligula* (Bristol, 1993), 125; A.A. Barrett, *Caligula: The Corruption of Power* (Batsford, 1989), 48.

15. Quint. *Inst.* 10.1.32: . . . *neque illa Livii lactea ubertas satis docebit eum, qui non speciem expositionis, sed fidem quaerit.* But cf. 10.1.101, where he expresses admiration for Livy's speeches.

16. See Walsh's analysis of Livy's methods in relation to Polybian expectations, in *Livy*, 138 f.

17. For Polybius' understanding of πραγματικὴ ἱστορία, see Walbank, *Polybius*, 66 f. Sempronius Asellio wrote a contemporary history that may have commenced with the destruction of Carthage and ended at about the end of the second century B.C.; his view was that a historian should give indication of plans and methods. Cf. Gellius *NA* 5.18.8; Walsh, *Livy*, 29 f.

minority, just as the methodological principles stated by Thucydides (1.20–22) made him an exception in historiography, rather than a model, despite his fame.

The traditions also contain evidence—albeit some of it anecdotal—attesting Livy's success. Seneca the Elder, in his discussion of the epitaph in historiography (*Suas.* 6.21), includes Livy along with Asinius Pollio and Cremutius Cordus in a comparison of their respective evaluations of the life of Cicero.[18] Pliny the Younger was a man of letters who enjoyed Livy, to the extent that having declined to share his uncle's (fatal) interest in vulcanology, he tried to read Livy's history in an attempt to distract himself from the seismic disturbances occurring at the time (*Ep.* 6.20). Pliny's admiration for the historian may also account for the story in the *Letters* (*Ep.* 2.3) of the Spaniard who journeyed all the way from Gades (Cadiz) to see Livy. Martial (14.190), like Caligula, complained about the size of Livy's work, but at least the epigram demonstrates that Livy must have been reasonably well known.

This book is not the place for a searching analysis on the reasons for Livy's public appeal, but one example in particular offers some insight. At 35.14 Livy describes a meeting that Scipio Africanus supposedly had with Hannibal at Ephesus some years after the Battle of Zama. The historian acknowledges that his tradition is Claudius (Quadrigarius), who in turn followed a history written in Greek by C. Acilius (cf. *FGrH* 813.F.5).[19] The tradition was early, but its reliability was uncertain, and Livy's main authority did not say anything about Scipio's presence on the embassy to Hannibal. The gist of the story is that Scipio asked Hannibal which general he ranked as the greatest general in history and that, after some procrastination, Hannibal finally (and cleverly) admitted that Scipio was in a class of his own, a far greater general than Alexander, Pyrrhus, or Hannibal himself.[20]

Historically, the tale is unlikely,[21] but it is significant for two reasons.

---

18. On the necrology format in historiography, see A.J. Pomeroy, "Livy's Funeral Notices," *G&R* 35 (1988): 173–83; see also Pomeroy, *Appropriate Comment*, 1–31.

19. Livy 35.14.5; the identity of Livy's source as Claudius Quadrigarius is supported by J. Briscoe, *A Commentary on Livy, Books XXXIV–XXXVII* (Oxford, 1981), 165.

20. The story is also told by Appian (*Syr.* 10.38–42) and Plutarch (*Flam.* 21). For a comparative analysis of the traditions, see K. Brodersen, *Appian's Antiochike* (Munich, 1991), 104–7.

21. Against authenticity, see M. Holleaux, *Études d'epigraphie et d'histoire grecques* (Paris, 1957), 184–207; H.H. Scullard, *Scipio Africanus: Soldier and Politician* (London, 1970), 198 and n. 163. See Briscoe (supra, n. 19), 166, for additional references.

It shows, first, Livy's willingness to admire a national hero and, second, his awareness of what the majority of his audience would probably enjoy. Polybius would have very likely deemed such an anecdote outside the boundaries of historical propriety. But to Livy, the tale, in addition to being a good story, was part of national tradition; like the legend of the Roman hero Regulus (cf. Horace *Odes* 3.5), it emphasized Roman character and the greatness of Roman achievement. In Livy's presentation, both Hannibal and Alexander were eclipsed by Rome; thus the historian's capacity to entertain while at the same time flattering Roman sensibilities and values would be very attractive to the majority of his audience.

It has often been remarked that Livy was a profound influence on Quintus Curtius, particularly in style. Linguistically, Curtius cannot be said to be strictly Livian, since in common with other Silver Age authors, he also displays his familiarity with Vergil, and Atkinson supported the suggestion of other scholars that Curtius' prose rhythm and his *clausulae* has more affinity with Cicero than with Livy or Tacitus.[22]

One could also say that Sallust's *Jugurtha* has common ground with Curtius' *Historiae;* both works are accounts of the careers of non-Romans, written by Romans. Jugurtha was likewise portrayed as a mixture of *virtus* and *vitia,* and Sallust's discussion of the role of *fortuna* has clear implications for Curtius' evaluation of Alexander. But, for all the charismatic and ambivalent portrayal of its subject, the *Jugurtha* was nevertheless a biting exposé of factional politics at Rome. Another early Augustan author who may have had a profound influence on Curtius was Pompeius Trogus, a possibility that will receive some consideration in another section of this chapter.

But Curtius probably comes closer to Livian style than to the historical styles of Sallust and Tacitus. Livian echoes in vocabulary, theme, and rhetorical topoi have often been noted.[23] As G.V. Sumner said, "nobody doubts Curtius studied Livy."[24] Leeman termed Curtius *Livianus,* a view

---

22. On Vergilian affinities, see Rutz, 2336; Atkinson, *Curtius* i, 39; Steele, *AJPh* 36 (1915): 410. There was also a dissertation by R. Balzer, "Der Einfluss Vergils auf Curtius Rufus" (Diss. Munich, 1971), which I have not been able to consult. On Ciceronian rhythms, see Atkinson, *Curtius* i, 48.

23. On Livy's influence, see Atkinson, *Curtius* i, 39 f.; Steele, *AJPh* 36 (1915): 404, 421, and *AJPh* 40 (1919): 43–46; Dosson, 276–77; Rutz, 2340; L. Braccesi, "Livio, Curzio Rufo e Petrarca (per la fortuna dell' excursus su papiro)," *Athenaeum* 65 (1987): 237–39. One may note the affinity between Livy 6.16.3 and Curtius 6.9.32, where the use of *attollere oculos* and *hiscere* occurs together; see Rolfe, 2:86.

24. Sumner, *AUMLA* 15 (1961): 37 n. 15.

echoed by A.J. Woodman, in *Rhetoric in Classical Historiography*, who himself omitted a specific analysis of the former.[25] Dietmar Korzeniewski took exception to this common view, although his arguments are on the whole unconvincing, particularly his view that Curtius' style has a "poetic character," a phenomenon that is found in Livy's first decades, but not in his later ones.[26]

However, Curtius did not have to reproduce exactly Livy's Latinity to have been influenced by him, and as for poetic character, it is difficult to accept that Livy entirely abandoned his love of image, description, and emotive power (or whatever constitutes poetic) in his later work.[27] It is also possible that in terms of a common interest in *regnum*, Curtius was mostly interested in Livy's early books. Even allowing for the conventionalized depiction of tyranny so prevalent in late republican and early imperial literature,[28] there are certain parallels between Curtius' development of *regnum* and its related motifs—*vis, fides, superbia, libertas, pietas*, and so on—and Livy's treatment of the kings in book 1.

Alexander's *vis* (force) has both positive and negative aspects: one may recall the *vis* of Romulus (albeit tainted with fratricide), which literally carves Rome out of the wilderness, as opposed to the *superbia* and *licentia* of Tarquinius Superbus or Sextus. One may also note a similarity between Curtius' Alexander and Livy's Romulus in the former's slaying of Cleitus and the latter's murder of his brother, Remus. Livy gives alternative versions of how Remus met his death, although his own emphasis is on Romulus' deed, via the historian's comment "the more common story is . . ." [vulgatior fama est . . .] (1.7.2). However, Livy does not stress the enormity of the crime or that it is *nefas*; more than forty years later, Romulus' disappearance, perhaps murdered at the hands of disgruntled *patres* as Livy suggests (1.16.4), was for different reasons.[29] In

---

25. Woodman, *Rhetoric*, 158–59 n. 149. Cf. Leeman, *Orationis Ratio*, 1:255 f.

26. Korzeniewski, "Die Zeit des Quintus Curtius Rufus," 81 f. "Poetic character" may apply to certain aspects of Tacitus' Latinity; he also borrowed particularly from Vergil. See Furneaux, *Tacitus*, 1:38 f., esp. 40 n. 2; cf. Syme, *Tacitus*, 1:357 f.

27. However, see Syme's obvious but lucid remark in *Historia* (1988): 366; 107 of Livy's books are not extant, and he may have modified his manner, especially in treating contemporary events.

28. One may note the parallel in Livy 1.54.6–10 (Tarquinius Superbus' silent demonstration to the messenger of how Sextus should treat the leading citizens of Gabii) with Thrasybulus of Miletus; cf. Hdt. 5.92. See also J.R. Dunkle, *TAPhA* 98 (1967): 151–71.

29. Cf. Livy 1.15.8; Romulus had become more popular with the common people than with the senators. On Livy's possible use of a pre-Caesarian source favorable to Romulus and on the exploitation of parallels with Caesar's assassination in other traditions, see R.M. Ogilvie, *A Commentary on Livy, Bks I–V* (Oxford, 1965), 85.

one very real sense, Romulus' removal of Remus was necessary, for although the gods had offered signs, the issue was undecided, and kingship cannot be dual. So Curtius says at 10.9.1, "kingship is indivisible..." [insociabile est regnum...], a phrase reminiscent of Tacitus (*Ann.* 13.17.1).

Alexander's murder of Cleitus is also an act of force and likewise violates obligations of *fides* and *pietas;* Cleitus' sister had been Alexander's wet nurse, and the man himself had once saved the king's life. But apparent Livian echoes, noticeable in one of Cleitus' jibes to Alexander,[30] are discernible in the king's brief, savage words to Cleitus as he kills him.

"Go, now," he said, "to Philip and Parmenion and Attalus!"

["I nunc," inquit, "ad Philippum et Parmenionem et Attalum!"] (Curt. 8.1.52)

Like Cleitus, Remus taunted a man of *vis;* Romulus' response was equally short.

Thus perish anyone else who leaps across my walls!

[Sic deinde, quicumque alius transiliet moenia mea!] (Livy 1.48.7)

Yet in Curtius (8.1.50–51), Alexander's action was premeditated; the murder was not the result of impulse as was reported in some historical traditions or even as was the case with Romulus. Curtius alone depicts Alexander's murder of Cleitus as deliberate *licentia regni;* in this respect, Alexander has become less like Romulus and more like Sextus Tarquinius. The portrayal of Alexander in Curtius' later books is very much the portrait of a king in moral deterioration; but while the historian may exploit a traditional—if not hackneyed—theme, he nevertheless demonstrates his Roman approach to it and his awareness of his own national, literary heritage.

Regnum also steadily declines in the first book of Livy's history. In a florid and emotive passage, Livy prepares his audience for what will be the reign of the worst king, Tarquinius Superbus, by describing how his ambitious wife, Tullia, crazed by the hounding furies of her murdered sis-

---

30. Curt. 8.1.37; cf. Livy 9.19.10–11. See also Braccesi (supra, n. 23).

ter and husband, drove her carriage right over her father's body. The historian comments that on the death of the penultimate king Servius Tullius, "just and lawful kingship" perished with him. *Libertas* and the res publica are established by the book's end. But paradoxically, despite Livy's anathema for *regnum*, the nature of the whole of the *Ab urbe condita* is cyclic.[31]

Rome's history begins and ends with kings. Scholarly views on Livy's attitude toward Augustus are contradictory, but it seems certain that like so many authors of the Augustan Age, Livy felt a genuine gratitude for the peace that the *princeps* established.[32] If Livy is keen to stress the refoundation of Rome at the end of book 5 and the identification of Camillus with Augustus (as some scholars believe), an attractive link can be drawn between his interpretation and Curtius' gratitude to another *princeps* who could also be said to have founded the city afresh.[33] Yet it should also be emphasized that both historians (along with many Greco-Roman authors) were only too well aware of the ambivalent power of kingship.

Stylistically, Curtius is not as complicated an author as Livy; in general he uses shorter sentences, his vocabulary contains few unusual words (although he does use common words in a strange sense), and he has a tendency to overuse a favorite construction or phrase—a stylistic weakness that was (and is) not unique to him.[34] But whereas Curtius does not have the same linguistic brilliance of Livy, he is also less difficult to read. Moreover, his prose is clear, and he can be effectively terse in an appropriate situation. For example, Curtius relates Alexander's violent solution to the puzzle of the Gordian knot in a concise but dramatic fashion.

---

31. This view is controversial, but see G.B. Miles, "The Cycle of Roman History in Livy's First Pentad," *AJPh* 107 (1986): 1–33.

32. Livy's attitude toward Augustus has been the subject of much debate; R. Syme, "Livy and Augustus," *HSCP* 64 (1959): 57–69 (cf. Syme, *The Roman Revolution*, 317 f., 463–64), claimed Livy was pro-Augustus, but Walsh, *Livy*, 10 f., and "Livy and Augustus," *PACA* 4 (1961): 26–37, argued Livy was more independent. Cf. H. Petersen, "Livy and Augustus," *TAPhA* 92 (1962): 440–52; E. Gabba, "The Historians and Augustus," in *Caesar Augustus: Seven Aspects*, ed. F. Millar and E. Segal (Oxford, 1984), 61–88. A more balanced appraisal may be found in T.J. Luce, "The Dating of Livy's First Decade," *TAPhA* 96 (1965): 209–240; cf. Luce, *Livy: The Composition of His History*, 290–92.

33. On Camillus and Augustus, see Miles (supra, n. 31), 14f, but see Walsh, *Livy*, 15–19.

34. Syme, *Historia* 37 (1988): 367–68 n. 51, cites the rare usage of *bacchabundus*; cf. infra, n. 37.

Alexander struggled in vain for a long time with the hidden knots. "It makes no difference," he cried out, "'how they are untied!" and having slashed through all the knots with his sword, he either tricked the oracle or fulfilled it.

[Ille nequiquam diu luctatus cum latentibus nodis; "Nihil," inquit, "interest quomodo solvantur," gladioque ruptis omnibus loris, oraculi sortem vel elusit vel implevit.] (3.1.18)

The previous context has established an atmosphere of tense expectation; the king must untie the knot, lest his failure be seen as an omen. One may note Curtius' word order; Alexander's cry in *oratio recta* and the emphatic placement of *nihil interest* underscore the message that what is important is the action of solving the problem, not the manner in which it is solved. The ablative of means and the ablative absolute neatly convey the simultaneous action of slashing the cords, and the *vel . . . vel* construction alerts us to the historian's own worldly view *(oraculi sortem . . . elusit)*. However, the final word placement of the verb *implevit* informs the reader that the anxieties of Alexander's audience in regard to the prophecy were set to rest.

One could argue that Livy's impact might be reduced if more had survived of other early imperial writers, such as Cremutius Cordus, Aufidius Bassus, and Servilius Nonianus, all of whom earned commendation from Quintilian (*Inst.* 10.1.102–4). It is interesting that Quintilian did not mention Curtius in his survey of Roman imperial historiography, which suggests that Quintilian either predated Curtius or did not consider him worthy of mention. But perhaps the omission is not so surprising. Quintilian's list is not exhaustive; he emphasizes that he has been selective and that there are other good writers. Although he says he has mentioned names according to *genera*, or types, the historians that he lists all wrote Roman history. He does not mention Trogus, and since the general essence of his argument is to demonstrate the equal talent of Roman writers and orators alongside their Greek counterparts, he refers to historians with Roman themes. Yet even here, he is not particularly expansive, and some of his other omissions of Roman historians are unexpected—he does not mention the histories of Pliny the Elder (*A fine Aufidi Bassi*; cf. *Ep.* 3.5.5), Cluvius Rufus, or Fabius Rusticus.[35]

---

35. On Quintilian's list, see J.J. Wilkes, "Julio-Claudian Historians," *CW* 65 (1972): 177–92, 197–203; cf. H. Lindsay (supra, n. 14), 9.

In the absence of the works of other early imperial historians, Livy provides the more obvious model. Despite the equally rhetorical nature of Velleius Paterculus' *Epitome,* Curtius has more in common with Livy than he has with Velleius. As Atkinson noted, any similar phraseology between the two authors suggests little beyond mutual knowledge of common rhetorical maxims.[36] For instance, Curtius' report of Alexander of Epirus' comment that he had encountered men in Italy whereas Alexander the Great had faced women (8.1.37) may well have been a deliberate Livian echo (cf. Livy 9.19.10–11). One may also recall the Curtian and Livian mutual usage of *comissabundus* to describe the drunken revel of Alexander's army through Carmania; the term is deliberately used by Curtius elsewhere, again within the context of licentious behavior.[37]

However, it is equally possible that each historian exploited common topoi from the rhetorical schools. Alexander of Epirus' alleged remark on the effeminacy of Asiatics remained popular in the traditions.[38] This does not necessarily mean that Curtius and Livy were contemporaries, since we know that in Roman rhetorical schools Alexander remained a popular subject for *declamatio,* or rhetorical exercise on a given theme. It is evident that in the early imperial period, Latin literature became increasingly influenced by this specialist form of rhetoric. Juvenal (*Sat.* 10.166–67) clearly exploited his audience's familiarity with *suasoriae* within a satirical context, alluding to topoi on Hannibal and Alexander.[39] Aspects of Curtius' relationship to rhetoricians and various rhetorical formats of the first century A.D. have also been considered before, as scholars have discussed the affinity between certain passages of Curtius' work and excerpts from Valerius Maximus and Seneca the Elder.

Undoubtedly the Alexander traditions were used by Roman rhetoricians and philosophers. Valerius Maximus did not write history, but he provided rhetorical exempla on historical characters for orators, who

---

36. Atkinson, *Curtius* i, 39 f. On Velleius Paterculus in general, see C. Starr, "The Scope and Genre of Velleius' History," *CQ* 31 (1981): 162–74.

37. Livy 9.17.7; Curt. 9.10.26, 5.7.10. According to the *OLD, comissabundus* is used elsewhere only by Pliny (*NH* 21.9).

38. See Gellius *NA* 17.21.3. See also W.B. Anderson, "Contributions to the Study of the Ninth Book of Livy," *TAPhA* 39 (1908): 89–103; his argument that Livy's digression at 9.17–19 was a youthful exercise is not persuasive. See F.W. Walbank, "Livy, Macedonia, and Rome," in *Ancient Macedonian Studies in Honour of Charles F. Edson,* ed. H.J. Dell (Thessaloníki, 1981), 335–56.

39. For the influence of declamation on Roman literature, see S.F. Bonner, *Roman Declamation,* 149 f.; J. Fairweather, *Seneca the Elder,* 304 f.

could exploit them in varying degrees of elaboration. He included Alexander as a model under several categories, including *patientia* (endurance), *constantia* (constancy), *amicitia* (friendship), *clementia* (compassion), *iracundia* (irascibility), *superbia* (arrogance), and *cupiditas gloriae* (lust for glory).[40]

However, as R.B. Steele noted, although Curtius and Valerius Maximus depict some Alexander stories in common, they differ in their presentation.[41] For instance, one may note Curtius 3.6 on Alexander's illness at Tarsus and its relationship with Valerius Maximus 3.8.ext.6, or one may note the two writers' depictions of Alexander's visit to Darius' family (Curt. 3.12.15–26; Val. Max. 4.7.ext.2). Curtius' treatment of each episode is very elaborate in relation to Valerius Maximus, Trogus, and other traditions. A detailed treatment does not seem necessary here. Alexander's sickness at Tarsus and his meeting with Darius' family have received thorough analysis in terms of composition and sources in other modern works; in the present study, the significance of both episodes for Curtius' development of *regnum* is discussed in chapter 5.[42] Valerius Maximus includes the Tarsus incident under the heading *constantia*. His emphasis is therefore appropriately given to Alexander's steadfast trust in his friend Philip the doctor; despite Parmenion's warning that Philip had been bribed by Darius, he drinks the medicine "without any delay" [sine ulla cunctatione], whereas in Curtius (3.6.5–7) the king indulges in an anxious soliloquy—which may be described as sheer rhetorical padding, obviously intended to heighten the dramatic tension.

Curtius' and Valerius Maximus' depictions of these episodes point not so much to one author's direct influence over another but to both authors' respective use of common ground. Curtius and his aural or reading public were well aware that an episode like the Tarsus incident presented a prime opportunity for rhetorical virtuosity, and it was up to the historian to make the best of it. Moreover, he exploits a number of complex themes in the episode, including Alexander's *fides* and *pietas* toward Philip and his relationship with Parmenion and his army.

---

40. Val. Max. 3.2.ext.1, *patientia;* 3.8.6, *constantia;* 4.7.ext.2, *amicitia;* 5.1.ext.1, *clementia;* 8.3.ext.1, *iracundia;* 9.5.ext.1, *superbia;* 8.14.ext.2, *cupiditas gloriae.* See also Leeman, *Orationis Ratio,* 1:255.

41. Steele, *AJPh* 36 (1915): 411.

42. On Alexander at Tarsus, see Atkinson, *Curtius* i, 146 f., especially his comparative tables of sources, 168–69; on his meeting with Darius' family, see ibid., 248 f.

Also, according to G. Maslakov, the rhetorician's organization of exempla on a variety of themes faces different problems from the historian, in terms of potential contradictions in both political and unresolved moral positions.[43] The historian follows an orderly narrative of events, a pattern that Curtius adopts. When he does diverge from a chronological sequence or decide to narrate one series of events as a unit (5.1.1–2), he explains his reasons for doing so. While Curtius' narrative of certain rhetorical episodes could stand as self-sufficient declamations (see, e.g., Alexander's meeting with the Greek mercenaries in 5.5.8 f., discussed later in this chapter), they are also part of a consistent, integral structure.

Nevertheless, certain parallels between Curtius and the rhetoricians are worth examining, and Seneca the Elder provides an appropriate case study.[44] The comparison in language and style between Seneca *Suasoriae* 1.1 and Curtius 9.4.18 offers an especially striking example of similarities in rhetorical phraseology and sentiment. The subject of the Seneca passage is a debate between several characters on whether Alexander should cross the ocean; the fears of the characters include the monsters of the deep and the unknown.

> The sea stands motionless, a sluggish mass of nature, as if failing by its own limits: strange and terrible shapes, great monsters even for Ocean, which that same deep emptiness nurtures; the light obscured by deep darkness, the day cut off by gloom; the sea indeed heavy and motionless; and the stars either nonexistent or unknown.
>
> [Stat immotum mare, quasi deficientis in suo fine naturae pigra moles; novae ac terribiles figurae, magna etiam Oceano portenta quae profunda ista vastitas nutrit, confusa lux alta caligine et interceptus tenebris dies, ipsum vero grave et defixum mare et aut nulla aut ignota sidera.] (Sen. *Suas.* 1.1)

---

43. G. Maslakov, "Valerius Maximus and Roman Historiography," *ANRW* II.32.1 (1984): 437–96, esp. 453–54.

44. The links between Curtius and Seneca the Elder have received considerable attention; see W.A. Edward, *The Suasoriae of Seneca the Elder* (Cambridge, 1928), 83 f.; Bardon, *LEC* 15 (1947): 125; Dosson, 244; Leeman, *Orationis Ratio,* 1:256. Within this context, studies on Curtius' affinities with Seneca the Younger may be noted; see Steele, *AJPh* (1915): 412; Atkinson, *Curtius* i, 26 f., 41; J.R. Hamilton, *Historia* 37 (1988): 445–56. Hamilton argues Seneca knew of Curtius.

In Curtius, Alexander's soldiers in *oratio obliqua* voice the same fears that occur in Seneca, complaining:

> They themselves were hurled before unconquered peoples, so that by their own blood they might open up Ocean for him; they were dragged beyond the stars and sun and forced to go to places that nature had removed from the sight of mortal men. Again and again, new enemies appeared with new arms. And if they should rout and put to flight all those enemies, what reward would there be for themselves? Gloomy darkness and perpetual night lying heavily on a deep sea, a sea filled with schools of savage sea monsters and unmoving waters where moribund nature had failed.

> [Indomitis gentibus se obiectos, ut sanguine suo aperirent ei Oceanum. Trahi extra sidera et solem cogique adire, quae mortalium oculis natura subduxerit. Novis identidem armis novos hostes existere. Quos ut omnes fundant fugentque, quod praemium ipsos manere? caliginem ac tenebras et perpetuam noctem profundo incubantem mari, repletum inmanium beluarum gregibus fretum, inmobiles undas, in quibus emoriens natura defecerit.] (Curt. 9.4.18)

In particular, the sea is depicted in both authors as a motionless, deep, dark expanse (note the repetition of *caligo* and *tenebrae*) that is inhabited by sea monsters and that nature has somehow failed or forsaken. It is possible that this description did not originate from the earlier Alexander traditions (there is no suggestion of either similar imagery or sentiment in any of the other extant, historical accounts) but was rather the result of a rhetorical exercise on a standard topos. Other echoes of Seneca occur elsewhere—Moschus (*Suas.* 1.2) warns *quod humanis natura subduxit oculis, aeterna nox obruit,* whereas in Curtius the soldiers complain about going where *mortalium oculis natura subdexerit.*

Another example of a rhetorical topos in the early empire is offered by the ominous description of the sea in an extract from a poem composed by Albinovanus Pedo, which is also quoted by Seneca.

> And now they see day and sun long left behind;
> Banished from the familiar limits of the world
> They dare to pass through forbidden shades

To the bounds of things, the remotest shores of the world.
Now they think Ocean, that breeds beneath its sluggish waves
Terrible monsters, savage sea-beasts everywhere . . .
               (Sen. *Suas*. 1.15–20; trans. M. Winterbottom)[45]

There are probable derivative Hellenistic elements in the description. The image of the dark, sluggish ocean is reminiscent of Homer's picture of the Cimmerians at the start of *Odyssey* 11, where the poet speaks of a dark, although not motionless, sea. Early lyric poetry could also have had some influence; Stesichorus depicted the sun descending into a wine cup that at night floats back over the ocean from west to east, so that by necessity the sea must be calm and still.[46]

The Romans knew of sharks, sawfish, and other large marine animals, but the term *sea monster* (*belua, pristis,* and so forth) could also refer to a whale. Arrian (*Ind*. 30.1) describes as "huge sea monsters" (Κήτεα δὲ μεγάλα) the cetaceans that Nearchus encountered on his return voyage from India, and he acknowledges that these animals were much bigger than those found in the Mediterranean. Whales were thus not unknown to an educated Greek or Roman, and both Aristotle and Pliny the Elder included sections on them in their natural histories.[47] However, *sea monster* would be an appropriate term for any Greco-Roman writer to use, given the extra advantage of increasing the emotional impact of the passage through adding a sense of foreboding and wonder.

Although there are features in common, the objectives of Curtius and the rhetoricians were different; the Seneca passage belongs to declamation, within the context of *suasoriae,* or speeches advising historical and

---

45. Seneca's text of the poem follows:

iamque vident post terga diem solemque relictum
iam pridem, notis extorres finibus orbis,
per non concessas audaces ire tenebras
ad rerum metas extremaque litora mundi.
nunc illum, pigris immania monstra sub undis
qui ferat, Oceanum, qui saevas undique pristis . . .

The translation of Seneca in text is from M. Winterbottom, trans., *The Elder Seneca* (*Suas*. 1.15 Cambridge, Mass., 1974), 2: 503.

46. Cf. D. Page, *Poetae Melici Graeci* (Oxford, 1962), 100, F 8 = Athen. (om. E) xi 469 E.

47. Aristotle *Hist. an*. 8.2; Pliny *NH* 9.2 f. Pliny's narrative is a mixture of fantasy and fact. Curtius (4.4.3) uses the vague term *belua,* presumably meaning a whale, rather than *balaena*.

mythological figures. Curtius may have known Seneca's work, and in a similar fashion, the Albinovanus Pedo poem, within its context of Germanicus' expedition to the North Sea in 16 A.D., may have been another model for him, as it possibly was for Tacitus. Pedo was probably one of Germanicus' officers on this campaign (see Tac. *Ann.* 1.60), and although a likely eyewitness, he also apparently used a considerable amount of imagination in his poem.[48] It is also possible that Curtius may have simply repeated phraseology from his education; for the sake of audience appeal, he deliberately incorporated elements from a Roman topos with which he was familiar and which may have even been known to his public. In Curtius, the description of the sea adds color to the historiographical framework. Tacitus likewise uses similar imagery in his discussion of the sea beyond the islands of the Suiones as a *mare pigrum ac prope immotum* (Tac. *Germ.* 45.1; cf. *Agr.* 10.4–5). One may again note the pervasive nature of rhetorical discourse in Silver Age literature. The similarities are there because of the emphasis on rhetoric in Roman education and Latin prose, particularly in Quintilian's canon of oratory, historiography, and philosophy. Finally, in view of what Curtius says himself in relation to his methods, his use of sources, and his structure, it is apparent that his aims were different from those of the philosopher or the rhetorician. In short, one should look to other models for Curtius.

Quintus Curtius and Pompeius Trogus

The *Historiae Philippicae* of Pompeius Trogus was certainly extant in the third or fourth centuries A.D., and Justin praises the author's style, describing him as *vir priscae eloquentiae* [man of old-fashioned eloquence] (J. praef. 1).[49] As we saw earlier, it is possible that Justin may

---

48. Tiberius' brother, Germanicus (Drusus the Elder), was the first to navigate the North Sea (see Suet. *Claud.* 1); his son's expedition (see Tac. *Ann.* 2.23–24) had disastrous results. See Furneaux, *Tacitus,* 1:259, 312, 387 f.; Winterbottom (supra, n. 45), 2:503 n. 4.

49. Justin's date is controversial. Syme summarized a selection of arguments in *Historia* 37 (1988): 359 f. He dates Justin to about 395 A.D., perhaps correctly, but some scholars prefer R.B. Steele's Antonine date (see Steele, "Pompeius Trogus and Justinus," *AJP* 38 [1917]: 19–41) or a date in the third century (see W. Kroll, *RE* 10 [1917]: 957). Syme (loc. cit., 360) sarcastically noted that Otto Seel, the editor of the Teubner texts (1935; 2d ed., 1972), evidently changed his mind from a late (third- or fourth-century A.D.) date, suggested in his 1935 edition (iii), to sometime in the second century (see Seel, *Eine römische Weltgeschichte* [Nurnberg, 1972], 346), without giving reason. More recently, J.C. Yardley has also argued for a second-century A.D. date; see the introduction to Heckel and Yardley, *Justin.*

have exaggerated the history's reputation; although apparently well known by early imperial authors, it seems to have fallen into relative oblivion by the fourth century.[50]

Still, Curtius was probably influenced by the *Historiae Philippicae.* Pompeius Trogus himself lived during the Augustan period, and his father had served as secretary to Julius Caesar (see J. 43.5.12). The younger Trogus was thus contemporary with Livy and certainly knew his work. In 38.3.11 Justin says he has faithfully reproduced Trogus' rendition in *oratio obliqua* of Mithridates' speech to his soldiers, as an example of Trogus' style and, in particular, his *brevitas:* Justin adds that Trogus criticized both Sallust and Livy for their practice—conventional in historiography from Herodotus and Thucydides—of fabricated direct orations. However, on this issue, Trogus differed vastly from Curtius and every other historian, including Polybius: the obsession with *oratio obliqua* appears to have been unique to Trogus himself.

It is difficult to gauge the original style of Trogus, since the extant text is anything from a seventh to a mere tenth of the original.[51] Moreover, Justin's role as editor and his criteria of selectivity are clearly stated in his preface.

> During a period of leisure in which we were occupied in the city, I made excerpts from the forty-four volumes of this material (for he published that many) having judged what matters were worthiest and having omitted those which were essential neither for the sweet joy of learning nor as valuable examples, and I made a short work, comprised of the choicest flowers as it were . . .
>
> [Horum igitur quattuor et quadraginta voluminum (nam totidem edidit) per otium, quo in urbe versabamur, cognitione quaeque dignissima excerpsi et omissis his, quae nec cognoscendi voluptate iucunda nec exemplo erant necessaria, breve veluti florum corpusculum feci.] (J. praef. 4; trans. T.J. Ryan)[52]

---

50. See chap. 1, n. 3.
51. See Syme, *Historia* 37 (1988): 358 n. 1; cf. F.R.D. Goodyear, "On the Character and Text of Justin's Compilation of Trogus," *PACA* 16 (1982): 1–24.
52. The translation in text is from T.J. Ryan, unpublished translation, University of Newcastle.

Justin's project has been viewed by some scholars as more like an anthology than a summary or an epitome. Justin decides what to include and what to omit, which must automatically change the emphasis of the original author.[53]

The extent to which Justin paraphrased or even rewrote the original, which would result in the inevitable contamination of his own thought, is difficult to determine; his term *florum corpusculum* suggests that his approach was "scissors and paste," in the sense of excerpting passages from Trogus, more or less untouched, with perhaps a sentence or two of his own to provide the transitions from one episode to the next. But there is evidence to indicate that he tampered with the original a good deal more, and other scholars have argued that Justin thought he was writing a creative work of his own.[54]

There is a certain degree of parallelism between Curtius' history and Justin—or, more appropriately, Trogus. Both historians had an interest in foreign history and wrote treatises of Alexander, the latter within the context of his universal history. Both appeared to have drawn on common traditions, with varying degrees of correspondence and differentiation.[55] Some scholars have also argued that specific similarities in phraseology between the two authors would indicate that Curtius knew and copied Trogus directly. Dosson set out tables giving parallel usages of words, and Otto Seel ascribed many extracts from Curtius to Trogus' Alexander books.[56] Not all these examples are convincing, and one has to take into account the influence of a common source or else rhetorical topoi; the same material may have simply produced similar paraphrasing. However, as will be argued in a later part of this chapter, in the conclusion of his own book 5, Curtius was probably influenced for structural reasons by Trogus' account of the death of Darius.

Moreover, as C. Edson and Atkinson have pointed out, Curtius could apply Trogus' phraseology to another context.[57] One can surmise that

---

53. See Syme, *Historia* 37 (1988): 358; Goodyear (supra, n. 51), 1 ff. Cf. P.A. Brunt's description of Justin as an "Epitome of an Epitome," in *CQ* 30 (1980): 487; see also Hornblower, *Hieronymus of Cardia*, 1.

54. See P. Jal, "A propos des Histoires Philippiques: Quelques remarques," *REL* 65 (1987): 194–209; cf. J.C. Yardley, "The Literary Background to Justin/Trogus," *AHB* 8, no. 2 (1994): 69–70.

55. See chap. 3, n. 1.

56. Dosson, 146–47 and n. 3; O. Seel, *Pompei Trogi Fragmenta* (Leipzig, 1956), esp. 84 f. Examples of other verbal echoes are suggested by Atkinson, *Curtius* i, 60.

57. Atkinson, *Curtius* i, 67; cf. C. Edson, review of *Pompei Trogi Fragmenta,* comp. O. Seel, *CPh* 56 (1961): 198–203.

Curtius may have imitated Trogus' phrasing in much the same way that he used Vergilian vocabulary or copied Livy, even to the point of echoing one of Livy's jests, just as Tacitus himself also copied literary precursors.[58] But such *imitatio* would not necessarily weaken the originality of the imitator. Although all Roman literature observed the *lex operis* (or "rules of the game") in terms of the conventions for respective genres, it was also remarkably flexible. Roman writers could freely borrow from their predecessors, provided that they made their own contributions, in which case the borrowed phrase or model enhanced the flavor of their work.

Neither Curtius nor Trogus acted as an apologist for Alexander, and both were capable of presenting certain episodes—especially those pertaining to the king's relationship with his courtiers—in a negative light. However, as a general observation, it could be said that despite certain rhetorical exaggerations, Curtius tends to offer a more balanced appraisal of Alexander's court. His characterization of the king as a man of excess, both in *virtutes* and *vitia,* is not inconsistent with an appreciation of political realities. In comparison, Justin/Trogus is consistently hostile toward Alexander.

In his lengthy treatment of the fall of Philotas, Curtius maintains an impartial stance on the general's guilt, beyond a cynical observation on the reliability of evidence obtained under torture (6.11.21). In Justin, even allowing for the truncated nature of the Epitome, the negative nuance is clear: "In the meantime Alexander began to vent his cruelty against his own men with a hatred appropriate not to a king but to an enemy" [Interea et Alexander non regio, sed hostili odio saevire in suos coepit] (12.5.1–4). Justin then presents the complaints of the soldiers against Alexander in *oratio obliqua:* "As a result, throughout the entire camp everyone began to murmur, bemoaning the fate of an innocent old man and his son, all the way saying that they, too, ought not to hope for anything better" [Fremere itaque omnes universis castris coepere innoxii senis filiique casum miserantes interdum se quoque non debere melius sperare dicentes] (J. 12.5.4).

Certain aspects of Curtius' treatment of the same episode provide some interesting comparisons with Justin/Trogus. Both Curtius and Trogus used at least one tradition in common. The dissent of the soldiers appears in each (cf. Curt. 7.1–4), as do Alexander's decisions to, first, monitor the correspondence of his soldiers and, second, place the dissi-

---

58. See chap. 3, n. 66.

dents into a separate cohort (see J. 12.5.6–8; Curt. 7.2.36–38). There are also considerable differences. Curtius' account is far more elaborate, since he turns the whole aftermath of Philotas' fall into a study of king and court, in his expansive treatment of the trials of Alexander Lyncestes and Amyntas. According to Curtius (7.1.4–5), both trials were arranged for show, as the king needed to restore his tarnished *auctoritas.* Curtius also probably deliberately gave the Amyntas trial a contemporary tone by incorporating elements reminiscent of the trial of Marcus Terentius, which appears in Tacitus (*Ann.* 6.8).[59]

However, even where the information in Justin and Curtius coincides, the emphasis is different on the part of each historian. In the former (12.5.4) the soldiers bemoan the fate of an *innoxius senex;* Curtius does not comment on Parmenion's guilt or innocence but rather specifies why Alexander owed Parmenion *gratia* (7.1.3). Again, in Justin, Alexander organizes the rebelliously minded soldiers into a separate cohort, in the hope of either destroying them or settling them in remote colonies. There is no hint of this reason in Curtius; the king separates the dissidents so that their talk might not influence others. Moreover, Curtius (7.2.37) notes the *ignominia* (disgrace) these soldiers would feel through having to camp separately. This emphasis may have been a Roman intrusion on Curtius' part; one may compare Corbulo's punitive action against the centurion Paccius Orfitus in Tacitus (*Ann.* 13.36.3), where the centurion and his disgraced cohort were forced to camp outside the army lines.

Curtius turns the episode into another example of Alexander's *fortuna.* Far from resulting in disaster, the new cohort becomes even more enthusiastic for war and distinguishes itself with regard to *virtus.* The latter sentiment recalls Livy 10.4.4; the dictator Quintus Fabius (ca. 302 B.C.), hearing news that his master of the horse, Marcus Aemilius Paulus, had suffered a rout, finds the survivors of the disgraced cohort camping separately outside of the fortifications, the army eager to wipe out the *ignominia.*

The structure and aims of Justin's *Historiae Philippicae* were also clearly different from Curtius' *Historiae,* and Hellenistic historiographical influences on Trogus' original were probably more pronounced.[60]

---

59. On Terentius' speech, see Dio Cassius 57.19.3–4. On the parallels between Tacitus and Curtius, see Devine, *Phoenix* 33 (1979): 142–59; Atkinson, *Curtius* ii, 251 f.

60. See A. von Gutschmid, "Trogus und Timagenes," in *Kleine Schriften* (Leipzig, 1894), 218–27.

Perhaps influenced by Theopompus' earlier work of the same title, Trogus' study traced the rise and fall of four kingdoms—Assyria, Media, Persia, and Macedonia—before the advent of Rome.[61] Theopompus' own history is thought to have derived its structure ultimately from Herodotus, and the same discursive format was evidently copied by Trogus, which is demonstrated by the prologues to each of the books. Thus, although the accounts of Curtius and Justin occasionally converge, the former author, both in his decision to write on a single subject and in the way he chose to structure his history, embarked on a divergent project from the universal historian.

Curtius' Structure: Some Basic Principles

In the area of the composition and structure of his history, Curtius displays more probable affinity with Livy and Tacitus. As indicated earlier, one long-standing criticism of Curtius has alleged that the *Historiae* was more or less a series of rhetorical, purple passages that, at best, were only loosely connected.[62]

Owing to controversies surrounding the transmission and division of our extant texts, ascertaining an ancient author's original arrangement of his or her work is always a difficult problem. One automatic and sometimes unanswerable question arises: did a particular author finish the text where we have it, or was there more? Extant ancient texts are often incomplete, either because the author possibly did not finish the work, as in the case of Thucydides, or because the rest of the text was lost. On the odd occasion, even an apparently complete text caused controversy. A famous example of a modern scholar who finished an ancient work is the Renaissance Italian humanist Maffeo Vegio, who, since he believed that Vergil had not intended that his epic should end with the death of Turnus, wrote a thirteenth book to the *Aeneid*, in which Aeneas celebrated his marriage to Lavinia.[63] Also, sometimes an ancient author suggested

---

61. See J.W. Swain, "The Theory of the Four Monarchies: Opposition History under the Roman Empire," *CPh* 35 (1940): 1–21; cf. J. Pendergast, "The Philosophy of the History of Pompeius Trogus" (Ph.D. diss., University of Illinois, 1961).

62. See chap. 1, 13.

63. See K.W. Gransden, *Virgil*, Landmarks of World Literature Series (Cambridge, 1990), 104. Vegio's edition was followed by Gavin Douglas in the first English translation of the *Aeneid* into English in the sixteenth century.

continuation of a monograph.[64] We shall return to the issue of complete texts shortly, insofar as it is pertinent to Curtius' *Historiae*.

Pointing to a hexadic structure in both the *Aeneid* and the *Annales* of Ennius, Syme argued that Tacitus divided both the *Historiae* and the *Annales* into hexads, or groups of six books—twelve in the former and eighteen in the latter. The theory applies very well to the *Annales,* but in view of the state of the text, it is more difficult to justify for the *Historiae*. The hexads were structured around a common theme, such as the reign of Tiberius in books 1–6.[65] Although Tacitus gives a lengthy narrative of events within the empire and outside of Rome, his characterization of Tiberius is the main subject. Germanicus' campaigns in Pannonia, the revolt of Tacfarinas in Africa, relief for earthquake victims in Asia, the growth of *maiestas* trials at Rome, and court intrigues are nevertheless all dominated by the personality of the emperor.

Livy's composition of his history is also a controversial issue; however, the common scholarly view is that Livy blocked out his material according to pentads and decads, and this method of organization is deemed the historian's own creation.[66] The pentad is Livy's basic unit of composition. Within this framework, Livy used two chief methods in designing his narrative. The first is thematic unity (especially prevalent in the first pentad)—for instance, the themes of *regnum* in book 1 or *libertas* in book 2. The second method, according to T.J. Luce, is "architectonic": Livy achieves a special focus or symmetry by placing carefully developed episodes at certain points within books or pentads. For example, book 5 is composed in two contrasting halves—the first concerning the conquest of Veii, Rome's greatest victory up to that point; the second concerning Rome's greatest defeat, the rout at the Allia and the Sack of Rome. Within this structure, the narrative is built around the demoralizing effects of *luxuria,* as with the looting of Veii and Rome's recovery after its own disaster.[67]

Thus, convention aside, there were good reasons for a historian to arrange his material into either pentads or a hexadic structure. On a

---

64. See D.S. Levene, "Sallust's Jugurtha: An Historical Fragment," *JRS* 82 (1992): 53–70.

65. See Syme, *Tacitus,* 1:253 f. and, more importantly, 2: app. 35; cf. R. Drews, "The Lacuna in Tacitus' *Annales* Book Five in the Light of Christian Traditions," *AJAH* 9 (1984): 112–22, who raises some interesting implications about the hexadic structure.

66. See Luce, *Livy,* 3. Cf. Walsh, *Livy,* 5–8; Woodman, *Rhetoric,* 134 n. 80.

67. Luce, *Livy,* 26–32. On the *luxuria* motif in Livy 5, see Miles (supra, n. 31), 5 f.

pragmatic level, it would facilitate control and unity, while at the same time serving aesthetic literary considerations in the opportunity for developing cameo scenes relating to the main themes.

The textual transmission of Curtius' *Historiae* is problematic; some manuscripts do not give any indication of books and chapters at all. Moreover, in the fifteenth and sixteenth centuries, certain scholars, such as Angelo Decembrio, issued editions with the text split into eight or a dozen books. However, as Dosson noted, most and better manuscripts of Curtius favor a ten-book division, and this structure has been adopted by modern scholars.[68]

Although there is substance to the idea of a division into twelve books (which would suggest that Curtius, like Tacitus, may have followed the Ennian and Vergilian model), other stylistic and structural considerations make ten books for the *Historiae* a more appropriate arrangement. Whatever scheme Curtius employed, book 5 was evidently conceived as a self-contained unit, and the death of Darius imparts a clear break. The division is suggested by two factors: the historian's comment on Alexander's triumph at Gaugamela (Curt. 4.16.33), which concludes the account in a rhetorical but definite fashion; and his statement at the beginning of book 5 that he will deliberately keep the Asian narrative together and return to an account of European events at another point—which he apparently did, as what we have of book 6 commences in the middle of Agis' war.[69]

It seems possible that Curtius may have adopted a structure similar to Livy's model and conceived the *Historiae* as a decade that was divided into two pentads. These pentads are in turn linked by the themes of *fortuna* and *regnum*. It should be noted that W. Rutz also commented on Curtius' use of pentads, particularly in the climax of book 5, the death of Darius, and in the portrait of Alexander in the post-Darius books.[70]

Under the ten-book division, the beginning and ending of each book has been so carefully designed that it is hard not to see the scheme as anything but the original design of the author. Each book closes with a climactic incident, and the opening of the sequential book, usually itself a rhetorical flourish, relates to the conclusion of the previous book. For

---

68. Dosson, 3 n. 2. On Decembrio, see ibid., 374.
69. One important contribution of Codex P (see chap. 1) was that its scribe recognized that there was a major lacuna in the text between the end of book 5 and the start of book 6; see Atkinson, *ANRW* II.34.4 (1997): section 1.
70. Rutz, 2335–36.

instance, in the modern editions, book 3 finishes with the sack of Damascus, whereas book 4 commences with Darius' flight. But the reference to the assassination of the city's governor, who had betrayed Damascus to Alexander, provides the link with book 4; the governor's *perfidia* is countered by the *fides* of his assassin, who was still conscious of the Great King's majesty. The name of Darius, the recipient of that loyalty, is the very first word of book 4, and the description of his shameful flight through solitary wastes enhances the irony of the assassin's action.

In the post-Darius books, book 6 finishes with the death of Philotas, while book 7 opens with the events in the wake of his execution: the trial of Alexander Lyncestes and Amyntas. The remaining books follow a similar, sequential pattern, with the breaks occurring smoothly and naturally, linking each book in theme; the beginning of book 8 underscores the importance of *fama* and *gloria,* important motifs in the second pentad, and at the same time reminds us of Alexander's *crudelitas* to Ariamazes, the commander of the rock fortress, who had defied him (7.11.27–28). Following the king's victory over Porus on the Hydaspes, book 9 opens on a note of joyful anticipation, with Alexander's belief that the East had been opened up to him; however, this splendid optimism is contrasted with the army's terrible crossing of the Gedrosia desert (9.10.8–16) and the ugly theme that surfaces at the end of the book: Alexander's elimination of satraps who have displeased him, irrespective of their guilt. Moreover, in a significant play on image, book 9 begins with a sacrifice to the sun and ends with a most unheroic revel in honor of Father Liber (Dionysus). If both these symbols may be linked with Alexander, the former represents kingship's capacity for *beneficia,* the latter its potential for destructiveness and caprice.

It seems reasonable that Alexander's conquest of Darius was the dominant theme of the first five books, with each of the three great battles against the Persians—at the Granicus, Issus, and Gaugamela—as obvious high points. The historian could also explore a comparison between Alexander and Darius as *reges* through a series of related episodes; for instance, in book 3, Darius' savage treatment of his guest and suppliant Charidemus may be contrasted with Alexander's *fides* toward his own retainer, the physician Philip. Once he had won the empire, Alexander's increasing tyranny and the deterioration of *libertas* formed the connecting thread of the second pentad.

The potential content of Curtius' lost, first two books has caused scholarly speculation since the Renaissance; more recently, Waldemar

Heckel offered a summary of books 1 and 2 in the Penguin edition.[71] Nevertheless, some brief observations may be offered here, particularly in relation to why certain topics and events may have interested the historian. Whether Curtius produced any account of Alexander's early life is hard to determine. Like Arrian, he clearly knew certain traditions about the king's youth, but since he elsewhere provides background information for the reader's benefit—for example, details about Hephaestion (3.12.16); Philip, the king's family doctor (3.6.1); Alexander's horse, Bucephalas (6.5.18); or his nurse, Hellanice (8.1.21)—it seems unlikely that Curtius wrote a substantial narrative of Alexander's boyhood. As with Arrian, the king's *erga,* or his res gestae, probably constituted his main focus.[72]

Equally problematic is how much attention Curtius would have given to Alexander's Balkan campaign; Diodorus (17.8.1–2) alludes briefly to the king's campaigns in Thrace, Paeonia, and Illyria, which were necessary for him to secure the Macedonian borders. How much detail the Balkan campaign received in the eyewitness or early accounts is hard to evaluate; Arrian's discussion (1.2–6) is the most elaborate, but because most of his information probably derives from Ptolemy,[73] the question of Curtius' treatment would depend on not only his use of that tradition but how much importance he placed on the expedition. Since Ptolemy does not seem to have been one of Curtius' major authorities,[74] he possibly did not relate a substantial narrative. But the Theban uprising, in view of its extensive coverage in the main sources,[75] would likely have provided a better dramatic opportunity, and so would the battle at the Granicus. It is possible that Curtius used the Granicus battle as an exciting conclusion to book 1, although this may have left him a little short of material for book 2.

However, given the historian's emphasis on the sieges of Tyre and Gaza in book 4, the main interest for the military narrative of book 2

---

71. See chap. 1, 4; *Quintus Curtius Rufus, the History of Alexander,* trans. J. Yardley, with notes by W. Heckel (Harmondsworth, 1984), 19 f.
72. See Bosworth, *HCA,* 1:14.
73. See ibid., 51.
74. See chap. 3, 74–76, 82, 84–85.
75. See Arrian 1.7–9; Diod. 17.8–14; Plut. *Alex.* 11–13; J. 11.3 f. Cf. Aeschines 3.239 f.; Dinarchus *Contra Dem.* 18–21. Diodorus' account, which was probably drawn from Cleitarchus, is very emotive and elaborate (Diod. 17.14.4; cf. *FGrH* 137.F.1 = *Athen.* 4.30.148 D–F; Hammond, *THA,* 13 f., 51); Arrian (1.9 f.) digresses on the significance of the disaster.

may have been based around the sieges of Miletus and Halicarnassus, Alexander's campaigns in Lycia, Pamphylia, and Pisidia, and his administrative arrangements. Curtius probably elaborated the assault on the rock fortress of the Marmares in Lycia (described only by Diodorus, at 17.28), perhaps drawing on a little of the attractive color offered by Livy's account of the fall of Sarguntum (21.14.3–4).[76]

In general, the traditions are uninformative about Alexander's operations from autumn 334 to spring 333 in Pamphylia and Pisidia. Diodorus' account (17.27 f.) is brief and garbled, and Arrian (1.24.4–29) is surprisingly unclear and vague in certain places; the routes that Alexander took are not elucidated, and his motives for the interior march are not known. Also, Arrian does not mention until 3.6.6 that Nearchus was appointed as satrap of Lycia and Pamphylia.[77] Curtius may well have been more expansive. Moreover, since he reminds us at 7.1.6 that he has already told us about the arrest of Alexander the Lyncestian, it is highly likely that this episode received substantial treatment, particularly in view of its political aspects.

The extant text of book 3 commences with Alexander's decision to recruit troops from the Peloponnesus and his own arrival at Celaenae.[78] But Curtius did not have to end a book with a battle; the Battle of Issus indeed provided a high point in book 3, but it did not preclude an exciting finish to the book. As I noted earlier, Curtius dramatically exploits relatively minor episodes, such as the sack of Damascus, with subtle emphasis on the motifs of *perfidia* and *fides,* which become increasingly important in the *Historiae*'s narrative.

In view of the historian's care with Darius' portrait in books 3–5, it is also not unreasonable to assume that he may have related the story of the Persian king's accession, probably in the lost book 1. Both Justin (10.3) and Diodorus (17.5–6) give some details about Darius' accession; Arrian (3.22.2 f.) is not helpful. Some speculation on Curtius' possible treatment is relevant for a number of reasons. We can gain some idea of the potential outline from Alexander's speech (Curt. 6.3.12)—which indicates that Curtius was aware of Bagoas' role—and more substantially from

---

76. I am grateful to Professor Heckel for the suggestion.
77. Cf. Plut. *Alex.* 17.2–18. See Brunt, *Arrian,* 1:100 f.; Bosworth, *HCA,* 1:156 f. On Alexander's route from Miletus to Phrygia, see F. Stark, "Alexander's March from Miletus to Phrygia," *JHS* 78 (1958): 102–20.
78. See Waldemar Heckel, *Hermes* 119 (1991): 124–25, who argues that the section may reiterate an event of winter 334/3 B.C.

Diodorus. Darius became Great King through the machinations of Bagoas, a eunuch and Chiliarch of Artaxerxes Ochus. Bagoas poisoned Ochus along with his sons, including the new king Arses and his offspring, thus extinguishing the whole male, direct line of the royal house. Darius was a relative of the royal family, whom Bagoas had selected to replace Arses, but instead Darius, in turn, poisoned Bagoas. Contrary to what Arrian has Alexander say in a letter to Darius (2.14.5), he did not usurp the throne, but it cannot be denied that he ascended the throne through the crime of someone else—as did Alexander himself.

We simply cannot know how Curtius treated the beginning of Alexander's reign or what parallel attention he may have given to Persian affairs. However, he apparently knew a reasonable amount of Achaemenid court history, since in certain places he provides additional information or refers to earlier events; for example, he discusses Ochus' refugee family members at the fall of Damascus (3.13.12–13) and Sisygambis' reflections of how her family had suffered under Artaxerxes Ochus (10.5.23). Sometimes the detail is given within the context of a prominent Persian's meeting with Alexander, as is the case with Ochus' granddaughter (6.2.7–8) and Nabarzanes' reference to Darius' murder of Bagoas (6.4.10).

Moreover, given that Curtius evidently relied on the same tradition as Diodorus for large sections of his work, it is very likely that he knew as much about Darius' accession as Diodorus. There was also an obvious parallel between Darius' and Alexander's accessions, which Curtius may have noticed: both kings gain the throne through assassination. Even if Curtius did not follow Trogus' interpretation (J. 9.7) and make Alexander an actual party to Olympias' murder of Philip, at the very least he possibly would have depicted the young king's accession as swift, dynamic, and forceful. Thus he would have likely stressed the elimination of Philip's murderers (cf. Diod. 17.2.1) and the identities and supporters of Alexander's relatives who were rivals for the throne (cf. Diod. 17.2.3–6).[79] For all of Diodorus' comments on Darius' bravery (17.6.1; cf. J. 10.3.3–5) or his removal of Bagoas (Diod. 17.5.6), Darius' accession was basically underhanded and cowardly. Alexander, in contrast, would be the man of *vis*.

Hence the essential elements of Curtius' characterization of both kings would have been established at the outset. Also, the irony of Darius'

---

79. Cf. Plut. *Alex.* 10.4 and *De fort. Alex.* 1.3.327c; Curt. 6.9.17; J. 11.2.1–3, 12.6.14.

removal of Bagoas and the depth of Alexander's later, moral decline was not lost on the historian; we can note Orsines' caustic remark to Alexander's own eunuch Bagoas at 10.1.37. Just as Alexander exceeded Darius as a king in his *fortuna*, as well as in the positive qualities of his *regnum*, so was the scale of his vice the more pronounced.

To return to Curtius' organization of his material, the so-called architectonic method of Livy, or his use of episodes, is also applicable to Curtius. Scholars do not deny that Curtius' structure is episodic, but it should be stressed that the episodes are placed with an eye toward thematic balance and unity. One may note, for instance, the contrast and balance between Darius and Alexander that Curtius achieves in books 3 and 4,[80] a possible bipartite division in books 5 and 10, and his placement of episodes in his depiction of Alexander as *rex, dux,* and *tyrannus* in books 6, 7, 8, and 9. Again, Curtius' plan for each book must be been given due consideration: he may have owed the overall concept to Livy, but his design and execution were his own.

Other structural issues are elaborated elsewhere in this study; however, an analysis of the respective schemes of books 5 and 10 may provide an example of his objectives in organization. If Curtius did adopt an arrangement of two pentads, both these books would have been of paramount importance to him. As the final book of the first pentad, book 5 would furnish a pivot of the *Historiae* by concluding the Alexander and Darius narrative and would at the same time give indication of some important themes for the second pentad, particularly in relation to Curtius' characterization of Alexander. It is perhaps no accident that the historian emphasizes Alexander's *licentia* in his treatment of the king's firing of Persepolis, since the portrayal of his moral deterioration constitutes a main area of interest in the latter five books.[81]

One obvious and immediate problem with any attempt to propose a scheme for these books is the state of the extant text; the end of book 5 has been lost, while book 10 is so riddled with lacunae that it renders any detailed study of the episodic arrangement very difficult. But enough emerges from what survives to suggest an overall pattern. Book 5 appears to fall into two definite parts. As we saw earlier, the importance of keeping the Asian narrative and hence the Alexander and Darius theme together as a cohesive whole is stated by the historian in his opening sentence. He then relates Darius' flight to Arbela, his speech to his followers,

---

80. See chap. 5.
81. See chap. 3, 95–99.

and his decision to go to Media. From that point, the focus switches to Alexander, whose activities occupy the narrative until 5.8, when the account returns to Darius at Ecbatana and his final days. At 5.13 f. our attention is focused on both the Persian and Macedonian kings. From the context of the narrative at the point where the text breaks off (5.13.25), together with the evidence offered by other texts, it seems reasonable to assume that at the finish of the book, Curtius would have brought Alexander and Darius together in some way, if only through the intermediary of Polystratus rather than the blatantly romantic meeting between the two kings that, according to Diodorus (17.73.3), appeared in certain traditions.

Justin (11.15) and Plutarch (*Alex.* 43) record that with his final breath Darius pledged Alexander as his successor through a soldier; neither missed the literary poignancy of a tradition that reported one dying ruler acknowledging the greatness of his successor. Furthermore, from the Great King's reported last wishes in Justin's text (11.15.7–13), Trogus clearly intended the death of Darius as the climax to book 11 and a natural dividing point between books 11 and 12. Since Trogus was also interested in the theme of *regnum*, he found an ideal structural conclusion to his book in the transition of rule from one *rex* to the next.

It seems plausible that Curtius would have exploited a similar opportunity: the two protagonists would be united, and so would the twin themes of the first pentad—the *fortunae* and *regna* of the kings. At the point where the text breaks off, Curtius' account has much of the tradition evidently used by Trogus and Plutarch;[82] the name of Polystratus appears in the latter, and it may have been edited out of Justin's account. But the setting of the meeting in Curtius has a closer affinity with Justin; a thirsty Macedonian soldier, searching for a spring, discovers the wounded Great King in his carriage.[83] In Curtius, the dying Darius would have made a speech to Polystratus. Certain elements of the speech from either Trogus' tradition or his own version may have also appealed to Curtius: Darius' emphasis on Alexander's *benignitas* toward his family, his prayer that rule over *terrarum omnium* would fall to Alexander, and his pledging of royal *fides* through the clasp of his right hand. Curtius (4.10.34) had already indicated Darius' acknowledgment of Alexander's *pietas*, and in the historian's account of the Great King's last days,

---

82. The source was probably Cleitarchus; see Hammond, *THA*, 101, 133, 137; cf. Hammond, *Sources*, 75; Heckel and Yardley, *Justin*, ad 11.15.5.

83. See Atkinson, *Curtius* ii, 163.

Darius perceived Alexander as an avenger (5.12.5); it would be appropriate for him to recognize him as his successor with his last breath. It is also likely that Curtius would have included an epitaph for the Achaemenid king, since in keeping with historiographical convention, he comments on the deaths of important men elsewhere.[84]

With the death of Darius, Alexander succeeds to a greater *regnum*, as all the indications throughout the first pentad have promised. Yet, as the king's violent solution to the puzzle of the Gordian knot and the burning of Persepolis suggest, the greater part of Alexander's conquest is still ahead, and with this achievement lies the scale of the king's *virtus* and *vitia*.

Like book 5, the structure of book 10 also seems to have been divided into two definite parts, and from its remnants, we can surmise that book 10 would have been a carefully developed narrative in its original form. We have no reason to doubt that Curtius abandoned the literary standards of his earlier books. Book 10 is the concluding book of the second pentad, but unlike Arrian, Curtius did not finish his account of Alexander's reign with the king's death; instead, the remnant of the narrative is occupied with the initial struggles of Alexander's generals over who is to rule the empire. The events described occupy a mere seven days, as the story is carried only so far as to establish the atmosphere of tumult caused by the power vacuum. On the thematic level, Curtius not only summarizes Alexander's *regnum*, which he does in his epitaph of the king at 10.5.26 f., but, in the symbolism of impending civil war, raises further provocative issues. Not one man among Alexander's talented generals could rule his empire alone; inevitably it must be partitioned. It is perhaps not surprising that Curtius should see contemporary overtones in a situation where the death of a strong head of state with no obvious heir or alternative was followed by civil chaos. The latter part of book 10 is particularly colored with Roman imperial overtones. From the debate of Alexander's generals over what is to be done and the reluctance of Perdiccas to accept *summa imperii* to the raising of Arridaeus and the famous digression on Rome's new *princeps*, it is evident that Curtius saw the aftermath of Alexander's death as an object lesson relevant to his own day.[85] In this didactic aspect, he was well within mainstream Roman historiography.

---

84. See Curt. 7.2.33–34; cf. the necrology format applied to cities (5.7.8, 4.4.19–21). See also supra, n.18, and cf. chap. 5, n. 2.

85. See Thomas R. Martin, *AJAH* 8 (1983): 161–90, but see my appendix.

The first part of book 10 opens with Alexander's deeds on his return from India. The subsequent execution of the king's governors, regardless of whether they are guilty or innocent, continues the grim tone raised at the end of the preceding book, where the historian sourly observed that the executioner followed Alexander's triumphal progress through Carmania; the satrap Astaspes, whom the king suspected of treason, was put to death.

At 10.1.21–28 Curtius uses the Orsines episode as an example of Alexander's injustice; however, just as the narrative turns to events in Europe, a lacuna interrupts the text. The history resumes with the news of Harpalus' death, Alexander's Exiles Decree, his payment of the soldiers' debts, and the dismissal of his veterans. The last event triggers the army's mutiny, but a large lacuna interrupts the account again, and the text does not recommence until the king is on his deathbed.

A new theme thus surfaces: who or what will replace Alexander's *regnum*? Yet the theme of the first part of the book, Alexander as *rex*, and the theme of the second, the struggle for succession, are united at the book's end. Ptolemy seizes the king's body and inters it, first in Memphis and later in Alexandria.

If I may return to an earlier point, both the apparent overall plan of book 10 and the phraseology of its final sentence suggest that Curtius finished the text where we have it. It may be carrying Curtius' *imitatio* of Livy too far to suggest that he deliberately followed Livy's lead by finishing his *Historiae* with a burial, just as the *Ab urbe condita* (incomplete or otherwise) finished with the death of Drusus. Curtius' conclusion bears a striking relation to the end of Alexander's necrology; at 10.10.20 Curtius remarks of the king's burial at Alexandria, "every honor was accorded to his [Alexander's] memory and his name" [omnisque memoriae ac nomini honos habetur]. We may compare this text to 10.5.37.

> therefore his name and the fame of his deeds spread kings and kingdoms throughout nearly the whole world, and those who had clung onto even the least part of such a great fortune were considered most famous.

> [itaque nomen quoque eius et fama rerum in totum propemodum orbem reges ac regna diffudit; clarissimique sunt habiti qui etiam minimae parti tantae fortunae adhaeserunt.]

The implication is apparent. Ptolemy's future *regnum*, sanctioned by Alexander's greatness through the appropriation of his body and the power of his name, will indeed bear the promise of success. The triumph of Ptolemy's regime and dynasty would not have been lost on Curtius' Roman audience.

Curtius' Use of Speeches

A few general observations should also be made on Curtius' use of speeches.[86] Composed speeches probably originated with Herodotus and remained conventional Greco-Roman historiographical practice. As Cicero remarked (*De oratore* 2.62–64), historiography was the branch of literary prose that came closest to oratory. It was expected that the *verus historicus* should tell the truth, and this convention extended to the accurate reporting of speeches;[87] other ancient critics elaborated views on the aesthetic, or rhetorical, purpose of such addresses, while retaining the general philosophy that speeches should at least retain the gist of what was said.[88] But from the time of Thucydides' problematic comment on speeches (1.22.1–2) forward, an apparent discrepancy between theory and practice inevitably prevailed; for instance, despite his theoretical statements, Dionysius of Halicarnassus evidently composed the speeches in the *Roman Antiquities* himself.[89] Given the Greco-Roman emphasis on oratorical and declamatory techniques in education, an audience would expect and probably enjoy speeches during the course of the historical narrative. Naturally, historians differed in the manner and the extent to which they employed such harangues: as Walsh pointed out, Livy's speeches actually adhere more to the principle of *brevitas* than do some of the "interminable compositions of Dionysius."[90]

Most of Curtius' extant books are indeed marked by one or more speeches in *oratio recta*, which are sometimes directly or indirectly paired for maximum rhetorical effect. The pairing of speeches on opposing

---

86. A specialized study is F. Helmreich, *Die Reden bei Curtius* (Paderborn, 1927), which, unfortunately, I have been unable to obtain.
87. See Fornara, *The Nature of History in Ancient Greece and Rome*, 142–68, esp. 143; cf. Bosworth, *FAA*, 94–96.
88. See Diod. 20.1.1–20.2.2; Fornara, *The Nature of History in Ancient Greece and Rome*, 147–51. See also Dio Chrys. 18.14–17, but as Bosworth (*FAA*, 94) notes, Lucian's criteria for speeches (*Hist. conscr.* 58) do not mention factual accuracy.
89. Dion. Hal. *Th.* 43 f. But see Bosworth, *FAA*, 95, 96, and n. 8.
90. Walsh, *Livy*, 230–31. See also T.P. Wiseman, *Clio's Cosmetics*, 29.

points of view was standard rhetorical practice; for example, both Curtius and Livy used the device as part of their literary and thematic structures.[91] Curtius' practice of *oratio obliqua* is also worth a comment. Frequently the historian is careful not to undermine by too many direct speeches the impact of what is obviously a showpiece oration. Thus at 8.5.10–12, Cleon's speech calling for divine honors for Alexander is given in *oratio obliqua*, which increases the dramatic impact of Callisthenes' direct response. Similarly, at 4.14.1–25, Alexander's exhortation to his soldiers before Arbela is reported indirectly, whereas Darius speaks his piece: Alexander is obviously the inevitable victor, and thus the irony and poignancy of the Great King's futile oration is enhanced. The direct orations take place in a number of situations, with differing speakers and to various audiences, which all add up to a diverse assortment of speakers and oratorical display: exhortations to troops or to Companions, deliberations at councils, drunken reproaches at banquets, warnings from barbarian envoys, advice from mercenary generals or philosophers, and indictments and defenses at trials.[92]

We do not have the first two books for scrutiny, but it is possible that Curtius deliberately designated more speeches for the second pentad. One may compare Arrian; most of his showpiece orations come in the latter books of his work, and there are very few speeches in books 1–3. Curtius most likely thought speeches were the most effective and dramatic way of highlighting both the internal challenges Alexander was facing after the final defeat of Darius and the developing political tensions between the king and his *nobiles*. Affairs like the so-called Philotas conspiracy, the *proskynesis* episode, or the conspiracy of the Pages lent themselves admirably to *genus iudicale* oratory, enabling the historian to display his rhetorical talents.[93]

However, Curtius' speeches are always thematically relevant: only once, in book 5, with the speeches of the Greek captives, does he appear

---

91. Cf. Curt. 7.7.10–19 with 7.8.12–30 (indirect pairing), and cf. 8.7.1–15 with 8.8.1–19 (direct pairing). On paired speeches in Livy, see Luce, *Livy,* 27; cf. in general K. Gries, "Livy's Use of Dramatic Speech," *AJPh* 70 (1949): 118–41.

92. Selected examples in Curtius include exhortations, 4.14.9–26 (Darius), 6.3.1–18, 9.2.12–30, 7.7.10–19 (Alexander); councils, 4.13.8–11, 6.8.4–9, 9.6.6–15; Alexander and his *nobiles,* 3.2.11–16, 5.8.6–9 (Darius and courtiers); drunken reproaches, 8.1.34–37 (Cleitus); barbarian envoys, 7.8.12–30; advice, 3.2.11–16 (Charidemus), 8.5.13–19 (Callisthenes); trials, 6.9.2–6.10.37 (Philotas), 7.1.18–40 (Amyntas), 8.7– 8.19 (Hermolaus).

93. On *genus iudicale* and other types of oratory, see Walsh, *Livy,* 220 f. On Curtius' "pride" in his speeches, see Tarn, *Alexander the Great,* 2:94–95.

to indulge in sheer rhetorical virtuosity for the sake of it. Yet, even here, although the historian is obviously conscious of his own artistry, the episode is still vital to Curtius' characterization of Alexander. The king's *beneficia* and *fides* toward the Greeks provides an appropriate transition for his call at 5.6.1 for his followers to take vengeance on the Persians by sacking Persepolis.

In fact, Curtius endeavors to make his speeches befit both speaker and occasion. This effort sometimes apparently produces inconsistency; for instance, when the king is wounded by an arrow in the breastbone at the fortress of the Indian Malli at 9.5.26, he is still able to ask his physician, Critobulus, why he is hesitating to remove the barb. Although it is not impossible that Alexander would be capable of speech, the point is literary: Critobulus' hesitation, out of fear of reprisals, recalls the plea of Alexander's family doctor, Philip, back at 3.6.10–11. In a similar fashion, the Alexander who urges his potentially mutinous troops to continue fighting at 6.3.1–18 is a different orator from the halting, angry, almost inarticulate king (6.9.2 f.) who reproaches Philotas for his broken *fides* or from the eloquent speaker at 9.2.12–34 who tries to convince his troops to cross the Hyphasis. Yet at 6.9, with Philotas' arrest, the situation calls for a different tone. Alexander's speech is deliberately contrasted with the glib oration of Philotas (6.10), which in fact proves to be the latter's downfall. On another occasion, the Scythian dialogue at 7.8.11 f., Curtius is forced to make some kind of explanation to make the incongruity of the speaker, a rough barbarian envoy, fit the polished eloquence of his words.

The historicity of the speeches, or indeed the extent to which they are independent compositions, is difficult to determine. In the matter of source material and the composition, Curtius probably allowed himself more freedom, although it should be noted that Sallust, Tacitus, and other authors rewrote certain speeches, even though they clearly had access to the originals. Livy's debt to Polybius or other sources in his speeches cannot be denied, but he does adapt his material for literary and rhetorical considerations as well, to produce a more dramatic atmosphere.[94] It has been alleged that Curtius fabricated most, if not all, his speeches. Such an allegation is probably true, but some qualifications need to be added. The other extant Alexander historians often indicate

---

94. Cf. Sall. *Bell. Cat.* 51 f.; Tac. *Ann.* 11.24. On the practice in general, see Bosworth, *FAA*, 96 f. On Livy, see Walsh, *Livy*, 219, 231 f.

that something was said in the original source, without necessarily producing a speech themselves.

A notable example of this practice is Curtius' version of the debate among the mutilated Greek prisoners at 5.5.5 f.;[95] it is likely that some form of exchange and the names of the speakers were in the original source, as Diodorus 17.69.6 also alludes to a discussion.[96] However, Curtius, probably through his own embellishment, turned his account into a declamatory exercise, where each party takes the polar opposite line of argument. The two speakers, named in Curtius as Euctemon of Cyme and Theaetetus of Athens, adopt pro-Asian and pro-Hellenic (or at least pro-Athenian) sentiments, respectively. Rolfe thought that the oratorical style was also appropriately suited to each speaker; hence Thaetetus declaimed in a "plain" or "Attic" fashion, as opposed to the "Asianism" of his rival. However, some scholars have been more cautious in accepting this view; overall, the speeches do not differ remarkably in type, and as Atkinson noted, the impact of Theaetetus' speech is reduced by the historian's use of *oratio obliqua*.[97] Since Euctemon's counsel prevails, it was logical for Curtius to give him the more dramatic speech.

According to Atkinson, Curtius also imbued the speakers with Roman imagery and values; Theaetetus speaks openly of returning to *penates* and *patria,* and Euctemon (5.5.13) refers to the *ergastulum*—in Roman terms, that unpleasant rural slave prison or workhouse where the Romans kept unruly slaves or convicts. Interestingly, some additional points could be added to Atkinson's suggestion that the *ergastulum* "has a distinct Roman association."[98] The evidence for *ergastula* is slight; Columella (1.6.3) has a good description of digging the pit where these slaves or prisoners were kept, and Suetonius (*Tib.* 8; cf. *Aug.* 32.1) refers to an imperial inquiry into such slave barracks during the reign of Augustus.[99]

---

95. The episode was also mentioned by Diod. (17.69.2–9) and Justin (11.14) but was omitted by Arrian. See Dosson, 244–46; Atkinson, *Curtius* ii, 104 f. Cf. Currie, "Quintus Curtius Rufus," 73–74.

96. The source may have been Cleitarchus. See P. Goukowsky, *Diodore de Sicile XVII,* 221; Berve, 2: nos. 316, 360; Heckel and Yardley, *Justin,* ad 11.14.12. But see Atkinson, *Curtius* ii, 108, who suggests Curtius may have introduced Theaetetus himself.

97. Rolfe, 1:374 (but see Fairweather, *Seneca the Elder,* 243); cf. Atkinson, *Curtius* ii, 107.

98. Atkinson, *Curtius* ii, 107.

99. The inquiry was not out of humanitarian reasons; admittedly some travelers were being unlawfully detained, but the primary objective seems to have been finding men who were avoiding military service. See J.M. Carter, *Suetonius, Augustus* (Bristol, 1982), 137; H. Lindsay, *Suetonius, Tiberius* (Bristol, 1995), ad loc.

The Roman word was a derivative of the Greek *ergasterion,* a more generic term for a workplace, or workforce, which in Latin evidently assumed a specialist function, with no exact Greek equivalent.

One must therefore ask whether the historian has taken some license with his source and fabricated a little extra Roman color. But Euctemon's opening comment (5.5.10), is that he and his fellow captives "were ashamed to emerge from the darkness of a prison [ex tenebris et carcere]," which suggests that Curtius' source may have mentioned an underground prison, perhaps located at Persepolis. Underground imprisonment in either quarries or mines would have been certainly familiar enough to Greek writers. Thus a reasonable explanation is that Curtius has used a Roman term to convey the frightful situation of the Greek captives vividly to his own home audience, and within its context, the word is certainly appropriate.[100]

It is clear that Curtius simply elaborated certain points from the original speech. The argument in Diodorus (17.69.6–7) that the Greek captives' misfortune would make them an object of embarrassment to other, luckier people back home and that they could find comfort in one another's mutual state is echoed in even more detail by Euctemon (Curt. 5.5.12, 16). Justin's brief account (11.14.11–12) also suggests a common tradition with Curtius and Diodorus, as it agrees in its main details with the other two; the Greek captives, as a result of their mutilation, preferred to stay and receive allotments of land rather than distress their relatives in Greece.

Another example of Curtius' possible debt to his original source is provided by Arrian's account of Hermolaus' trial (4.14.2–3). Citing an alternative tradition, Arrian says Hermolaus made a speech before the Macedonians condemning Alexander's new, unpleasant changes in his behavior. The subject matter of this harangue is similar to the full-scale direct oration Hermolaus is given in Curtius (8.7.1 f.); we may compare Hermolaus' condemnation of Alexander's hubris in Arrian to his opening statement in Curtius, ". . . because you have begun not to rule over us as freeborn men but to dominate us as if we were slaves . . ." [. . . quia non ut ingenuis imperare coepisti, sed quasi in mancipia dominari . . .].

---

100. Diod. 3.12–13, drawing probably on Agatharchides, describes the working conditions in Egyptian mines for convicted criminals and prisoners of war during the Ptolemaic dynasty; on *ergastula,* I am grateful for certain issues pointed out in correspondence with Professor Brian Bosworth and Dr. A.J. Pomeroy; see also J.C. Fitzgibbon, "Ergastula," *Classical News and Views* 20 (1976): 55–59.

Further points of correspondence between the two speeches are references to the deaths of Philotas, Parmenion, and Cleitus and Alexander's adoption of Median costume (cf. Curt. 8.7.4; Arrian 4.14.2). Arrian reported Hermolaus' speech indirectly, as it was evidently outside his preferred traditions. Yet he also felt bound to offer some explanation of the boys' motive, and although he noted that his main authorities on the episode, Ptolemy and Aristobulus, portrayed the Pages as impressionable disciples of the high-principled but insidious Callisthenes (4.14.1), he was well aware of the weight of alternative opinion that alleged Callisthenes was innocent. He explicitly stated that the man's *parrhesia* (frankness) made it only too easy for his enemies to accuse him (4.12.7).[101]

However, Arrian's own attitude toward Callisthenes is ultimately negative. In Arrian's view (4.10.1) Callisthenes may have been morally right to protest against Alexander's increasing orientalism, especially in the king's desire to have Macedonians and Greeks perform *proskynesis*. His speech (4.11.2–9) is an eloquent and effective reply to Anarxarchus' call for divine honors. But of Callisthenes' subsequent behavior, such as his disruption of the king's feast through his refusal to perform the obeisance, Arrian remarks that while the historian disapproved of Alexander's hubris, Callisthenes likewise displayed stupidity (or "tactlessness"—σκαιότης). The historian's own judgment is that a courtier should show moderation in his conduct and be prepared to exalt a king as far as it is practicable.

It also seems not unreasonable to surmise that Arrian, who was steeped in philosophical ideas himself, may have even resented that Callisthenes wasted a chance to influence the king for the better. Arrian's prejudice against Callisthenes prior to his narrative of the man's opposition is demonstrated by the *logos* in which Philotas earlier asked the historian who was held in most honor by the Athenians. Callisthenes' response had been to praise the tyrannicides Harmodius and Aristogiton. As the audience would be well aware, Philotas was later executed for treason. Arrian presents Callisthenes' idealism as misguided, but Callisthenes also becomes guilty by association. Arrian's depiction of Callisthenes' conversation—apocryphal or not—with a would-be regicide is deliberately provocative. Arrian thus may have simply summarized what he thought were the main points of Hermolaus' complaints, and his

---

101. Cf. Plut. *Alex*. 55.1; Curt. 8.6.1; J. 12.7.2. See also Bosworth, *HCA*, 2:90 f.

exposition relates to his endorsement of the traditions alleging that Alexander already hated Callisthenes and so readily believed his complicity in the plot.

In Curtius (8.7.8–10), Callisthenes' innocence is openly stated by Hermolaus. Curtius, drawing perhaps in part or even to a large degree from his source, wrote up an oratorical display in the form of a debate between Hermolaus and Alexander on *regnum*. Both speeches are analyzed in relation to this theme in chapter 6; suffice it to say here that Alexander's eloquent defense of his *regnum* was probably largely composed by Curtius. Certainly the king's observations on *clementia* (8.8.8), a double-edged term for a Roman, would carry contemporary meaning for the historian's audience. Heckel noted that Curtius, in another rhetorical tour de force, namely, Amyntas' oration (7.1), may have retained historical elements in Amyntas' original speech while blending them with contemporary aspects—in this case, the Marcus Terentius trial.[102] As with Tacitus' account, the topos of the Amyntas speech is the same; far from denying his friendship with the convicted Philotas, Amyntas turns it into his defense. The general issues associated with a court society were as relevant to Curtius as they were to Tacitus, but it is idle to speculate which *princeps* Curtius had in mind. Ultimately the study of power interested him; for a people used to *libertas*, the end result is the same regardless of whether the ruler is called *princeps* or *rex*.

As indicated earlier, it is also probable that Curtius fabricated certain speeches outright, such as the speech of Darius to his *nobiles* at 5.8.6–17, the speech of Cobares (or Gobares) at 7.4.10–18, and Alexander's oration to his young mountaineers at 7.11.8–12, prior to their ascent of Ariamazes' Rock. With each of these examples, there is no suggestion of a speech made in other traditions, which together with the rhetoric and the reoccurrence of favorite motifs, such as *libertas* or *licentia regni*, suggest that some of the material may have been contributed by Curtius himself.

Cobares' speech to the regicide Bessus (Curt. 7.4.1–19) can be taken as a case example. The episode of Bessus' banquet where a violent argument broke out between Bessus and one of his friends is also recorded by Diodorus (17.83.7–9). In Diodorus' account, there is an important variation in the name of Bessus' adviser (Bagodarus), and the story is compressed, as one would expect, into a few lines. But enough similarity

---

102. W. Heckel, *AClass* 37 (1994): 67–78.

remains to suggest at least elements of a common tradition. In Curtius the incident could be interpreted as another manifestation of the "advice" scenario, where a subject imparts his forthright, if unwelcome, opinions to his king. One may recall the Charidemus (3.2.11–16), Nabarzanes (5.9.3–8), or Cleitus (8.1.34–37) episodes—where, as in the case of Bessus and Cobares, each king's response was violence. Only in the case of Nabarzanes, whose advice masked a treacherous intent, was Darius' anger justifiable.

One could say that Diodorus' more stringent editorial tendencies may have simply omitted any reference to a speech in his account of the quarrel between Bessus and Bagodarus, but Curtius' narrative provides some clues as to its composition. The structure of Cobares' address (7.4.10 f.) is unusual. He starts off in *oratio recta*, but at 7.4.13 the speech is broken by an intrusion into *oratio obliqua*. Curtius comments that Cobares added some aphorisms popular among the barbarians,[103] which Curtius says he has recorded to show barbarian wisdom—a sentiment similar in tone to what he says of the Scythians at 7.8.10–11. On this occasion, Curtius states the traditional nature of the speech, which he says he has reproduced "more or less" without change.[104]

It seems likely that the Bactrian proverbs in Cobares' speech may have been in Curtius' source, and Cobares himself may well have been a historical character; but probably purely Curtian elements in the direct speech include the rhetorical emphasis on *moderatio* (7.4.12) and the contrast between Alexander and Bessus in terms of the former's superior *virtus* (7.4.14). Moreover, in keeping with what was apparently an aphoristic tone in the original, Curtius adds another proverb to Cobares' conclusion:

a thoroughbred horse is ruled by only the shadow of a whip; a useless mount cannot even be roused by the spur.

[nobilis equus umbra quoque virgae regitur; ignavus ne calcari quidem concitari potest.] (7.4.18)

Curtius' direct speech composition in this example thus appears to be a free elaboration of an original intervention. Perhaps not surprisingly,

---

103. Curt. 7.4.13: *canem timidum vehementius latrare, quam mordere, altissima quaeque flumina minimo sono labi.*
104. See chap. 3, 87–89.

Bessus does not respect the *libertas* he granted to Cobares or his *consilium fidele*. He draws his scimitar on the Mede in a drunken parody of Darius' previous anger against Nabarzanes. Likewise, Alexander, also drunken and with his friends trying to restrain him, will draw a weapon on Cleitus—with the important difference of success. Thus the setting and the elements of the Cobares episode are derivative and may even be historical; however, Curtius has also exploited the episode to his own literary advantage and given words to a character that have rather less credibility than what they may have had.

For the most part, Curtius was clearly uninterested in reproducing or trying to approximate for historical purposes what was actually said, and rarely does he preface a direct oration with stylistic formulae, such as *in hunc modum locutus fertur*. In short, the purpose of the history's speeches is artistic: they are outward, dramatic manifestations of political and literary themes.

As we have seen, Curtius' interest in *regnum* bears a certain affinity with Livy's symbolic depiction of the kings in book 1. His treatment of episodes like the trials of Amyntas and Hermolaus and his emphasis on the *libertas* of a Charidemus, Cleitus, or Callisthenes appear to reflect the politics of the Roman imperial court, while his eulogy of Rome's new *princeps* has similar aspects with the panegyric of Pliny the Younger.[105] But unlike Livy's history, which was an undeniable success, or Tacitus' works, which allegedly inspired the third-century A.D. Roman emperor of the same name, the impact of Curtius' work cannot be known. As we know from the literary soirees of Pliny (*Ep.* 8.12), many books of the first century A.D. were published predominantly through an oral presentation and were composed with a listening audience in mind.[106] Curtius' tendencies to be epigrammatic or to draw an appropriate *sententia* on character or a moral not only indicate rhetorical influence but perhaps suggest a narrative appropriate for a live presentation.[107] He appears to be aware of his audience, and at one point (5.1.38), he even pauses to acknowledge their tender sensibilities ("with respect to your ears" [honos auribus habitus sit]), before describing the climax to Babylonian female

---

105. For the similarities between Curtius' eulogy (10.9.1–6) and Pliny's panegyric, see Bosworth, *CPh* 78 (1983): 150–61, and my appendix.

106. See Juvenal 3.9.

107. See Curt. 5.4.31; Atkinson, *Curtius* ii, 101. See also Curt. 3.3.2, 6.5, etc; Atkinson, *Curtius* i, 69.

striptease.[108] The rhetorical excursus at 10.9 on the timely accession of the new *princeps* is analyzed in the appendix: although an integral part of the literary structure, it was also probably deliberately aimed at the audience and the persona of the emperor, whoever he was. Given the contemporary political connotations that the historian imparts to his interpretation of Alexander's reign, it seems likely that his work was aimed at the senatorial and equestrian body and perhaps the traditional, or long-established, families. But both the subject and Curtius' approach need not necessarily have resulted in his work reaching a narrower audience than Livy's.

However, there is one fundamental difference between the two authors: Livy wrote a history of his own people and was thus drawing on and appealing to national experience. Even Trogus' treatment of Alexander was contained within a study that sought to highlight the degeneracy of world empires prior to the rise of Rome. By writing a specialized history of a Macedonian king, Curtius parted company with mainstream Roman historiography, which made Rome its theme, and joined a minority of Roman authors—for instance, Nepos, who concentrated on the achievements of non-Romans in his encomiastic biography, *Datames,* or the *Eumenes.*

In modern times, Curtius' portrayal of Alexander has been criticized for its sensationalism and at times "stage-tyrant" depiction of the king.[109] However, paradoxically, in view of hostile attitudes toward Alexander expressed in Latin literature elsewhere, it could well be that Curtius' history may have been too fair an appraisal of the Macedonian king. His audience may have been expecting a far more vituperative account. But perhaps such an observation oversimplifies the tastes and intelligence of the historian's reading or aural public.

Nevertheless, one indication of reaction to the unsatisfactory nature of the bulk of Alexander historiography is Arrian. In his first and second prefaces, Arrian acknowledges that while there is no shortage of Alexander traditions, no one account had done its subject justice—until the advent of himself. Although Arrian is undoubtedly including the Alexander historiographical tradition as a whole in his statements, it is plausible that he thought the more negative picture that the Romans apparently

---

108. Cf. Apuleius *Apol.* 75; Quint. *Declam.* 3.1. See also Atkinson, *Curtius* ii, 47.
109. See J.R. Hamilton, *Alexander the Great* (London, 1973), 103.

found so appealing needed correction. To Arrian, only a sophisticated, well-known historian, philosopher, and, moreover, fellow Hellene could write a definitive history of the great Macedonian.

It is important to take the *Historiae* of Quintus Curtius within its contemporary context. As the next chapter emphasizes, one commendable aspect of modern scholarship has been to recognize how much any historian is a product of his or her times.[110] Any historian's depiction of Alexander is inevitably influenced by the historian's own society, values, and attitudes. "Roman" Curtius' study of power remains a provocative analysis, and his characterization of Alexander as king, general, and tyrant is a brilliant and feasible interpretation. Yet to highlight the individuality of Curtius' own voice, it is necessary to survey his sources and methodology.

---

110. See most recently Hornblower, *Greek Historiography*, 71.

Chapter 3

Quintus Curtius' Sources and His Historical Methods

In modern times, the issue of Curtius' sources has received more scholarly attention than any other aspect of the author, apart from the apparently insoluble question of his date.[1] Unlike Arrian, Curtius only makes three specific references to any sources, but his history contains a lot of information often not found elsewhere, which suggests that Curtius may have either extracted more from his sources or consulted different authorities from the other extant traditions.[2] Conversely, large sections of parallel narrative between Curtius and other accounts, particularly Diodorus, indicate a common tradition, but at the same time, the origins of this shared tradition remain a matter of deep controversy.[3]

---

1. See Rutz, 2329–30. See Dosson, 101–61; E. Schwartz, *RE* 4 (1879): 1873 f.; A. Fränkel, *Die Quellen der Alexanderhistoriker* (Breslau, 1883; reprint, Aalen, 1969). For bibliography prior to 1972, see Seibert, 31–34. More recent treatments include R. Egge, *Untersuchungen zur Primärtradition bei Q. Curtius Rufus*; Atkinson, *Curtius* i, 58–67; Hammond, *THA*; Porod, 2–48. Tarn's theory (*Alexander the Great*, 2:100 ff.) that Curtius used an "anonymous mercenaries' source" along with the more conventional primary traditions may be discounted. See R.K. Sinclair, "Diodorus Siculus and the Writing of History," *PACA* 6 (1963): 36–45; J.R. Hamilton, "Cleitarchus and Diodorus 17," 126 n. 3; Atkinson, *Curtius* i, 67.

2. See Atkinson's remarks (*Curtius* i, 58) on *contaminatio* in Curtius and the examples listed. He does acknowledge the problems created by inconsistency in interpretation rather than fact. See also Hamilton, "Cleitarchus and Diodorus 17," 127–28.

3. The parallels between Diod. 17 and Curtius are listed in E. Schwartz, *RE* 4 (1879): 1873–75; Dosson, 138–40; Fränkel (supra, n. 1), 395 f. (who also gives the differences, at 407 f.); Atkinson, *Curtius* i, 64 f. The discussions on the common tradition are too numerous to cite here, but the controversy, essentially founded on the nineteenth-century theories of Schwartz and Jacoby, is based on whether Cleitarchus was the main source for the Alexander vulgate; for a summary of the argument, see E.N. Borza, *PACA* 11 (1968): 25 f. Cf. M.J. Fontana, "Il problema delle fonti per il xvii libro di Diodoro Siculo," *Kokalos* 1 (1955): 155–90; C.B. Welles, introduction to *Diodorus of Sicily*, vol. 8 (Cambridge, Mass., 1963). Borza himself argued against Cleitarchus as Diodorus' major source in book 17. More recently, on the affirmative, see P. Goukowsky, "Cleitarque Seul?" *REA* 71 (1969): 320–37; F. Schachermeyr, *Alexander der Grosse*, 658–62; Hammond, *THA* (who also identifies a supplementary tradition); Hamilton, "Cleitarchus and Diodorus 17";

57

It is not the aim of this study to carry out a systematic exercise in *Quellenforschung* in the sense of identifying the source or sources behind particular sections in Curtius' narrative. Such dissection can be valuable in that it attempts to determine what source an ancient writer is following at a certain point and hence the extent of that author's derivation as opposed to his own contribution. However, in view of the paucity of extant fragments of the lost traditions, naming the original source or ascertaining its nature can often be dubious. Usually all we have is a scattered collection of references to a lost author or a series of quotations taken out of context, and the material may sometimes appear trivial or designed to illustrate the literary point of its excerptor. Often the name of a lost source, such as Diyllus, Timagenes, or the elusive Cleitarchus himself, appears to offer tantalizing prospects of major influence, particularly when later traditions have made comments about them; but without substantial evidence, the extent of their impact remains speculative. Moreover, critical comments passed by one author on another can in themselves be prejudiced, ambivalent, and misleading.[4]

The mere name of a source is useless unless we have a general idea of its characteristics and reliability, and this information is best offered by continuous narrative in traditions that can be safely assumed to be using the source. Yet, without secure identification, there is some degree of limitation to *Quellenforschung*. In the case of the Alexander vulgate, as J.R. Hamilton has demonstrated,[5] analysis of parallel, continuous accounts may suggest certain characteristics of a particular, shared tradition, and intelligent guesswork may even venture a name for the original source,

---

Bosworth, *FAA*, 7 f. On Curtius' use of Cleitarchus, Atkinson (*Curtius* i, 64 f.) and Egge (*Untersuchungen zur Primärtradition bei Q. Curtius Rufus*) are cautious, while Porod concludes that Curtius did not read Cleitarchus in the original. Badian's careful remarks on the problem generally, in "Alexander the Great, 1948–67," *CW* 65 (1971): 39, are still worth noting.

4. Hammond, in *THA*, argues that the obscure historian Diyllus was used extensively by Diodorus in book 17, but only six fragments of that author survive. On Timagenes, see infra, n. 69; on Cleitarchus, see infra, nn. 77, 78. Scholars have tried to "reconstruct" lost primary traditions from the extant accounts. Examples are the attempts of H. Strasburger and more blatantly E. Kornemann (see infra, n. 8) to recover Ptolemy's history almost entirely from Arrian. See Bosworth, *HCA*, 1:16 n. 1, and *FAA*, 14. On the problem in general, see also L. Pearson, "Lost Greek Historians Judged by Their Fragments," *G & R* 11–14 (1943): 43–56; P.A. Brunt, *CQ* 30 (1980): 477–94.

5. Hamilton, "Cleitarchus and Diodorus 17."

perhaps with a reasonable degree of probability. But given the complexity of Alexander historiography, the possible *contaminatio* of alternative accounts, and the personal aims of the historian using the traditions, any certainty of identification or large degree of recovery of an individual source appears unlikely.

As the extant text of Curtius is peppered with lacunae, we cannot be sure that in the missing sections the historian did not make other comments on his authorities (as he does on Ptolemy and Cleitarchus at 9.5.21) or discuss his main sources together with his aims, in his preface. This latter point seems particularly unlikely, since in general, ancient historians did not emphasize their choice of a particular source, and when they did acknowledge earlier writers, even anonymously, they were often critical.[6]

As we have seen, Roman historians were not interested in their traditions to the same extent as a modern scholar; while they were aware of issues like historical veracity, they were far more concerned with moral didacticism and its presentation.[7] In view of the exhibitionist and rhetorical nature of Roman historiography, Curtius would inevitably adapt and distort his source material in his search for stylistic elegance, which again makes any attempt at retrieving the original source particularly difficult.

However, a survey of the early accounts is useful at least to indicate what was available to Curtius and the type of sources that may have appealed to him. Moreover, to suggest what is creative or idiosyncratic about Curtius' use of traditions, it seems worthwhile to explore the

---

6. See Livy's hostile remark at 9.18.6 (= *FGrH* 88.T.9). *Levissimi ex Graecis* is thought to refer to Timagenes, because of the latter's contempt of Rome and Augustus. See G.W. Bowersock, *Augustus and the Greek World* (Oxford, 1965), 109–10; T.J. Luce, "The Dating of Livy's First Decade," *TAPhA* 96 (1965): 209–40, esp. 220 ff. See also infra, n. 69. Cf. Curtius' own critical comments at 9.5.21 (quoted later in this chapter) and Polybius' criticisms of earlier writers like Theopompus and Timaeus (8.9 f., book 12, etc.). On source acknowledgment in ancient historiography, see F.W. Walbank, *Commentary on Polybius*, 1:27; and see more recently Hornblower, *Greek Historiography*, 54 ff. Given the likely chronological proximity, Tacitus' use of sources may also be suggestive of Curtius' methodology; Tacitus does not make a regular practice of naming his authorities, and he does not adhere to his one statement of principle at *Ann.* 13.20.2–4. See Furneaux, *Tacitus*, 1:13 f. and 26 n. 1; Syme, *Tacitus*, 1:289 ff. (who states at 291 n. 4 that Tacitus may have decided that the method was "impracticable and inartistic").

7. On Roman awareness of the need for truth in historiography, see Cic. *De or.* 2.15.62; T.P. Wiseman, *Clio's Cosmetics*, 48 f.; A.E. Wardman, *Rome's Debt to Greece* (London, 1976), 101 f. But see A.J. Woodman, *Rhetoric*, 10, 70 f.

author's own opinions on historiography and compare his methodology with his fellow Alexander historians in a series of examples.

The ancient historiography of Alexander the Great is a vast area.[8] It includes five main historical narratives—not one of them contemporary with its subject—and considerable sections of Strabo's work on geography, especially in relation to Alexander's campaigns in India.[9] The extant authors were separated chronologically and motivated by different purposes to write about Alexander's life and exploits. Diodorus' account, dated sometime between 55 and 30 B.C., was the earliest; Strabo belonged to the late Augustan era; Curtius was probably first century A.D.; and Plutarch and Arrian wrote during the first half of the second century A.D.[10] Pompeius Trogus' *Historiae Philippicae* was also a product of the Augustan Age, but, as noted earlier, it survived only through Justin's *Epitome*.[11]

We know of a formidable collection of lost, literary traditions on Alexander. These sources include all of the eyewitness accounts; contemporary or near-contemporary authors, such as Cleitarchus, Megasthenes, and Hieronymus of Cardia; and subsequent, derivative Hellenistic histories, such as the works of Hegesias of Magnesia or geographers like Eratosthenes.[12] There was also an apparent abundance of docu-

---

8. For earlier bibliography, see Seibert, 1–61; Badian (supra, n. 3), 37–83; J.M. O'Brien, *Alexander the Great: The Invisible Enemy*, 286–89. Jacoby's collection of the lost Alexandrian fragments in *FGrH* 117–53 is translated in C.A. Robinson, *Alexander the Great*, vol. 1. For a selection of specialized treatments on the lost traditions, see Fränkel (supra, n. 1); H. Strasburger, *Ptolemaios und Alexander*; E. Kornemann, *Die Alexandergeschichte des Königs Ptolemaios I von Aegypten*; T.S. Brown, *Onesicritus: A Study in Hellenistic Historiography*; Pearson, *LHA*; P. Goukowsky, *Essai sur les origines du mythe d'Alexandre*, 1:131–59; Pédech, *Historiens*; Hammond, *THA*, and its Companion, *Sources*; and Brunt's discussions of the primary traditions in Brunt, *Arrian*, vols. 1 and 2. For an excellent general introduction, see Bosworth, *CE*, 295–300, and *HCA*, 1:16–34.

9. See Strabo 15–17; P. Pédech, *GB* 2 (1974): 129–45.

10. Plutarch was the earlier source, but it is controversial as to whether Arrian's history was written early or late in his career; see A.B. Bosworth, *CQ* 22 (1972): 163–85 (for an early date, ca. 115 A.D.), and *HCA*, 1:10–13. More recently Bosworth has reinforced his argument (*HCA*, 2:257). But see Brunt, *Arrian*, 1: app. 28 (for a later date, ca. 128/29 A.D.); Stadter, *Arrian of Nicomedia*, app. 5 (for a late date, ca. 137 A.D.).

11. The date of Justin is also controversial; see chap. 2, n. 49.

12. Hegesias of Magnesia was a Greek orator of the early third century B.C.: see Dion. Hal. *De comp. verb.* 18 (= *FGrH* 142.F.5); Plut. *Alex.* 3.3; Cic. *Brut.* 286 and *De or.* 226. Hieronymus of Cardia was evidently used by Diodorus for books 18–20 (see Hornblower, *Hieronymus of Cardia*) and possibly by Curtius in book 10 (see R.M. Errington, *JHS* 90 [1970]: esp. app. 1, 72 f.). But see F. Schachermeyr, *Alexander in Babylon und die Reichsordnung nach seinem Tode* (Vienna, 1970), who suggests Cleitarchus was the primary source. Other universal histories, such as Timagenes', may have had some impact particularly on Curtius.

mentary material that dated either to Alexander's reign or shortly after, including correspondence,[13] works of a technical nature,[14] and propagandist pamphlets—such as those composed by Ephippus and Nicobule on the deaths of Hephaestion and Alexander, as well as the tradition represented by the *Liber de morte testamentumque Alexandri Magni,* which is appended to the *Metz Epitome.*[15] The narrative of the *Metz Epitome,* dating from late antiquity, was a summary of an earlier history, which in its extant fragmentary form covers only Alexander's campaigns between Hyrcania and southern India. A very controversial source is the *Ephemerides,* or the king's daily journal; however, this problematic document will be considered later in the context of Ptolemy's alleged use of it.

In addition to the historical and technical accounts and propagandist documents, one may note the Alexander Romances, a somewhat generic term used to describe a miscellany of traditions derived from cultures and time periods as diverse as the ancient, medieval European, and Islamic worlds. These traditions were either derived from or related to a Greek prose biography of the king. Known as Pseudo-Callisthenes, this biography was based very loosely around a quasi-historical framework consisting mostly of fabulous stories emphasizing Alexander's heroic deeds and travels.[16] The earliest romances were not given form until possibly the

---

13. The authenticity of the letters is problematic. Many of them are cited in Plutarch without corroboration by other sources. Some correspondence is thought genuine; some—for example, in the Alexander romances—is pure fantasy. See A.M. Zumetikos, "De Alexandri Olympiadisque Epistularum Fontibus et Reliquiis" (Diss. Berlin, 1894). Other correspondence, such as the letters between Alexander and Darius, are probably literary embellishments by the later traditions on earlier sources; see chap. 5. See also Bosworth, *CE,* 299; L. Pearson, "The Diary and Letters of Alexander the Great," *Historia* 3 (1955): 419–55; J. Hamilton, "The Letters in Plutarch's *Alexander,*" *PACA* 4 (1961): 9–20.

14. Alexander's bematists, or surveyors, Baeton, Diognetus, and Amyntas, wrote on distances, ethnography, flora, and fauna. See *FGrH* 119, 120, 122. See also F. Pfister, "Das Alexander-Archiv und die hellenistisch-römische Wissenschaft," *Historia* 10 (1961): 30–67, for a prosopographical study of Alexander's scientists.

15. For Ephippus and Nicobule, see *FGrH* 126–27. The relationship of the *Liber de morte* to the *Metz Epitome* is controversial. See F. Pfister, *Kleine Schriften zum Alexanderroman* (Meisenheim am Glan, 1976), 17–52. But see L. Ruggini, "L'Epitoma rerum gestarum Alexandri Magni et il Liber de Morte Testamentoque Eius," *Athenaeum* 39 (1961): 285–357; E.J. Baynham, *Antichthon* 29 (1995): 60–77.

16. See R. Stoneman, *The Greek Alexander Romance* (Harmondsworth, 1991). Cf. the Armenian version, *The Romance of Alexander the Great,* trans. A.M. Wolohojian (Columbia, 1969). See E.A. Budge, *The Alexander Book in Ethiopia* (Oxford, 1933), for the Ethiopic text and other derivatives.

second century A.D. and were to continue, in one version or another, well into modern times.[17]

Some of these tales may have arisen spontaneously during Alexander's lifetime, while others drew on more traditional material or local folklore. It is not uncommon to find deeds that Alexander performs also attributed to Gilgamesh and other heroes. A common observation is that through the romances, different ethnic groups tend to make Alexander one of their own according to individual culture, although this concept is not unique to the Alexander Romance. According to Herodotus (3.2), the Egyptians tried to claim kinship with the house of Cyrus by making Cambyses Egyptian. Similarly, in the Egyptian-based Pseudo-Callisthenes, Alexander is the son of Nectanebo, the last pharaoh of Egypt, whereas in the *Iskandarnamah,* a Persian medieval romance, he is the son of the Persian king and the half brother of Darius—a good Muslim who punishes the infidel for refusing to embrace Islam.[18] Yet Pseudo-Callisthenes also used apparently historical sources, and the work contains occasional information that sounds plausible,[19] whereas, by way of contrast, the accounts of the extant Alexander historians can be insidiously manipulative in varying degrees, in their efforts to sustain literary and historiographical aspirations. Peter Green rightly emphasized that all the Alexander traditions warrant careful evaluation and that subjectively labeling some as "good" or "bad" is misleading, if not hazardous.[20]

E. Badian succinctly remarked:

A survey of interpretations of Alexander for any period is no dreary exercise. It is a mirror of changing modes of thought and historical interpretation as formed by the history and experience of the gen-

---

17. On the formation of the romance traditions, see Budge (supra, n. 16), xv ff.; Stoneman (supra, n. 16), 8 f. Cf. P.M. Fraser, *The Cities of Alexander the Great* (Oxford, 1996), 205–26; Merkelbach *Die Quellen des Griechischen Alexanderromans;* Cary, *The Medieval Alexander,* 9 ff.

18. See Tarn, *Alexander the Great,* 1:143 f.; Stoneman (supra, n. 16), 2. See *Iskandarnamah,* trans. Minoo S. Southgate (Columbia, 1978), 20–21.

19. Antipater's role in Alexander's acclamation by the Macedonian Assembly (Ps.-Call. 1.26) is often cited as authentic by modern historical studies, as is the king's crowning at Memphis (1.34). On the historicity of the latter, see L. Koenen, *Eine agonistische Inschrift aus Aegypten und frühptolemäische Königsfeste,* Beiträge zur klassischen Philologie 56 (Meisenheim am Glan, 1977), but see S.M. Burstein, "Pharaoh Alexander: A Scholarly Myth," *Ancient Society* 22 (1991): 139–45; cf. A. Stewart, *Faces of Power: Alexander's Image and Hellenistic Politics,* 174. See Stoneman (supra, n. 16), 10, for other examples.

20. Green, *Alexander of Macedon,* 479.

erations and individuals surveyed. Not only has every scholar (as Wilcken said) his own Alexander, but ever since antiquity the figure of the great Macedonian has been a universal symbol—as A. Heuss put it—a bottle *(Schlauch)* that can be filled with any wine: it attracts and embodies the philosophy of a person or of an age as no other ancient figure has—not even Caesar—and perhaps none at all.[21]

Yet the *Schlauch* encompasses more than the concept of the king as a bottle for the "wine"—or the personal interpretation—of an individual historian. Also implicit is a general principle of historiography: the historian as the "wine maker," or, more specifically, the idea of process—the source methodology and literary skill through which the historian blends and composes the final product. The question of literary style as opposed to a "scientific" approach has dominated historiography since antiquity; although modern methods have favored and developed the latter,[22] it is also true that the most careful research is useless unless presented in a lucid and effective manner. Theodor Mommsen, Sir Ronald Syme, and Ernst Badian, while all great historians, were (and are) also great stylists.

The equally polarized and idiosyncratic interpretations of Alexander by Sir William Tarn and Fritz Schachermeyr provide striking, modern manifestations of the Alexander *Schlauch*. The following brief digression is intended to illustrate certain principles that, while relevant to historiography in general, have especially stamped both modern and ancient approaches to Alexander. These aspects include the importance of personal background and philosophy, literary style, and the use of evidence.

Tarn could be termed a "gentleman" by the definitions of culture, refinement, urbanity, and social status. Born in 1869 into a world of privilege, he was educated at Eton and Cambridge. Although a barrister by profession, Tarn maintained his productivity in classical scholarship

---

21. See E. Badian, "Some Recent Interpretations of Alexander," 280. See also C.B. Welles' (favorable) review of F. Schachermeyr's 1949 biography, *Alexander der Grosse, Ingenium und Macht,* in *American Journal of Archaeology* 55 (1951): 433–36.

22. The general concepts of modern historical research, prevalent from the nineteenth and twentieth centuries in relation to the ancient world, are sensibly stated by E.N. Borza in *The Impact of Alexander* (Hinsdale, 1974), 5: ". . . the rational analysis of texts, the fuller understanding of language use, the criticism of evidence, the corroboration of archaeological discoveries and the application of principles drawn from the newly-emergent social sciences, especially economics." It hardly needs to be said that each of these areas raises its own difficulties.

both during his career and after his early retirement from the bar, to the extent that his original biography of Alexander was first published in the *Cambridge Ancient History* in 1926. He was a product of an age that yielded other wealthy, private scholars, such as the famous excavator of Knossos, Sir Arthur Evans—a time when publishing on the ancient world was not dominated by the university academic to the same extent as it is today.[23]

Tarn's *Alexander* biography was reissued in 1948, largely unchanged, but supplemented with a study on the ancient sources and related historical topics. His influence in English scholarship was probably at its highest in the immediate post–World War II period, yet in the late 1950s a critical reaction led by Badian exposed Tarn's Alexander for what he was, namely, a reflection of Tarn's own class ethics and Victorian idealism—a generous, dashing, but self-disciplined king who "never had a mistress" (but who was certainly not homosexual) and who was driven by an almost Christian vision of the "Brotherhood of Man."[24]

It could be said that Tarn was entitled to his view of Alexander as much as anybody else. But although this is not the place for a critique of Tarn's historical methods, the revelation of his weaknesses, especially in relation to his dismissal or distortion of the ancient evidence, has seriously challenged the scholastic value of his work.[25] Also relevant to the present study is not only the blatant subjectivity of Tarn's interpretation but the stylistic power of his presentation. One cannot deny the creative inspiration of Tarn's thrilling prose, which renders his work seductive and, at the same time, because of his faulty methodology, all the more insidious, particularly to the unwary, as the following excerpt from his well-known thesis on Alexander's plans for the unity of mankind demonstrates.

> The second thing is his belief that he [Alexander] had a divine mission to be the harmoniser and reconciler of the world, to bring it to

---

23. On Tarn's life and methods, see A.B. Bosworth, "The Impossible Dream: W.W. Tarn's Alexander in Retrospect," *Ancient Society Resources for Teachers* (Macquarie Ancient History Association) 13, no. 3 (1983): 131–50, esp. 132 f.

24. Tarn, *Alexander the Great,* 2:319 ff., esp. 323. On Tarn's worldview generally, see Green, *Alexander of Macedon,* 483 ff.; Badian, "Some Recent Interpretations of Alexander," 287 f.

25. Tarn's methods drew some initial uneasiness from A.R. Burn in his review, in *JHS* 67 (1947): 141–44. But Tarn's thesis on Alexander's vision of civilized unity was finally demolished by Badian; see *Historia* 7 (1958): 425–44. Equally devastating was Badian's examination of Tarn's methodology in *CQ* 8 (1958): 144–57. Cf. Bosworth (supra, n. 23), 134 f.

pass that all men, being brothers, should live together in *Homonoia,* in unity of heart and mind. This was a dream, or an inspiration; it was something which had come to him and was struggling for expression; he gave it expression for the first time at Opis, tentatively, in the form of *Homonoia* between all men, and one who was there crystallised it in the metaphor of a loving-cup in which all men were mixed.[26]

The late Fritz Schachermeyr first published his study *Alexander der Grosse: Ingenium und Macht* in 1949. The book was written in difficult circumstances, as its author had been deprived of his university chair in the aftermath of World War II.[27] It was very much a personal project, and in Schachermeyr's own autobiographical reminiscences, produced in his extreme old age, he commented on the monograph's demands.[28] Schachermeyr totally rejected Tarn's approach, particularly his treatment of the vulgate traditions as opposed to the "reliable" tradition of Ptolemy and Aristobulus. His interpretation of Alexander was the very antithesis of Tarn's. To Schachermeyr, Alexander was a "Titan," a dark, complex conqueror, a man of *kriegerische Kraft* (warlike power) and *Brutalität,* who was all too capable of bloody reprisal and atrocity. According to Schachermeyr, Alexander's vision was for world empire, tempered by benign despotism, provided his autocracy was accepted.

Ironically, Schachermeyr's concept was as extreme and romantic as Tarn's, and it is not surprising that the irresistible parallels that could be drawn between his presentation of Alexander and the Third Reich rendered his views equally vulnerable to critics.[29] Also, using ancient historiography as a model, Schachermeyr was devoted to literary style, and again perhaps not surprisingly, his compositional techniques, featuring a

---

26. Tarn, *Alexander the Great,* 2:447–48. His very elaborate and personal interpretation was based largely on Arrian 7.11.9, which he also mistranslated; see Badian, *Historia* 7 (1958): 428 f.

27. On Schachermeyr, see Badian, "Some Recent Interpretations of Alexander," 282 f.; Bosworth (supra, n. 23), 140 f.; I also owe much of my discussion to Professor Bosworth's paper (which he kindly supplied in advance), "Ingenium und Macht: Fritz Schachermeyr and Alexander the Great," *AJAH* 13 (1996): 56–78. An updated version of Schachermeyr's biography with some additions and greatly expanded footnotes was published in 1973; but he did not revise his central thesis.

28. F. Schachermeyr, *Ein Leben zwischen Wissenschaft und Kunst,* ed. G. Dobesch and H. Schachermeyr (Vienna, 1984), 174–76.

29. A.R. Burn likened Schachermeyr's Alexander to a "young Nazi let loose in the Alps"; see review of *Alexander der Grosse: Ingenium und Macht,* by F. Schachermeyr, *CR* 1

rich, florid narrative illustrating a principle he called *Kunstprosa,* or "elevated prose," provoked a critical response.[30]

But unlike Tarn, Schachermeyr's literary presentation and personal insight rested on a solid foundation of evidence; although his contradictory Alexander caused concern for some scholars,[31] his careful (if conservative) source criticism ultimately renders his interpretation durable. Admittedly, Schachermeyr's prose would be difficult to translate into English and likely unpalatable; nevertheless, his Alexander should be acknowledged as potentially far-reaching and certainly more formidable than Tarn's or perhaps any other modern biographer's.

Tarn and Schachermeyr represent extreme examples. However, in terms of the Alexander *Schlauch,* what was true of the poetic interpretations of Tarn and Schachermeyr in modern times was equally applicable to the ancient, extant Alexander historians. They also imposed their own personalities and values on their presentations of the king, used the evidence to suit their interpretations, and, in the case of Curtius or Arrian, wrote with as much literary flair.

Before we can approach the primary sources or indeed the arcane figure of Alexander himself, it is imperative (as Bosworth noted) to understand the methodology of the traditions we have.[32] Although the extant

---

(1951): 101. Cf. C.B. Welles (supra, n. 21): 433; E. Meyer, review of *Alexander der Grosse: Ingenium und Macht,* by F. Schachermeyr, *MH* 7 (1950): 244–46, esp. 254. Despite certain provocative overtones, such as Alexander's "hypnotic effect" on his courtiers, which may recall a similar quality attributed to Adolf Hitler, it is important to note (see Bosworth, "Schachermeyr" [supra, n. 27]) that Schachermeyr's Alexander evolved over a number of years, long before Hitler's regime, and that the historian's vision of world empire is similar to the nineteenth-century interpretations of Wilcken and others. Schachermeyr's racial views, which were heightened by the Third Reich (see *Lebensgesetzlichkeit in der Geschichte: Versuch einer Einführung in das geschichtsbiologische Denken* [Frankfurt, 1940], 63–65; cf. *Indogermann und Orient* [Stuttgart, 1944]) and in particular his condemnation of Alexander's encouragement of racial integration as spoiling the vigor and "purity" of his own people perhaps predated Nazism, as Bosworth suggests, but likely drew on the same philosophical pools that spawned Nazi ideology.

30. On *Kunstprosa,* see Schachermeyr (supra, n. 28) 175. His style was criticized as inappropriate for serious scholarship; see H.U. Instinsky, review of *Alexander der Grosse: Ingenium und Macht,* by F. Schachermeyr, *HZ* (1952): 559–62. But see Schachermeyr's answers to his critics, in *Alexander der Grosse: Das Problem seiner Persönlichkeit und seines Wirkens,* 16–21.

31. See T.S. Brown's review of *Alexander der Grosse: Ingenium und Macht,* by F. Schachermeyr, *AJPh* 72 (1951): 74–77; but see Badian's comment in "Some Recent Interpretations of Alexander," 300 and 282, where he hails Schachermeyr's Alexander as "the leading one of our age."

32. Bosworth, *CE,* 300.

tradition provides us with the raw material we need for *Quellenforschung*, it must also be evaluated on its own terms and in the light of its contemporary interests. Judgment on the merits of the historian's presentation is passed by his audience, and criteria have varied according to the century.

As we saw in the previous chapters, Curtius' own Roman audience and the audiences of the Middle Ages looked for style, rather than historical accuracy. Paradoxically, in modern times, Arrian's effort to inform us of his sources has won him high praise from critics, who have tended to concentrate on this aspect, whereas his own creativity has been less emphasized; thus, he has been labeled the "most reliable" of the Alexander historians. Yet Arrian's stated principles of source methodology in his proem (praef. 1) emphasize his role as editor. While he believed that a compound narrative drawn from Ptolemy and Aristobulus would be the most reliable, his own selectivity, based on what he considers is the "more trustworthy and worth telling," determines the version he chooses to present when his main authorities happen to differ.[33] In addition, he tells us (praef. 3) that he uses supplementary material, which he believes is worth recording and not unreliable, but "only as stories [ὡς λεγόμενα μόνον] told about Alexander." However, as he does not cite his sources for these tales, it is difficult to tell whether he is using detail from supplemental sources, either directly or secondhand, or from his main authorities.[34] It is also evident that the *logoi* had an integral part in Arrian's overall literary structure, either for enhancing his portrayal of the king, if they were favorable, or for demonstrating to his audience his readiness to include alternative traditions, albeit sometimes negative or sensationalist, about which he could express skepticism or steadfast denial.[35]

---

33. On Arrian's compound method, see Stadter, *Arrian of Nicomedia*, 61.

34. Arrian's use of subsidiary traditions and the application of the *logos* formula is a complex part of his methodology. See Schwartz, *RE* 2: 1240–43; Bosworth, *HCA*, 1:20 f. Cf. Stadter, *Arrian of Nicomedia*, 72–76, 105–10.

35. Arrian 2.12.5 f. is explicit that the story of Sisygambis' confusion of Hephaestion for Alexander is not from Ptolemy and Aristobulus but is a *logos* that he approves; he is skeptical about the *legomena* relating the king's Dionysiac activities in India (cf. 5.2.7, 5.3.1) but openly denies the tale of Alexander's showy bacchanalian procession through Carmania (6.28.1–2) and the romantic story of Roxane preventing a dying Alexander from throwing himself in the Euphrates (7.27.3; cf. Ps.-Call. 3.32). Cf. Arrian's mixed judgments on the stories about Hephaestion's death, at 7.14.2–8. For other examples, see Bosworth, *HCA*, 1:20–21; Stadter, *Arrian of Nicomedia*, 105–10. A substantial use of *legomena* in book 4 occurs on the *sophrosyne* theme, where Arrian is compelled to address the well-known stories of Alexander's excesses.

Arrian was just as interested in style and presentation as Curtius. Frequently he displays his knowledge of various topics in academic discussion, such as his digressions on Heracles and Melqart (2.16.1–6), the sack of Thebes (1.9.1–8), and how Alexander bridged the Indus (5.7–8.2).[36] His use of a theme or philosophical concept—for example, of destiny in book 7 or the *sophrosyne* issue (4.7.5–14)—is ample demonstration of his literary intent.[37] Arrian seems to have perceived himself as Alexander's historical Muse; this perception is at least suggested by the tone of his second preface at 1.12.1–5.[38] His written works were clearly important to him (1.12.5), and his confidence in his own ability and in the impact of his literary production was reflected not only in his history of Alexander but in his minor studies.[39] Arrian's historical and literary methods have been discussed in far more depth elsewhere, and the general observations offered here are only intended to support the conclusion of more recent scholarship: far from being a mere conduit for Ptolemy and Aristobulus or other traditions, Arrian's history is a sophisticated blending of his own source selection, arrangement, and literary structures.[40]

All of the extant Alexander historians lived at a time when Rome was the dominant power in the West and when the Parthian dynasty in the

---

36. On Arrian's style generally, see Bosworth, *HCA*, 1:34 f.; on Heracles, 235–38; on Thebes, 84–89. Pearson, *LHA*, 11 n. 26, draws attention to the parallel offered by Xerxes and suggests that Arrian is exploiting the theme of Alexander's hubris. Arrian's principal authorities, Ptolemy and Aristobulus, had not described how Alexander bridged the Indus, and he is interested in the problem from a technical point of view, hence he offers an exposition of the Roman method. But his references to Herodotus also suggest his awareness of his literary heritage and his own artistry.

37. On Arrian's literary methods and use of themes generally, see Stadter, *Arrian of Nicomedia*, 60–88.

38. Arrian is very conscious of the potential of great subjects to create great literature and hence of the importance of style; cf. Quint. *Inst.* 2.4.1–20. The digression's importance and its difficulty are well explored: see G. Schepens, *Ancient Society* 2 (1971): 254–68; Brunt, *Arrian*, 2:538–40; Stadter, *Arrian of Nicomedia*, 62–66; Bosworth, *HCA*, 1:104–7, and *FAA*, 32 f.; J. Roisman, *RSA* 13–14 (1983–84): 253–63; J.M. Marincola, *JHS* 109 (1989): 186–89; V.J. Gray, "The Moral Interpretation of the "Second Preface" to Arrian's *Anabasis*," *JHS* 110 (1990): 180–86.

39. Arrian 1.1.3, 1.12.5, 6.11.2. His confidence in his work is most apparent in *Cynegeticus* 5.6, where he records the name of his bitch, Horme, for posterity. See Stadter, *Arrian of Nicomedia*, 54–55; Bosworth, *ANRW* II.34.1 (1993): 226–75.

40. This conclusion is all too apparent from the appendixes of Brunt in the recent Loeb editions of Arrian and from the multiple and incisive studies of Bosworth; Stadter, in *Arrian of Nicomedia*, also emphasizes Arrian's independence. See also G. Wirth, *Historia* 13 (1964): 209–45.

East held sway over much of what had once been conquered by the king. By the time Diodorus Siculus wrote, even the power of the last great Successor kingdom, governed by the Ptolemies in Egypt, was in decline. In view of the passage of history between 323 B.C. and the time when the surviving historians wrote, each must have faced potentially immense difficulties in trying not only to sift through a huge amount of conflicting material about Alexander but also to evaluate the apparently contradictory nature of the king himself.

One difficulty is that the Alexander *Schlauch* has a tendency to narrow, as successive historians concentrated on certain aspects while omitting others. Even Arrian, Curtius, and other writers who went back to the eyewitness or early accounts rather than simply use a more general history, such as Timagenes', could not help but be influenced by a more narrowed tradition. On particular occasions, both Arrian and Curtius express dissatisfaction with their primary and later sources, and from what incomplete impression we can obtain of the lost traditions, neither historian was altogether unjustified.[41] The surviving Alexander historians certainly faced no dearth of sources, although some were probably more accessible or better known than others.[42] The lost eyewitness traditions include Callisthenes, Onesicritus, Polyclitus, Nearchus, Chares, Medius of Larissa, Aristobulus, and Ptolemy. Cleitarchus, another important early authority, was widely recognized and used by later traditions, although it is generally deemed that he did not journey with Alexander.[43]

Individual personality, motive, a sense of literary heritage, bias, selec-

---

41. Curtius' comment, 9.5.21, is discussed in a later section of this chapter; Arrian 6.11.2 seeks to correct historical inaccuracies from other traditions, but he expresses concern (4.14.4) when his two reliable authorities contradict one another over what should have been public knowledge.

42. We can speculate on what traditions were accessible and well known from the number of secondary authors who quote them, but this evidence is hardly a reliable guide. Gellius *NA* 9.4.1–3 (= *FGrH* 134.T.12) tells a lively anecdote about finding a collection of books for sale in poor condition (but cheap), including Ctesias, Onesicritus, and Hegesias. On the availability of Ptolemy, see infra, n. 67.

43. See Pearson, *LHA*, 216 f.; Pédech, *Historiens*, 9 f. But see Bosworth, *HCA*, 1:32. Cleitarchus' date is controversial, but contrary to Tarn, *Alexander the Great*, 2:16–29, and Pearson, *LHA*, 242, Cleitarchus almost certainly wrote before Ptolemy. See J. Hamilton, "Cleitarchus and Aristobulus," *Historia* 10 (1961): 448–58; F. Schachermeyr, *Alexander in Babylon und die Reichsordnung nach seinem Tode* (Vienna, 1970), 211 f. (who argues a date ca. 316–305, accepted with modification by Brunt, *Arrian*, 2:555); Badian, "Some Recent Interpretations of Alexander," 35. On Cleitarchus' reputation, see Bosworth, *FAA*, 7; infra, n. 78.

tivity, and creativity were just as relevant to the methodology of the early accounts as they are to the extant traditions. It is difficult to determine the extent to which the first generation of historians also created their own "Alexanders," as opposed to merely recording their own roles in the expedition and their limited impressions of the king.[44] But propagandist aims and literary artistry were likely to have been more prevalent in some accounts. Diogenes Laertius remarked on the parallels between Xenophon's quasi-fictitious *Cyropaedia* (On the education of Cyrus) and Onesicritus,[45] while other fragments of Onesicritus' work suggest a blend of factual reporting and imagination, possibly conditioned by his philosophical outlook.[46]

In the *Hellenica,* Xenophon's bias against Thebes and his tendency to favor his hero, the Spartan king Agesilaus, are prominent.[47] In a similar fashion, the accounts of militaristic, memorialist writers, such as Nearchus and Ptolemy, glorified their own achievements, while remaining silent on or even depreciating the deeds of their rivals.[48] Bosworth raises the general issue of the desirability of truth in the face of public opinion, especially where events had been viewed by "tens of thousands."[49] But one may ask what the distribution of the audience was likely to have been at the time of Nearchus' composition, the extent of his readership, the amount of circulation any eyewitness account had among the other participants, and whether its author would have been very worried about any contradictory opinion. Although the more politically oriented early historians may have avoided outrageous false-

---

44. See Pearson, *LHA,* 19–20.
45. Diogenes Laertius 6.84 = *FGrH* 134.T.1.
46. See Pearson, *LHA,* 110–11. Cf. Brown, *Onesicritus,* esp. 24 f., on Onesicritus' philosophical views. See Pédech, *Historiens,* 71, for references. Strasburger's entry in *RE* 18: 460–67 is still relevant.
47. Xenophon's dislike of Thebes is well known; however, much of the "orthodox" view that Xenophon's attitudes include a simple pro-Spartan bias and Panhellenism have recently been challenged by C.J. Tuplin, *The Failings of Empire: A Reading of Xenophon Hellenica 2.3.11–7.5.27, Historia* Einzelschriften 76 (Stuttgart, 1993).
48. E. Badian, *YCS* 24 (1975): 147–70, argued that Nearchus falsely changed the scene of his crowning by Alexander to when the fleet and army were reunited (Arrian *Ind.* 42.9 = *FGrH* 133.F.1, but see Arrian 7.5.6). Cf. Brunt, *Arrian,* 2:429 n. 3. On the bias of Ptolemy, see infra, nn. 95, 98.
49. A.B. Bosworth, "Nearchus in Susiana," in *Zu Alexander dem Grossen: Festschrift G. Wirth,* ed. W. Will (Amsterdam, 1988), 541–56, 559 f. Cf. E. Badian, "The Death of Parmenio," *TAPhA* 91 (1960): 324–38, who argues that Callisthenes undermined Parmenion's reputation—which is plausible during the period after his murder, but not, as Badian would suggest, during Parmenion's lifetime.

hood to keep some credibility, it still seems likely that they had plenty of license.

Ptolemy's work likewise was probably not the dry, factual history that it was once thought. Over thirty years ago, Badian, pointing to the exaggerations, omissions, and biases inherent in the Ptolemaic tradition, suggested that it was composed with a deliberate aim in mind: the presentation of its author as Alexander's true successor.[50]

Callisthenes of Olynthus, the king's court historian, is the only author who is known to have been writing during the campaigns, and he did not survive the king. One might expect his account to have been truly firsthand evidence, untainted by inaccuracy of memory or bias. In fact, Callisthenes was already a prolific writer of some fame prior to the expedition, and it is very likely that he was deliberately employed to publicize the campaign in an extravagant and propagandist fashion, although Bosworth suggests that this feature of his work may have been overemphasized by later authors.[51]

As the man who protested against Alexander's attempt to introduce *proskynesis* at his court, Callisthenes' fall appears to have impressed the extant Alexander historians. According to Tarn and others (in an erroneous argument), Callisthenes' arrest and execution were the main reasons for the hostility of the Peripatetic school and the establishment of a vitriolic tradition about the king, stressing the degeneration of his reign into tyranny.[52]

---

50. E. Badian, review of *The Lost Histories of Alexander the Great*, by Lionel Pearson, *Gnomon* 33 (1961): 660–67; cf. *CQ* 8 (1958): 149 f. Strasburger, *Ptolemaios und Alexander*, 50 f., also noted Ptolemy's selectivity. Cf. W. Schwahn, "Die Nachfolge Alexanders des Grossen," *Klio* 23 (1930): 211–38, esp. 228; more recently, W. Ellis, *Ptolemy of Egypt* (London, 1994), 17–22. See also infra, n. 95, for additional bibliography on Ptolemy's biases.

51. A number of works were attributed to Callisthenes, including a *Hellenica*; see *FGrH* 124.F.1–59 for the fragments (not all of them are certain), and see Pédech, *Historiens*, 18 f. Polybius 6.45 censures Callisthenes for inaccuracy, but cf. 12.12.17–22. Strabo 17.1.43 refers to Callisthenes as a flatterer; cf. Cic. *Ad. Q.* fr. 2.11.4. The story of Alexander's fortuitous passage along the shore of Pamphylia was well known: see *FGrH* 124.F.31 and cf. Plut. *Alex.* 17; Arrian 1.26; Strabo 14.3.9; Josephus *AJ* 2.348. The other often cited propagandist example is Alexander's prayer at Gaugamela that if he was the son of Zeus, he would be granted victory (Plut. *Alex.* 33 = *FGrH* 124.F.36). See Pearson, *LHA*, 36 ff.; Badian, review of *The Lost Histories of Alexander the Great* (supra, n. 50), 661; Hamilton, *Plutarch*, 44, 87; Bosworth, *FAA*, 4 f.; Bosworth, "Alexander and Ammon," esp. 57 f.

52. See Tarn, *Alexander the Great*, 2:95–99, supported by T.S. Brown, *AJPH* 70 (1949): 225–48. But see Badian, *CQ* 8 (1958): 144–57; E. Mensching, *Historia* 12 (1963): 274–82; Fears, *Philologus* 118 (1974): 113–30.

Yet whether each of the Alexander historians believed Callisthenes to have been guilty or innocent of the charges for which he was condemned, their attitudes toward him as a historical figure remain, at best, ambivalent. Plutarch, who undoubtedly admires Callisthenes' stand over a principle, also recognizes that it cost him his life. Arrian paints a picture of unbridled and imprudent insolence toward Alexander on Callisthenes' part, whereas Curtius' qualifying description of the historian "as if he were a champion of the public liberty" [veluti vindex publicae libertatis] recalls the Tacitean Thrasea Paetus.[53]

We do not know how Callisthenes' history of Alexander was preserved. He may have sent installments back to Greece as he wrote (although there is no evidence that he did), or his work may have been taken over by someone else after his arrest. One can only guess at the extent of the influence Callisthenes' account had on the other primary traditions. They may well have made their own notes during the journey, but as there is some affinity between Aristobulus' version of Alexander's journey to Siwah and Callisthenes' (via Strabo 17.1.43), it is possible that Callisthenes' history was available and that some of the eyewitness traditions made good use of it. However, it is also possible that other historians, such as Ptolemy, may have drawn on official records or their own memory. P. Pédech argues that Ptolemy ignored Callisthenes out of national pride and bias and instead based his account on the *Ephemerides,* but perhaps this point may only be taken so far: Philip had incorporated foreigners in his *hetairoi,* and Callisthenes himself, through his relationship to Aristotle, must have been well known to Alexander and his associates.[54]

The dates for the composition of the other eyewitness accounts are uncertain but apparently varied considerably. We can be reasonably confident that Aristobulus wrote after the Battle of Ipsus in 301 B.C. and probably in his old age, whereas Onesicritus and Nearchus may have written earlier, in the period of the Diadochoi.[55] Nearchus was an advi-

---

53. Plut. *Alex.* 54; Arrian 4.10.1–2, 4.12.6; Curt. 8.5.20. On the term *vindex publicae libertatis,* see chap. 6, nn. 53–54.

54. Pédech, *Historiens,* 248 f. On the preservation of Callisthenes' history, see Pearson, *LHA,* 23; Hammond, *Alexander the Great, King, Commander, and Statesman,* 198. On the Siwah passage, see Pearson, *LHA,* 33–36; Bosworth, "Alexander and Ammon," 68–75. See also Bosworth, *HCA,* 1:24 n. 31, on the use of archival material in the other traditions besides Arrian.

55. On Aristobulus' age, see *FGrH* 139.T.3; on the Battle of Ipsus, see Arrian 7.18.5. See also Bosworth, *FAA,* 3 n. 7. For dates of Onesicritus and Nearchus, see Badian, review of *The Lost Histories of Alexander the Great* (supra, n. 50), 663; Badian (supra, n. 3), 39 f. But see Heckel, *Marshals,* 232–33.

sor to Demetrius Poliorcetes in 313/2 (Diod. 19.69.1),[56] and he may have finished his history around this time, although he had evidently begun it earlier, since, according to Plutarch (*Alex.* 76.3), he entertained Alexander during his last illness by reading him an account of the voyage from India. The date of Ptolemy's history is a far more controversial issue, which essentially revolves around whether he also wrote early (prior to 317), while still trying to establish his rule or at another time.[57]

As indicated earlier, there was also considerable and significant variation in the identity, occupation, and probable motive of all these authors, which should have affected the history each produced. Some were closer to the king than others; Nearchus and Ptolemy had been associates of Alexander's youth, and both had held important positions of command, whereas Chares was Alexander's court chamberlain.[58] It is less discernible how close the Thessalian writers Medius and Polyclitus were to the king, although traditionally the onset of Alexander's fatal illness occurred shortly after Medius' party.[59] Onesicritus and Aristobulus, Alexander's chief pilot and technician, respectively, were probably further removed from the inner circle of the court, but this distance certainly did not result in more objective histories.[60]

Of more significance are the interests and selectivity of the secondary traditions, which have affected the amount and the type of material preserved from the original sources. For instance, the eyewitness accounts of Nearchus, Onesicritus, Polyclitus, and Aristobulus and of early (or Hellenistic) writers like Cleitarchus, Megasthenes, and Eratosthenes apparently contained extensive information on Asia and India. This informa-

---

56. See R.M. Errington, "Diodorus Siculus and the Chronology of the Early Diadochoi, 320–11 B.C.," *Hermes* 105 (1977): 478– 504.

57. Critical opinion once maintained that Ptolemy could not have written before 284, but see Badian's remarks (supra, n. 3).

58. On Nearchus and Ptolemy, see Arrian 3.6.5; cf. Plut. *Alex.* 10.5. On Chares, see Plut. *Alex.* 4.6. See also the respective, prosopographical entries in Berve, 2: nos. 544, 668, 820; and see the similar studies in Heckel, *Marshals*, 222–33.

59. Only ten fragments survive of Polyclitus' history (*FGrH* 128.F), most preserved by Strabo, suggesting a geographical and anecdotal nature of the work. On Medius, see Arrian 7.24.4–7.25.1, cited as a *legomenon*, which describes Medius as one of Alexander's "most persuasive" Companions. Cf. *FGrH* 117.F.3, 127.F.1; Diod. 17.117.1; J. 12.13.7. Medius was also involved in the purported poisoning of Alexander: see Arrian 7.27.2; Ps.- Call. 3.31; *FGrH* 134.F.37 = *Liber de morte* 97.

60. On Onesicritus, see *FGrH* 134.T.4, 5 a–c, 6. Aristobulus has traditionally been seen as Alexander's architect or engineer, based largely on his restoration of Cyrus' tomb (Arrian 6.29; cf. Strabo 15.3.7 [730] = *FGrH* 139.F.51b): see Pearson, *LHA*, 150 ff.; Pédech, *Historiens*, 385 ff.; Brunt, *Arrian*, 2:556. More cautious are Bosworth, *HCA*, 1:27, and Stadter, *Arrian of Nicomedia*, 69.

tion appealed to secondary writers with specialist concerns in geography or natural history, including Strabo, Pliny the Elder, Plutarch, Arrian, Artemidorus, and Aelian. In view of their dilettantish interests, Athenaeus, Gellius, Pliny, and Plutarch extracted from Chares and other sources material of an anecdotal nature on Alexander's court.

Opinion on the worth and dependability of the primary traditions also varied among the later sources, again according to individual tastes and criteria. Onescritus and Aristobulus were both criticized for either fabrication or apologist tendencies; conversely, Nearchus was praised by Arrian for his reliability.[61] Two sources, Ptolemy and Cleitarchus, who are both named by Curtius himself, may be used as brief examples of primary traditions challenged by later sources, if only to highlight the controversies associated with these lost authors and to surmise why Curtius may have found them appealing or unsatisfactory as authorities.

Curtius acknowledges Cleitarchus twice. At 9.5.21 he censures both Cleitarchus and Timagenes for inaccuracy, and at 9.8.5 he cites the former as an authority for the massacre of eighty thousand Indian natives in the territory of King Sambus.[62] Naming a source does not automatically ensure that the author consulted that tradition himself. It is evident that authors like Arrian and Strabo sometimes echo remarks made by others on particular sources, without consulting those sources for themselves.[63] Thus Curtius could have simply repeated a critical remark that he found in a secondary authority. The historian's reproval follows his description of the Macedonians' capture of the Indian Malli fort, where the king was severely wounded.[64] The passage is controversial and therefore worth examining in detail.

---

61. On Onesicritus, see Plut. *Alex.* 46 = *FGrH* 134.T.8; Strabo 15.1.28 = *FGrH* 134.T.10. On Aristobulus as a flatterer, see *FGrH* 139.T.4–5; but see also P.A. Brunt, "Notes on Aristobulus of Cassandreia," *CQ* 24 (1974): 65–69. Aristobulus' sympathetic portrait of Alexander has received considerable attention: see Pédech, *Historiens*, 348 f.; Pearson, *LHA*, 157 f.; Bosworth, *HCA*, 1:28–29. On Nearchus, see Arrian 5.5.1 and *Ind.* 17.6; cf. Strabo 2.1.9.

62. The figure of eighty thousand is not certain; some manuscripts read eight hundred, but corruption of the numerals is likely. See Bosworth, *FAA*, 45–46.

63. See Bosworth, *FAA*, 45–46; Arrian (*Ind.* 6.8) and Strabo (15.1.13 [691] = *FGrH* 134.F.7) echo Eratosthenes' citations without reading the original sources. Cf. Arrian's rebuke of Onesicritus, at 6.2.3, which Brunt, *Arrian*, 2:445, says may have come from Ptolemy.

64. Curtius mistakenly attributes the siege to a town of the Sudracae (9.4.26); cf. Arrian 6.11.3. See also Bosworth, *FAA*, 76–77.

According to the authorities, Cleitarchus and Timagenes, Ptolemy, who reigned after these events, was present at this battle, but he himself, who was hardly inclined to depreciate his own glory, has set on record that he was absent, as he had been sent on an expedition. Such was the carelessness of those compiling the old records of history or, an equal failing, their credulity.

[Ptolomaeum, qui postea regnavit, huic pugnae adfuisse auctor est Clitarchus et Timagenes, sed ipse, scilicet gloriae suae non refragatus, afuisse se, missum in expeditionem, memoriae tradidit. Tanta componentium vetusta rerum monimenta vel securitas vel, par hic vitium, credulitas fuit.] (Curt. 9.5.21)

Curtius' construction is stylish and rhetorical. He has linked together as "the authority" two traditions, Cleitarchus and Timagenes—one early, the other comparatively recent. His use of the singular *(auctor est)* is not only appropriate for the chronology but also subtly insults Timagenes, by implying that he is a mere echo of Cleitarchus. The historian counters their allegation of Ptolemy's presence at the battle by a reference to Ptolemy's own text *(sed ipse, scilicet gloriae suae non refragatus, afuisse se, missum in expeditionem, memoriae tradidit).*

Although Curtius' use of Ptolemy is discussed at a later point in this chapter, it seems appropriate here to consider whether Curtius' statement means that he consulted that author directly. Linguistically, the presence of the perfect indicative in *memoriae tradidit* (he has set on record), as opposed to an impersonal and vague expression like *traditur* (it was said),[65] could indicate a personal knowledge of what Ptolemy actually wrote in his text, but it does not prove that Curtius had the original before him. Bosworth argues that the historian's sarcasm on Ptolemy may have been a standard topos, much like the parallel comments offered by Livy on Cato (34.15.9) and by Tacitus on Nero (*Ann.* 11.11.3).[66] However, this argument assumes that Ptolemy himself must have been reasonably well known as an author; a premise that, in view of his appar-

---

65. Suet. *Gaius* 55.3 uses *traditur* in a very general sense, of the story that Caligula intended to make his horse Incitatus a consul.
66. Bosworth, *FAA,* 80–81. Tacitus' phraseology offers a more striking parallel to Livy than Curtius' version: cf. Livy 34.15, *haud sane detractator laudium suarum,* with Tac. *Ann.* 11.11.3, *nam ipse, haudquaquam sui detractor.* See also Syme, *Tacitus,* 1:349 n. 12.

ent obscurity, seems hard to accept.[67] It seems more likely that the phrasing of Livy's appealing witticism was imitated by Curtius and Tacitus to suit themselves. Moreover, a certain amount of audience involvement and flattery is present in all three authors; Livy's sly jibe is at the expense of a national icon, Nero's lunacy in general was known to everybody (or at least to those who mattered), and Ptolemy (as Curtius reminds his audience) was a king. A Roman audience would expect a king to brag, without the audience's necessarily knowing or caring to know a lot more.

It was part of ancient historiographical practice to set right previous historical inaccuracies; as Zumpt observed, every age boasted of its own attention to accuracy, because it could always find something to correct in writers of earlier times.[68] Curtius thus criticizes Cleitarchus and Timagenes for *securitas* (carelessness) and *credulitas* (credulity), with both remarks perhaps more pointedly aimed at Timagenes as the secondary authority for passing on the inaccuracy.[69]

The other vexing question is whether Curtius used Cleitarchus directly. Corroboration from another source (Diod. 17.102.5-7) favors a firsthand knowledge,[70] while the surrounding context in Diodorus and

---

67. Apart from Arrian, Ptolemy is not extensively quoted; he is cited once by Pliny the Elder (*NH* 1.12–13 = *FGrH* 138.T.2), Strabo (7.3.8 = *FGrH* 138.F.2), Curtius (9.5.21), and Synesios (*FGrH* 138.F.11, a bizarre story) and twice by Plutarch (*De Alex. fort.* 1.3 [327 D–E] = *FGrH* 138.F.4; cf. *Alex.* 46 = *FGrH* 138.F.28a), Stephanus Byzantius (*FGrH* 138.F.5, 31 [uncertain]), and Geographus Ravennas (*FGrH* 138.F.28c, 32 [uncertain]). See also Bosworth, *HCA,* 1:22; Stadter, *Arrian of Nicomedia,* 67.

68. C.G. Zumpt, *Q. Curtii Rufi, De Gestis Alexandri Magni* (Edinburgh, 1849), 303 n. 7. Historiographical emendation of past error may be traced back to Hecataeus; see Bosworth, *FAA,* 75–76 n. 63.

69. On Timagenes, see *FGrH* 88. There are very few fragments of his surviving. He was brought to Rome in about 55 B.C. as a slave (Sen. *Contr.* 10.5.22), eventually established a friendship with Augustus, and was brought into his household to record his *acta,* but when Timagenes made too many sharp or flippant remarks, he was banished. He lived with Asinius Pollio (Sen. *De ira* 3.23.4–8), which may explain Livy's hostility; on Pollio and Livy, see Syme, *The Roman Revolution,* 485, but see Walsh, *Livy,* 268, and A.B. Bosworth, "Asinius Pollio and Augustus," *Historia* 21 (1972): 445–46. For Timagenes' possible impact on Trogus and Curtius, see A. von Gutschmid, "Trogus and Timagenes," *Rhein. Mus.* 37 (1882): 548 f., and Atkinson, *Curtius* i, 58–61; but in view of the scanty remnants of Timagenes' work, the examples Atkinson cites of influence on Curtius seem hard to justify. It is also possible that Curtius may have taken his information from Trogus. But Curtius probably read Timagenes, and as he was influenced by Livy, his scathing comment (like Livy's) was likely calculated for audience appeal; Timagenes was famous for his anti-Roman sentiments. See Heckel's discussion in Heckel and Yardley, *Justin,* introduction, part II.2. On Timagenes in general and for further references, see M. Sordi, "Timagene di Alessandria: Uno storico ellenocentrico e filobarbaro," *ANRW* II.30.1 (1982): 775–97.

70. Diodorus does not name Cleitarchus as an authority for book 17, but he does cite him on Semiramis' palace at 2.7.3 (= *FGrH* 137.T.5). See also Bosworth, *FAA,* 9 n. 33.

Curtius suggests in detail a chronological sequence. Diodorus (17.98–99) also describes the assault on the Indian fortress, but he does not mention Ptolemy. It is doubtful if Diodorus knew Ptolemy's own version, but his omission does not necessarily mean that the historian was not following Cleitarchus.[71] On the contrary, Curtius and Diodorus contain much detail in common, including both a tree that protects Alexander and the dramatic attack on the king by a native, who shoots and fells the king, but who is killed by him when he tries to strip his body. Likewise, in both accounts, Peucestes is the first to appear over the wall, and he covers Alexander with his shield. My feeling is that Diodorus has simply compacted his account, omitting much of the additional detail that Curtius supplies (such as the names of the rest of the men who come to Alexander's aid), while keeping Peucestes as the savior of the king. Curtius does not mention that Cleitarchus attributed any heroics to Ptolemy,[72] and it is possible that Ptolemy's presence at the assault was all that was noted. We may compare another story common to both Curtius and Diodorus, which probably also derives from Cleitarchus: Ptolemy was wounded by an Indian poisoned weapon but made a subsequent miraculous recovery through the help of Alexander's dream and its obliging serpent.[73] Such a tale, with its baggage of Ptolemaic propaganda, snakes and all, undoubtedly had more appeal for Diodorus. He could include this story and gloss over a passing reference to Ptolemy in Cleitarchus' account of the Malli campaign.[74]

The originality of Curtius' research and statement remains a difficult question. It does seem unlikely that Cleitarchus' mistake had not been detected before, but the so-called notoriety of a specific Cleitarchan and Ptolemaic controversy may be a little dubious. Assuming that Curtius is an early imperial author, he is the earliest known source who cites

---

71. Hamilton, "Cleitarchus and Diodorus 17," 143, argues Diodorus may have deliberately rejected Cleitarchus at this point. P. Goukowsky, *Diodore de Sicile XVII*, 257, and Hammond, *THA*, 65, suggest that Diodorus deliberately suppressed Ptolemy's name because Cleitarchus' lie was "common knowledge." But see Bosworth, *FAA*, 81 n. 91.
72. Pace Hammond, *THA*, 65.
73. See Diod. 17.103.4–8; Curt. 9.8.20–28; J. 12.10.1–3. Cf. Strabo 15 (723); Cic. *De div.* 2.135. See Goukowsky (supra, n. 3); Hamilton, "Cleitarchus and Diodorus 17," 143–44; Heckel, *Marshals*, 226.
74. Another comparable example of Diodorus' selectivity is his omission of the Roman embassy to Alexander in 324/3, which is attributed to Cleitarchus in Pliny *NH* 3.57 (= *FGrH* 137.F.31). Arrian (7.15.5–6) names Aristus and Asclepiades as the sources. Cf. Diodorus' and Justin's treatment of the embassies, at Diod. 17.113.2 and J. 12.13.1 Both authors possibly omitted the story out of considerations of space, or in Justin/Trogus' case, national pride; see Bosworth, *FAA*, 83–93, esp. 90 n. 115.

Cleitarchus' error; it was clearly unknown to Diodorus and apparently missed by Strabo.[75] Certainly Arrian's introductory comment to his elaborate critique of the Malli siege (6.11.2 f.) indicates that the incident itself was often inaccurately related, and it seems unlikely that both he and Curtius made a similar remark about the same episode by pure chance. But Arrian's emphasis addresses a later, embellished and apparently widely known tradition on the siege, in which Ptolemy was not only present at the fortress but saved Alexander's life and earned his title *Soter*. This story appears with variations in several writers of the imperial period, including Plutarch, Pausanias, and Pseudo-Callisthenes.[76] There is no reiteration of the elaborated version in Curtius' account; the only hint that he may have known of alternative traditions that enlarged Ptolemy's role lies in the sarcastic jibe at his *gloria*. However, such a statement may be nothing more than an indication of the nature of Ptolemy's history; Curtius may well have found Ptolemy boastful in general, and had he been at the siege where his king received a near-fatal wound, he would have said so. Whether Curtius discovered a historiographical "exclusive" cannot be proven, but he did have an outstanding example of one primary source (Cleitarchus) contradicted by another primary source (Ptolemy), who himself happened to be the subject of the first. It was simply too good an opportunity for the historian to miss; he could exploit his audience's probable familiarity with Cleitarchus and Timagenes at the same time as displaying his own knowledge. Conversely, regular source criticism does not appear to have been part of Curtius' compositional technique, apart from the odd occasions in the text where he does appear to evaluate the historicity of his sources (see "Some Principles of Curtius' Methodology" later in this chapter).

If we assume that Curtius drew on Cleitarchus and Ptolemy as authorities, the historian's reasons for choosing them warrant some exploration. There is very little that we can confidently assert about Cleitarchus today. The thirty-six extant fragments of his work and discerning (although divided) ancient critical opinion suggest an author who, despite his literary ambitions, had a tendency for the rhetorical, col-

---

75. Strabo mentions the Malli only in passing, at 15.1.33 (701).
76. Plut. *De Alex. fort.* 1.2 (327B), 2.13 (344D). Cf. Paus. 1.6.2; Ps.-Call. 3.4.14–15. See Bosworth, *FAA*, 82. It is doubtful (contra Pearson, *LHA*, 214) that the story of how Ptolemy earned his title came from Cleitarchus. Rather, it was probably a later embellishment. See Brunt, *Arrian*, 2:134–35 n. 6; Bosworth's full discussion in *FAA*, 79–83.

orful, and bizarre.[77] Yet Cleitarchus was a well-known author, and his *History of Alexander* (his only attested work) was evidently a substantial affair, consisting of some twelve or more volumes.[78] Thus he was likely to have been for Curtius a readily available source who presented him with a wealth of information with potential audience appeal, if the digression on the Hanging Gardens at Babylon or the visit of the Amazon queen (which Curtius shares with Diodorus) may be traced back to Cleitarchus.[79]

It is also possible that Cleitarchus provided a more detailed—albeit sensationalist—treatment of the unpleasant aspects of Alexander's personality and reign. Allowing for Roman ambivalence to the Macedonian and the fact that Alexander's negative qualities were well explored in the rhetorical schools, Curtius may have still sought an early source with a more balanced appraisal as opposed to the apologist accounts of Aristobulus and Ptolemy. The fall of Philotas may be taken as a case in point. Arrian unequivocally accepted the "official" version of Ptolemy, corroborated by Aristobulus, and Ptolemy, who benefited from the execution of Philotas and others, certainly had his own reasons for keeping his account to a minimum.[80] Elsewhere, the anti-autocratic tone of the Scythian oration (discussed later in this chapter) and the negative aspects of *regnum* suggested by the Charidemus (3.2.11–18) and Dioxippus

---

77. On Cleitarchus' worth and style, see Quint. *Inst.* 10.1.74 (= *FGrH* 137.T.6). Philodemus (*FGrH* 137.T.11) groups Cleitarchus with rhetoricians; cf. Demetrius (*FGrH* 137.T.10) and Cic. *De leg.* 1.2.7 (= *FGrH* 137.T.13) and *Brut.* 42–43 (= *FGrH* 137.F.34). See also Bosworth, *FAA*, 7. The fragments also abound in geographical and zoological detail; Cleitarchus is frequently cited by Strabo, Aelian, and Pliny.

78. Pliny (*NH* 10.136 = *FGrH* 137.T.4) calls Cleitarchus a *celebratus auctor*. Diogenes Laertius (1.6 = *FGrH* 137.F.6) refers to a twelfth book of Cleitarchus. As Cleitarchus was still on the Indian narrative, it seems reasonable to assume he would need two or three more volumes to complete the work, but we have no evidence on the length of the books.

79. For the Hanging Gardens, see Diod. 17.64.3–6 and Curt. 5.1.10–45; see also Hamilton, "Cleitarchus and Diodorus 17," 138–40. For the visit of the Amazon queen, see Curt. 6.5.24– 32; Diod. 17.77.1–3; Plut. *Alex.* 46.1–2; J. 12.3.5–7. Cf. Strabo 11.5.4 (505) = *FGrH* 137.F.16. According to Plutarch, a number of traditions recorded the incident, but certain corroborative details in the vulgate (a thirteen-day visit, the rivers Phasis and Thermodon) suggest Cleitarchus as the ultimate authority. See Hamilton, *Plutarch*, 124, but he is more cautious about Cleitarchus in "Cleitarchus and Diodorus 17," 136.

80. Ptolemy was promoted into Alexander's prestigious bodyguard after the fall of Philotas. See Arrian 3.27.5. Cf. Curt. 6.7.1– 7.2.38; Diod. 17.79–80; Plut. *Alex.* 48–49; J 12.5.1–8; Strabo. 15.2.10 (724). For additional data, see Bosworth, *HCA*, 1:359; my chap. 6, n. 11.

(9.7.19–26) episodes, which may have also been Cleitarchan, provided Curtius with a core tradition that he could adapt or embellish.[81]

It is possible to suggest other traces of Cleitarchus in Curtius, although with varying degrees of plausibility. For instance, the historian displays an interest in the Persians and in figures like Sisygambis, the mother of Darius III.[82] Cleitarchus' father, Dinon of Colophon, wrote a *Persica*, and it seems likely that Cleitarchus' own work would have exploited this study. Curtius' elaborate description of Darius' army on the march (3.3.8–25) is clearly based on a source or sources with specialist knowledge of Persian customs. But there is no corresponding digression in Diodorus, and it is equally possible that Curtius may have used Persian material derived from other authorities, including Ctesias, Dinon himself, and Herodotus.[83]

Curtius shares several stories about Sisygambis with Diodorus; of particular note are the Persian queen mother's mistaken identification of Hephaestion for Alexander (Diod. 17.37.3 f.; Curt. 3.3.22) and her decision to commit suicide after his death (Diod. 17.118.3 f.; Curt. 10.5.19–25; J. 13.1.5).[84] The former tale was evidently well known in the Alexander traditions, since it appears in Arrian as a *logos* (2.12.6–8) and in Valerius Maximus' treatment on friendship (4.7.ext.2). In Curtius, the story precedes the historian's rhetorical excursus (3.12.18–21) on the king's *continentia* and *fortuna*, which foreshadows the decline of Alexander's *regnum* into tyranny. However, while it does seem likely that the episode was a standard topos in the Roman schools, two elements in particular suggest that Diodorus and Curtius used a common source. Sisygambis is named in only these historians; although Ptolemy may have recorded anecdotes on Alexander's relations with the queen mother, she is never specified.[85] *Fortuna*, or *tyche*, *continentia*, and *phronesis* appear as the important motifs

---

81. For Charidemus, see chap. 5, 139. Brunt, *Arrian*, 2:564–65, is doubtful that the Cleitarchan picture was overly hostile, but allowance is made by Bosworth in *FAA*, 11.

82. For Macedonian customs, see Curt. 4.7.31, 6.8.25, 10.9.12; see also Tarn, *Alexander the Great*, 2:10 f. For Persian customs, see Curt. 3.3.8 f., etc; cf. my chap. 2.

83. Cleitarchus' use of Dinon's *Persica* is suggested by the frequency of Persian terms, such as *gangabae* or *gaza* (treasure), *tigris* = *sagitta*, and *doryphoroe* (perhaps *dorophoroe*); on the confusion of the latter term, see W. Heckel, "*Doryphoroe* in Curtius 3.3.15 Again," *RhM* 135 (1992): 191–92. See also Atkinson, *Curtius* i, 120 f., esp. 134–35. For the fragments of Dinon, see *FGrH* 690; Pearson, *LHA*, 226 f.

84. See also Diod. 17.59.7; Curt. 4.15.5–11, 5.3.12–15 (cf. Arrian 3.17.6). The story of Alexander's faux pas in giving the Persian queen some wool to weave is unique to Curt. 5.2.18 f.

85. See Bosworth, *HCA*, 1:221, 323–24. Darius' mother is incorrectly named as Stateira at Ps.-Call. 2.22. The Valerius Maximus passage was very likely derived from Trogus; see O. Seel, *Pompei Trogi Fragmenta*, (Leipzig, 1956), F 80c.

in each historian's moralizing comments on Alexander's action, which suggests that they may have been present in the original source; yet Curtius' digression is also part of a literary series of authorial commentaries on the king's character, culminating in the rhetorical obituary on Alexander at 10.5.26–37. It was stylistically and thematically appropriate for Curtius to use the story of Sisygambis' suicide as an appropriate transition for the epilogue; both the excursus in book 3 and the summary in book 10 deliberately balance and complement each other.[86] The original source for the Sisygambis material may have been Cleitarchus, but Curtius certainly exploited the stories to his own advantage.

Curtius has been credited with using a variety of sources, and he may have known Nearchus and Onesicritus, since at 10.1.10–12 he records their reported statements. Yet the phraseology there—"they told of some things they had heard, others they had discovered" [nuntiabant autem quaedam audita, alia comperta]—is more indicative of secondary excerption than of direct consultation, and the same context of reported stories is given in Diodorus (17.106.6).[87] The description of the fleet's encounter with the whales and Curtius' account of the so-called Ichthyophagi, or "Fish-Eaters" (9.10.8–10), has some affinity with the other traditions, which ultimately were based on Nearchus and Onesicritus.[88] But it seems more likely in view of the brief treatment both episodes receive and the similarity between Curtius and Diodorus that their accounts were derived not from Nearchus and Onesicritus but rather from another authority that had some elements in common with those sources.

Within the same context, Curtius' account of the Gedrosia desert crossing and its hardships (9.10.5–19) is also worth a comment in terms of the original tradition. Like Strabo, Arrian probably derived his account of the desert journey from Nearchus.[89] Certain elements in Arrian's narrative (6.25.2–3) are corroborated in Curtius (9.10.12). But overall, Curtius' version is much closer to Diodorus' (cf. Diod. 17.105.3–5 and Curt. 9.10.8–10; Diod. 105.6–7 and Curt. 9.10.17), and

---

86. On Curtius' necrology of Alexander and on the excursus in book 3, see chap. 4.
87. Cf. Strabo 16.3.5 (767).
88. Hammond, *THA*, 128, 137, 151, 159, identifies some eight sources in Curtius. Diodorus (17.106.6 f.) includes the story of the tides in this context, which is given more detailed treatment in Curtius (9.9.9–25) and Arrian (6.19.1). For the whales, see Diod. 17.106.6–7; cf. Arrian *Ind.* 30 and Strabo 15.2.11–13. See Bosworth *FAA*, 42. For the Ichthyophagi, see Diod. 103.3–5; cf. Arrian *Ind.* 29.9 f. and Strabo 15 (721). See Hamilton, "Cleitarchus and Diodorus 17," 142; Hammond, *THA*, 69. On Curtius' possible consultation of Onesicritus, see Atkinson, *Curtius* i, 64.
89. Arrian 6.24 f.; cf. Strabo 15.2.5 (722). See also A.B. Bosworth, *Alexander and the East*, 166–85.

it seems more likely that they shared a common source who was not Nearchus but who may have been Cleitarchus. It is possible that the latter knew Nearchus' work, but it is more likely that his account was composed from other sources. Like Nearchus, Cleitarchus may have talked to survivors of the crossing, but that would hardly mean he would receive or record exactly the same information.

Arrian's tradition contains details like a devastating flash flood (6.25.4–6; cf. Strabo 15.2.6 [722]), which does not appear in Curtius and Diodorus. More importantly, the famous story of Alexander's refusal of water that his army could not share, which according to Arrian's source took place in the Gedrosia (6.26.1–3), was attributed to a different location in the vulgate; in Curtius (7.4.9–12)—and possibly in Diodorus—the incident happened in a desert in Sogdiana. Arrian admitted that there were other versions that placed the story elsewhere and at an earlier time. Nearchus, probably Arrian's source for the episode, did not experience the Gedrosia journey himself, but he may have exploited another tradition that was probably already in circulation. If so, Nearchus could have had a strong propagandist motive for placing the episode where he did; according to Arrian and Strabo, Nearchus explained one of Alexander's motives for making the expedition as a desire to emulate his predecessors Cyrus and Semiramis. He did not want the king's desert crossing to be perceived as a disaster; by inserting the story of Alexander's refusal to drink, Nearchus (and Arrian) would enhance the heroic and quasi-divine aspects of Alexander's leadership and emphasize the superiority of his achievement over the achievements of Cyrus and Semiramis.[90]

Another controversial issue is whether Curtius used Arrian's other main authorities. It has been suggested that Curtius may have drawn on Ptolemy and Aristobulus for a piece of description, while data that Curtius and Arrian share in common, such as details of certain battles (at Gaugamela, Tyre, etc.) or of military and civil administration, may derive from the Ptolemaic tradition. But apart from Curtius' well-known reference to his sources at 9.5.21, nothing else suggests direct consultation.[91]

---

90. On Cyrus and Semiramis, see Arrian 6.24.2–3; cf. Strabo 15.1.5 (686) = *FGrH* 133.F.3. For Alexander's refusal of the water, see Plut. *Alex.* 42.5–8; Front. *Strat.* 1.7.7; Poly. *Strat.* 4.3.25; Arrian 6.26.1–3. Diodorus' treatment is lost, but we know from the index to his work that Alexander lost many of his men in the Sogdian desert crossing. For an alternative analysis of the traditions, see Hammond, *Sources*, 274 f.

91. For Curtius' use of Ptolemy and Aristobulus, see Hammond, *THA*, 123; Atkinson, *Curtius* i, 61 f.; Tarn, *Alexander the Great*, 2:107, 185 f.; Pearson, *LHA*, 198. Strasburger, *Ptolemaios und Alexander*, 6 f., collected a number of parallels between Arrian and Curtius but was noncommittal on the tradition.

However, even if we do accept that Curtius may have known and used Ptolemy's work directly, his attitude toward that author raises some interesting questions.

As indicated earlier, Ptolemy appears to have been relatively unknown as an author in antiquity. Yet Arrian's high reputation as the "most reliable" of the extant Alexandrian traditions has rested in modern times not only on the explanation of his historical methods but on his choice of the eyewitness accounts of Ptolemy and Aristobulus as his principal authorities. Tarn remarked, "Ptolemy had better opportunities of knowing than most people and was able to use the Journal and other official material."[92] This statement, with its roots in nineteenth-century German research, once represented the "orthodox" view: that when Ptolemy wrote his history, he had access to the *Ephemerides,* or the royal journal.[93] The authenticity of this document and the problems created by the scanty fragments and their homogeneous nature have been too well explored to reiterate here.[94]

Certainly Arrian does not say he selected Ptolemy because of his use of archival material. It seems possible, particularly if one accepts Hammond's arguments (cited in note 94), that Ptolemy acquired the *Ephemerides,* along with Alexander's body, weapons, and other paraphernalia, when he intercepted the king's funeral carriage at Damascus. According to Arrian (*Succ.* F 24.1; cf. F 1.25), Ptolemy's interference increased Perdiccas' ardor for an invasion. But Ptolemy may have also obtained the archives at any time, perhaps after his own departure from Babylon or even after the death of Perdiccas. Moreover, if Ptolemy did use the *Ephemerides* or records of some kind, there still remain the controversial issues of when he wrote, his motives for writing, and how much of his account was propaganda justifying his reign—all issues that would have affected his reliability.[95] A certain amount of subjectivity inevitably seems to creep into any attempt to ascertain Ptolemy's motives; for instance, opinion on the matter is influenced by whether one

---

92. Tarn, *Alexander the Great,* 2:1.

93. See A.B. Bosworth, "Arrian and the Alexander Vulgate," 3; Green, *Alexander of Macedon,* 482.

94. Bosworth, *FAA,* 158 f., gives a concise but substantial statement of the problem, together with full bibliography. Pédech, *Historiens,* 246–51, supports the traditional view, and Hammond is also consistent: see *THA,* 5–11; "The Royal Journal of Alexander," *Historia* 37 (1988): 129–50; "Aspects of Alexander's Journal and Ring in His Last Days," *AJPH* 110 (1989): 155–60; "A Note on Royal Journals," *Historia* 40 (1991): 382–84.

95. See Badian, *CQ* 8 (1958) 149 f.; Bosworth, "Arrian and the Alexander Vulgate," 10–29, and *HCA,* 1:25 f.; Brunt, *Arrian,* 1:xxxiv and 2:560; R.M. Errington, *CQ* 19 (1969): 233–42.

wants to believe that Ptolemy genuinely admired Alexander, that he was concerned about all the untrue stories that were being told about the late king, and that he wrote in his old age, as king of Egypt, to "set the record straight," relying on either his memory or the journal or both.[96]

Ptolemy's exploitation of his own association with Alexander is shown by his appropriation of the king's body and the subsequent establishment of the official Ptolemaic state cult of Alexander.[97] Undeniably, Ptolemy would have been eager to glorify Alexander's achievement and his own association with him. Elements of propaganda that appear in the traditions, such as the stories that Ptolemy was Alexander's illegitimate half brother and that snakes guided the king to Siwah, probably derive from Ptolemy's history or some other pro-Ptolemaic source.[98]

As a Roman, how would Curtius have viewed Ptolemy? One could suggest that the taint of anti-Ptolemaic propaganda still current in the first century A.D. may have influenced Curtius adversely, but such influence is impossible to prove.[99] Overall, the historian's own comment on Ptolemy *(scilicet gloriae suae non refragatus)* contains the clearest indication. Curtius was at least conscious of the self-congratulatory tone of Ptolemy, and a reason he may have been wary to use Ptolemy as a major source could be the very reason Arrian gave for choosing him (praef. 2), namely, Ptolemy's position as king. Despite a general Roman awareness of the need for truth in rulers, Curtius was also conscious of the power of kings to suppress rumor, as well as the danger faced by a subject who spoke the truth to the king (10.10.18–19).[100]

---

96. See Pearson, *LHA*, 193 f.; Hammond, *THA*, 10. The *Ephemerides* may have contained useful information about itinerary; see C.A. Robinson Jr., *The Ephemerides of Alexander's Expedition* (Providence, R.I., 1932).

97. See R.M. Errington, "Alexander and the Hellenistic World," in *Alexander le Grand, image et réalité,* Fondation Hardt, *Entretiens* 22 (Geneva, 1976), 141–45, 171–72.

98. See Curt. 9.8.22; cf. Paus. 1.6.2. See also J. Bousquet, "La Stèle des Kyténiens au Létôon de Xanthos," *REG* 101 (1988): 12–53, who argues for the authenticity of Ptolemy's Argead descent via his mother. For the snakes, see Arrian 3.3.5; see also Bosworth, *HCA,* 1:272–73. Brunt, *Arrian,* 2:510 is more reserved about Ptolemy's depreciation of Perdiccas; see also J. Roisman, *CQ* 34 (1984): 373–85.

99. See Lucan 8.610 f., although his disgust is centered on foreign meddling in Roman affairs. But cf. his remarks on Ptolemy XIII, at 8.770 f.

100. Arrian's choice of Ptolemy on the grounds of his royal status and hence Ptolemy's desire to avoid the shame of being caught in a lie because he was a king has caused much comment. On his "naivety," see Brunt, *Arrian,* 1:xxxi and 2:535. But see Badian review of *The Lost Histories of Alexander the Great* (supra, n. 50), 666; Bosworth, *HCA,* 1:43; Hammond, *Alexander the Great,* 5. On Curtius' treatment of *libertas,* see chaps. 5 and 6.

Unlike Arrian, it is doubtful if Curtius decided on a systematic format of evaluating the primary traditions, based on considered criteria. He probably judged each source on its merits, excerpted and adapted what he wanted from it, and discarded what did not appeal to him. He had different interests from Arrian, but he took his own aims and work just as seriously.

Some Principles of Curtius' Methodology

The following discussion explores Curtius' attitudes toward historiography and his methods by comparison with the other extant accounts. Together with Diodorus, Justin, and the *Metz Epitome*, Curtius has long been labeled as part of the Alexander vulgate, which, at the label's most innocuous definition, assumes the presence of a common source in these authors that is different from the Ptolemy and Aristobulus tradition of Arrian.[101]

It has often been noted that Diodorus especially provides an important basis for cross-referencing with Curtius. A large amount of Diodorus' *Bibliotheca* is extant, which enables some evaluation of his methodology. The standard view is that Diodorus tended faithfully to follow one source for large sections of his narrative, without undue creativity or distortion on his part.[102] Diodorus thus provides a useful control: the use of a common tradition is indicated wherever Curtius and Diodorus' book 17 run parallel, whereas variation in the accounts suggests either another source or adaptation on the part of one historian. There are some difficulties and limitations with this cross-comparative approach. Even with the lacunose state of Curtius' text, his work is still the longest surviving version of the vulgate. Diodorus, like Trogus, was writing a world history, which means that he would have edited his sources considerably and restricted his narrative of Alexander's reign out of necessity. Also, a large lacuna that occurs in the extant text after the execution of Bessus (17.83) robs us of Diodorus' treatment of such key episodes in Curtius as the death of Cleitus, the fall of Callisthenes, and

---

101. See Hammond, *THA*, 1 f.; cf. Bosworth, *FAA*, 8–9.
102. On Diodorus' methodology in general, see Hornblower, *Hieronymus of Cardia*, 20 f. Kenneth S. Sacks, *Diodorus Siculus and the First Century*, 3–8, has argued a case for Diodorus' own independence and creativity, but his focus is not Diodorus' Alexander narrative.

the king's marriage to Roxane (all of which we know Diodorus covered, from the summary of his history's contents, in book 17).[103]

Arrian is also an important model, because in addition to indicating what traditions were available to Curtius, his own virtuosity and subjectivity provide a revealing comparison with Curtius in their respective treatments of certain episodes.

Apart from the well-known passages where Curtius refers to his authorities directly, the historian provides occasional comments on his traditions and explanations of his methods during the course of his narrative. Tarn was annoyed by what he perceived as the author's "advertised" lack of historical principle, erroneously using as justification for his comments Curtius' own opinion at 9.1.34.[104]

> For my part, I hand on more than I believe, for I do not venture to make categorical assertions on matters that I doubt, nor do I leave out what I have learned.
>
> [Equidem plura transcribo quam credo; nam nec affirmare sustineo de quibus dubito, nec subducere quae accepi.]

Such a sentiment is surely Herodotean in tone. Herodotus states several times that he records traditions without necessarily believing them, and Curtius has merely expressed his own endorsement of this principle.[105] If he was as cynical about historiography as Tarn claims, one wonders why he would offer such an explanation. Traditions may be dubious, but that does not mean that a historian should deny the reality of their existence. The context of Curtius' statement is also worth noting. It follows his description of Indian fighting dogs that were so tenacious that they held on to their quarry even while being dismembered, a story that Diodorus (17.92), Strabo (15.1.31 [700]), and the *Metz Epitome* (66–67) record without any judgment on its authenticity. Although Aristobulus is cited by Plutarch (*FGrH* 139.F.40) on a breed of Indian dog that preferred to

---

103. Elsewhere the table of contents of Diodorus 17 provides some indications of his treatment of similar episodes: Ὡς οἱ πρωτεύοντες Σογδιανῶν ἀπαγόμενοι πρὸς τὸν θάνατον παραδόξως ἐσώθησαν (cf. Curt. 7.10.4); cf. τῶν φίλων πολλοὺς ἔπεισε γῆμαι τὰς τῶν ἐπισήμων βαρβάρων θυγατέρας = *Metz Epit.* 30–31. This reference was apparently omitted in Curt. 8.

104. Tarn, *Alexander the Great*, 2:92; cf. his remarks on Curt. 5.6.8–9, on which now see Atkinson *Curtius* ii, 115–16.

105. Hdt. 2.123, 4.5, 7.152; cf. Curt. 10.10.11.

fight lions, it seems more likely that Cleitarchus was their authority for the tale, particularly in view of his apparent dominance as Diodorus' and Curtius' source for the Indian narrative.[106] Curtius' skeptical remark may have also been made for the benefit of his audience, given many Romans' repellent interest in bloodsports.

Curtius shows considered evaluation of his sources on occasion. At 5.6.8–9 he finds the amount of money that Alexander captured in Persepolis "almost beyond belief" [prope ut fidem excedat] but acknowledges that he would have to doubt other details in the tradition, which by implication he believes credible, or else accept the figure of 120,000 talents. His awareness of conflicting sources is demonstrated not only by his remarks on Ptolemy and Cleitarchus but also at 10.10.5, where he corrects an erroneous tradition on the distribution of provinces from Alexander's will. His comment "I have found the report of such a matter, although handed down by some authorities, unsubstantiated" [sed famam eius rei, quamquam ab auctoribus tradita est, vanam fuisse comperimus] suggests that he had done some additional research himself.

One particularly problematic comment relating to Curtius' historiographical principles is expressed at 7.8.11, with his introduction of the Scythian envoy's speech. At first sight, his statement seems a patent show of rhetorical artificiality.

> Thus what they said concerning the king, which has been handed down to posterity, is perhaps not to the taste of our customs and our orators, who have been allotted more cultivated times and intellects. But although their speech may be scorned, yet our fidelity [fides nostra] ought not to be; we will quote what was said that, in whatever manner, has been passed down without adulteration.

> [Sic, quae locutos esse apud regem memoriae proditum est, abhorrent forsitan moribus oratoribusque nostris, et tempora et ingenia cultiora sortitis. Sed, ut possit oratio eorum sperni, tamen fides nostra non debet; quae utcumque sunt tradita incorrupta proferemus.]

Prior to this statement, Curtius commented on the nobility and intellectual integrity of the Scythians, noting that "some of them were not without *sapientia* in so far as a race that was always under arms [gens armata]

---

106. Hamilton, "Cleitarchus and Diodorus," 129 f., is most convincing.

was capable of philosophy." Such a concept is hardly unique to Curtius. While the exploration of Scythian tribes and customs from an anthropological view had fascinated Herodotus, the idea of certain Scyths as "virtuous savages" was also a well-known literary topos. It is apparent from traditions as early as Homer, as Arrian noted (4.1.1), that the Abian Scythians were considered the "most just of men" [δικαιοτάτους ἀνθρώπους], which may have had some impact on philosophical ideology in Alexander's time.[107] The tradition was continued in the Roman period, when Scythian nomads were celebrated as more virtuous than landed peasants.[108] Yet Curtius is also emphasizing in very strong—if not almost technical—terms, manifest in his use of *fides* and *tradita incorrupta*, that he has reported at least the essence of the speech—if not its words—just as it was written in his source.[109] Curtius records what he calls "barbarian wisdom" in other sections of his narrative (cf. 7.4.13); however, nowhere else in his history (as we have it) is either an introduction to a speech or a comment on the positive worth of his source so forcibly expressed.

The question of Curtius' source for the speech is a relevant issue. Allowing that the speech was clearly intended as a rhetorical display, some scholars have suggested that Curtius fabricated the oration himself, in which case his statement becomes a mere device to give a veneer of traditional appearance. Hammond, while acknowledging the historian's remark, nevertheless calls the speech "fictitious" and "packed with Senecan epigrams."[110] It is possible that sources closer to Curtius' time could have tampered with the speech, since the sentiments on *amicitia* (7.8.27–29) and *fides* appear more Roman than Greek.[111] It is also pos-

---

107. Hdt. 4.1–144. On the Abii, see Homer *Iliad* 13.6; cf. Curt. 7.6.11, *Iustissimos barbarorum constabat*.
108. Cf. Horace *Odes* 3.24.9; Arrian *Bithyn*. F. 54 (*Scripta Minora et Fragmenta*, ed. A.G. Roos [Leipzig, 1968]). On the Scythian *mirage nomade*, see P. Briant, *État et pasteurs au Moyen-Orient ancient* (Cambridge and Paris, 1982), 102–11. Tacitus also exploits the ideal of the noble barbarian in the magnificent speech of the British chieftain, Calgacus, at *Agr*. 30–32.
109. Cf. Tac. *Hist*. 1.1, *sed incorruptam fidem professis neque amore quisquam et sine odio dicendus est*.
110. Hammond, *THA*, 143. See also Tarn, *Alexander the Great*, 2:94.
111. Rolfe, 2:202, points out the parallel between Curt. 7.8.19, . . . *ad latrones persequenos venire, omnium gentium quas adisti latro es*, and Cic. *De rep*. 3.14 and Aug. *De civ. dei*. 4.4.25, the reply of a captured pirate to Alexander: . . . *ut orbem terrarum; sed quia id ego exiguo navigio facio, latro vocor; quia tu magna classe, imperator*. Similar phraseology likening Alexander as a "robber of the world" is used of the Romans by Tacitus in Calgacus' speech, at *Agr*. 30; however, the motif of the rapacious nature of Roman imperialism is evident in Mithridates' letter to Arsaces (Sall. *Hist*. fr. 4.69.5 M).

sible that Curtius himself may have made some slight modifications to bring out his own points of interest; *utcumque* (7.8.11) is sufficiently vague as to allow a little license.

However, in view of the unique nature of Curtius' assertion, it seems not unreasonable to take the historian at his word. That Curtius elsewhere concocts speeches or appears to use his sources freely to suit his literary aspirations only enforces the truth of his point that he has not done so here. If the historian did not compose the speech himself and has said as much, who was a likely original source for it? The speech contains Herodotean-sounding material on the Scythians (7.8.17).[112] Its tone is cautionary, with references to proverbs (7.8.14–16) and the issue of divinity (7.8.26), and the oration as a whole is dominated by the themes (naturally translated into Latin) of *ambitio, imperium, gloria,* and *fortuna*. One of the Cleitarchan fragments (*FGrH* 137.F.48: ὥσπερ ὑπὸ τοῦ ἰοῦ τὸν σίδηρον, οὕτω τοὺς φθονεροὺς ὑπὸ τοῦ ἰδίου ἤθους κατεσθίεσθαι) although admittedly listed by Jacoby as "doubtful," is comparable to a moral aphorism in the Scythian speech (7.8.15: *leo quoque aliquando minimarum avium pabulum fuit et ferrum robigo consumit*). The context is different in each; the point of the Scythian proverb is that the powerful are brought down by the small, whereas the alleged Cleitarchan saying is concerned with the destructive power of envy. The simile of rust consuming iron could be common property, yet the number of proverbs attributed to Cleitarchus in Jacoby, if authentic, suggests that he had a penchant for pithy maxims. Cleitarchus is thus a possible candidate for Curtius' source,[113] but ultimately judgment is arbitrary; it is revealing that the historian was impressed enough by a traditional speech and by the closeness of its themes to his own literary development that he made the Scythian oration an integral part of book 7.

Under examination and cross-comparison, Curtius' methodology reveals several characteristics: his personal selectivity, a probable tendency for a composite arrangement of sources, an adaptation or distortion of source material to suit literary considerations, and overall a marked imposition of his own personality and values on his narrative. Curtius often expresses opinions, sometimes in propria persona (e.g.,

---

112. Cf. Hdt. 4.3.6; see W.W. How and J. Wells, *A Commentary on Herodotus* (Oxford, 1912), 1:304.

113. See Pearson, *LHA*, 222 n. 42; Professor Heckel has suggested to me that Hegesias might also have been a source for the Scythian speech. Curtius seems to have known of Hegesias' rhetorical and sensationalist account of Betis (Batis) at the fall of Gaza (see my chap. 5), and *FGrH* 142 demonstrates that Hegesias also had a talent for apt expression.

5.4.31; 4.6.17) or sometimes as moral *sententiae*.[114] On occasion, he favored a "blending" of sources to enhance a descriptive narrative. One striking illustration of this technique is Curtius' account of the siege of Tyre. However, since that episode has received considerable scholarly attention elsewhere, it does not seem worthwhile to examine here.[115] The following episodes are revealing examples of Curtius' use of his sources.

The Gordian Knot

At Curtius 3.1.14–18, Alexander is confronted with the Gordian knot and decides to slash the thongs with his sword. Strangely, Diodorus omitted the episode, but the versions found in Arrian, Plutarch, and Justin help illuminate Curtius' approach.[116] The historian's treatment incorporates elements common to the other accounts, as well as his own emphasis on additional motifs that are consistent with his characterization of Alexander as king and general.

Since the Phrygian natives had declared that whoever solved the puzzle of the knot would rule Asia (3.1.16), the king is seized with *cupido* (lust or strong desire) for fulfilling the prophecy. *Cupido* and its Greek equivalent, *pothos*, occur fairly often in the Alexander traditions as an explanation of the king's driving motivation—either for a difficult achievement or for a journey to an exotic place. Alexander's *cupido* to fulfill the oracle is also given in Justin, and we may compare Arrian's variation (2.3.1), in which, when Alexander reaches Gordium, he feels *pothos* to see Gordius' wagon and its knot. Curtius uses *cupido* in other places, and it seems likely that it was a traditional motif that appealed to him.[117] He also emphasizes the Macedonian fear at Alexander's rash self-confidence *(fiducia ex temeraria)*. Alexander's *temeritas* per se was hardly unique to Curtius, but it is certainly an important theme in his characterization of the king, since it relates to the historian's develop-

---

114. See McQueen, 30; Atkinson, *Curtius* i, 69

115. On Tyre, see Rutz, "Zur Erzählungskunst des Q. Curtius Rufus: die Belagerung von Tyrus," *Hermes* 93 (1965): 370–82; Atkinson, *Curtius* i, 293–319; Porod, 108–30.

116. Plut. *Alex.* 18.204; Arrian 2.3; J. 11.7.3–16. Cf. Marsyas of Philippi, *FGrH* 135/6.F.4. See Hamilton, *Plutarch,* 46–47. See Bosworth, *HCA,* 1:184 f., for additional references. See also Atkinson, *Curtius* i, 84 f.; Porod, 62–74.

117. For *cupido* in Curtius, see 4.7.8, 4.8.3, 7.11.4, 9.2.9, 9.2.12, etc. *Pothos* and an equivalent, *epithumia*, are used by Arrian; see Bosworth, *HCA,* 1:62 f. V. Ehrenberg, *Alexander and the Greeks,* 52–61, believed that the term was Alexander's, to explain what motivated him, and was picked up by the primary traditions, but other scholars are skeptical; see also Brunt, *Arrian,* 1:469 f.

ment of Alexander's *virtus* and *fortuna*, concepts that are explored in depth elsewhere in this study.[118]

Alexander tries to undo the knots, and the expectant throng is concerned lest the king's failure appear as an omen. The same psychological element is present in Arrian, with a slightly different emphasis; Alexander was unable to untie the knot but unwilling to leave it tied, in case doing so caused "commotion" [*kinesis*] among the crowd (2.3.7).

Curtius' presentation of Alexander's solution is different from the other versions. As we saw earlier, the king struggles for a while with the tangle and then cuts the knot with his sword, crying out dramatically as he does so. The other three accounts record the sword story with some variations. According to Plutarch (*Alex*. 18.3) and Justin (11.7.16), once Alexander had cut the knot, he found the ends concealed inside. Arrian cites the sword version under the *logos* format, adding that "Alexander said it was now untied," and then gives Aristobulus' alternative (also recorded by Plutarch) that the king simply took out the pole pin that held the knot together and so released the yoke from the pole. Arrian remarks that he is not sure exactly how Alexander solved the problem but that certainly the king and his followers believed that the prophecy had been discharged, because it is said that a thunderstorm confirmed it that very night.

In terms of its source(s), the Gordian knot episode is an open question. Cleitarchus has been suggested as an authority for the sword version, but several traditions evidently recorded the event, and Ptolemy himself may have related the sword story in some form.[119] However, Curtius' own selectivity and his use of this story are very clear. Certain details that would detract from the historian's emphasis or clutter the narration are deliberately omitted. He says nothing about the more intellectual solution of Aristobulus or even that Alexander found the concealed ends of the knot once he had cut it. Curtius is also silent on the background story of Midas and the wagon that is given in Arrian and Justin; yet elsewhere in his history, he is quite happy to digress. Given the common elements between Curtius and his fellow historians in the Gordian knot episode, it seems highly unlikely that he did not know the variant details that the others record.[120] Instead, the historian's presentation is kept short and

---

118. See Atkinson, *Curtius* i, 91; on *temeritas*, see also my chap. 4, 115–16.
119. See Pearson, *LHA*, 157, on Aristobulus. See also Atkinson, *Curtius* i, 90–91; Bosworth, *HCA*, 1:185, 187.
120. Hammond, *THA*, 145, attributes the *pothos/cupido* motif to Aristobulus; if he is right, Curtius' deliberate omission of Aristobulus' version is quite blatant.

sparse, with a tendency for dramatic effect. Curtius has chosen the version that suits him. Alexander's violent solution fits one aspect of his portrayal of the king as the man of *vis,* in much the same way as do his burning of Persepolis, dragging of Betis alive behind his chariot, and crucifixion of Ariamazes. The references to Alexander's supreme self-confidence and indeed the oracle itself remind us of the omnipresent theme of *fortuna.* Alexander indeed held *fortuna in potestate* (Curt. 10.5.35).[121]

The Siege of Ariamazes' Rock

It has been suggested that Curtius' account of Alexander's capture of Ariamazes' Rock at 7.11 followed one main source, with some *contaminatio*—or incorporated elements—from another authority.[122] The narrative is one of three incidents involving the capture of rock fortresses in the Alexander traditions. It presents complicated problems in source analysis, since there is conflict between Arrian and the vulgate accounts, with confusion and conflation of detail—in location, chronology, and the identity of the commanders. As Bosworth has noted, in addition to the siege of Ariamazes' Rock (328 B.C.), which was north of the Oxus, there was the siege of the Rock of Sismithres at Nautaca and the surrender of Chorienes, who offered hospitality to the king and his men.[123]

The most detailed parallel to Curtius' narrative is offered by Arrian (4.18.4–4.19.4), whom we may assume is following Ptolemy and Aristobulus, since he does not cite any variant *logoi*. Both historians locate the rock fortress in Sogdiana, but it is commanded by Oxyartes in Arrian and by Ariamazes in Curtius.[124] Cophes, the son of Artabazus, acts as an envoy in Curtius but does not appear in Arrian. Curtius (7.11.3) is more informative about the number of men in Ariamazes' force (thirty thousand) and the rock itself: he describes a cavern and deep recesses[125] and gives its height and dimensions, whereas Arrian (4.18.5) remarks that it was "precipitous everywhere" [πάντῃ ἀπότομον]. In Curtius (7.11.3) the

---

121. Curt. 10.5.35. See chap. 4, 128–29.
122. See Hammond, *THA,* 144–46.
123. Bosworth, *HCA,* 2:124 ff. On the Rock of Sismithres, see Curt. 8.2.19–33; Plut. *Alex.* 58.3; Strabo 11.11.4 (517). On Choriennes' surrender, see Curt. 8.4.1–22; cf. *Metz Epit.* 24– 31.
124. On Ariamazes, see Berve, 2:112. Cf. Polyaenus in *Strat.* 4.3.29; *Metz Epit.* 17–18.
125. Curt. 7.11.3: *In medio altitudinis spatio habet specum, cuius os artum et obscurum est; paulatim deinde ulteriora panduntur, ultima etiam altos recessus habent.*

barbarians' water supply is provided by ubiquitous springs; in Arrian (4.18.5), by the deep falls of snow. Both historians remark that the Sogdianians had stored provisions sufficient to stand a long siege. Curtius gives Alexander's motive as *cupido* to wear out even *natura*—perhaps a pointed echo of the Scythian warning that Alexander would wage war with the elements (Curt. 7.8.13). He also says the king's desire to take the rock was increased by the Sogdianian leader's boastful remark asking if Alexander could fly, a detail corroborated by Arrian (4.18.6). In both narratives, Alexander calls for volunteers experienced in mountain climbing and offers money to those who are first to the top.[126]

There are further points of correspondence between the two accounts for the actual climb: the number of the mountaineers (300) and their method of ascent through the use of pitons, either the *ferrei cunei* (iron wedges) that Curtius mentions[127] or the tent pegs of Arrian; the number of casualties they take; and their means of signaling Alexander by waving linen cloths. Curtius elaborates his narrative by including a direct speech and descriptive elements during the climb (7.11.16–17), to highlight the tension and drama. The historian also says that the climbers were armed with spears and lances, whereas Arrian is silent on weaponry. Arrian's narrative is far more concise; his mountaineers achieve the summit in a night, whereas in Curtius they take two nights and a day.

It is possible that Curtius may have followed the same sources as Arrian for the actual ascent of the rock, while still retaining his core narrative and adding his own rhetorical contributions for the sake of literary style. But this assumes Curtius found the Ptolemy and Aristobulus account more vivid or informative on the climb, and one alternative suggestion is that the "Ariamazes" source may have simply corroborated Arrian's tradition, with some variations. Polyaenus' account—with a variation in the name to "Ariomazes" (*Strat.* 4.3.29)—and *Metz Epitome* 16–18, although both heavily abbreviated, may have also used the "Ariamazes" source, and they provide some revealing points of comparison and contrast. The springs are corroborated by Polyaenus, and the number of young men who were experienced rock climbers (three hundred) is the same in all the traditions. In Polyaenus, Alexander reconnoiters the rock by riding around it (as he does at Curtius 7.11.14) to find the best approach, and when the young men reach the summit, they wave their

---

126. Twelve talents in Arrian (4.18.7); ten talents in Curtius (7.11.12), on a sliding scale of rewards.
127. Cf. *Metz Epit.* 16 *(clavi ferrei)*.

girdles—given as *candida vela* [white cloths] in Curtius (7.11.11, 21) and as *lintea candida* in the *Metz Epitome* (16). Another corroborative element in Polyaenus is the shout that the Macedonians send up (cf. Curt. 7.11.25). There are some differences between Polyaenus and Curtius; for instance, the men are unarmed in Polyaenus' account. The major point of departure is the heavy forestation of the rock. According to Polyaenus, the young men scale the crag by climbing up through the trees, fastening small cords to the boughs—an element that is clearly at variance with Arrian, Curtius, and the *Metz Epitome*.

Thus while a composite arrangement of sources is possible, it is equally possible that Curtius followed the vulgate fairly closely, without *contaminatio* and with only some minor embellishment. The absence of Diodorus' version in this particular instance renders Curtius' method of source extraction difficult to confirm. He was certainly following the "Ariamazes" account for the capture of the fortress, and there are literary reasons why Curtius overall should prefer this source.

The respective emphases of Arrian and Curtius are very different. Arrian stresses not only Alexander's *philotimia* and his ability psychologically to outmaneuver the enemy but also his mercy at their surrender and his *sophrosyne* in marrying Roxane (4.19.6). Curtius' emphasis is on Alexander's *ambitio*—highlighted during the Scythian speech (7.8.12), introduced again at 7.11.1 and 7.11.5, and stressed during the king's exhortation to his young mountaineers (7.11.10). Yet up until the final moment, the victory depends only on bluff and Cophes' mendacity. Alexander, relying once more on his *fortuna* and incensed *(infensus)*[128] by Ariamazes' arrogance, calls for an unconditional surrender. This act sets the tone for what is surely the Curtius' own observation at the beginning of book 8: "Alexander, having brought the rock under his control more by his reputation than by glory . . ." [Alexander, maiore fama quam gloria in dicionem . . .].

According to the *Metz Epitome* (18), Ariamazes was killed by his own men, who were then pardoned by Alexander. It is possible, as Bosworth suggests, that this tradition confused a source that alleged that Ariamazes was forced to surrender by his soldiers. But Curtius' version of Ariamazes' death may have been his own deviation from the standard vulgate. In Curtius, the king's scourging and crucifixion of Ariamazes and

---

128. *Infensus* was added in I, the Codices Interpolati, but retained by modern editions. It does make sense from the context.

his nobles is consistent with his treatment of Betis (4.6.27 f.), who, like the former, was not of royal rank and who displayed *contumacia*. Alexander's *crudelitas* to an expendable enemy also provides a contrast with the equally dramatic ending of book 8, where it is politically expedient for Alexander to make a friend of his peer King Porus and thus leave behind him a loyal kingdom rather than a potentially dangerous realm.

The Burning of the Achaemenid Palace at Persepolis

The final episode worth analyzing for this chapter is the destruction of the royal palace of Persepolis.[129] Three main narratives, those of Plutarch, Diodorus, and Curtius, represent the departure of the vulgate from the Ptolemy and Aristobulus tradition of Arrian, over the circumstances and the motive for the arson. The role of Thais in the vulgate narratives may be traced back to Cleitarchus, yet it is difficult to isolate what else may be "Cleitarchan," since the three traditions vary in detail and literary emphasis.[130] All four narratives are revealing in terms of the concerns and methods of the authors, but Curtius' own subjectivity and interests are especially conspicuous.

Prior to the story of the fire, Diodorus (17.71.4–8) describes the palace of Persepolis and its furnishings, before mentioning Alexander's banquet, where a "frenzy" [*lyssa*] seized the drunken guests. Curtius has omitted any descriptive information on Persepolis. His account of the blaze, which he intended as a climax in book 5, is introduced by an authorial flourish emphasizing what will be the important themes in his narrative (5.7.1).[131]

> However, Alexander's great qualities of mind, that character in which he surpassed all other kings, that steadiness in undertaking

---

129. On the traditions, see Pearson, *LHA*, 218 f.; E. Mederer, *Die Alexanderlegenden bei den ältesten Historikern*, 71 f.; Hamilton, *Plutarch*, 99–101. For a summary of the main historical issues, see Bosworth, *HCA*, 1:331 f. Important recent treatments include E. Badian, "Agis III: Revisions and Reflections," 258–92; E.F. Bloedow, "'That Great Puzzle in the History of Alexander': Back into 'the Primal Pit of Historical Murk,'" in *Rom und der griechische Osten: Festschrift für Hatto H. Schmitt*, ed. Ch. Schubert and K. Brodersen (Stuttgart, 1995), 23–41.
130. Cf. Curt. 5.7.1–12; Diod. 17.72; Plut. *Alex.* 38; Arrian 3.18.11; Strabo 15.3.6 (730); Cleitarchus, *FGrH* 137.F.11 = Athenaeus 13.37 (576 D–E).
131. Cf. Curt. 3.12.18–22, 6.2.1–5, 6.6.1–12, 10.5, etc.; see my chaps. 4 and 5.

dangers, his speed in forming and carrying out plans, his good faith toward those who surrendered, his mercy toward prisoners, and his moderation in allowable and usual pleasures, he stained by an excessive desire for wine.

[Ceterum ingentia animi bona, illam indolem qua omnes reges antecessit, illam in subeundis periculis constantiam, in rebus moliendis efficiendisque velocitatem, in deditos fidem, in captivos clementiam, in voluptatibus permissis haud tolerabili vini cupiditate foedavit.]

Authorial digressions on the king's character are an integral part of the narrative. Here the language is strong, and the tone is obviously rhetorical and exaggerated, but the implication is serious. Alexander's *virtutes* are disgraced by *cupido vini*. For someone who normally exercised great control over personal desires, the king's behavior at Persepolis is badly timed, pure self-indulgence, political folly, in fact, outright *licentia regni*. As the historian says, at a time when the Persians were hostile and Darius was preparing to renew the war, "Alexander held banquets" (Curt. 5.7.2).

Historically, banquets were an important part of Macedonian court and social practice.[132] In Curtius' history, the setting of a banquet in various episodes, although traditional, is also exploited by him to establish an atmosphere of license that usually has a negative result. The king's hypocritical treatment of Philotas, Gobares' warning to Bessus, Alexander's murder of Cleitus, the marriage to Roxane, Callisthenes' speech on divine honors, the Pages' assassination attempt, and the Dioxippus episode are all based around a *convivium*.[133]

Curtius stresses decadence at the Persepolis banquet by his emphasis on the drinking and, more specifically, by the presence of *pelices* (concubines) described as "women, not indeed those whom it would be a crime to violate" [(feminae) . . . non quidem quas nefas violari esset] (5.7.2). Tarn, who evidently misinterpreted the historian's statement, remarked that Curtius' comment was a "curious definition of a respectable woman."[134] In fact, Curtius' emphasis is that these women were simply

---

132. See E.N. Borza, "The Symposium at Alexander's Court," AM 3 (1983): 45–55.
133. For the *convivia*, see Curt. 6.8.16, 7.4 f., 8.1 f., 4.22 f., 5.9–24, 6.14, 9.7.1–15.
134. See Tarn, *Alexander the Great*, 2:93.

there as sexual commodities. Yet Thais, one of the *pelices,* urges Alexander to burn the royal palace.

The other vulgate traditions that mention Thais do not portray her in quite so unfavorable a light as does Curtius, in addition to giving her a central part. Diodorus describes Thais as an Athenian *hetaira,* or courtesan, who urges the king to lead a *komos* and burn the palace in an act of vengeance. She is the first after the king to hurl her torch into the palace.[135] Diodorus' interpretation brings out certain literary elements; in an atmosphere of almost religious frenzy, manifested in the Dionysiac imagery, Xerxes' impious act of burning the Acropolis of Athens is repaid by "one woman and in sport."[136] In Plutarch (*Alex.* 38.2), Thais is the mistress of the future king Ptolemy, which gives her some degree of respectability, despite his comment about the impropriety of her remark to Alexander. The theme of women punishing the Persians appears in his account, expressed in equally romantic terms, although without the Dionysiac elements. Plutarch adds that the Macedonians were delighted at the blaze, since they believed Alexander would now return home.

Curtius omits any background information about Thais. She is an *ebrium scortum* (drunken tart) who gives her opinion on a matter of state importance.[137] Her speech has an implicit political tone. Burning the palace would win Alexander the *gratia* of the Greeks whose cities had been destroyed. Urged on by the others and "more greedy for wine than able to carry it" [avidior vini quam patientior] (Curt. 5.7.4), Alexander listens to her; thus the responsibility for burning the palace rests with him alone. The king kindles the fire, and when the conflagration arouses the soldiers, they see Alexander fueling the flames and join in.

Arrian's brief version of events may be summarized at this point. Alexander burns the palace against the advice of Parmenion, who tries to

---

135. Diodorus' word order emphasizes this aspect (17.72.6): αὕτη δὲ μετὰ τὸν βασιλέα πρώτη τὴν δᾷδα καιομένην ἠκόντισεν.

136. See Hamilton, *Plutarch,* 99.

137. This characterization may have been a traditional element in view of Plutarch's similar remark, but Curtius is quite blunt. In Latin, *scortum* appears to have negative and demeaning overtones, originally deriving from a word meaning "skin" or "leather." *Scortum* was also used of male prostitutes; Curtius uses *scortum* of Bagoas in a clearly hostile context (cf. 10.1.29, 42). In general, see J.N. Adams, *Latin Sexual Vocabulary* (London Duckworth, 1982), 217, and "Words for *Prostitute* in Latin," *RhM* 126 (1983): 321–58. Conversely, while *hetaira* could be given a negative nuance, it was normally a more euphemistic expression than *scortum;* see R. Just, *Women in Athenian Law and Life* (London, 1989), 52–53.

warn him that he is destroying his own property and that the Asians will believe he is only there as a transient conqueror. The king replies that he wants to punish the Persians for laying Athens in waste and burning Greek temples during their invasion. Arrian (3.18.12) concludes that in his view the action was futile and that Alexander did not show wisdom or common sense.

Arrian's treatment provides some interesting revelations of his method. Thais has been omitted—perhaps deliberately dropped—by Arrian's source Ptolemy; however, the vulgate theme of retribution for the destruction of Greek temples appears in Alexander's reported remark.[138] Ironically, Parmenion's advice echoes Alexander's most recent policy. By his reappointment of Persian satraps, the king was already demonstrating that he was prepared to incorporate Iranians into top administrative positions, which was hardly the act of a transient victor. Historically, the real Parmenion may have been only too happy to see Persepolis burn: in view of his usually conservative attitudes, Parmenion perhaps had only envisaged a limited expedition from the outset.

The Persepolis episode seems to bother Arrian. He has not referred to any variant *logoi,* and even if he did not use Cleitarchus' work directly, he was surely familiar with the story of the party from secondary authorities.[139] Perhaps in keeping with the principles expressed in his preface, he omitted a *logos* that he did not believe or consider worth mentioning.[140] In its place, he recorded a final and lame example of the Parmenion and Alexander "conflict motif"[141] and attached a note of censure onto an essentially apologetic treatment.

Arrian's assertion that the fire was deliberate policy is supported by many modern critics, particularly in view of corroborative archaeological

---

138. Robin Lane Fox, *Alexander the Great,* 263, offers a romantic but speculative explanation on Thais' omission.

139. Although Arrian records *logoi* that are common with the vulgate and may ultimately derive from Cleitarchus (see, e.g., 2.12.3 f.), most scholars accept that Arrian did not use Cleitarchus, (see Brunt, *Arrian,* 2:540, 546, 548; Bosworth, *HCA,* 1:32) although he was well aware of his work (see Pearson, *LHA,* 213). Cleitarchus continued to be cited by other second-century A.D. authors, such as Athenaeus and Aelian, and it is possible that in view of earlier accounts—including those of Diodorus, Trogus, and Curtius—Arrian deliberately avoided him.

140. Arrian 1.3. His role as the editor of supplementary material is clearly stated; see Bosworth, *HCA,* 1:16 f.

141. On the Parmenion and Alexander conflict motif, which may go back to Callisthenes, see Bosworth, *HCA,* 1:115. See also C. Bearzot, "La tradizione su Parmenione negli storici di Alessandro," *Aevum* 61 (1987): 89–104.

evidence that suggests that the palace had been systematically stripped and that the fire had been concentrated in the three buildings erected by Xerxes.[142] Both Plutarch (*Alex*. 38.8) and Curtius were evidently aware of the literary traditions that maintained the fire was deliberate; however, Curtius (5.7.10–11) has buried this explanation in his own moralistic manner, consistent with the *cupido vini* motif of his introductory *oratio*. The Macedonians, out of shame that the famous palace had been destroyed by a *comissabundus rex* (reveling king) convince themselves that the act was appropriate. The historian adds that Alexander regretted his action when he came to his senses, remarking that the Greeks would have been more severely avenged if the Persians had been forced to see him on the throne of Xerxes. This latter remark is traditional, since it is well represented with variant details in other sources.[143]

Obviously the party was a romantic (at least for Diodorus and Plutarch), colorful, and dramatic story that appealed to three of the five Alexander historians. Once more, Curtius' portrayal of Alexander has taken priority in his interpretation. He does not condone the action, and the arson is not the work of a *dux* but the wanton, destructive caprice of a *rex*. The historian's rhetorical epilogue on the city at 5.7.8–9 emphasizes the contrast between the former power of the place and its utter destruction. Alexander's action, the result of *licentia regni*, is *vis* on the grandest scale, which at once symbolizes the end of the old regime and the nature of the new. Thus the epilogue provides an appropriate transition for Curtius to commence his account of Darius' final days.

Allowing for the derivative nature of extant Alexander historiography as a whole, the extent of Curtius' originality will always remain controversial. However, the preceding cross-comparative analysis aimed to enforce Curtius' creativity in his presentation of the Alexandrian tradition and to demonstrate how his themes are given first importance. In summary, while Curtius may have favored one authority more readily than others for large sections of narrative, it seems that regardless of his source or sources, he would omit or embellish details to suit himself. Yet the historian also appears to have read widely on his subject. He provides an abundance of geographical, zoological, and ethnographical detail that he probably drew from a source like Cleitarchus, possibly supplemented by

---

142. For references, see supra, n. 129. Curtius' text at 5.6.9–11 seems to indicate that the city had been emptied of its treasure, a detail supportive of an intentional act of arson.
143. See Plut. *Alex*. 37, *Ages*. 15.4, *Mor*. 329d. See also Hamilton, *Plutarch*, 99.

other authorities, such as Aristobulus or Macedonian sources.[144] He was capable of making discerning use of Cleitarchus, and he was apparently cautious of Ptolemy.

Arrian's history of Alexander finished with the death of its subject; he treated the history of the Diadochoi in a separate monograph, which survives only in the excerpts of Photius. But Curtius followed up Alexander's demise with a kind of epilogue that relates a short account of the immediate activities of Alexander's generals. Although the narrative only occupies some seven days, it is clear from his forward-looking comments that the historian knew a good deal more.[145] He certainly would have needed alternative authorities to Ptolemy and Aristobulus, as their histories evidently finished with Alexander's death (Arrian 7.26.3). He may have used the tradition of Hieronymus of Cardia, who wrote a history of Alexander's successors that, although lost, is thought to have been reliable.[146] The first seven days following Alexander's demise and the subsequent civil turmoil offered opportunities for a concluding statement on *regnum* that he could relate to his own time, and they allow his considerable rhetorical talents full rein.

Curtius was not interested in a definitive history of Alexander as much as in the literary, rhetorical, and moral prospects his reign presented. In the process of vintaging his wine for the Alexander *Schlauch*, he naturally used sources for which a scholar may venture a guess, just as a connoisseur may detect the grape varieties behind a particular style of wine in a blind tasting, with varying degrees of ease or difficulty according to the style. But ultimately, the taste of the final blended product, the wine itself, stays on the palate. We must consider Curtius the *vigneron* a little further; it therefore seems appropriate to examine his themes and aspects of his structure in the remaining three chapters.

---

144. See Curt. 6.2.12–14; 6.4.4–9, 16–23; 7.3.5–12; 7.4.26–31; 8.9.1–37. See also McQueen, 18.
145. See Curt. 10.5.37, 10.8.23, 10.9.1–2, 10.9.19, 10.10.18–19.
146. See supra, n. 12.

Chapter 4
Fortuna

At Curtius 10.5.25, Sisygambis, Darius' aged mother, starves herself to death supposedly due to her immense grief over the death of Alexander. In truth, Sisygambis' death was well timed. In view of the lack of an acceptable heir and the coming struggles between the generals, she was in an insecure position, and it is unlikely that she would have received the same generous treatment from them that Alexander had accorded her. Curtius himself (10.5.18–25) emphasizes her vulnerability prior to the matriarch's decision to kill herself.[1] Nevertheless, Curtius, impressed by this *magnum documentum* [firm evidence] of Alexander's *indulgentia* [lenience] and *iustitia* [fairness] and in keeping with standard historiographical practice, launches into his necrology of the king, in which he gives a brief summary of Alexander's achievement, as well as passing judgment on his character and career.[2]

Tarn's criticism of Curtius as the "gifted amateur" is noticeable in his comments on the eulogy. In Tarn's opinion, the historian sacrificed consistency of character portrayal for the sake of eloquence: "[Curtius] proceeds to contradict and stultify nearly everything he has said. . . . Nothing can fit the summary to the body of the book."[3] While Curtius' supposed inconsistency in his characterization of Alexander in the necrology is treated at a later point in this chapter, for the moment an examination of the opening lines is very important. The first line, 10.5.26, is thus: "And by heaven! It is clear to those judging the king in a fair manner that his strengths were attributable to his nature and his vices to fortune or to his youth."

A similar idea is also expressed in Arrian's *peroratio* (7.29.1 f.), where, though he says he personally does not consider Alexander's misdeeds

---

1. On Sisygambis' death, cf. Diod. 17.118.3.
2. On the necrology convention, see chap. 2, n. 18.
3. Tarn, *Alexander the Great,* 2:100; for "gifted amateur," see 91. Cf. Dosson, 203–6. See also my chap. 1, 5.

important, he asks others to consider the king's youth, his unbroken good fortune, and the fact that he was surrounded by flatterers.[4] Arrian and Curtius could well have drawn on a common source for these opinions,[5] but the instability of youth is a common enough theme in Greco-Roman literature. Sallust, for instance, describes Jugurtha (*Bell. Iug.* 6.1) as "endowed with great strength, with handsome looks, but especially with a powerful intellect, who did not let himself be spoiled by luxury or idleness."[6]

At *Jugurtha* 1.1–4, Sallust states that when the *animus* [mind] of an individual pursues *gloria* by the path of *virtus*, it does not need *fortuna*, since *fortuna* is not capable of giving *probitas* [honesty] or *industria* or *aliaeque bonae* [other good qualities] to one individual or of taking them away from another. However, a mind can be enslaved by *prava cupido* [perverse desire], and thus Jugurtha's *ambitio* is fired by Romans who are *clari magis quam honesti* [more famous than honest] and who flatter him and tell him *Romae omnia venalia esse* [everything at Rome is for sale]. Thus for all his formidable qualities, the Numidian prince is essentially corruptible and malleable. Likewise, the youthful followers of Catiline (cf. *Bell. Cat.* 14.4) are called *molles* [soft, pliant] and *fluxi* [weak] and are captured by crafty wiles without any difficulty. Sallust himself indicates that he was himself ambitious when he was young but that *ambitio* brought him the same *fama* (in the negative sense) and *invidia* as other less scrupulous rivals.[7]

Cicero, in his defense of Caelius Rufus, also emphasizes the vulnerability of youth to corrupting influences or bad company. He argues youth is weak in itself and so is especially endangered by the *libidines aliorum* [appetites of others]. In Caelius' case, Catiline was already a nasty influence, who was capable of even deceiving Cicero himself—for a short while. Thus Sallust and Cicero speak of youth's apparent aptitude for

---

4. Curt. 10.5.26: *Et, hercule, iuste aestimantibus regem liquet bona naturae eius fuisse, vitia vel fortunae vel aetatis.* See Pomeroy, *Appropriate Comment*, 71 f.; more expansive is Bosworth's analysis of Arrian's encomium, in *FAA*, 135 f.

5. So argues Bosworth, *FAA*, 136, who acknowledges the similarities between the two necrologies but stresses divergences in content and emphasis; he also (143 f.) stresses Arrian's contribution in the disposition of his own encomium.

6. Sall. *Bell. Iug.* 6.1: . . . *pollens viribus, decora facie, sed multo maxime ingenio validus, non se luxu neque inertiae corrumpendum dedit.* On Jugurtha's *ambitio*, see ibid. 8. On the character of Jugurtha, see D.C. Earl, *The Political Thought of Sallust*, 66 f.; G.M. Paul, *A Historical Commentary on Sallust's Bellum Jugurthum* (Liverpool, 1984), 29.

7. On Sallust's *ambitio*, see *Bell. Cat.* 3.3–4.1; on his rejection of a political career, see *Bell. Iug.* 4.3–4. See also Paul (supra, n. 6), 14–15.

corruption, especially by less socially acceptable people. Yet there is also a strong sense of danger; the pretty young men who form Cicero's last class in his description of Catiline's supporters are insidious, precisely because they are young—they are the future.[8]

However, in Curtius' necrology (10.5.34), Alexander is not corrupted by any outside human element. Curtius uses the word *aetas,* rather than *iuventus* or *adulescentia,* because the entire span of Alexander's life was, in fact, his youth. To Curtius, the king's *vitia,* his *iracundia* [irascibility] and his *cupido vini* [love of wine] were inflamed by his *iuventa,* and thus *senectus* [old age] might have softened them. This latter point may be a somewhat qualified concession on the historian's part, since throughout the *Historiae,* Curtius has stressed the contradictory traits of Alexander's nature, and there is nothing to indicate that ordinary old age would have modified the king's disposition. Yet the idea that age brought a decline in physical abilities and an inevitable mellowing of a person's nature seems to have been conventional: for instance, in Plato's version of the conversation between Socrates and an elderly metic, Cephalus (*Repub.* 1.328c–330a), the latter says that physical pleasures have lost their intensity; and Galba comments (*Hist.* 1.15) that Piso has already passed the passions of his youth.[9] There is also Justin's comparison of Alexander to Philip (9.8.14)—Alexander was clearly seen as the more hot-blooded and intense of the two.[10]

According to Curtius (10.5.33 f.), Alexander's *vitia* were also due to *fortuna,* and determining the historian's interpretation of this term is a complex undertaking. *Fortuna* is a dominant theme of the *Historiae,* inextricably linked to the development of *regnum.* However, before examining Curtius' treatment of *fortuna,* it is necessary to establish, to some extent, its background in Greco-Roman literature. The following examples from various authors chosen for discussion mostly date from

---

8. Cic. *Pro Cael.* 4.10. Cf. *In Cat.* 2.22–23. Cicero's negative views on youth in the *Pro Caelio* did not necessarily apply to what he says elsewhere: at *Brut.* 92.318, he says how industrious and hardworking he was in his own youth.

9. On old age, see Arist. *Rhet.* 2.1389b. See in general B. Richardson, *Old Age among the Greeks* (New York, 1933); W.K. Lacey, *The Family in Classical Greece* (London, 1968); T.M. Falkner and J. de Luce, ed., *Old Age in Greek and Latin Literature* (New York, 1989); T.G. Parkin, "Age and the Aged in Roman Society: Demographic, Social, and Legal Aspects" (D. Phil., Oxford University, 1992).

10. On Justin's comparison, see Pomeroy, *Appropriate Comment,* 67–70. Alexander's own youth caused certain people to underestimate his ability: see J. 11.3.4 (the Athenians); Diod. 17.7.1 (Darius); Plut. *Dem.* 23.2; Aeschines 3.160; and Marsyas of Pella, *FGrH* 135/6.F.3.

the third century B.C. through to the first century A.D. and are intended to highlight certain aspects and interpretations of *fortuna,* rather than to provide a comprehensive analysis.

A Survey of *Fortuna*

Fortuna and its Greek counterpart, *tyche,* have a long tradition in Greco-Roman literature and religious beliefs, and it would need a far more detailed study than is permissible here to trace its development.[11] The evidence for early ideas on *tyche* is relatively scanty; Hesiod refers to Tyche as one of the offspring of Tethys and Oceanus (*Theog.* 360), and *tyche* appears in two of the Homeric hymns.[12] According to Pausanias (7.26.8), Pindar placed Tyche among the Fates, where she is described as being "more powerful than her sisters."[13] On a few occasions in Greek tragedy, she appears as a personified force in association either with the power of fate or with chance.[14] To the great rationalist Thucydides, *tyche* appears to represent chance, in the sense of an inexplicable situation that sometimes occurs, regardless of foresight or planning, and that provides human beings with a convenient excuse to blame something other than themselves.[15]

In the fourth century B.C., aspects of *tyche* assumed an integral part in philosophy. Plato discussed the principle of chance in the tenth book of

---

11. On *tyche* and *fortuna*, see K. Latte, *Römische Religionsgeschichte* (Munich, 1960), 175 f.; there is also a monograph by A.A. Buriks on the development of *fortuna* in the Roman world (Diss. Leiden, 1948), which unfortunately, I have been unable to obtain. In general, see also M. Nussbaum, *The Fragility of Goodness: Luck and Ethics in Greek Tragedy and Philosophy* (Cambridge, 1986).

12. See *Homeric Hymn to Demeter* 420; cf. *Homeric Hymn to Athena* 11.5, where *tyche* is used in the sense of "good fortune."

13. Cf. fr. 41 in *Pindari Carmina*, ed. B. Sneel (Leipzig, 1964): Μοιρῶν μίαν εἶναι τὴν Τύχην καὶ ὑπὲρ τὰς ἀδελφάς τι ἰσχύειν.

14. See Soph. *OT* 977, 1080; Eur. *Ion* 1514 and *Hec.* 777–86. The latter reference is a particularly brutal manifestation of blind, careless chance; by pure coincidence, Hecuba's handmaid finds the body of Polydorus washed up on the beach. Despite the obligations of *xenia,* he had been murdered by his host.

15. Thuc. 1.140.1; cf. 6.23.3, 5.16.1. At 5.104.1 and 5.112.2, the Melians claim that divine *tyche* will help them withstand Athenian aggression, but rather than championing their piety, Thucydides' cynicism at their folly may be all too plain; cf. A.B. Bosworth, "The Humanitarian Aspect of the Melian Dialogue," *JHS* 113 (1993): 30–44. On Thucydides' attitude toward *tyche* in general, see Lowell Edmunds, *Chance and Intelligence in Thucydides* (Cambridge, Mass., 1975).

the *Laws,* Epicurus elaborated *tyche* in physics,[16] and the Peripatetic school brought it into ethics.[17] Moreover, the existence of Plutarch's moral essay, ΠΕΡΙ ΤΥΧΗΣ, indicates, as with his other discussions on the fortunes of the Romans and indeed of Alexander the Great himself, its popularity as a rhetorical topos.[18]

During the Hellenistic period, *tyche* was firmly recognized as a pervasive entity who controlled the destinies of cities, kingdoms, and their rulers.[19] It is also clear that Roman literary concepts (discussed in the following section of this chapter) were heavily influenced by Hellenistic ideas on *tyche* that are not easily defined. For instance, *tyche,* as part of an inherited tradition, plays a complex role in Polybius, ranging from a simple sense of "happenstance," to a capricious or vengeful force, to a power akin to fate or Providence.[20]

According to Plutarch (*Quaest. Rom.* 281.E [74]; cf. Ovid *Fast.* 6.569 sq.), Servius Tullius first deified the power of *fortuna,* because, despite his servile origins, he had been raised to the kingship; yet the original Roman—or rather Italian—goddess Fortuna was perhaps a deity of fertility, whose name was probably derived from *ferre,* "to bring."[21] She was also associated with women; according to Livy (11.40.10-12; cf. Dion. Hal. *Rom. ant.* 8.55.2-3), a temple was built and consecrated to Fortuna Muliebris after the successful pleas of Volumnia and Veturia to Coriolanus. Like Greek Tyche, Fortuna evidently supervised the unpredictable element in life, and there were a number of shrines dedicated to her in Rome and throughout Italy, including important temples at Praeneste and Antium, supposedly from primitive times. Plutarch comments (*De for. Rom.* 318E) that even in his own day Rome had no shrine of Wisdom, Prudence, Magnanimity, Constancy, or Moderation, but to Fortuna or Tyche there were "splendid and ancient shrines, all but coeval

---

16. Epicurus *Epistle* 3.133.

17. See Aristotle *Ethica Nichomachea* 1100b8-30, 1153b17, and *Physics* 198a5; cf. A.A. Buriks, "The Source of Plutarch's Περὶ Τύχης," *Phoenix* (1950): 60 n. 7.

18. See Plut. *Mor.* 2.97C; cf. *Mor.* 4.316B, 326D. See S. Swain, "Plutarch's *De Fortuna Romanorum,*" *CQ* 39 (1989): 504-16. On the traditional nature of the *De fortuna Romanorum* and on Plutarch's use of stock themes, see C. Jones, *Plutarch and Rome* (Oxford, 1971), 68 n. 7. For the Alexander treatise, see S. Schroeder, *MH* 48 (1991): 151-57.

19. See G. Herzog-Hauser, *RE* 14: 1673-82; Buriks (supra, n. 17), 59 n. 1.

20. See Walsh, *Livy,* 56 n. 1; Walbank, *Commentary on Polybius,* 1:16 f. Cf. Walbank, *Polybius,* 58-65.

21. See Columella 10.316; Fortuna is praised by gardeners when they sell their produce.

with the foundation of the city."[22] Several important shrines were also erected during the imperial period. Tiberius, as Syme notes, was one emperor who did not earn his fame from his construction program; yet his temple erected to Fors Fortuna on the right bank of the Tiber (see Tac. *Ann.* 2.41.1) suggests a Claudian deference to the family's Sabine origins and a desire to extend urban *clientela*. Nero built a temple of Fortuna within the environs of the Golden House, and Domitian built a temple of Fortuna Redux in the Campus Martius.[23]

Ennius and Pacuvius provide some indication of early Roman literary attitudes toward *fortuna*. Ennius (*Ann.* 8.4) particularly draws attention to its caprice in a military context.

One day brings about many things in war,
And once more many fortunes lie low by chance
In no way has Fortune followed anyone always.

Fortuna is also capable of casting down a mortal from the highest *regnum*, so that he becomes the "lowest house-servant" [famul oltimus] (Enn. *Ann.* 9.10). To Ennius, *fortuna* is also an indiscriminate force, punishing those who do not deserve it, as Antiochus laments in his defeat.[24]

Pacuvius also elaborates on one view of *fortuna* as a senseless and unpredictable force, blind and brutish because it is unable to distinguish between who is worthy and unworthy.

Philosophers assert that Fortune is senseless
and blind and brutish and declare that she stands

---

22. On Plutarch's inaccuracies in relation to the temples and monuments in Rome, see Swain (supra, n. 18), 510 f.

23. On the temple of Fors Fortuna, see R. Syme, *Roman Papers,* vol. 1, ed. E. Badian (Oxford, 1979), 310 f., esp. 313. On the temple of Fortuna Seiani, built by Nero, see Pliny *NH* 36.163. Cf., on Sejanus and *fortuna,* Syme, loc. cit., 309. On the temple of Fortuna Redux, see Martial 8.65. See also S. Platner and T. Ashby, *A Topographical Dictionary of Ancient Rome* (Oxford, 1929), 218–19.

24. Ennius *Ann.* 8.4:

Multa dies in bello conficit unus,
Et rursus multae fortunae forte recumbant
Haudquaquam quemquam semper fortuna secuta est.

See *The Annals of Q. Ennius,* ed. O. Skutsch (Oxford, 1985), 93, and Skutsch's discussion on 440. This passage is from a speech in which Aemilius Paullus refuses to follow up a success won by Terentius Varro. For Antiochus, see 14.8. The text of 9.10 is uncertain, see Skutsch's note at loc. cit., 97.

on a revolving stone globe, because wherever
chance drives that stone, there, they state,
Fortune falls. They say she is senseless, because
she is cruel, unpredictable, unstable. They reiterate
that she is blind, because she discerns nothing about
where she will direct herself; brutish, because she is
unable to distinguish between a worthy and unworthy man.
There are, however, philosophers who, on the other hand,
deny that Fortune exists in any form but declare that
all things are governed by accident. This is more like
the truth practice teaches, in reality, from experience;
just as Orestes at one moment was a king, at another was
made a beggar.

[Fortunam insanam esse et caecam et brutam perhibent philosophi,
saxoque instare in globoso praedicant volubilei.
qua quo id saxum impulerit fors, eo cadere Fortunam autumant.
Insanam autem esse aiunt quia atrox incerta instabilisque sit;
caecam ob eam rem esse iterant quia nil cernat quo sese adplicet;
brutam qua dignum atque indignum nequeat internoscere.
Sunt autem alii philisophi qui contra Fortunam negant esse ullam
sed temeritate res regi omnes autumant.
Id magis verisimile esse usus reapse experiundo edocet;
velut Orestes modo fuit rex, factust mendicus modo.]
(Pacuvius 37–46 = Cic. *Ad Herenn.* 2.23, 36)[25]

Thus one view maintains that the personified goddess Fortuna is governed by *fors* in the sense of chance. Chance will decide what she does. To use a modern analogy, if one wins a prize on a lottery wheel, one may thank Lady Luck, but chance has determined where the wheel stopped. Thus, in Pacuvius' first interpretation, *fors* directs Fortuna. The images of the revolving stone globe,[26] the goddess's blindness, and her *atrocitas* (brutality) and instability emphasize that she is an uncontrollable force. Yet Fortuna is still accorded entity.

---

25. *Remains of Old Latin*, ed. E.H. Warmington (Cambridge, Mass., 1936). The translation quoted here is by T.J. Ryan.

26. The globe was a common image associated with Fortuna in literature. See Plut. *De for. Rom.* 318F and Dio Chrysostom *Orat.* 63.7; the latter explains the various symbols. On the power of Fortuna, see Horace *Odes* 1.35; see also R.G.M. Nisbet and M. Hubbard, *A Commentary on Horace Odes Book 1* (Oxford, 1970), 390 f.

However, as Pacuvius notes, another view asserts that *fortuna* does not exist at all and that all *res* are governed by *temeritas*. In this second interpretation, *temeritas*, like *fors*, carries the sense of "chance" or "happenstance," but the implication is that there is no entity, force, or, by extension, order to the universe at all—that all that occurs happens by accident. The more common meaning of *temeritas* in Latin literature is "rashness" or "thoughtlessness." Curtius himself uses *temeritas* mostly in this latter sense; only once (5.11.10) does he employ the adverb *temere* in its sense of "by happenstance" or "by chance." Yet Alexander's *temeritas* is closely linked to his *felicitas*, or his good luck. Curtius reproves the king for his rash or dangerous actions but also recognizes that because Alexander was so lucky, his impulsiveness never resulted in his death. The issue of Alexander's *temeritas* will become pertinent at a later point in this chapter.

Whether mere happenstance or personified entity, *fortuna* is a power one can do little about, which is how it tends to be depicted in art. A statue of personified Roman Fortuna in the Vatican displays two of her attributes: the rudder symbolizing the course of life and the horn of plenty that she distributes in her erratic fashion. She is also associated with a wheel, and other typical emblems are wings, the libation bowl, and the blindfold. All these symbols are testimony to her perceived nature of fickleness and mutability and indiscrimination—and also to Roman consciousness of her importance.[27] In a similar vein, Pliny the Elder notes (*NH* 2.22) that *fortuna* was universally invoked among his contemporaries, either to be praised or blamed.

Sallust and Cicero adopt a far more sophisticated attitude toward *fortuna*, and although, at least according to one scholar, the latter is inconsistent in his views, his final judgment is that *fortuna* is nothing but a word in which men can hide their ignorance.[28] If we may return once more to the context of Sallust's discussion of *fortuna* in the *Jugurtha*, he also declares that *dux atque imperator vitae mortalium animus est* [the mind is the leader and commander of mortal life] (*Bell. Iug.* 1.3). This statement is not entirely contradicted by his declaration in the *Bell. Cat.* 8.1 that *Sed profecto fortuna in omni re dominatur* [Without doubt, fortune holds sway over all matters]. The historian in this instance is empha-

---

27. Ferguson, *The Religions of the Roman Empire*, 86, 117. On Tyche in art, see S.B. Matheson, ed., *An Obsession with Fortune: Tyche in Greek and Roman Art,* Yale University Art Gallery Bulletin (New Haven, 1994).

28. Cic. *Acad.* 1.7.29; cf. Walsh, *Livy*, 58 n. 1.

sizing the importance of historiography. The deeds of the Athenians were sufficiently distinguished and magnificent, but it was chiefly because Athens produced writers of great talent that the achievements of Athens became celebrated. In other words, the *fortuna* of Athens was to have writers of genius; Fortuna is crucial in that she produces the individuals who possess sufficient *ingenium* to immortalize the distinguished achievements of great men. One may recall Pindar's comment on Odysseus in the *Nemean Odes* (7.21), which has a similar depreciatory edge; Odysseus and his suffering would be unknown but for Homer.[29] According to Sallust, *fortuna* does not produce *virtus*, but *virtus* can overcome the changes *fortuna* may bring. In a similar fashion, Catiline's mistake is that he places too much trust in *fortuna* as a force and not enough in initiative.[30] Sallust's thought was hardly homogeneous; but it could be said that Livy and the other Augustan writers possibly adopted a far more conservative attitude in trying hard to reconcile Fortuna with the traditional deities, relating her power to the power of the gods.[31]

Greek *tyche* and Roman *fortuna* are basically particular. Either can favor cities and individuals. For the Hellenistic world, Alexander the Great was the epitome of how an individual's *tyche* was so great that he was virtually invincible. One may note other Hellenistic usages of the idea, such as the famous statue of Tyche by Eutychides at Antioch, which became a model for subsequent depictions of a city's *tyche*;[32] Strabo's reference to the royal oath at Ameria (12.3.31); and the Ptolemies' exploitation of the *agathe tyche* of their queens. The king's *tyche* would

---

29. The concept of immortality through literature is exploited by Arrian in his so-called second preface, 1.12.1–5; for bibliography, see chap. 3, n. 38.

30. Cf. Sall. *Bell. Iug.* 1 and *Bell. Cat.* 8. See D.J. Stewart, "Sallust and *Fortuna*," *History and Theory* 7 (1968): 298–317, esp. 304 f. On the character of Catiline in relation to *virtus*, see Earl, *The Political Thought of Sallust*, 85 f.

31. See Walsh, *Livy*, 58 f.; I. Kajanto, *God and Fate in Livy* (Turku, 1957).

32. According to Pausanias (4.30.6), a sculpture of Tyche was portrayed in Archaic times by Bupalus of Chios. On the Tyche of Antioch, see Tobias Dohrn, *Die Tyche von Antiochia* (Berlin, 1960); C. Havelock, *Hellenistic Art* (London, 1971), 19; J.J. Pollitt, *Art in the Hellenistic Age* (Cambridge, 1986), 2–4. But there may have been earlier precedents; cf. a marble stele (now lost) with an inscription honoring the Athenian Phylarchos from the Arcadian League, which is dated to sometime between 368 and 361 B.C. It depicts a relief of Tyche holding a helm in her left hand, with her right touching a trophy. However, the date of the inscription is controversial: see M.N. Tod, *A Selection of Greek Historical Inscriptions* (Oxford, 1950), 2: no. 132, pp. 98–102; cf. J. Roy, "Arcadia and Boetia in Peloponnesian Affairs," *Historia* 20 (1971): 569–99, and "Postscript on the Arcadian League," *Historia* 23 (1974): 505–7.

naturally affect his subjects and would thus be of some concern.[33] A city's *fortuna* was equally important; Pindar (fr. 39) referred to Fortune as the "protector of cities" [Τύχα φερέπολις], and one may recall Juno's command at Horace *Odes* 3.3.61–62 that Rome must not rebuild Troy lest the city inherit the same ill-starred *fortuna* and suffer the same fate.[34]

Plutarch, in the *De Fortuna Romanorum* (*Mor.* 4.316), argued that Rome owed more to *fortuna* than to *virtus*, although this was apparently an old conflict in Greco-Roman historiography.[35] Yet Plutarch also notes (*Mor.* 4.318D) that Lucius Cornelius Sulla was called *felix* in Latin and *epaphroditus* in Greek. The former term conveys the ideas of fecundity and productivity, as well as that of being fortunate. *Epaphroditus* covers a range of meanings from "loveliness" or "charm" to the idea of being favored by Venus, as in Sulla's epithet. The metaphor was drawn from the game of dice; hence there is a link between Venus and good fortune, or *felicitas*. Both *felix* and *epaphroditus* can mean being favored or blessed. The opposite of *felix*, *infelix*, emphasizes barrenness and ill fortune, as in Vergil's epithet for Dido.[36]

Julius Caesar frequently notes the importance of *fortuna* on the battlefield and seemed aware of his own personal favor in this direction. Suetonius claims (*Div. Iul.* 83) that Caesar bequeathed a temple of Fortuna to the people, and the anecdote Plutarch tells (*Mor.* 4.319D) of Caesar bidding a nervous pilot to trust Caesar and Caesar's *fortuna* seems indicative of the man's confidence in the inevitability of his success or at least of his reputation. The story appears in other traditions,[37] but perhaps the most forceful expression of it occurs in Lucan, where Caesar arrogantly claims that the storm is but a mere indication of *fortuna*'s favor.[38]

The aforementioned examples of Hellenistic and Roman usages of *tyche* point to a very public identification, exploited in literature and the visual arts. Similarly, an emphasis on personal *fortuna* and good fortune would be very necessary for Roman commanders, themselves military and political figures. Plutarch (*Mor.* 4.320) names Octavian as an example of someone who enjoyed such favor, and again one may note that,

---

33. On *agathe tyche*, see P.M. Fraser, *Ptolemaic Alexandria* (Oxford, 1972), 1:241–43.
34. See C. Witke, *Horace's Roman Odes: A Critical Examination* (Leiden, 1983), 40 f.
35. Plut. *De for. Rom.* 317B–C; cf. Dion. Hal. *Rom. Ant.* 1.4–5.
36. Vergil *Aen.* 4.68, 450, 596; cf. 4.326–30, where Dido laments she has no child by whom she could remember Aeneas.
37. Cf. Plut. *Caes.* 38.5; Appian *BC* 2.57; Florus 2.13.37.
38. Luc. 5.592–93; cf. 5.582–83.

like cities, individuals could inherit *fortuna;* Octavian became heir to Caesar's *fortuna* as well as his name. Mark Antony, constantly beaten at cockfights and dice by the young Octavian, was warned to keep away from the youth, because Antony's *fortuna* was not as great as that of Octavian. The idea of personalized *fortuna,* the particular good or bad luck of everyman, is a dominant aspect of Curtius' treatment of the concept; hence he comments in Alexander's eulogy (10.5.35), "However, it must be allowed that, although he owed much to his own virtues, he owed more to *fortuna,* which he alone of all mortal men had under his control."[39]

Curtius' Attitude toward *Fatum* and His Philosophical Views

Essentially, Curtius' development of *fortuna* in his history is related to three concepts: Alexander's personal *fortuna* in the sense of an inevitable success or good luck, which is connected, in turn, to the historian's ideas on *fatum* (destiny), and finally unfailing *fortuna*'s capacity to corrupt the *ingenium* of its subject. However, to appreciate Curtius' treatment of *fortuna,* it is appropriate to first evaluate his philosophical concepts, which is not altogether easy.

Curtius displays aspects of several philosophical schools, without appearing to adhere to any particular one. It would have been hard for any educated Roman of Curtius' time not to have encountered Stoic philosophy; indeed, according to certain opinion, Roman historiography from Cato to Tacitus is colored by Stoicism.[40] McQueen lists certain parallels between Curtius' attitudes and Stoic beliefs: respect for kingship, approval of *gravitas* and of equality of high and low, death as the ultimate release, and obedience to the *ius gentium* (convention of nations). At least one of these parallels may be questioned.[41] However, as McQueen also acknowledges, Curtius' Stoicism is most noticeable in his evident belief in destiny, in something akin to Stoic predeterminism. His use of the word *fatum* is thus important. Curtius can use *fatum* to mean "fate" (4.6.17) or as another word for death (8.9.32) or for the

---

39. *Fatendum est tamen, cum plurimum virtuti debuerit, plus debuisse fortunae, quam solus omnium mortalium in potestate habuit.*
40. See Walsh, *Livy,* 50.
41. See McQueen, 32–33. Particularly questionable is the example McQueen cites for Curtius' views on *gravitas:* 8.5.13. As analysis of the Callisthenes episode shows, Curtius is ambivalent toward the historian; see chap. 6.

inevitability of death or fate. This latter aspect is particularly true of Curtius' comment on Orsines at 10.1.30 (cf. 9.6.27). Yet by far, in the majority of passages in which *fatum* occurs, it means something like "fate" or "destiny." Darius, at 5.12.11, says he will await the "the decree of my fate." Alexander comments at 9.6.19 that even the lazy have no control over *fata*. Similarly, at 10.9.1 civil wars were inflicted on the Macedonians by Fata (the Fates).

A problematic passage at 5.11.10 would probably clarify Curtius' belief in a predetermined and inevitable course of events, were it not for textual difficulties that allow alternative readings—especially in relation to *nexuque*—and hence different interpretations. The Rolfe edition, based on Hedicke's text, makes Curtius criticize both the Epicurean and Stoic doctrines.[42]

> Eludant fidem licet quibus forte temere humana negotia volvi agique persuasum est nexuve[43] causarum latentium et multo destinatarum suum quemque ordinem immutabili lege percurrere.
>
> [Those may scoff at my belief who haply are convinced that human affairs roll on and take place by mere chance, or that each man runs his ordered course in accordance with a combination of hidden causes determined long beforehand by an immutable law.] (trans. J.C. Rolfe)

As this text reads, Curtius seems to suggest that both Epicurean and Stoic philosophies would probably scoff at Patron's simple loyalty. If, according to an Epicurean, life is a lottery and the actions of any individual have no effect on events, one might question whether it is worth doing anything at all; in a similar fashion, as a Stoic might see it, what is destined to happen will happen, regardless of what one does. But it is difficult to determine what Curtius' emphasis originally was. A long, conjectural insertion before *nexuque* in Mützell's text (and other older texts), *equidem aeterna constitutione crederim* . . . [as far as I am concerned, I believe that, by eternal decree . . .], albeit attractive, has dubious authenticity.[44] Bardon's text adopted Vogel and Dosson's supplement of *nec serie* prior to *nexuque*, which appears to give Curtius Stoic sympathies.

---

42. Cf. Tac. *Ann.* 6.22.1–2, where Tacitus seems to advocate a middle course.
43. *Nexuve* is offered by Jeep and Hedicke; *nexuque* by the Codices B, F, L, P, S, and V.
44. Cf. Rolfe, 1:408 n. 5.

Eludant videlicet, quibus forte temere humana negotia volvi agique persuasum est, <nec serie> nexuque causarum latentium, ex multo ante destinarum, suum quemque ordinem immutabili lege percurrere.

[Naturally, this would be ridiculed by those who feel certain that the affairs of mankind are governed by chance rather than that each person is destined by an immutable law to a life-cycle governed by an interconnected series of invisible causes pre-ordained long in advance.] (trans. J.C. Yardley) [45]

It is true that Curtius' point in the Darius and Patron scene and indeed for the remnant of Darius' days, is that the Great King has in fact surrendered to what he believes is his fate. Once his own people are prepared to betray him, he has already lived too long, as he says, and so, by implication, any action to avoid what is destined for him is futile and unkingly.[46] Yet, at the same time, although Curtius seems to allow for destiny's determinate force, individuals are able to affect an outcome, for good or evil. Darius might well be doomed; still, he can make a personal decision that allows him to exit with some dignity. In view of this interpretation, Hedicke's reading could stand.[47]

However, perhaps the most important guide to the historian's attitudes may be found in Curtius' eulogy of Alexander. At 10.5.36 he says, "She [Fortune] likewise decided on the same end for his life and for his glory; the Fates waited for him while, having subdued the East and reaching Ocean, he achieved everything of which a mortal was capable."[48] Alexander's *fortuna* and the Fates determined the length of his life and achievement. Significantly, the king does not outlive his *gloria;* there is no humiliating end for him as there was for Cyrus, Pyrrhus, Hannibal, or Pompey.[49] Similarly, throughout his work, Arrian (7.30.2) believes that providential design guided Alexander's career and that some divine power was clearly associated with him.

---

45. See McQueen, 41 n. 28; Duff, *Silver Age*, 89–90 (who accepts the *equidem . . . crederim* interpolation). The Stoic view is also preferred by Bardon (154 n. 2) and Atkinson (*Curtius* ii, 148–49).
46. For Darius' fatalism, see Curt. 5.11.11–12, 5.12.8, 5.12.11.
47. I am grateful to Professor Bosworth for the suggestion.
48. *Vitae quoque finem eundem illi, quem gloriae, statuit. Expectavere eum fata, dum Oriente perdomito aditoque Oceano quidquid mortalitas capiebat impleret.*
49. Cf. Livy 9.17.6; see Swain (supra, n. 18), 514 n. 54.

114   *Alexander the Great*

Nevertheless, Curtius has no all-encompassing, deep commitment to Stoicism.[50] In particular, like the Academics or Epicureans, he rejects the view of neo-Stoicism that the future may be foreseen through oracles, dreams, portents, augury, and divination, the media of the gods. In this rejection the historian clearly differs from Arrian (who appears to express a genuine belief in what he sees as the manifestation of divine will, and who believes that proper rites should be paid to the appropriate deity) or even from Tacitus (who despite his own skepticism, believed in the art of astrology provided its practitioners were genuine).[51] Instead, throughout the *Historiae,* Curtius is skeptical about oracles and divination and about people who practice them. He is rational and open-minded about dreams or what appear to be supernatural happenings, and although he attacks Alexander's *superstitio,* he is also cynically aware that the king can exploit it.[52]

Curtius' treatment of the siege of Gaza (4.6.12) provides further insight into his views on fate. The seer Aristander interprets an omen, offered by the actions of a raven, to mean that Gaza would fall but that the king himself would be wounded. Apart from the *fides* and *virtus* of Betis, Curtius' emphasis is on Alexander the general—his *superstitio, temeritas, virtus, ira,* and treatment of defeated enemies. The omen of the raven and hence, in Curtius, the motif of *superstitio* was evidently in the original sources, since it appears, with variations, in Arrian and Plutarch.[53]

Naturally, Alexander, like any army commander, pays attention to signs from the gods; despite his own exploitation of *superstitio* during the siege of Tyre, he is nevertheless affected by it himself. In fact, the king's manipulation of superstition and his own disregard for and yet, at times,

---

50. Cf. Kajanto (supra, n. 31), 55.

51. See Arrian 7.30.2, 7.16.7–8; Brunt, *Arrian,* 1:x (cf. 2:539), and *Athenaeum* 55 (1977): 30 f. Brunt denies Stoic coloring in the *Anabasis* and argues that the influence of Epictetus had faded; cf. Bosworth, *FAA,* 146 f., but see Stadter, *Arrian of Nicomedia,* esp. 109 f. On Arrian's religious convictions, cf. Arrian 2.3.8, 7.30.2–4, and *Cyneget.* 35.1; Bosworth, *ANRW* II.34.1 (1993): esp. 238 f., 241. For Tacitus' positive comments on the art of astrology, see chap. 1, n. 35.

52. For Alexander's manipulation of *superstitio* and his occasional contempt of it, see 4.10.7, 9.4.28–29. For Alexander's own *superstitio,* see 5.4.1, 7.7.8 f.

53. Arrian 2.26.4; Plut. *Alex.* 25.3. In Arrian the bird is described as "carnivorous"; it drops a stone on Alexander's head as he is sacrificing. In Plutarch the bird drops a clod of earth, which hits the king on the shoulder: the bird is then caught in the ropes of the siege engines.

fear of omens are recurrent motifs throughout the *Historiae*. However, Curtius' treatment of the Gaza incident is ironic. Despite the warning, Alexander insists on exposing himself to danger, and as soon as he has avoided an Arab assassin (4.6.16), he believes he has discharged the prophecy. Yet he is wounded once he starts fighting: as Curtius says, *Sed, ut opinor, inevitabile est fatum* [But in my opinion, fate is inevitable] (4.6.17).

In view of the cynicism he has expressed about the reliability of omens earlier, Curtius' statement at first sight appears inconsistent. However, throughout the *Historiae*, the historian's doubt is uniform. The context thus becomes crucial. First, by *fatum*, Curtius is probably not referring to the concept of *fortuna* in its personalized sense or even to *fata* as in the idea of destiny. Although the historian may believe in these concepts, he does not necessarily have to believe in open manifestations of them, or what people believe are obvious signs of destiny. Certainly there is no special reason to interpret the word differently from its normal meaning of "fate,"[54] but as the historian makes very clear, Alexander is wounded because of his own actions, that is, *quippe dum inter primores promptius dimicat* [while he was fighting too readily among the foremost] (4.6.17). Taken in this context, Curtius' earlier statement is thus a little sarcastic: by increasing his odds of being hit, Alexander has helped fulfill the prediction. If one may use a modern parallel, it would be like someone receiving a warning about being hit by a truck, managing to avoid one accident, and then promptly standing in a multilane highway.

Alexander's *temeritas* is, of course, a key note of Curtius' characterization of the king. It is closely related to Alexander's *virtus*, since his desire to be always at the forefront and his prowess there inspires his men. This thirst for *gloria* and concern for his image occasionally results in *temeritas* where Alexander, through excessive personal risk, endangers his men, as at 3.6.14, at Tarsus, and at 9.5, at the fortress of the Malli. There are many examples of reckless generals in history, many of whom have earned the censure of historians or rhetoricians. Valerius Maximus (9.7), for instance, comments on the dangers of sudden and thoughtless action. The death of the Roman general Marcellus in 208 B.C. provides an obvious illustration. Plutarch and Livy condemn Marcellus' reckless-

---

54. Scholars normally take *fatum* at 4.6.17 as referring to "fate": see Atkinson, *Curtius* i, 339; McQueen, 41 n. 28. On the wounding of Alexander, cf. Arrian 2.27.1–2.

ness for being out of keeping with his age and experience; Polybius emphasizes his failure as a general.[55]

Although the other Alexander historians recognize Alexander's reckless nature, they do not especially condemn him for it. Arrian (6.13.4) accepts this aspect as part of what made up his hero: he admits Alexander's passion for glory was such that he had not the strength of mind to keep out of the thick of the fighting,[56] and indeed Alexander's great achievement in his military conquests underpins much of Arrian's admiration in his eulogy.[57] The consequential difference between a Marcellus and Alexander is that while Alexander is no less impulsive than Marcellus, he is not killed as a result of his actions, although there are many occasions where his recklessness should have meant his death.

Temeritas is a frequent motif in Curtius, and there is a close relation between the king's *fortuna, virtus,* and *temeritas.* For instance, Darius, in his battle speech prior to Arbela, comments on Alexander's recklessness (4.14.18), in the vain hope of convincing himself and his audience that Alexander would very likely be killed. The historian himself sums up the king's *audacia* after the army has crossed the Tigris (4.9.23); because Alexander succeeded at everything that he did, there was never opportunity to say that he had acted rashly.

To return to Curtius' apparent lack of comprehensive Stoic conviction, he does not see suicide as an honorable way of death; both Alexander and Darius say they prefer to die by the crime of someone else. Thus, in terms of his philosophical outlook, Curtius appears to have been what Dosson terms a "philosophe éclectique."[58] Although apparently not a particularly religious man, Curtius could accept the idea of destiny and believe that Alexander's success was due not only to his own great *virtus* and *ingenium* but to the favor or design of some inexplicable power. Alexander was indeed *fortunatus* (blessed or plain lucky), but the course of his life and his great achievement was governed by Providence.

---

55. Livy 27.27.11; Plut. *Marc.* 28.3; Polybius 10.2.7–12. See E.M. Carawan, "The Tragic History of Marcellus and Livy's Characterisation," *CJ* 80 (1984/85): 131–41; A.J. Pomeroy, "Polybius' Death Notices," *Phoenix* 40 (1986): 407–23, esp. 413.

56. Cf. Plut. *Alex.* 40.4, 41.1. In Arrian the theme occurs as part of a debate, where according to Nearchus, Alexander, after sustaining his serious injury at the Malli fortress, was reproached by his friends for running such a personal risk in advance of the army. A similar case is more tactfully (and rhetorically) expressed by Craterus; cf. Curt. 9.6.8 ff.

57. See Bosworth, *FAA,* 156.

58. Dosson, 266. Curtius' Alexander may be seen as a *fatalis dux,* although the historian does not use this term.

One last issue pertaining to Curtius' development of *fortuna* in his history remains: to what extent his use of *fortuna* as a theme may have been influenced by his source or sources. Here Diodorus provides a useful comparison. In several episodes, *tyche* plays a dominant role. Examples include the capture of Darius' family (the reversal of *tyche* for them); Alexander's appointment of Ballonymus as ruler of Tyre, which corresponds to the appointment of Abdalonymus of Sidon in Curtius and Justin; Alexander's use of Darius' table as a footstool; and his meeting with the Greek captives whom the Persians had mutilated.[59]

Although some of these incidents are discussed in more detail in chapter 5, it may be said that only in one of these episodes, namely, the capture of Darius' family, is Curtius especially close to Diodorus, and even here, there are variations in emphasis. For instance, although both historians describe the plight of the Persian women, wives of the king's relatives and friends, Diodorus stresses prudent Macedonian sympathy for the women because they are an example of *tyche's* vicissitude, whereas Curtius sees the irony of *fortuna* in that those who once adorned Darius' tent were now guarding it for Alexander. Again, while both historians note the attention given to Darius' family, Diodorus simply reiterates the reversal-of-*tyche* theme, but Curtius prefers to emphasize the personal aspects of Darius' mother, wife, and little son, who had been born to the hope of a great *fortuna* that his father had just lost. Thus, through a variation, the poignancy of the scene is enhanced by the latter historian.

Moreover, there are certain episodes, such as the Charidemus incident (cf. Curt. 3.2.10–19; Diod. 17.30) or the capture of Porus (discussed later in this chapter), where *fortuna* features very strongly in Curtius but not so in Diodorus. Even more striking is the difference in the moral digressions of both historians after Alexander's noble treatment of Darius' family;[60] whereas Curtius launches into a diatribe on how Alexander is corrupted by his *fortuna,* Diodorus comments generally that successful people may become arrogant and unable to cope with their good fortune. Alexander, however, showed wisdom in his treatment of Darius' family and should therefore be praised for his good qualities. Thus, although *fortuna* is a common element, each historian's emphasis is very different.

Tyche may have been a prominent theme in the source (perhaps

---

59. For the capture of Darius' family, see Diod. 17.36.2; cf. Curt. 3.11.24. For Ballonymus, see Diod. 17.46.6–47; cf. Curt. 4.1.15–25 and J. 11.10.8–9. For Darius' table, see Diod. 17.66.3–7; Curt. 5.2.13–15. On the Greek captives, see chap. 2, 49–50.

60. Cf. Curt. 3.12.18–21; Diod. 17.38.4–6.

Cleitarchus) regularly used by Diodorus and Curtius, but *tyche's* influence as a motif appears to have had a fairly even distribution in Diodorus outside of book 17, and it is likely that such moralizing was Diodorus' own contribution.[61] Given the impact of Alexander's personal good fortune in particular, this moralizing is perhaps to be expected, but nevertheless, Curtius made the concept an integral part of his work. Although using material and even ideas that were hardly new, the historian's rhetorical arrangement of the theme and adaptation of the sources appears to result in something quite original.

Alexander, *Fortunatus Rex;* Darius, *Infortunatus Rex*

At its most simple level, *fortuna* in Curtius is used in the sense of "lot," "circumstance," or "state," as at 3.12.23, where the historian remarks that Alexander ordered that the Persian royal family was to retain all insignia of its former *fortuna*. Similarly, *fortuna* also appears with the general meaning of "happenstance" or, loosely, "fate."[62]

However, in his first pentad, Curtius develops the theme of the personal *fortunae* of two kings, Alexander and Darius. Essentially, in two aspects these kings are the antitheses of each other. In *ingenium,* Alexander is the man of *vis,* whereas Darius is *ignavus* (cowardly); and, more importantly, Darius is *infelix* or *infortunatus,* whereas Alexander is the *fortunatus rex.*

This characterization immediately marks Alexander out. His personal *fortuna* is not only his success or good luck but an unfailing success, one that, as we have seen, carries more than a hint of divine favor or providential design. However, on a few occasions, Alexander's *fortuna* seems to retain a more traditional appearance of caprice. For instance, when Alexander falls sick at Tarsus (3.5.11), he finds that *fortuna* has brought an unexpected turn of events: "'You can perceive,' he said, 'at what a crucial time in my affairs fortune has caught me. . . . I seem to hear the clash of hostile arms and I—who on my own accord started the war—am now being challenged.'"[63] In this case, the king, through sufficient *fides*

---

61. See J.I. McDougall, ed., *Lexicon in Diodorum Siculum,* vol. 2 (Olms, 1983).
62. See Curt. 3.13.12, 4.1.29, 7.7.28.
63. Curt. 3.5.11: *"In quo me,"* inquit, *"articulo rerum mearum fortuna deprehenderit, cernitis. Strepitum hostilium armorum exaudire mihi videor, et qui ultro intuli bellum iam provocor."* The poetical *exaudire . . . videor* recalls Horace *Odes* 2.1.21; cf. another likely Horatian echo (of *Odes* 2.17.4, 1.12.46) at Curt. 9.6.8.

in his physician Philip, meets and overcomes the particular challenge of *fortuna*.

Similarly, shortly before the Battle of Issus (3.8.20), Alexander's *fiducia* turns to anxiety, and he is reminded of fortune's mutability.[64] Yet Issus is still a relatively early event for Curtius' Alexander and a momentary lapse of confidence on his part serves to increase the dramatic tension, without really taking away the feeling of his coming success. Alexander's resolution is that he would die nobly and with great glory. Thus the historian's emphasis is on Alexander's *virtus*. Curtius' point is that Alexander is worthy of his *fortuna*. In fact, in books 3–5, *fortuna* is a steady, inevitable accumulation of the king's success where the fate of peoples or cities depends on his activities. Even *fortuna* in a more general sense becomes, at times, identified with Alexander. Commenting on the importance of the siege of Tyre (4.1.40), Curtius says that *fortuna*'s attention was focused on this contest and that the fate of everything else rested on the result. Alexander's onslaught at 5.6.15 is termed an *impetus fortunae* (onset of fortune). As Alexander crosses the Tigris prior to the battle of Arbela (Gaugamela), the army, vulnerable as it was, could have been destroyed, but the *perpetua fortuna regis* (perpetual fortune of the king) turns the enemy away from the place, and the historian remarks that the king's *audacia* (boldness) is liable to underestimation (4.9.22–23).[65]

Even Alexander's *temeritas*—which, as we have seen, was normally condemned in a commander in antiquity from the classical historians to Augustus—turns out well for him. This result may seem to render as an ironic expression of wishful thinking Darius' statement at 4.14.19: "Though good luck may seem to favor you, in the long run it does not sustain rashness."[66] Darius' observation would be true of anyone else, but Alexander's *felicitas*—an aspect of his *fortuna*—is so great that whatever he does, rashly or otherwise, or whatever happens by chance will favor him. I shall return to Alexander's *felicitas* very shortly. In contrast, Darius is the unlucky and unsuccessful king. He is warned by the Greek mercenaries (3.8.2–3) that he should divide his forces, so as not to allow

---

64. Curt. 3.8.20: *Illam ipsam fortunam, qua adspirante res tam prospere gesserat verebatur* . . . ; cf. 3.8.21–22.
65. Curt. 4.9.23: . . . *audaciae quoque, qua maxime viguit, ratio minui potest, quia numquam in discrimen venit an temere fecisset.*
66. *Licet felicitas adspirare videatur, tamen ad ultimum temeritati non sufficit.* For Augustus, cf. Suet. *Div. Aug.* 25.

his entire kingdom to fall under one stroke of *fortuna*. The advantageous objective of Darius' battle plan for Issus (3.8.30) is shattered by *fortuna, omni ratione potentior* [more powerful than any reckoning]. At Arbela (4.16.10), *fortuna* piles up the resources of an empire as well as an age and in a single day transfers them to the victor. Curtius has voiced such a sentiment at 3.11.23 and repeats it again, in a different context, at 5.2.8, where Abulites of Susa sends gifts to Alexander. The contrast between Alexander's *fortuna* and Darius' is also emphasized at Susa in the anecdote of Darius' table; the former casually rests his feet on a table, a part of Darius' *domus*, which now symbolically has become Alexander's own household.[67]

A vivid reversal of fate for an individual was a well-known theme in ancient literature, and historiography was no exception. Despite Polybius' criticisms of historians who favored a sensationalist narrative, dramatic reversals of fortune recur often in his own history. Frequently *tyche* decides important issues by small margins, or its erratic nature spells a complete turnabout for an individual. For instance, Hannibal, besieging Mathos in Tunes, is captured and, in an ironic twist, crucified on the very cross on which Spendius, a former enemy, had been left hanging. Polybius views this episode as an instance of *tyche* designing a competition in cruelty, allowing both sides the opportunity for vengeance.[68] Polybius' idea of greatness is the individual who, even in the midst of supreme success of self and city, acknowledges that *tyche* is mutable—as in Scipio Aemilianus' moment of keen perception and personal horror at the sack of Carthage, when he comments that some day the same destruction could befall his own city. One of Polybius' moral lessons is that prosperity cannot last and that a prosperous individual should practice moderation (which is, after all, proper conduct for a human being), so that in the case of misfortune, the individual will be looked on more kindly by his fellows.[69]

So in Curtius, Darius' speech to his nobles outside Ecbatana (5.8.15), in which he says he expects a change on the part of *fortuna*, is, on the surface, a reasonable statement. Yet the tone is also reminiscent of Nicias' rather desperate exhortation to the Athenians and their allies at Syracuse (Thuc. 7.77.3–4) or of Catiline's address prior to the final battle in Sal-

---

67. Cf. Curt. 5.2.13–15; Diod. 17.66.7.
68. Polybius 1.86; see Walbank, *Commentary on Polybius*, 1:18.
69. Polybius 38.21; see Walbank, *Commentary on Polybius*, 1:19 n. 11.

lust's *Bellum Catilinae* (58.21). Catiline's equally bleak speech urges that if *fortuna* should be unfavorable to his men's *virtus*, by fighting like true men they would leave their enemies a painful and costly victory. Similarly, Darius says that if the gods do not favor "just and dutiful wars" [iusta ac pia bella], it will still be permissible for brave men to die honestly. However, he adds an interesting qualification. He urges his followers to assume the courage worthy of their fame and nation and to meet whatever *fors* will bring them with the same resolute spirit they have shown in the past. The Persians have the strength to withstand the challenges of *fors*, and it is significant that Darius uses the impersonal sense of chance, rather than personalized *fortuna*. Darius' Persians can meet the trials of universal *fors*, but for Darius himself, either a glorious victory or his downfall will confer eternal fame: *me certe in perpetuum aut victoria egregia nobilitat aut ruina*.[70]

Darius is isolated from his men. His *fortuna* has singled him out, and the placement of *ruina* as the final word in his speech indicates only too clearly what the outcome of such an ultimate contest with Alexander would be. The utter hopelessness of Darius' *fortuna* is further enforced by Nabarzanes' answer (5.9.3–8) to his Great King's speech. Curtius does not admire Nabarzanes, whom he sees as a *proditor* (traitor) and a *parricida* (regicide), but he gives the noble a pointed argument. *Pertinax fortuna* (tenacious fortune), says Nabarzanes, does not cease to oppress the Persians. Darius' personal *fortuna* is ill-starred, and because he is the Great King, his bad luck must invariably affect his followers. Thus Nabarzanes advises Darius to hand over the auspices and rule to someone who will only be called "king" until the enemy should withdraw from Asia; this person would then hand the throne back to Darius. The idea of a Great King abdicating was ludicrous; such an insidious proposal provokes an angry response from Darius, but his ineffectual wrath is symbolic of his weakness in general.

At 5.12.20, Darius, betrayed by his nobles, ultimately becomes the plaything of *fortuna*—as his captors, out of honor, bind him in shackles of gold, an ironic symbol of his former and present status. Justin (11.15.1–2) is the only other source who mentions the golden fetters; but whereas Curtius is interested in the reversal of Darius' *fortuna*, Justin

---

70. Curt. 5.8.17. *Ruina* for *pugna* is a textual emendation by Hedicke; the Bardon and Mützell editions read *pugna*, which, although acceptable, does not have the same dramatic effect as the contrast between *victoria* and *ruina*.

emphasizes a different, historical irony. The Persian kingdom is brought to an end in the territory of the Parthians, the later heirs of *imperium*.[71] Darius' misfortune is a main theme of Arrian's necrology on the king.[72] In Curtius (3.12.24), even Darius' mother acknowledges that Alexander has surpassed such a Great King in *aequitas* (fairness) and *felicitas* (good luck), the very hallmark of Alexander's *fortuna*.

Cicero, at *Pro lege Manilia* 10.28, claims that the best military commanders possess four essential qualities: *scientia rei militaris* (knowledge of military affairs), *virtus* (excellence), *auctoritas* (authority), and *felicitas*. The first three qualities are due to the general's *ingenium,* but the last is the gift of *fortuna*. Alexander's *felicitas* is his uncanny, sheer good luck, which sometimes proves to be the difference between success and failure. At the Cilician Gates (3.4.11), the king marvels at his *felicitas* when his army is not overwhelmed with rocks from above. Ironically the situation is reversed at 5.3.22, the only time when the king's *felicitas* is brought to a standstill. Yet on this occasion, Alexander's qualities as a commander overcome the setback. At 4.16.20–27, during the aftermath of Arbela, a potentially dangerous situation for the victorious king is surmounted by a combination of his *perpetua felicitas, virtus,* and soldiers. These situations are variations of a point stated earlier: Alexander is a capable general. However, there are many instances, both in and out of a military context, where Alexander is helped by his good luck alone. Alexander's *fortuna* and *felicitas* are just as prominent themes in the second pentad as they are in the first. At 8.3.1 f., *fortuna* saves Alexander the trouble of tracking down Spitamenes. *Fortuna* and the company of the diners cause the king to prolong a banquet and so avoid assassination by the Pages (8.6.14). *Fortuna* safeguards Alexander by having him land near a tree when he jumps into the Malli fortress (9.5.3), and it twice protects the king and his army when they indulge in bacchanalian revels— once at 8.10.20 and again at 9.10.27–28, when, owing to good fortune, a disordered procession of a drunken and sick army through Carmania becomes a source of astonishment to the barbarians.[73]

Alexander is keenly aware of his *fortuna,* since in the post-Darius

---

71. On the golden fetters, see Heckel and Yardley, *Justin,* ad 11.15.1–2; Heckel argues they were intended as a mark of respect. Cf. Mark Antony, who paraded Artavasdes in his triumph at Alexandria (Vell. 2.8.2–3; Dio 49.40.4). See also A.J. Woodman, *Velleius Paterculus: The Caesarian and Augustan Narrative* (Cambridge, 1983), 211.

72. Arrian 3.22; cf. Bosworth, *HCA,* 1:346 f.

73. *Crapula graves* here (9.10.27) probably approximates our term *hangover;* cf. Livy 9.30.9.

books it enhances his renown. His reputation becomes a significant factor in causing the surrender of many hill fortresses in Sogdiana, because the natives are convinced Alexander is invincible. The king trusts his *fortuna* in bluffing Ariamazes into accepting unconditional surrender (7.11.27). At 9.9.2, when Alexander decides to sail down an unknown river, the sole consolation for his nervous men is his *perpetua felicitas*.

Just as Darius' bad luck affected the morale of his followers, so Alexander's consistent good fortune extends to his men and is as much a source of inspiration to them as his *virtus*. The historian comments at 3.6.18 on the Macedonians' enthusiastic acclaim: "First of all, it seemed that he undertook no task without divine aid; for since Fortune was on hand everywhere, even his rashness had resulted in glory."[74] Similarly, Parmenion (3.13.14) relies on the *felicitas* of Alexander prior to the surrender of Damascus. During the battle against Porus (8.13.13 f.), two rash Macedonian youths, Hegesimachus and Nicanor, aroused by the *perpetua felicitas* of their side, swim out to an island in the Hydaspes and kill many of the enemy until they are themselves surrounded and dispatched. However, Alexander is also warned to be wary of his *felicitas*, a theme that relates to the last area of Curtius' development of *fortuna*— its capacity for the corruption of moral character in the long term.

The Corrupting Effect of *Fortuna*

Warnings on the transitory nature of *fortuna* occur frequently throughout the *Historiae*, from the statement of Darius to the speech of the Scythian envoys.[75] Alexander's defeat of Porus (8.14.40 f.) provides a unique and important example of Curtius' emphasis on this theme. The meeting between Porus and Alexander is depicted in a dramatic fashion in two of the other five main historical traditions, Arrian (5.19.1–2) and Plutarch (*Alex.* 60.14), and is described less directly in the *Metz Epitome* (61). The incident may have ultimately derived from eyewitness sources; for instance, even though it is given as a *logos* in Arrian, he appears to follow Ptolemy's account from 5.15 and may have still been using him.[76] In any case, even if the two kings did meet in the manner in which they

---

74. Curt. 3.6.18: *Iam primum nihil sine divina ope adgredi videbatur; nam, cum praesto esset ubique fortuna, temeritas in gloriam cesserat.*
75. See Curt. 4.5.2; cf. 7.2.19, 7.8.24.
76. Arrian's use of this format does not preclude Ptolemy as his source; on the complex issue of *legomena* in general, see chap. 3, n. 34.

were supposed to, any oral report of what was said between them would have been liable to distortion, since they could have only communicated through interpreters. Porus' alleged proud and brave response to Alexander, "Treat me as king" [βασιλικῶς μοι χρῆσαι], clearly appealed to Plutarch and Arrian, who were both steeped in philosophical ideologies and appreciated the neatness of an aphorism that encapsulated Alexander both acting like a king and treating Porus as one.[77] Interestingly, the tradition was also evidently part of the vulgate, as it is represented with only a slight variation in emphasis in the *Metz Epitome:* . . . *de se ipso ut animo regio consuleret obsecrare coepit* [as for his own person, he now began to beseech Alexander to consult his own feeling as a king] (trans. J.C. Yardley). In comparison, in the text of Pseudo-Callisthenes (3.4) and its various derivatives, Porus is an enemy to be killed. He is a Goliath who is literally stabbed in the back in most of these fabulous versions, while in the *Iskandarnamah,* he refuses to convert to Islam and so is beheaded by a Muslim Alexander.[78]

Alexander's questioning of Porus is not mentioned by Diodorus and Justin, which may have been an editorial omission, but it appears in Curtius. Yet instead of giving a response similar to the versions quoted by Plutarch and Arrian, Porus replies in Curtius, "What this day tells you to do . . . the day on which you have discovered how transitory good fortune is" (8.14.43).[79] In Curtius, Porus is an example of fortune's vicissitudes. Such a reply could well have been due to a free adaptation of his source on the historian's part or could even reflect the source. Curtius could well have fabricated Porus' answer himself, for literary effect, but whatever the origin, he has made good use of it. It is strange that Diodorus did not reproduce a similar ending, since, as noted earlier, the reversals of *tyche* are a favorite theme of his elsewhere. In Curtius, Porus clearly intends that Alexander should learn from his calamity. Yet in Alexander's case, such warnings on the transitory nature of *felicitas* seem futile. Alexander's *felicitas,* although it may slip (cf. 5.3.22), never fails him. Thus for Alexander, Porus' admonition as well as warnings from other sources are more likely indicative of another, subtle and dangerous aspect of *fortuna*—the morally corruptive effect of unbroken success.

Alexander's meeting with Sisygambis and her family (Curt. 3.12.15 f.)

---

77. See Bosworth, *HCA,* 2:310.
78. See E.J. Baynham, *AHB* 9, no. 1 (1995): 1–13.
79. Curt. 8.14.43: *"Quod hic,"* inquit, *"dies tibi suadet, quo expertus es quam caduca felicitas esset."* See also Hammond, *THA,* 43.

provides the historian with an opportunity to digress on the gradual deterioration of the king's character and to indicate what his future Alexander will be. In view of the episode's relevance to the theme of *fortuna* and the necrology in book 10, it seems appropriate to examine it here. The story of the Persian queen mother's mistake in paying homage to Hephaestion before Alexander appealed to Diodorus, Arrian, and the rhetorical schools, as well as, in a much later era, to sixteenth- and seventeenth-century ideals of heroic behavior, if the paintings of Paolo Veronese and Charles Le Brun may be used as examples.[80] In Curtius, Alexander (3.12.17) displays *pietas* toward Sisygambis by calling her *mater*, a title he confers formally on her, with the added endearment of *dulcissima*, at 5.2.22.[81] His *fides* to Hephaestion is evident in that he not only does not take offense at having his friend accorded royal honors before himself but actually acknowledges the man as an alter ego. This character is the ideal Alexander *rex*: thus Curtius embarks on his didactic, rhetorical sermon, contrasting the future Alexander with the present one. The passage is worth quoting from 3.12.18–21.

> Equidem hac continentia animi si ad ultimum vitae perseverare potuisset, feliciorem fuisse crederem, quam visus est esse, cum Liberi patris imitaretur triumphum ab Hellesponto usque ad Oceanum omnes gentes victoria emensus. Sic vicisset profecto superbiam atque iram, mala invicta, sic abstinuisset inter epulas caedibus amicorum, egriosque bello viros et tot gentium secum domitores indicta causa veritus esset occidere. Sed nondum fortuna se animo eius superfuderat: itaque orientem tam moderate et prudenter tuli, ad ultimum magnitudinem eius non cepit. Tunc quidem ita se gessit, ut omnes ante eum reges et continentia et clementia vincerentur.

> [Had he been able to maintain this degree of moderation to the end of his life, I would certainly consider him to have enjoyed more good fortune than appeared to be his when he was emulating Father Liber's triumph on his victorious march through all the

---

80. On Sisygambis' mistake, see Arrian 2.12.6–8; Diod. 17.37.4–5; Val. Max. 4.7.ext.2; *Itin. Alex.* 39. Arrian gives the story as a *logos*, unlike the episode of Leonnatus' visit, which he says was from Ptolemy and Aristobulus; see Bosworth, *HCA*, 1:220 f. For Veronese, etc., see chap. 1, n. 7.

81. Cf. Diod. 17.37.6; see Atkinson, *Curtius* ii, 68–69.

nations from the Hellespont right through to the Ocean. For then he would surely have overcome the defects he failed to overcome, his pride [superbia] and his temper [ira]; he would have stopped short of killing his friends at dinner, and he would have been reluctant to execute without trial men who had distinguished themselves in battle and had conquered so many nations with him. But good fortune had not as yet overwhelmed him: while it was on the increase, he bore it with self-restraint and abstinence, but eventually he failed to control it when it reached its peak. At this particular time, certainly, his actions were such that he outshone all previous kings in self-control and clemency.] (trans. J.C. Yardley)

Since Diodorus (17.38.4–6) also moralizes on Alexander's character after the meeting with Sisygambis, a digression of some kind was probably in the original source. *Tyche* appears in a most general and conventional fashion; Diodorus observes that good fortune produces arrogance. But his theme is Alexander's *phronesis*—prudence or common sense—and unlike Curtius, he does not digress on what Alexander later became.

Curtius' chief theme is stated in the opening line of his digression: Alexander failed to practice *continentia animi,* which is unlikely to mean self-restraint in the sexual sense, as it does at 3.12.21–22,[82] but rather, in view of the following context about Father Liber, simply the abstinence from excessive self-indulgence, at all levels. *Superbia* and *ira* are dominant traits of the Alexander *tyrannus* character, which might have emerged in the lost books, with Curtius' characterization of the king at Thebes or the siege of Halicarnassus, but which definitely surfaces in the later books, beginning in book 4, with the sieges of Tyre and Gaza and the visit to Siwah. Similarly, those two traits and excessive indulgence—namely, *cupido vini*—lead to Alexander's murder of Cleitus in book 8.

Above all, the excursus relates to the historian's necrology. This relationship is indicated first by context and the placing of both the moral digression and the eulogy. Each time, Sisygambis plays a prominent role. The former follows Alexander's gesture of respect to her; the latter, her suicide on his death. In terms of content, the *vitia* of the obituary recall the crimes stated in the digression. Alexander did put to death "men who had distinguished themselves in battle," such as Parmenion, Philotas, and

---

82. Cf. Curt. 4.10.24, where the historian remarks that the beauty of Darius' wife had been an incentive not to *libido* but to *gloria*. On *continentia* in the sense of sexual self-restraint, see Livy 26.50, but cf. Gellius *NA* 7.8.3 = Valerius Antias fr. 25 [HRR ed. Peter]; see A.J. Pomeroy, "Hannibal at Nuceria," *Historia* 38 (1989): 162–76.

Cleitus. Moreover, *domitores secum* is indicative of the king's position and that of his Companions. Originally, as a Macedonian king, he was considered by the nobles as a primus inter pares, and he could not have conquered Asia without their help.[83] After Alexander has become lord of Asia, the conflict between the king and the Macedonian high command emerges as a major political theme of the second pentad.

The digression relates to the obituary in other ways. In the former, Alexander surpasses all other kings at that time in *continentia* and *clementia*, whereas in the necrology, he surpasses all other kings in *fortitudo*, even among those whose sole virtue it is. Alexander has been singled out from this lonely crowd. His courage, which is the basis of his *vis*, is his most consistent and yet most significant characteristic. Finally, the role of *fortuna* is emphasized in both passages; I shall return to the context of its use.

The digression in book 3 is not an isolated piece of rhetorical moralizing. It has been structured into the development of the *Historiae* and can be considered a second preface to the ensuing narrative of Alexander's *regnum*, just as the necrology can be considered a summary of it. The pattern has been established. Alexander the king and general will be interspersed with Alexander the tyrant. As his power grows, the king will give full rein to his *mala invicta* (unconquered faults).

Sisygambis' reply to Alexander's *clementia* is dignified and perceptive. The matriarch is aware that Alexander is superior to Darius. She has no illusions about her true status—*famula* at 3.12.25 can have negative associations,[84] but she also knows that Alexander's mercy is politically expedient: as she says, it is better that Alexander's power be attested by clemency rather than cruelty. Despite the ambivalence of *clementia*, the comment is later enforced by episodes with a moral point that contain warnings pertinent to Alexander, such as the Abdalonymus story at 4.1.15–25,[85] and by further digressions from the historian in book 6, appropriately the first book of the second

---

83. Alexander kills Parmenion without a trial, although he is accused at Philotas' trial; Cleitus is tried posthumously. See Curt. 6.9.4, 8.2.12; cf. Diod. 17.80.1. The nature of Macedonian kingship is controversial. But on the primus inter pares, see J.R. Ellis, *Philip II and Macedonian Imperialism* (London, 1976), 24; E.D. Carney, *PP* 211 (1983): 260–72.

84. Cf. Cat. 63.89–90.

85. Abdalonymus, raised to kingship of Sidon by Hephaestion on the recommendation of two noble youths, is warned by these same young men not to forget his humility: see Diod. 17.47 (Ballonymus and Tyre), who uses the story as an instructive example of *tyche*'s mutability. Cf. J. 11.10.8–9, where Alexander, not Hephaestion, appoints Abdalonymus as king, to remind the Sidonian nobility who had the real power. In Curtius, Abdalonymus is clearly intended as an ideal of kingship, of which Alexander falls short.

pentad.[86] The implication is that the king lacked the strength of mind to resist the temptations that total power brought, just as the same *licentia regni* prompts Darius to execute Charidemus in book 3. Curtius' comment, echoed by Charidemus himself, is that *plerumque fortuna* perverts *etiam natura*. Since Alexander's *fortuna* exceeds that of Darius, so does his potential for evil.

The idea that Alexander became corrupted by his success was hardly new; as we saw earlier, the tradition was strong in the rhetorical schools and in Roman literature generally; Alexander was considered unable to have managed his prosperity.[87] In the necrology at 10.5.33, Curtius attributes to Alexander's *fortuna* these negative qualities: "to equal himself with the gods and to aspire to divine honors, to put faith in oracles advising such behavior, to be more angry than was appropriate with those who scorned to venerate him, to change his dress to that of foreign nations, and to imitate the customs of the conquered peoples, which he had rejected before his victory."[88] The same list of vices is also present in Arrian's catalogue and may have been commonplace.[89] But with Curtius, the common denominator is *superbia*. Due to *fortuna,* Alexander's power becomes absolute and unchangeable. Yet the historian says at 10.5.35 that Alexander, alone of all mortals, held *fortuna* itself *in potestate* (in his power). Such a curious statement requires some explanation, since it seems at odds with the statement in the earlier digression that the king could not withstand *fortuna. In potestate habere* has a strong legal sense that suggests a relationship akin to the control exercised by a *dominus* (master) over a *servus* (slave) or to the authority of the *paterfamilias* over his own family.[90] Curtius' text could imply that Fortuna was

---

86. Cf. Curt. 4.6.29, 6.2.1–4, 6.6.1–11. See also chap. 6, 169–71.

87. It was a strong biographical tradition and rhetorical topos that Alexander, although initially noble in character, became corrupted by success; cf. Cic. *Tusc.* 3.21 and Livy 9.18.1–2. J. Stroux (*Philologus* 84 [1928/29]: 233–51), Tarn (*Alexander the Great*, 2:32, 69, 96), and Brown (*AJPh* 70 [1949]: 225–48) suggested that the topos was the product of the Peripatetic school, but their arguments were refuted by Badian (*CQ* 8 [1958]: 153) and E. Mensching (*Historia* 12 [1963]: 274–82).

88. *dis aequare se et caelestes honores accesere; et talia suadentibus oraculis credere, et dedignantibus venerari ipsum vehementius quam par esset irasci; in externum habitum mutare corporis cultum; imitari devictarum gentium mores, quos ante victoriam spreverat.* Cf. 10.5.35.

89. Cf. Arrian 7.29.3–4. Arrian's elaborate apology recalls the digression on Alexander's excessive behavior in Arrian 4.7.3–14; see Bosworth, *FAA,* 145 f.

90. The power of a father over his offspring or that of a master over a slave is termed *potestas,* along with the power of a husband over a wife if married *cum manu.* Curtius' readers may well have thought of all three relationships. *Potestas* (sc. *patria*) is the word for

Alexander's slave in that she did everything for him. Alexander's *perpetua felicitas is* an aspect of his control over *fortuna*, and likewise, as we have seen, fate ordains his *gloria* and the length of his life. There is something more. Curtius, overall, is interested in the exercise of power, of how an individual measures up to his success. But the king's choice of action remains his responsibility, and equally Alexander may have been as powerless to resist his slave Fortuna as the emperor Claudius was to withstand the manipulation of his freedmen Narcissus and Pallas.

Curtius' depiction of Alexander is not simply a portrait of an initially morally upright king who becomes a cruel tyrant. Granted, a portrayal of the changing nature of Alexander's character and *regnum* is at the heart of the historian's work. At first, this portrayal may seem contrary to the ancients' usual depiction of character as something static or unchanging. An individual's personality did not develop but instead revealed inherent traits, although Hamilton adds the modification that while *phusis*, or nature, did not change, character, *ethos*, could alter, depending on external influences.[91] Yet in Curtius the negative aspects of Alexander are also there right from the start; *fortuna* simply gives them scale and sanction.

Moreover, the dichotomy inherent in Alexander's *regnum* is evident in the eulogy, which, contrary to the usual view, is not a contradiction of the historian's characterization. Despite the rhetorical nature of the necrology, its tone is subtle, ironic, and sophisticated. Three of Alexander's positive qualities—his *vis incredibilis animi* (incredible strength of mind), *laboris patientia* (endurance of effort), and *virtus* (10.5.27 f.)— sound conventional. One may seem to hear Livy on Hannibal (21.4.3–9) or Sallust on Catiline (*Bell. Cat.* 5). Yet just as these two historians outweigh the good characteristics of their respective antiheroes with the bad, so Curtius' evaluation of the king's worthy points is qualified. Even the proviso on Alexander's endurance, *propemodum nimia,* is close to outright criticism. Moreover, Alexander's *clementia in devictos* recalls his treatment of Betis of Gaza (4.6.29), Ariamazes (7.11.28), or the leader of the Musicani (9.8.16),[92] as much as his treatment of Porus, Darius' family (3.12.13–26), or the Sogdianian nobles (7.10.4–9).

---

a father's dominion over his son, whereas *potestas* (sc. *dominica*) and more precisely *mancipium* cover master and slave. See D. Daube, *Roman Law: Linguistic, Social, and Philosophical Aspects* (Edinburgh, 1969), 75–76.

91. Hamilton, *Plutarch*, xxxviii–xxxix n. 2. Cf. C. Gill, CQ 33 (1983): 469–87; S. Swain, *Phoenix* 43 (1989): 62–68.

92. He is called King Musicanus in Diodorus (17.102.4); cf. Arrian 6.15.5–7, 6.17.1–2.

Similarly, in Curtius' statement on Alexander's policy of bestowing kingdoms, one can see a twisted echo of the historian's own, recent, sour comment following the Orsines episode (10.1.42): *arbitrio scorti aliis regna daret, aliis adimeret vitam* [on the judgment of a catamite, he gave kingdoms to some people and took life from others]. Curtius' reference to the king as having *liberalitas saepe maiora tribuens quam a dis petuntur* [a generosity often bestowing greater gifts than are requested from the gods in prayer] contains a critical irony in that it encompasses both Alexander's divine aspirations and his excess, while Curtius' use of *fere* (almost) in *omnes fere amicos benignitas* [his kindness to almost all his friends] is truly a brilliant touch. The dramatic, rhetorical development is sharply undercut by that one word, which clearly brings to mind the fates of Alexander's *amici* who, for whatever reason, fell victim to his *vis*.

It is also easy to think of examples of Alexander's *magnitudo animi*: his refusal of water brought to him in the desert (7.5.9 f.), though there are clear political advantages behind why he acts so; his heroic activity in rousing his frozen soldiers in the wastes of Gazaca (8.4.1–17); or his acknowledgment of his entire army on his deathbed (10.5.1–5). However, Alexander's *pietas* toward his parents is an ambiguous issue. His desire to consecrate Olympias, expressed earlier at 9.6.26 and in the obituary at 10.5.30, hints at Roman imperial apotheosis, but Alexander as the avenger of Philip is a little more doubtful. Cleitus provokes Alexander to *rabies* by mocking Alexander's adoption of Zeus Ammon as his father instead of Philip. Yet as Curtius probably dealt with Philip's assassination in the lost first book, we can never be sure what he would have made of Alexander's role in the whole affair.[93]

In short, Curtius says nothing in his obituary that he has not indicated in the *Historiae*. The nature of *regnum* is intrinsically ambivalent, and Alexander, given his youth and tremendous *fortuna*, is the epitome of this ambivalence.

Yet Curtius respects and admires his subject. Despite the potential of *regnum* for evil—*licentia, superbia*, or excessive behavior of any sort—strong kingship is necessary. The latter part of book 10 is devoted to emphasizing the contrast between Alexander and the lesser men who succeed him. Curtius' judgment is summed up at 10.5.37.

---

93. See chap. 2, 41.

For this king [rex] and commander [dux] a successor was sought; but it was a greater burden than was possible for one man to uphold; therefore his name and the fame of his deeds distributed kings and kingdoms throughout almost the entire world, and those were deemed most famous who had retained even the smallest part of such a great fortune [tanta fortuna].[94]

Alexander's *regnum* and *fortuna* are deliberately united. The historian's emphasis is on *rex* and *dux*, the king and general. A study of Curtius' development of this characterization in the *Historiae* is the purpose of the remaining two chapters.

---

94. *Huic regi ducique successor quaerebatur; sed maior moles erat, quam ut unus subire eam posset. Itaque nomen quoque eius et fama rerum in totum propemodum orbem reges ac regna diffudit; clarissimique sunt habiti, qui etiam minimae parti tantae fortunae adhaeserunt.*

Chapter 5

Regnum in the First Pentad: Alexander and Darius

As stated earlier, Curtius' chief unit of structure in the *Historiae* is the pentad, which is dominated by the themes of *fortuna* and *regnum*. In chapter 4 we saw how *fortuna* affected the lives and careers of the two major protagonists, Alexander and Darius. In books 3–5 Curtius develops a series of contrasts and balances between the two kings, and just as each was the opposite of his rival in terms of his *fortuna*, so too, Alexander and Darius are antitheses in character.

Alexander is the superior king because he is the man of *vis* (force), whereas Darius is portrayed as a weak figure. Alexander is young, Darius a more mature man. Alexander is the better *dux* on the battlefield against Darius. He is also the better politician and diplomat, which is illustrated in his treatment of his own officers and staff, as well as in his correspondence with the Great King in book 4. Initially, he is the better character morally—a model of self-restraint, dignity, and excellence. Darius, although not without some merit as a strategist, cannot hold his army together, and worse, he twice proves himself, very publicly, to be a coward. In his relationship with his followers, he is at times vain and arrogant, forgetful of sound advice or the considerations of loyalty, and prey to luxurious living and *superbia*. Curtius deliberately emphasizes the deep *fides* (loyalty) the Persians have for their king at the outset of his confrontation with Alexander, as well as the deterioration of the strength of this loyalty. Book 3 opens and concludes with episodes illustrating the *fides* Darius commands, yet by the beginning of book 5, his hold on the loyalty of even the closest of his followers has begun to slip; by the book's end, his own people have betrayed him.

Curtius has devoted an almost equal share of attention to Darius as he has to Alexander in the surviving first three books. In fact, only in Curtius is Darius given anything like individuality or a clearly defined and important role.[1] An intriguing prospect is that Trogus may have also given more attention to the Achaemenid monarch; in Justin both the narrative of Persian history and Darius' accession in book 10, as well as the account of his death in book 11, suggest a higher profile for Alexander's opponent in Trogus' original. In the other Alexander historians, Darius does occasionally appear in a cameo performance designed to illustrate some moral point—for instance, in Diodorus' version of the Charidemus episode (Diod. 17.30.2–7) or in Arrian's condemnation of royal flatterers (2.6.5–7).

Arrian is not particularly concerned with Darius' kingship as a prominent theme. He accepts that Darius was fated to lose and that his hero, Alexander, was destined to conquer Asia; consider his comments on the fate of the Persian Empire (2.6.7). Moreover, Arrian's use of τὸ δαιμόνιον [some divine power] (2.6.6) and his general sentiment that this force led Darius into a strategically inadvisable position at Issus is remarkably reminiscent of Herodotean language. Darius is portrayed as not only unlucky but also unworthy to rule—such is the tone of Arrian's sorry catalogue of disasters at 3.22, which forms Arrian's necrology of the Persian king.[2]

Moreover, Arrian has a tendency to use Darius stories only where they are relevant to Alexander. For instance, the famous anecdote of Darius' prayer for Alexander to succeed him is placed wildly out of chronological context by Arrian, at 4.20.1–3, where he uses the tale to illustrate Alexander's self-restraint around women.[3] It is a mere *logos* that allows Arrian to pass moral observation on enemy sensitivity. In Curtius, as we shall see, the story forms part of the integral portrayal of the two rulers. The different methodologies of each historian are clearly evident. Arrian may doubt the tradition, but he can use it for its symbolic importance and its relevance to his protagonist's character, which in this instance is wholly consistent with his stated aims at 1.3. To Curtius, however, the study of Alexander's *regnum* would be enhanced by systematic comparison with other kings and leaders; hence he emphasizes Darius in the first pentad and Agis, Bessus, Porus, and ultimately Perdiccas and Ptolemy in

---

1. See W. Rutz, "Das Bild des Dareios bei Curtius Rufus," *WJA* 10 (1984): 147–59.
2. Cf. Hdt. (on predestination) 8.13 fin., 7.10e. Herodotean coloring is also present in Curtius' account; cf. the section in this chapter on Charidemus. On Arrian's necrology of Darius, Bosworth, *HCA*, 1:346 f. highlights its bland nature and deficiencies.
3. Cf. Plut. *Alex.* 30.6 f. and *Mor.* 338F; Athen. 13.603C. See Bosworth, *HCA*, 2:133–34.

the second. Darius' last days provide a pertinent example. For instance, as we saw earlier, the structure of book 5 in Curtius is divided between Alexander and Darius. In Arrian (3.19.4, 3.21.1 ff.) the description of the pursuit of Darius is presented as a series of reports to Alexander, whereas in Curtius the narrative is concentrated on the Great King himself.

Obviously, certain aspects of the traditional tyrant figure, so long a favorite in philosophy, historiography, and declamation, appear in Curtius' depictions of Darius as well as of Alexander himself, particularly in the second pentad. These aspects include arrogance, cruelty, excessive self-indulgence, and even generosity. Their appearance in Curtius does not necessarily mean that literature in general and Curtius in particular were always hostile toward kingship. To some extent, Curtius' portrait would be influenced by his source, particularly if (as argued earlier) Cleitarchus was one of Curtius' main authorities. Cleitarchus' attitude was either more hostile or at least a better source of unsavory material than some of the other pro-Macedonian accounts, such as those of Ptolemy, Aristobulus, and Marsyas of Pella.[4] Negative elements of the tyrant portrait, particularly savagery and cruelty, appear in the other Alexander historians, especially in Trogus' depiction of Alexander. Yet Curtius is far too subtle a writer to present his characterization of either king as a mere stereotype. He presents Darius as an unfortunate, if not tragic, figure. He was a kind-natured man—Curtius frequently describes the king with words like *sanctus* (virtuous) and *mitis* (mild)—yet he lacked strength of personality. The historian may sympathize, but he does not condone.[5]

Throughout the first pentad, Alexander and Darius each display positive as well as negative qualities. Curtius' depiction of Alexander is built around the king and general in episodes that emphasize his excellence and extraordinary good luck in the field as well as his political and military relationship with his officers and soldiers. The positive aspects of their respective kingships include valor *(virtus),* reciprocal *fides* and *pietas* between king and subject, *clementia* (mercy), and *continentia* (self-restraint). Yet kingship can also be stained with *luxuria* (luxury, self-indulgence), *ira* (rage), *superbia* (arrogance), *dissimulatio* (deception), and *licentia regni* (license of royal power). Some of these qualities may themselves be ambivalent; for example, to any upper-class Roman from the late republican or early imperial period, *clementia* and *gratia* (grati-

---

4. See chap. 3, 71, 74.
5. See Curt. 3.2.17, 3.8.4, 5.10.14.

tude) are two-edged, implying the intrinsic superiority of the individual who exercises the former and the obligation of the latter. In Curtius' history, the ambiguity of *clementia* surfaces several times: in Alexander's illness at Tarsus (see discussion later in this chapter), in the account of Philotas' fall in book 6, and in the Conspiracy of the Pages in book 8.[6]

Book 5 marks the climax of the Alexander and Darius theme, as the historian tells us himself in the opening sentence. One might compare Diodorus' account narrating Agis' war after the battle of Arbela. Rather than interrupt his focus on the two kings, Curtius has deliberately favored literary aesthetics, yet he does not lose sight of historically significant events already indicated in his text. The events in book 5 include the surrender of Babylon and Susa to Alexander, the capture of the Persian (Susian) Gates, an expedition against the Mardi, the sack of Persepolis and burning of the palace, and the betrayal and arrest of Darius, as well as Alexander's pursuit of the former Great King and his captors. Compared with other sources, Curtius' narrative is by far the most elaborate; for instance, Arrian has compressed the equivalent account of events into six chapters of his book 3. One conclusion is that Arrian's account is overabbreviated; another, that Curtius' is overblown. However, one should always keep in mind the latter's agenda. When one considers the deliberate placement of episodes, the careful interplay of theme and image, and the rich use of irony, the indictment of excess becomes hollow. Analysis of the possible structural scheme for book 5 and of certain important episodes has been provided elsewhere in this book.[7]

It seems worthwhile to examine several episodes from books 3–4 as test cases for Curtius' thematic preoccupations. Since Curtius apparently intended Darius to be a foil to his Alexander, the incidents illustrating Darius' treatment of his courtiers offer particular interest, especially in relation to the qualities of kingship highlighted earlier in this discussion. The following diagram, which is based on book 3, depicts a structural pattern in terms of episodes and motifs subrelated to the major themes of *regnum*, showing the relationship of the selected incidents to each other. The episodes on the left may be contrasted with or paralleled by those on the right.

---

6. The advantages of *clementia* are apparent at Curt. 7.6.17, 7.9.18; on Philotas, see chap. 6; on the Pages, see especially 8.8.8 and chap. 6.
7. For the structure of book 5, see chap. 2, 42–45; for Darius' last days, chap. 4, 112–13, 120–21; for the burning of Persepolis, chap. 3, 95–99.

Chapter	Episode	Motif	Chapter	Episode	Motif
2	Charidemus	*Libertas Licentia regni*	5–6	Alexander at Tarsus	*Fides Pietas*
7	Sisines	*Dissimulatio* Alexander's *vis*	8	Darius and the mercenaries	Darius' *clementia*

The court behavior of Alexander and Darius also provides an effective preparation for Curtius' narrative of the Battle of Issus, which forms the climax of his third book and emphasizes the generalship of each king; Alexander's *virtus* is sharply contrasted with Darius' *ignavia* (cowardice). In addition to discussing the episodes in the preceding diagram, the following sections of this chapter also explore from book 4 the diplomatic exchanges between the two kings, Alexander's treatment of Betis (the defeated governor of Gaza), and the king's visit to Siwah, all of which highlight the *dux, rex,* and *tyrannus*.

Charidemus

The Charidemus incident is crucial to Curtius' development of *regnum*, not only in the first pentad, but in the sequential five books. Alexander will later commit the same offenses as Darius and refuse to respect *libertas*.

The scene is set in Babylon. Darius, having lost a talented commander in Memnon and disgusted by the apparent incompetence of his own generals, assembled his forces outside of Babylon in a vast array. The impressive list of soldiers and nationalities at 3.2.2–9 is undermined by the historian's own dry comment that sheer numbers *(multitudo militum)* were what Darius lacked least; at the same time, the Great King's courtiers *(purpurati)* inflate his confidence.

The evil of flattery where a king or tyrant was concerned was not an uncommon theme in Greco-Roman literature. In the *Republic* (567b–68a), Plato notes that after a tyrant had eliminated those who helped him to power, he would by necessity surround himself with a gang of admiring bodyguards. In the *De amicitia* (24.89), Cicero remarks that complaisance is unworthy of both *libertas* and friendship. Condemnation of flattery was also well represented in the Alexander historians. Plutarch is aware that Alexander was influenced by flatterers (*Alex.* 23.7); so, too, Arrian himself emphasizes the harmful effect of flattery on both Darius and Alexander (2.6.5, 4.8.6, 7.29.1). In particular, Arrian seems embarrassed by the implicit parallel between the kings and hence mitigates his reaction to Cleitus (4.9.1), whom he condemns for his hubris; Curtius seems far readier to let the similarities speak for themselves.

Seneca, a contemporary of Curtius', asserts in the *De beneficiis* (6.30 ff.) that what rulers need most is someone who will tell them the truth. Curtius obviously did not like flatterers either. At any court, the attendants who simply comply with the ruler to maintain his goodwill should be separated from the professional parasite, who deliberately flatters the king for a living or as the result of prearrangement—like the Sicilian Cleon in Curtius (8.5.8). Yet speaking the truth, however good for the king's moral fiber, carries its dangers for the courtier. The risk is amply illustrated by Charidemus' fate and the fates of other equally outspoken followers of Alexander.

In Curtius, Darius, expecting an affirmative response on the might of his army, turns to Charidemus, an Athenian described as "experienced in war," who had been expelled from Athens on Alexander's order. Thus, although Charidemus has no love for the king himself, he shows frankness and honesty in his open admiration of the high quality of the Macedonian army. However, at the same time, he forgets that he is a suppliant and guest at an oriental court; above all, he forgets royal arrogance. Although the Athenian general admits that Darius might not like what he is going to say, he persists with his genuine, if unwelcome, advice. He contrasts the Macedonian army, although *torva* (fierce) and *inculta* (unkempt), with the *luxuria* of the Persians; in short, his counsel is that Darius should hire mercenaries from Greece or Macedon. The Great King does not react kindly. At 3.2.17, Curtius underscores one of his major themes: the corrupting effect of *fortuna* on character. Darius, seized by the license of royal power that is his because of the high position in which *fortuna* has placed him, orders the Greek's execution, thereby violating all consideration of *libertas*, *fides*, and *pietas*. Charidemus was a guest and a suppliant and therefore deserved the protection of his patron; moreover, he was a free man, who had been asked for his opinion.

As he is being dragged off to his death, Charidemus shouts prophetic words, in what amounts to an echo of an earlier comment made by the historian, that fortune corrupts human character, "You, indeed, so suddenly changed by the license of royal power [licentia regni], will be an example to posterity that men, when they have surrendered themselves to Fortune, forget even their very natures." (Curt. 3.2.18) Ironically, the Macedonian king will unwittingly avenge Charidemus' death, yet the latter's warning to Darius is also later pertinent to Alexander. Darius feels remorse after Charidemus' execution; Alexander later regrets the deaths of Cleitus (8.2.2–11) and Callisthenes (8.8.23). Ironically, too, like Sophocles' Creon or Shakespeare's King Lear, Darius learns the consequences of his actions too late. Alexander, in contrast, is not cast in such a tragic mold.

Curtius' treatment of the episode should be compared with the only other surviving account, that of Diodorus (17.30.2– 7).[8] In Diodorus, as in Curtius, the story takes place after the death of Memnon. However, the setting is different in the former; Darius calls a council of war rather than displaying his forces. Darius' courtiers urge him to take personal command, but Charidemus, described as a "comrade-in-arms" of Philip, advises Darius to divide his army and appoint a proven commander for a detachment of one hundred thousand men, one-third of which should include Greek mercenaries.[9] Darius was rather inclined to favor Charidemus' argument, but the king's nobles opposed Charidemus. They cast suspicion on the Athenian. Charidemus, angered by their attacks, immediately insults them, mocking their lack of manliness, which parallels Charidemus' advice in Curtius that Darius should hire some "real" soldiers. In Diodorus, these insults annoy Darius—blind to his own interests—to the point of ordering Charidemus' execution. Charidemus was in part to blame for his own death, because of his acid tongue (as Diodorus himself points out), but in Curtius his mistake was to forget the pride of kings. Both sources record that Charidemus shouted that an avenger was on hand, and both say Darius regretted his action, although in Diodorus, the king's sorrow results from realizing that he had lost a valuable soldier.

Some elements in Diodorus' version of the Charidemus story correspond to Curtius' treatment of a later episode, namely, the Greek merce-

---

8. Arrian mentions (1.10.4–6) that Charidemus was an Athenian general whom Alexander demanded after the sack of Thebes and subsequently ordered into exile. Charidemus took refuge at Darius' court, but Arrian is silent on any other details. Moreover, in Arrian (2.6.3 ff.), Amyntas, son of Antiochus (cf. Berve, 2:58), serves the same Herodotean warning function as Charidemus.

9. Cf. Diod. 17.30.2 with Welles, 201 n. 2; but see G.S. Shrimpton, "Theopompus' Treatment of Philip in the Philippica," *Phoenix* 31 (1977): 133.

naries' counsel (3.8.2) prior to Issus, particularly the suggestion that Darius divide his army and hence the subsequent Persian suspicion. Yet Curtius' and Diodorus' accounts are still close enough on the Charidemus story to suggest a common source, which may have been Cleitarchus.[10] Heckel might be right to suggest that Diodorus' account is closer to the original version; Curtius very likely adapted his source to suit a literary theme with added contemporary implication for the historian's own audience. At a later point, he blended the warning of Diodorus' Charidemus (17.30.2), perhaps representing Cleitarchus' version, with that of the Greek mercenaries, brought by Thymondas. The latter story probably derived from Ptolemy; in Curtius, the mercenaries, echoing the advice given by Amyntas in Arrian (2.6.3) and Plutarch (*Alex.* 20.1–4), urge that Darius return to the spacious plains of Mesopotamia or, if he disapproves of that plan, at least divide his forces, lest the entire strength of his kingdom fall under the one stroke of *fortuna*.[11]

Both the march-past of Persian forces and Curtius' context for the Charidemus episode recall the famous incident of the exiled Spartan king Demaratus and his advice to Xerxes in Herodotus (7.101–5). Of course, Demaratus was not executed for his equally blunt exposition, which is, in effect, a virtual celebration of the Spartan ethos; nevertheless, as Jürgen Blänsdorf argued, Curtius may have owed a considerable debt to Herodotus in the composition of this episode. However, as Heckel noted, Curtius was simply attempting to impart some Herodotean coloring and would not distort details beyond necessity.[12] Moreover, Charidemus' remarks on the tough austerity of the Macedonians as opposed to the softness of the Persians, along with similar sentiments Cleitus later expresses (8.1.30–37), are common enough topoi.[13]

Curtius' creativity builds the Charidemus episode into a statement on *regnum*. Charidemus, the antithesis of the subservient *purpurati*, exercises *libertas,* which in this context means the right to free speech. One should note that *parrhesia* is a prominent aspect in Diodorus' version and

---

10. See Heckel, *AClass* 37 (1994): 67–78.
11. See Bosworth, *HCA,* 1:202; Atkinson, *Curtius* i, 193–94.
12. J. Blänsdorf, "Herodot bei Curtius Rufus," *Hermes* 99 (1971): 11–24; Waldemar Heckel, "One More Herodotean Reminiscence in Curtius Rufus," *Hermes* 107 (1979): 122–23.
13. Cf. Hdt. 9.122; Arrian 5.4.5; Livy 9.19.10–11. All three sources stress that hardy men are considered better fighters than those who live luxuriously—a fate that befell the Persians once they became dominant. On *truphe* as a Hellenistic motif, see A. Passerini, "La τρυφή nella storiografia ellenistica," *SIFC* 11 (1934): 35–56.

may have originated with Cleitarchus. But for Curtius and his age, the theme also had particular relevance. One might recall Tacitus *Annals* 14.12.1, where dissentient silence is interpreted as *libertas;* however, Thrasea Paetus' act of walking out of the Senate also earns censure from Tacitus. Within that context, Tacitus interprets Thrasea Paetus' *libertas* as dangerous to himself and futile. Plutarch was likewise concerned with the limits of free speech. In his treatise on how to tell a flatterer from a friend (*Mor.* 1.48E f.), Plutarch's basic premise is that one negative aspect of self-love is its tendency to cloud self-judgment. Yet he is also aware (1.66B) that within certain contexts, frankness can be as harmful as flattery and therefore should only be exercised at the appropriate time.[14]

Diametrically opposed to the concept of *libertas/parrhesia* is the power of the absolute ruler. The king's power can only be governed by his own sense of responsibility, which in Curtius sometimes fails Darius and later Alexander. Seneca warns Nero in the *De clementia* (1.8.5) that the anger of the *princeps* will invariably affect all those around him, "because you cannot strike anyone else, unless whatever happens to be around him is shaken too."[15] The implication of this blatant statement of power is that all *libertas* must come from the king. It is dangerous to speak one's own mind, even if one believes the advice is for the sovereign's good, as Charidemus, Cleitus, Callisthenes, and Gobares do in Curtius' history; servility, borne out of the need to survive, perpetuates a cycle of flattery and *licentia regni*. When freedom of speech results in punishment, it produces flattery to win the favor of whoever or whatever holds power. Ironically, in Curtius, Darius himself will later express a similar principle, in his rebuke to his courtiers over the advice of the Greek mercenaries.

Thus, in summary, the Charidemus episode is important for several aspects: as a statement on *regnum* and its inevitable conflict with *libertas* and *fides;* as an example of how Curtius may adapt his sources to suit a literary idea and for its irony, both on the simple level of Charidemus' warning about his avenger; and as a signpost for what Alexander will do. Finally, Curtius is clearly in tune with first-century political attitudes, analyzed by Seneca and expressed so forcefully by other imperial authors, such as Tacitus and Plutarch.

---

14. Cf. Plut. *Mor.* 1.67E, 1.68D, 1.70E.
15. Cf. Suet. *Gaius* 29.1.

Alexander at Tarsus

The episode of Alexander's illness at Tarsus complements the Charidemus incident in that it demonstrates Alexander's treatment of one of his retainers.[16] Having passed through the Cilician Gates, the king arrived at the city of Tarsus. The river Cydnus, noteworthy for its extreme cold, flowed through the middle of the town. Alexander—hot, dusty, and just as concerned about his image as Darius, but in a different sense—stripped off in full view of his army, and, "thinking that it would also be fitting if he should show that he was contented with care of his body that was simple and readily at hand, he jumped into the river." This particular explanation for Alexander's plunge is unique, but Curtius is no worse than Arrian or Justin in trying to elucidate why Alexander jumps into a frigid and potentially harmful stream. Undoubtedly, Curtius wants to stress the king's qualities as a commander in that he is tough enough to bathe in the icy cold water, in much the same way that both Livy and Sallust emphasized the self-abnegation in a military context of Hannibal and Catiline. Curtius also draws an effective contrast between the description of Darius' elaborate attire and Alexander's simplicity, which reminds his audience of Charidemus' comments and his own assessment of the Macedonian army (3.3.26). However, Alexander's swim almost cost him his life, since he collapsed with a chill shortly after entering the water.[17]

Fides and *pietas* are prominent motifs in Curtius' treatment of this episode; but this time the king is placed in a position of having to trust his very life to one of his followers. Curtius introduces Philip, Alexander's family doctor, at 3.6.1. There Philip, an Acarnanian, is described as "excessively devoted" [*admodum fidus*] to Alexander, since he had looked after his health from boyhood and loved him, not just as a king, but as an *alumnus* (foster son). Such a self-contained story is a favorite technique in Curtius. It marks the next section by checking the pace of the narrative and provides the reader with some vital background information.[18] Philip is not just a well-known doctor but a faithful family retainer of long standing. The king could expect the same degree of *fides*

---

16. In general, see N. Holzberg's analysis, *WJA* 14 (1988): 185–201.
17. Cf. Arrian, 2.4.7–11; J. 11.8.3–9; Diod. 17.31.4–6; Plut. *Alex.* 19.2–5. On the variant details, see Atkinson, *Curtius* i, 163–69.
18. See Atkinson, *Curtius* i, 151. The Argead family also used female members of noble families to look after royal children (cf. Curt. 8.1.21; Arrian 4.9.3). In Curtius, Philip is mentioned only once more, at 4.6.17.

from him that a Roman noble would expect from a loyal family client. One might compare Arrian's version of the story (2.4.8), where Philip is described as being greatly trusted in medical matters and respected for his military prowess, and Diodorus' brief account of him (17.31.5) as "Philip the Acarnanian." Curtius wants to stress the family link and Philip's loyalty and dependency.

The *fides* and *pietas* dilemma surfaces at 3.6.4 f. as the king ponders alternative choices of action. By giving Alexander an inward soliloquy, Curtius uses a favorite device of rhetoricians for representing mental turmoil.[19] He is faced with the problem of having to trust either his doctor, who has promised to cure him with a potion that he is not to drink until the third day, or his "most faithful courtier" *[fidissimus purpuratorum]* (Curt. 3.6.4), Parmenion. Curtius has already informed us (3.5.16) that Darius had decreed he would reward the slayer of Alexander; while the king waits for his medicine, Parmenion warns him in a letter that Philip had been bribed by Darius to poison him. In fact, Alexander knows there is really only one choice—to trust Philip. If he followed Parmenion's advice, there was a good chance he would die from the sickness anyway, and hence he would be a victim of his own timidity (*metus noster* [my own fear], Curt. 3.6.6). He would die if Philip proved disloyal, but if he were poisoned, the doctor himself probably would not live for very long. This fact is very clearly brought out at 3.6.10, when Philip says, *servatus a me vitam mihi dederis* [saved by me, you will have given me life].[20] Such a statement anticipates the fear of another physician, Critobulus, who removes the Malli arrow from his king only after a command from Alexander himself (9.5.25 f.). Within such a context, the comment of Paulus of Aegina (6.88.5) becomes especially pertinent. He recommends that a physician should withhold surgery if a missile penetrates a vital organ; any attempt to remove the object would not help the patient and would only expose the doctor to the abuse of laymen. If one's patient was a king, the chances of abuse or even death for the physician were all the greater. Indeed, another noteworthy example is the fate of the unfortunate doctor Glaucias, who failed to save his patient Hephaestion and was crucified by a distraught Alexander.[21] But in trusting Philip, Alexander would be seen to show *fides* toward an equally *fidissimus* family friend.

In comparison, trusting Parmenion would contain too much risk.

---

19. See McQueen, 31.
20. Cf. Plut. *Alex.* 19.8; the doctor vehemently protests his innocence.
21. Plut. *Alex.* 72.2; cf. Arrian 7.14.4.

Alexander's conclusion at 3.6.6 that "it was better to die from another's crime [alieno scelere]" can refer to one of two crimes: on the one hand, Philip's potential crime; on the other, Parmenion's—by putting Alexander into danger, even though to all appearances, he was trying to keep the king from danger. This interpretation is also supported by Philip's comment at 3.6.11. Another inference that can be drawn is that if Alexander rejected Philip's help and still lived, he would owe *gratia* to Parmenion. The general would undoubtedly take some credit for saving his king's life, even though the doctor's innocence or guilt would be impossible to prove. For Alexander to be under obligation to such a powerful Macedonian *nobilis* would not be a desirable state of affairs. Ironically, considerations of *gratia* later persuade the king to persecute Philotas, when he is reminded by Craterus (6.8.7–8) in a sophistic argument (which has no parallel in the other sources) that the king cannot show such a great concession as a pardon to Philotas. Such an act of *clementia* would place both Philotas and his father in a position of intolerable *gratia*. Cato at Utica faced a similar dilemma in relation to Julius Caesar's mercy and decided suicide was the appropriate action to preserve his *dignitas*.[22] The role of Parmenion in the Philip story does not appear in Diodorus. The other Alexander historians, together with Valerius Maximus (3.8.ext.6), use the story as an example of Alexander's courage and trust in his friends: the sole exception is Justin.

The last significant aspect of the Alexander at Tarsus incident is the reaction of the Macedonian soldiers when they hear of the king's recovery. They hasten to grasp Philip's right hand. Curtius then digresses (3.6.17–20) to explain the soldiers' intense affection for their king. Not only is Alexander the favorite of *fortuna*, but his exploits are enhanced by his youth and his impressive qualities as a *dux*, "bodily exercise among them, attire and bearing differing little from the ordinary citizen, a soldier's energy" (3.6.19). These characteristics make Alexander *carus* (beloved) and *venerandus* (venerated). Moreover, the reference to his military qualities and the affection of his soldiers recall the reason that he had jumped into the Cydnus in the first place (3.5.2), out of concern for his military image. Such recapitulation enforces another major theme of the *Historiae*: Alexander's ability to impress and hold the loyalty of his men. Thus the episode appears to end on a very positive note for the king:

---

22. On the implications of *beneficia*, see Seneca *Ep.* 81.31–32; Atkinson, *Curtius* ii, 223. On Cato, see E. Wistrand, *Caesar and Contemporary Roman Society* (Goteburg, 1979).

he has shown trust in a close friend's advice, which Darius had failed to show toward Charidemus. Yet underneath the image is a very cool and calculating king. The Sisines episode, shortly following that of Alexander at Tarsus, shows only too clearly the *dissimulatio* and *vis* Alexander can exercise when he deems it necessary.

Sisines

Sisines, a Persian noble, appears at 3.7.11 in an incident unique to Curtius.[23] Again, a self-contained story precedes the account. Sisines had previously been sent to Philip by the governor of Egypt but had been persuaded to defect. He was held to be among Alexander's faithful allies. While Alexander's forces are camped at Issus, a Cretan soldier (traditionally, Cretans often received hostile press)[24] hands Sisines a letter that contains a message from Nabarzanes, urging him, in ambiguous terms, to assassinate Alexander. Sisines, described by Curtius as an innocent man, tried many times, without success, to inform the king, who was busy with war preparations. He waited and earned the suspicion of harboring criminal intent, as Alexander already knew about the letter and was deliberately testing the Persian's loyalty. Alexander has Sisines murdered—by the Cretans. If Alexander had truly trusted Sisines, he would have informed him that he knew about Nabarzanes' letter, but straightforwardness is not always the method of kings.

Certainly Curtius' narrative carries a hint of Roman imperial intrigue, a point noted by Atkinson.[25] In Tacitus (*Ann.* 2.42.2–3), Tiberius enticed Archelaus, via a letter from his mother, to Rome and death. Sisines' status was probably closer to a foreign *cliens* (client) than a guest-friend, hence Curtius uses *socius* rather than *hospes* or *amicus*. At 6.5.1–5, Alexander accords Artabazus the kind treatment befitting an old guest-friend, but in addition to the long-standing *xenia* between the Argead

---

23. On Sisines, see Berve, 2:710. The man was a historical figure, but it is not certain whether the same individual is at issue in all the sources. Arrian (1.25.3–4) connects a Sisines with the plot of Alexander Lyncestes, while Justin (11.7.1) claims that Alexander learned of the conspiracy from "a captive," presumably a Persian. In Diodorus (17.32.1), Olympias warns the king about Alexander Lyncestes.
24. See Atkinson, *Curtius* i, 184.
25. Ibid., 185.

kings and the satrap's family (which is historically attested), it is important to note that by then Alexander had adopted Persian costume and protocol.[26]

In summary, the Sisines episode, along with offering a balance to Alexander's behavior at Tarsus and a contrast to Darius' treatment of his Greek mercenaries, is a significant example of Alexander's methods. Whether the king believed he had good cause to suspect Sisines or not is irrelevant; the king casually removed a potential threat. Also, the Sisines incident heralds a major episode in book 6, the Philotas affair, where Alexander's statecraft is used against his own Companions. Sisines' nondisclosure of the letter (despite good intentions) is later paralleled by Philotas' failure to inform Alexander of a plot against him. In the latter episode, the irony is all the more sharpened by Alexander's pledge of his right hand to Philotas (6.7.35) as a sign of renewed *fides*.

Darius and the Greek Mercenaries

The incident of Darius and the Greek mercenaries, reported at 3.8.1–8, is appropriately juxtaposed with the Sisines episode. Again, as in Diodorus, the mercenaries' advice causes a hostile response from Darius' *purpurati*. As indicated earlier, Darius' rebuke, in *oratio obliqua,* has a sardonic undertone that, contrary to certain opinion, is probably deliberate irony on Curtius' part.[27] The historian describes Darius here with nearly the same epithet ("upright and mild") that he used prior to the Charidemus incident, but this time Darius appears to behave wisely. He respects the free speech of both Greeks and Persians. The Great King says that no individual should be executed for offering idiotic advice, because this would mean that no one would offer honest counsel at all, "if to have advised were dangerous."

However, although the principle is the same, there is a considerable difference between destroying one individual, in a fit of pique, and slaughtering a whole company, especially if one is relying on them. As Curtius says, the mercenaries were Darius' "principal and almost only hope." Darius can mouth platitudes when it suits him. Curtius will also use Darius' words in another future ironic contrast. At 5.9.12, after

---

26. On the *xenia* between Artabazus' family and the Argead house, see Berve, 2:152.
27. Cf. Heckel, *AClass* 37 (1994): 67–78, who argues that Curtius' structure creates an "unfortunate contradiction."

Nabarzanes has urged that Darius abdicate, Artabazus reminds Darius of his own sentiments about bearing stupid advice with patience.

The last part of Darius' speech, 3.8.11, is pure bravado. Darius likens Alexander to a wild beast and ironically refers to the Macedonians as cowards. However, his sentiments also provide a transition to the preliminaries of Issus and the narrative of the battle itself. Since the contrast between Alexander and Darius as generals is notably marked during the battle, it is worthwhile to examine Curtius' depiction of Alexander the commander before discussing the actual confrontation between the Macedonian and the Persian.

Alexander *Dux:* The Battle of Issus

Alexander's superiority as a commander is heralded long before the Battle of Issus. In his account of the siege of Celaenae, Curtius contrasts the young king's insight and his dynamic force with Darius' complacency. The Great King does not even send aid to his loyal, besieged subjects. Additional elements of the Alexander *dux* portrait, notably, as we have seen, the king's *felicitas* and his austerity, appear prior to the Battle of Issus. Other features include his *pietas*—which he displays at Soli (3.7.3–4; cf. Arrian 2.5.8) by proclaiming a holiday and games in recognition of the vows made for his recovery—as well as his strategic acumen. He is willing to take the advice of Parmenion (3.7.8–10) over the choice of battleground, in contrast with Darius, who for all his noble sentiments about speaking freely, does not actually heed the warning of the Greek mercenaries. The Parmenion and Alexander conflict as a motif, although prominent in Arrian, is given different treatment in Curtius. This aspect, significant for what it reveals of each historian's approach, will be discussed at a later point in this chapter. All signs point to Alexander's victory—even the king's moment of unease (3.8.20–21; cf. J. 11.9.1) only serves to underscore the value he places on *gloria*.

Curtius' narrative of the preliminaries to the Battle of Issus (3.8.13 ff.) is not without problems. In particular, he is vague about the geography of the place.[28] After apparently accepting Parmenion's advice, it appears that Alexander left Issus. For instance, Sisines is killed *in agmine* [on the march] (3.7.15). The king arrives at the entrance to Syria just as Darius, coming through the Amanican Gates, slips in rearward of Alexander and captures his wounded men who had been left behind at Issus. Alexander

---

28. Cf. Curt. 3.7.10, 3.7.15, 3.8.13–24. Arrian (2.5–7.3), is more lucid on the movements of Darius and Alexander.

is forced to retrace his steps: the battle is still fought within narrow quarters. Curtius' phrase back at 3.7.10, *angustias saltus* [mountain narrows], was probably intended to refer to the region as a whole, but Alexander's movements are not satisfactorily explained. Although Curtius describes the composition of each army and the movement of its troops (3.9–11), his account is not as detailed (or as helpful militarily) as Arrian's (2.8–11). The former's chief interest does not lie in precise reconstruction of the battle: rather, his flair lies in dramatic image.[29]

However, the credibility of Curtius' account is not an issue here. What emerges, as indicated earlier, is the contrast between Alexander and Darius as generals. In comparison, Arrian comments that the Persian Empire was destined to fall and accordingly presents Darius as a lackluster and spiritless leader (2.10.2, 2.11.4). In Curtius (3.8.22–24; cf. Arrian 2.8.1), despite a potentially dangerous situation, Alexander (after his momentary lapse of confidence) is shown to be a calm commander, who orders his men to eat and then advance steadily on Darius.

Even though Darius' strategy, indicated at 3.8.27–28, is sound, the Persian army itself is disorganized and chaotic. Unlike Alexander, Darius cannot present a united front. The superior military discipline of the Macedonians is further emphasized at 3.10.3, when Alexander leads his men forward, checking their advance by a movement of his hand. At this point (3.10.4–10), Alexander gives his prebattle speech, which in Arrian (2.7.3–9) had occurred some time earlier and was spoken only to the king's officers.

The oration has features in common with both Arrian and Justin (11.9.4–6): notably, in all three historians, Alexander addresses the three national groups of his army in terms that would appeal to each. There are also considerable differences, especially between Arrian and Curtius. In the former, Alexander praises himself as a commander and elaborates on the strategic advantages the Macedonians enjoy. As Atkinson has noted,[30] the main variation in Curtius' speech is Alexander's emphasis on forthcoming conquests. While this may be due to Roman influence, Alexander's quest for domination over *totius orbis* (the whole world) is central to the historian's characterization of the king. It becomes an increasingly important motif of the portrait of Alexander as *dux,* particularly in the second pentad, where the king's speeches reflect his imperialist aims.[31]

---

29. Cf. Diod. 17.33–34 with Hammond, *THA* , 117 f.
30. Atkinson, *Curtius* i, 222–25.
31. Cf. Curt. 6.3, 7.7.10–20, 8.13–14 (Scythians), 9.2.11.

There are also conventional elements in Curtius' battle narrative; for instance, prebattle speeches and war cries are common in traditional battle scenes.[32] Also, the Persian nobles fall with their wounds to the front (cf. Diod. 17.33.7), which is a customary acknowledgment of bravery. In Sallust (*Bell. Cat.* 61.2–3), Catiline and his followers die in such a manner, and they of course were Roman citizens, not slaves or barbarians. However, the dramatic and vivid descriptions of hand-to-hand fighting are the key elements in Curtius' account. The Persians open the battle with a cavalry charge to the Macedonian left, which Alexander counters by reinforcing his wings. The description then shifts to the heavy infantry engaged in a rugby-like scrum.

> Then indeed there was great carnage; for the two lines were thus so intermingled that their arms clashed against arms and they directed their blades at each other's faces. Nor were the weak or the cowardly allowed to give way, foot to foot, as if they were fighting one against one, standing in the same spot until they might make room for themselves by conquest. Only then, therefore, they were moving ahead, when they had struck down the enemy. (3.11.5–6)

The historian introduces a decisive cavalry charge led by Alexander (3.11.7 f.; cf. Diod. 17.33.5 f.). A significant difference between Curtius' text and Arrian's is that the former seems to place the charge earlier and makes the clash of the two kings almost a reality. Arrian's cavalry charge (2.10.3 f.) occurs in a different context, and his description of Darius, who turns tail as soon as his left wing is routed (2.11.4), portrays the Great King as a craven leader. One may note Arrian's own comment later in his history (5.18.4) when he contrasts Porus' military bravery with Darius' cowardice. Also, the characterization of Alexander is reminiscent of the critique of the king recorded by Nearchus (6.13.4). Curtius emphasizes the *virtus* of individuals, such as Oxathres (3.11.8–10), but especially Alexander himself:

> Alexander was pursuing the obligations of no more a commander than a soldier, seeking the rich glory [opimum decus] of having slain the king; for Darius, carried on high in his chariot, was promi-

---

32. For war cries, see Curt. 3.10.1. Cf. Diod. 17.33.4; Livy 22.47.1; Verg. *Aen.* 9.504; Jos. *Bell. Jud.* 3.250; Atkinson, *Curtius* i, 215.

nent, a great incentive to his own men to protect him and to the enemy to attack.

The king's desire to slay Darius personally is also implied by Diodorus, and certainly history testified to the leaders of respective armies trying to slaughter each other. According to Xenophon (*Anab.* 1.8.26–27), Cyrus attempted to kill his own brother, Artaxerxes, at the battle of Cunaxa; likewise, the Theban general Pelopidas, in a fit of rage, made a personal attack on Alexander, the tyrant of Pherae (Plut. *Pelop.* 32), and paid for his recklessness with his life. However, Atkinson argues that Curtius has played down the desire for personal *gloria* on Alexander's part and has instead presented the king (as Livy or Caesar depict a Roman general) as a leader who gives personal moral and physical support to his men.[33] While this may be so—Alexander is forced to shame his men into action at the Sudracae fortress (9.4.30)—Curtius is not reticent about stressing Alexander's personal thirst for glory elsewhere. The image of Alexander seeking the *spolia opima*—the personal glory a Roman commander won by slaying the enemy's commander with his own hands—is reminiscent of Romulus at Livy 1.10.7. As we have seen, parallels between Livy's Romulus and Curtius' Alexander occur elsewhere in the *Historiae:* at 7.4.40 Curtius uses the unusual expression *decus opimum* to describe Erigyius' victory over the rebel satrap Satibarzanes. The term is used only by Curtius but was clearly borrowed from Livy.[34]

Alexander's *vis* and the courage of Darius' nobles, "slain by a glorious death before the eyes of their king" [ante oculos regis egregia morte defuncti] (Curt. 10.11.9), is intended to provide a striking contrast with Darius' cowardice. Not only have the nobles confounded the image of softness, with which they had been associated, but they have died trying to protect Darius. Yet he is not worthy of such *fides*.

Curtius' attitude toward the Great King is very clear; Darius, having abandoned his chariot, "shamefully" [indecore] casts away his royal insignia, lest they betray him in his flight (3.11.11). The battle quickly becomes a rout, and the Persians' camp is overrun by the victorious Macedonians.[35] The Roman historian does not miss the opportunity for a poignant description of Macedonian brutality and of the plight of the

---

33. Atkinson, *Curtius* i, 229–30
34. See chap. 2.
35. See Curt. 3.11.19–27; Diod. 17.34.8; Arrian 2.11.7–10.

Persian women. No doubt this description would hold contemporary audience appeal, but as such a scene appears even more graphically in Diodorus (17.35), Curtius has not overindulged himself. Darius' family is taken captive. His cowardice is again enforced toward the end of the battle narrative; ironically, the Great King's family members bravely assert that they are not captive while he still lives, when he is already far away from them. Similarly, his discarded cloak will cause his family to believe him dead, and, in turn, their grief and loyalty will affect Alexander.[36]

Yet book 3 concludes with a reference to Darius. The sack of Damascus (3.12.27 f.) is historically important in that Alexander seized a considerable hoard of money, and it is thematically significant for three reasons. Parmenion is depicted as a competent general, while the emphasis on the waste of war (3.13.9–11) occurs again in later books. However, the major motif is the loyalty Darius still commands. Earlier in the narrative, the inhabitants of Celaenae remained loyal; here the governor of Damascus betrays the city to Parmenion (cf. Arrian 2.11.10; Plut. *Alex.* 24.1–3) but, in turn, is himself killed by a faithful associate of Darius (3.13.17). Various thematic signposts, such as the slashing of the Gordian knot and the digression at 3.12.18–22, herald the confirmation of Alexander's supremacy. But despite the ironic tone of the opening line of book 4, the extent to which ground covered in Darius' retreat is still under Persian control foreshadows another confrontation.

Book 4: Diplomacy between Alexander and Darius

The rhetorical flourish of the opening sentence in book 4, displays an effective irony and contrasting images.

> Darius, king of an army only lately so great, who had entered battle on high in his chariot, rather more in the fashion of celebrating a triumph rather than waging a war, was fleeing through places—which he had once filled with nearly countless forces—now empty, void, an enormous wasteland.

The historian neatly reminds his audience of the *eminens* image he has used previously (3.11.7, 3.2.10), while the reference to the solitary wastes and Darius' once-vast numbers emphasizes the great loss the king

---

36. See chap. 4, 124–25.

has suffered; simultaneously, he recalls the Great King's extravagant confidence at the march-past in Babylon, which makes his present situation all the more pointed.

Within this context, Alexander, while he is at Marathus on the Phoenician coast, receives the first peace offer from Darius. The traditions on the negotiations are problematic, varying not only on the number of offers but in details of location and chronology and in contents. Justin and Curtius mention three attempts at settlement, Diodorus and Arrian refer to two, and Plutarch only acknowledges one.[37] Moreover, any cited correspondence in historiography invariably questions the authenticity of the original documentation and other related issues.[38] In Curtius all three exchanges should be viewed as a composite whole, with each providing insight into the diplomatic skills of the two kings and the historian's characterization.

Darius' first offer (4.1.7–10) is arrogant in tone. His second, after Alexander's siege of Tyre (4.5.1–8), albeit an admonition on the transitory nature of *fortuna*, shows a marked desire to grant concessions. His third attempt, prior to the final confrontation at Arbela (4.11.1–21) and supposedly initiated by reports of Alexander's *continentia*, is conciliatory, perhaps even humble. From an offer that was at best a bluff and one that he probably did not expect to work, Darius' overtures for a peace settlement become genuine and, for a Persian king, increasingly generous. Alexander remains confident and adroit throughout all the negotiations.

The first offer of a settlement is also recorded by Diodorus (17.39), Justin (11.12), and Arrian (2.14), although only the latter corroborates Curtius in locating the proposal at Marathus. According to Diodorus, Alexander kept the genuine letter from Darius a secret and substituted a forgery in his own interests. The contents of Darius' real letter in Diodorus is similar to the second offer he makes in Curtius and Justin.[39]

---

37. J. 11.12; Diod. 17.54.1–6; Arrian 2.25.1–3; Plut. *Alex.* 29.4.
38. Alexander's correspondence with Darius is a well-explored area: see W.B. Kaiser, "Der Brief Alexanders des Grosse an Dareios nach der Schlacht bei Issos" (Diss. Mainz, 1956); G.T. Griffith, "The Letter of Darius at Arrian 2.14," *PCPS* 14 (1968): 33–48; Seibert, 102; E. Mikrojannikis, "The Diplomatic Contacts between Alexander III and Darius III," in *Ancient Macedonia* (Thessaloníki, 1970) 1:103–108; Atkinson, *Curtius* i, 278 f.; Bosworth, *HCA*, 1:227–29; R. Bernhardt, "Zu den Verhandlungen zwischen Dareios und Alexander nach der Schlacht bei Issos," *Chiron* 18 (1988): 181–98; E.F. Bloedow, "Diplomatic Negotiations between Darius and Alexander: Historical Implications of the First Phase at Marathus in Phoenicia in 333/332 B.C.," *AHB* 9, nos. 3/4 (1995): 93–110.
39. Schwartz, *RE* 4 (1879): 1884, argued that there were three attempts at a peace settlement in Diodorus; cf. Hamilton, *Plutarch*, 76.

Curtius' text is closer to Arrian's, suggesting on this occasion the use of a common tradition; also, each quotes the content of Darius' letter indirectly and highlights Alexander's response in *oratio recta*. The former places more emphasis on Alexander's reaction before revealing the contents of the letter: "he was extremely offended by its arrogant tone" [quibus ut superbe scriptis vehementer offensus est] (Curt. 4.1.7). Curtius' use of *superbe* is significant. Darius has demonstrated arrogance before; before the end of book 4, Alexander will have also shown *superbia*, in relation to a defeated enemy and the political sensibilities of his Companions.

Both historians underscore Alexander's sophistry in the justification of his invasion. Darius' accession is presented as illegal; in Arrian (2.14.4–9), the Macedonian king claims Darius murdered his predecessor Arses with the help of Bagoas and seized the throne. However, in Curtius, Alexander says that Darius has assumed the same name as Darius the Great: this statement implies that the present Darius is not worthy of the title and at the same time links him to the destruction Darius I and Xerxes caused in Greece. In both accounts Alexander blames Darius as the aggressor, and likewise common to both is the former's accusation that the Great King or his agents were responsible for Philip's assassination. Arrian has Alexander demand that Darius should already acknowledge him as lord of Asia; in Curtius he arrogantly demands that henceforth Darius should remember he is "writing not only to a king but to your king" (Curt. 4.1.10).

Moreover, Alexander's statement "I know both how to conquer and how to treat the conquered" provides a yardstick for Curtius' audience to measure Alexander's *regnum*. This parameter is also enforced prior to the last peace offer: Darius, impressed by Alexander's *continentia*, prays that if his rule is fated to end, then his kingdom should pass to none other than this enemy and victor who was so just and merciful (4.10.34). Alexander's worthiness to rule is a recurrent theme that was probably also emphasized in Curtius' account of the Great King's death in book 5.

Finally, the motif of *fides* or its Greek equivalent *pistis*, in the sense of giving and receiving pledges, is a dominant aspect of both versions. Also like Arrian, Curtius presents both kings as unwilling to see each other as equals; rather, each endeavors to assert his superiority over the other. In Roman terms, in any *amicitia* one party or the other will assume an inferior status, a situation that neither king could be expected to tolerate. It is true that *amicitia* was sufficiently ambiguous as to encompass both equals and unequals. Darius does not use the demeaning *cliens*, but in his patronizing offer of *societas* (alliance) and money (4.1.8), he clearly wants to put Alexander on a lower footing.[40] Alexander emphasizes his own status from the outset, addressing himself as "King Alexander to Darius," which historically, he may have been unlikely to do, as he customarily used his name without a title.[41] Furthermore, Darius should come to Alexander as a suppliant (4.1.13; cf. Arrian 2.14.3, 8–9).

Thus both historians stress Alexander's superior diplomacy or "one-upmanship" in the Marathus correspondence. It satisfies Arrian. In the next attempt at settlement, Arrian (2.25.1–3) is more concerned with Alexander's ambition as opposed to Parmenion's conservatism. Only Curtius elaborates the differences between Alexander and Darius as kings throughout all three instances of negotiation. Curtius' thematic use of *fortuna* in Darius' second attempt at a settlement was discussed in chapter 4; however, some additional points warrant further comment.

Darius attempts another peace settlement after Alexander's important victory at Tyre (4.5.1–8), when, having gained control of the Phoenician fleet, the Macedonian was in an even stronger position. This time the Great King offered Alexander his daughter, Stateira, in marriage and was prepared to concede all the territory between the Hellespont and the Halys River. Historically, such an offer from an Achaemenid king would have been unprecedented; in Curtius, Alexander's reply was that Darius was merely offering him his own property. Instead, he recalls and reverses Darius' phrase in his first letter (4.1.8); sovereignty of the empire would be settled on the field of battle (4.5.7). His confidence in his own superiority is again very evident.

According to Curtius and Justin, Darius' third offer (second if we accept Diodorus' compressed account) occurred prior to the Battle of Arbela. In Diodorus, the offer is made before the death of Darius' wife, whereas in the other two accounts, Darius made a final attempt at peace in response to Alexander's respectful treatment of the Great King's deceased spouse. Again, in Roman terms, the attempt was motivated by Darius' recognition of Alexander's *pietas*; thus he was prepared to offer *amicitia* on an apparently equal basis, conceding all territory between the Hellespont and Euphrates, a marriage alliance, thirty thousand talents in

---

40. On *amicitia*, see R.P. Saller, *Personal Patronage under the Early Empire* (Cambridge, 1982), 11 f.

41. Whether Macedonian kings used the title *basileus* is controversial; see N.G.L. Hammond, "The King and the Land in Macedonia," *CQ* 38 (1988): 382–91, esp. 390.

gold for the return of his family, and even his own son Ochus as a hostage for his *fides*. However, Alexander shrewdly realizes that if he accepts peace, it will be Darius' victory. His response (4.11.18) is to remind the envoys of Darius' assassination attempts; only recently his men had intercepted letters from the Persian king that urged the Greek soldiers to murder Alexander (4.10.16). He claims Darius is "not an honorable enemy" [non iustus hostis] (4.11.18)—an ironic reversal of the Great King's words (4.10.34) when he heard of Alexander's *clementia*. The contest for empire can now only be decided on the field of battle, and "each [contestant] will have what the fortune of tomorrow [proximae lucis fortuna] shall allot to him" (4.11.21). The expression "fortune of tomorrow" is rather reminiscent of Vergil *Aeneid* 10.107, where Jupiter announces that destiny will decide the outcome between the Trojans and the Rutulians. Since Curtius uses Vergilian imagery and expressions elsewhere, an allusion to the poetic parallel offered by Aeneas and Turnus might be intentional and calculated for the audience's appreciation. However, within Curtius' own thematic development, the explicit reference to *fortuna* enhances and foreshadows the inevitability of Alexander's success; he remains Darius' superior.

It is worthwhile, at this point, to consider Arrian's account of Darius' final peace offer, which occurs while Alexander is still besieging Tyre (2.25.1–3). The content of this offer is similar to the versions already mentioned: concession of territory west of the Euphrates to the Aegean, marriage to Darius' daughter, and friendship and alliance, but ten thousand, rather than thirty thousand, talents. However, Arrian is more interested in the story for its famous sequel—namely, Parmenion's advice that if he were Alexander, he would accept the settlement, and Alexander's reply that he would do the same if he were Parmenion—which sharply differentiates the personalities of the two men. One is cautious, old, conservative; the other is young, brash, and dynamic. This contrast between Parmenion and Alexander is a favorite motif of Arrian's, and whatever its source, it is always at Parmenion's expense.[42]

The contrast between Alexander and his general also features in the other three versions of the final peace offer. Yet generally, in Curtius' extant first three books, the motif is not as heavily emphasized as it is in Arrian. For instance, on two occasions (3.7.8, 4.10.7) Alexander takes

---

42. See Arrian 1.13.2–7 (cf. Plut. *Alex.* 16.3), 1.18.6–91, 3.10.1–2, 3.18.2. The motif possibly originated with Callisthenes; cf. Plut. *Alex.* 33.6, and see Bosworth, *HCA*, 1:115. For other sources on Parmenion's advice to Alexander to accept Darius' offer, see Plut. *Alex.* 29.4; Curt. 4.11.10–15; Diod. 17.54.4.

Parmenion's advice; he also rejects it when he deems that strategy (4.13.1–13) or political circumstances (3.6.4 f.) warrant alternative action. Curtius is not so much trying to present Parmenion as the polar opposite of Alexander; rather, Parmenion is simply what the historian describes him as, "the most experienced among the commanders in the art of war" [peritissimus inter duces artium belli] (4.13.4).[43] However, like Darius, ultimately Parmenion is politically and militarily inferior to the Macedonian king.

Two other episodes are vivid depictions of the more somber aspects of Alexander's *regnum*. It is not surprising that book 4, as the penultimate book of the first pentad, should elaborate several important aspects of Alexander's character. Not only does the famous visit to Siwah affect the king profoundly, heralding future confrontation between himself and the Macedonian aristocracy, but his savage treatment of the defeated governor of Gaza marks a dark side of his personality that becomes increasingly prevalent during and after book 6.

Betis of Gaza

Curtius' portrait of Alexander as a man of *vis* and *ira* features in the aftermath of the siege of Tyre.[44] Although the account is dramatic and rhetorical, the historian never plays down Tyrian resistance and Macedonian casualties. Indeed, the final assault, despite the personal excellence of the king himself (4.4.11) is hard and bloody. Alexander needed a combination of luck, skill, leadership, and sheer hard work to take the city, but at Tyre's fall, he had done no more than any Roman proconsul. Even the execution of two thousand Tyrians, which is also mentioned by Diodorus (17.46.4), would not have seemed unusual to a contemporary audience, who had only to recall Varus' treatment of Jewish insurgents in 4 B.C.; he also crucified some two thousand rebels. Apart from the strategic considerations, Alexander had good cause to attack the place, owing to the Tyrians' slaughter of his heralds in violation of the unwritten *ius gentium* (law of nations) in relation to safety of envoys.[45]

---

43. Cf. Curtius' necrology of Parmenion, 7.2.33, discussed in chap. 6, 184.
44. For modern discussions of Curtius' account of the siege, see chap. 3, n. 115.
45. For Varus, see Jos. *BJ* 2.75 and *AJ* 17.295. On Roman brutality in war, see W.H. Harris, *War and Imperialism in Republican Rome, 327–70 B.C.* (Oxford, 1979), 50–53; A.J. Pomeroy, "Hannibal at Nuceria," *Historia* 38 (1989): 166 f. See also M.M. Westington, "Atrocities in Roman Warfare to 133 B.C." (Ph.D. diss., University of Chicago, 1938), which, however, I have not been able to consult.

Yet Alexander's *ira*, appropriately flagged at the beginning of the siege (4.2.5) and at the end (4.4.17), is a characteristic hallmark of the siege and is all the more prominent in the historian's account of the siege of Gaza (4.6.7–31). The historian's narrative corresponds approximately to Arrian's (2.25.4–27): only these authors treat the campaign in any detail. Diodorus (17.49.1) and Justin (11.10.14) give it cursory treatment, while Plutarch (*Alex.* 25.3–5) concentrates on two anecdotes. Also relevant to Curtius' account is the late fourth-century account of the rhetorician Hegesias, which was preserved by Dionysius of Halicarnassus (*De comp. verb.* 18 = *FGrH* 142.F.5) as an example of rhetorical and sensationalist excess—in effect, how *not* to write history.

Curtius' literary skill is evident in his introduction of Betis of Gaza (4.6.7), who is described as a man of *eximia fides* (exceptional loyalty) to his king. Yet, immediately prior to Betis' appearance (4.6.1–6), Curtius returned briefly to Darius' activities in Babylonia, particularly his plan to mobilize the vast forces of Bactria and his mistrust of its satrap, Bessus, whom he suspected of harboring treacherous intent. Thus the *fides* of Betis, who is of lesser rank than Bessus, is sharply contrasted with someone who is close to the king and who aspires to royal power. The threat of internal challenge is an inevitable consequence of kingship, especially if there is a viable, ambitious alternative and if the current *rex* provides his followers with good cause.

In the second pentad, Alexander himself faces a challenge from his aristocratic Companions. Not only has Curtius established the ground for a final confrontation between Bessus and Darius at the end of book 5, but in the contrast between Betis and Bessus, he shows the difference between *fides* and *perfidia*. Betis proves to be the more worthy servant, yet his loyalty coupled with his stubborn opposition *(contumacia)* to Alexander result in a horrific end for him. Ironically, the Gaza episode ends on the motif of *fides*. Alexander sends Amyntas back to Macedonia (4.6.31) for a massive levy of fresh troops because less confidence was felt in the loyalty of the "soldiers from the conquered nations" than in that of the soldiers from home. This comment in itself is a somewhat peculiar addition; at that time, it is unlikely that Alexander had recruited many local troops, except Phoenicians or Syrians who were used during the great sieges of 332. Since there is nothing comparable in Diodorus (17.49.1), the comment may well have been Curtius'. Yet, at 10.3.7, in the wake of the Macedonians' mutiny at Opis (or Susa in the vulgate), Alexander acknowledges the *pietas* of the Iranians toward their kings; at that stage, he is truly the sovereign of Asia.

Arrian (2.25.4) depicts Betis (Batis) as a eunuch in command of a group of Arab mercenaries; he appears as an independent ruler or tyrant, who for his own reasons decided not to surrender Gaza to Alexander.[46] Moreover, whereas Arrian explains the city's strategic importance (2.25.4–2.26.1) prior to his narrative, Curtius provides Alexander's motive, almost in passing, during his account of the siege (4.6.13). Using brief, spare phrases, the historian sketches the bare essentials of the military setting. Betis was able to defend a strongly fortified city with only a moderate force; Gaza was surrounded by light, sandy soil, which, although easy to work, bogged the wheels of the siege towers (4.6.8–9).

There are several facets to Curtius' presentation of Alexander in this episode. In addition to his consistent valor, the Roman historian emphasizes the king's superstition and his *temeritas* (rashness). As we saw earlier, *temeritas* is another key note in Alexander's characterization;[47] however, the most significant feature of Curtius' Alexander during this campaign is his rage. As the siege progressed, the king received two wounds (4.6.17, 24), which did not improve his temper; furthermore, an assassination attempt by an Arab soldier may have also increased his anger—although Curtius himself does not say so. Pace Atkinson's interpretation, the text does not specify that the Arab acted under Betis' orders; rather, the description (4.6.15) suggests he acted spontaneously.[48] Interestingly, Hegesias supplies the story that Betis employed an assassin, and other variations between Curtius and Hegesias indicate that there may have been more than one version of the tale.[49]

As soon as Betis was brought alive to Alexander (4.6.25), Curtius' first point is the king's youth (also a prominent aspect of the historian's necrology) and *insolens gaudium* (arrogant joy). Curtius openly says that the king's behavior toward Betis was not customary: he comments that on other occasions, Alexander admired *virtus*, "even in an enemy," while at 4.6.29 he remarks that already Alexander's recent fortune suggested foreign habits.

Curtius' description of Betis' response to Alexander at 4.6.27 is very significant: "He [Betis], gazing at the king with an expression that was not unterrified but defiant, said not a word in reply to his threats." This

---

46. On the historical problem of Betis' identity, see Atkinson, *Curtius* i, 334–36; Bosworth, *HCA*, 1:257–58.
47. See chap. 4, 115–16.
48. Curt. 4.6.15: *Quo conspecto Arabs quidam, Darei miles, maius fortuna sua facinus ausus*. . . . Cf. Atkinson, *Curtius* i, 343– 44.
49. Cf. Hammond, *THA*, 127–28; B. Perrin, "The Genesis and Growth of an Alexander Myth," *TAPhA* 26 (1895): 56–68.

description is the first instance of Curtius' use of *contumacia* (stubborn defiance) in terms of confrontation between the king and an individual. It features prominently in future conflicts between Alexander and his followers: at the Macedonian response to the king's claims after Siwah, during Craterus' speech indicting Philotas (6.7.3), in the description of Callisthenes (8.6.1), and finally in the description of the Macedonian army itself (10.2.10). In each of these examples, the *contumacia* of either individual or group is associated with *libertas,* but a *libertas* exercised without prudence or care, which usually results in death or punishment. Tacitus likewise highlights the dangers and futility associated with both *contumacia* and ill-advised or ostentatious *libertas,* and hence he commends his father-in-law, Agricola, (*Agr.* 42.4) for his moderate behavior and self-control out of consideration of Domitian's authority. From the point of view of the *princeps,* we might compare Trajan's attitude toward *contumacia* (Pliny *Ep.* 10.57.2), where he advises Pliny to arrest a man who had tried to ignore a previous sentence of exile, thereby flouting the authority of the court and, by extension, that of the emperor.

Betis' defiance results in his death, as Alexander's *ira,* fired by the prisoner's apparent haughtiness, turns to uncontrolled rage *(rabies).* As a defeated enemy, Betis was not entitled to any of the obligations Alexander may have felt toward his followers. Yet Alexander will honor King Porus, out of respect for his valor on the field as well as his rank. He also honors a Persian noble like Artabazus, again due to his rank, but also due to his *fides* to Darius and due to considerations of guest-friendship (6.5.1–5). He will show *clementia* to Nabarzanes out of expediency and because of the appeal of Bagoas (6.5.23). However, Alexander later hands the regicide and rival claimant Bessus over to Oxathres for execution (7.5.40 f.) and orders the crucifixion of the Sogdianian chieftain Ariamazes (7.11.28). The reason for Bessus' execution is obvious: Alexander could not afford to leave a regicide and potential threat alive, and he needed to reconcile the Persian nobility. Ariamazes' punishment, however, relates directly to the execution of Betis.[50] Unlike Porus or Artabazus or even Nabarzanes, neither of these men were of royal or high rank. More importantly in Curtius' text, each either displayed *contumacia* or openly mocked the king, thus provoking *saevitia.*

Also, Curtius' comment that already Alexander's recent fortune was suggesting foreign customs raises another theme: *superbia.* Hence one

---

50. See chap. 3, 94–95.

more point warrants consideration, namely, Alexander's actual execution of Betis. Alexander has displayed *ira* before; at Tyre and possibly, depending on Curtius' lost treatment, at the sack of Thebes. However, the king's treatment of Betis is excessive. It is the result of the same *superbia* or impulsive *licentia regni* that prompted Darius to execute Charidemus and that Alexander himself displays in the post-Darius books. The additional irony is that the king boasts that his method of killing Betis was in imitation of his ancestor Achilles (4.6.29).

Although some scholars have accepted the execution, others have dismissed Curtius' account as sensationalism.[51] Arrian does not mention such a story. Generally, his narrative is close to Curtius', although there are some variant details.[52] Yet as 2.27.5 and 7 would indicate, the siege was harder than the overall impression Arrian wishes to create. If Curtius is right, the difficulties of the siege, coming so soon as it did on the heels of Tyre, in addition to the wounding of Alexander and the defiance of Betis, seems more than sufficient to have provoked the king into a violent rage.

It is not my purpose to establish the authenticity of the incident. Curtius' thematic emphasis is clear. Alexander is already displaying the negative aspects of kingship associated with Darius. His success ensures that these are given full rein as the absolutism of his power increases. Yet the imitation of Achilles—and there were even traditions that suggested Hector was still alive, like Betis—also points to a savage inheritance.[53] Alexander's future decline is perhaps not so much a matter of change in itself, since *saevitia* appears to lurk beneath the surface of any *regnum*, but rather, with the abandonment of *continentia, fides,* and *pietas,* a matter of change in degree, method, and scale.

Siwah

In Curtius, Alexander's journey to Siwah (4.7.6–32) takes place shortly after his arrival in Egypt amid an atmosphere of joy from the Egyptians, since they perceive him as a liberator. Mazaces the Persian governor at

---

51. Scholars who have rejected the historicity of Betis' execution include Tarn (*Alexander the Great,* 2:267 f.) and Perrin ([supra, n. 49], 65 f.). It is accepted by Bosworth (*CE,* 68), Green (*Alexander of Macedon,* 193), and Lane Fox (*Alexander the Great,* 193), among others.

52. See Bosworth, *HCA,* 1:258 f.

53. On Hector, see Soph. *Ajax* 1031 and Eurip. *Andr.* 399, with Green, *Alexander of Macedon,* 541 n. 58.

Memphis promptly surrenders to Alexander. The king shrewdly exploits his advantage by taking care in his administrative arrangements not to change any native custom.[54]

As an oracle, Siwah was extremely well known and revered among the Greeks up to Alexander's time.[55] The surviving Alexander historians would have been using purely Greek sources, and as Siwah appeared to have such a profound effect on the king, it is not surprising that each gave the episode appropriate emphasis. Yet Curtius and Justin (or Trogus) display a more skeptical, if not cynical, attitude toward the incident, which is very different from Arrian, Plutarch, and Diodorus.[56] In Justin, Alexander, wishing at once to acquire a divine origin and to clear his mother of the infamy brought about by a charge of *stuprum* (sexual depravity), actually instructs the priests secretly in advance as to the kind of response he wanted. One should first note that Curtius' account of the journey is similar in terms of description to Arrian's, Diodorus', and Plutarch's and is certainly no less detailed.

Perhaps influenced to a certain degree by Greco-Roman literary convention, Curtius put geographical and ethnographical detail to good use.[57] The barren waste of the desert is contrasted with the lush density of the oasis. The exotic nature of the place is enhanced by the description of the Fountain of the Sun, an unusual but widely known spring, along with the account of the image of the god and the unusual method of how he was consulted. Similarly the neighboring peoples are strange and distant—Ethiopians, Trogodytes, and Lucan's Nasamones.

However, Curtius' cynical tone is prevalent from the outset, eventually culminating in the expression of his own opinion of the whole affair at 4.7.29–32. For instance, after describing the potential hazards of the journey, Curtius deliberately juxtaposes a comment that the Egyptians were exaggerating the difficulties, on the one hand, and, on the other, Alexander's being seized by *ingens cupido* (an enormous desire) to go visit the oracle to confirm his divine paternity: "but a huge desire was

---

54. Cf. Arrian 3.1–4; Diod. 17.49.2.

55. See Hdt. 1.46.3, 2.54; Plut. *Lys.* 25. See also C.J. Classen, "The Libyan God Ammon in Greece before 331 B.C.," *Historia* 8 (1959): 349–55; Bosworth, "Alexander and Ammon," 41–75, and *HCA*, 1:269.

56. Cf. Arrian 3–4; Diod. 17.49.2–51; Plut. *Alex.* 26.6–27; J. 11.11. See Atkinson's table on the corroborative and variant details, in *Curtius* i, 360–61. For a concise summary of the historical problems concerning the visit, see Hamilton, *Plutarch,* 69–70; Brunt, *Arrian,* 1: app. 5.

57. On Curtius' use of geographical representation, see Rutz, 2341–43.

goading his mind for the purpose of visiting Jove, whom Alexander, not content with mortal eminence, either believed or wanted others to believe, was responsible for his own parentage" (4.7.8). The idea of a hard journey whets the king's desire all the more, presumably to prove himself worthy; yet the sour comment on the Egyptians sets a tone of false pretense. In Curtius, *cupido* in certain contexts can precede some great undertaking (as in Alexander's solution to the Gordian knot or his decision to take Ariamazes' Rock) or else a wish to visit some bizarre and out of the way place (e.g., the king's desire to visit Ethiopia at 4.8.4 or his wish to explore an unknown river in 9.9.1). The motif of challenge, coupled with the idea of an Alexander driven to push his own achievement beyond the parameters of normal humanity, is inherent in each of these episodes.

It is significant that an issue that becomes such a prominent theme in the second pentad and that the historian rightly perceives as being a source of discontent to the king's Macedonian officers, namely, Alexander's godhead, should be twice founded on doubt—first, on the aspersions cast on the journey itself; second, on the claim to divine paternity. However, important emphasis is placed on the historian's qualification that Alexander either believed his divine origins himself or wanted others to believe them. Alexander will impose his desire for divine lineage on his followers, *nobiles* and army alike, for the sake of politics. His image must be more than *mortale fastigium* (mortal eminence). The ultimate irony is that in book 10, given the extent of Alexander's achievement and the quality of the kings who succeed him, his claims to godhead are well and truly justified.

As we saw earlier, Alexander's *cupido* and its closest Greek equivalent, *pothos*, is a well-explored theme in both ancient and modern Alexander historiography.[58] However, no matter how much the concept was a product of the original sources, it is still important to consider the context. For instance, in relation to Siwah, Arrian uses *pothos* as an explanation for Alexander's wish to visit the oracle (3.3.1). He further elaborates that the oracle had a reputation for infallibility and that it had been consulted by Alexander's ancestors, Heracles and Perseus, whom he sought to rival. Also, Ammon was in the king's lineage. Arrian, at this point, as Bosworth emphasizes, is not questioning Alexander's claim to divine parentage—unlike Curtius. Thus, whereas in Curtius, Alexander's

---

58. See chap. 3, n. 117.

cupido is based on politics, in Arrian, Alexander's *pothos* is a heartfelt longing, the result of a keen consciousness of heritage.

However, Arrian is aware of other aspects, as he comments at 3.3.2 that Alexander undertook the journey to obtain information about his origins or at least to say that he had. Thus Arrian also appreciates the importance of image, a point that he openly expresses in his necrology of the king at 7.29.3. Yet at 7.30.2 he says that some divine agency must have been associated with Alexander's birth, and although he stresses that the rain and the miraculous guidance of crows and snakes during the journey were believed by Alexander and his men to be signs of divinity, he asserts that he believes the king received divine assistance of some kind but that he does not know exactly what.

Curtius (4.7.15), along with Arrian (3.3.4–5), Diodorus (17.49.4–5), Plutarch (*Alex.* 27.1–3), and Strabo (17.1.43), mentions rain and ravens, or crows, that help Alexander and his followers on their journey. Citing Ptolemy as an authority, Arrian also adds that two snakes guided the army.[59] However, whereas the rain and crows appear as heaven-sent aid in the other historians, an air of rationality pervades Curtius' account (4.7.13). Similarly, his description of the ravens (4.7.15) is phrased in such a way as to explain the suggestion that they were acting as guides: also, unlike in the other accounts, there is no mention of the wind and sand that had obscured the track and hence made the birds' behavior very timely.

Curtius' critical tone is evident in his description of Alexander's questioning of the priest at 4.7.25 ff. The king is *humanae sortis oblitus* [forgetful of his mortal state]. In response to Alexander's inquiry as to whether rule over the whole world is destined for him, the seer is *aeque in adulationem compositus* [equally inclined toward flattery]. Alexander's godhead is implicit: the perpetrators of the crime against Philip had suffered punishment, but Alexander's father could suffer no man's crime. Finally, the historian's pronouncement at 4.7.29 on the reliability of the oracle's obviously ambiguous responses betrays open authorial contempt.

> In a true and sound estimation, these silly replies would certainly have made a joke of the oracle's credibility [fidem oraculi], but For-

---

[59]. The sources were Callisthenes and Aristobulus; see chap. 3, n. 54. On the significance of Ptolemy's variation, see Bosworth, *HCA,* 1:272–73; Hamilton, *Plutarch,* 71; Pearson, *LHA,* 207 n. 17.

tune makes those whom she compels to believe in herself alone, more greedy for glory, for the most part, than with the capacity for it [avidos gloriae magis quam capaces facit].

One should note that Arrian is also vague on exactly what Alexander said to the oracle and what reply he received (3.4.5), possibly because he doubted the authenticity of both the question and the answer he may have found in his sources. In any case, he implies that the king consulted Ammon in private.

Yet in Curtius' text, Alexander fulfills the essence of these very prophecies, and the irony would not have been lost on him. As the Scythians later emphasize at 7.8.12 f., Alexander was aiming at *totius orbis imperium*. Moreover, at the conclusion of the history, Alexander's body is taken back to Egypt, the home of Ammon. The somber effect of this success is implicit in a clause of the preceding quotation, *avidos gloriae magis quam capaces facit*, which underscores the dichotomy of Alexander's *ingenium*, also a prominent theme in the future books. One may conclude that Curtius deliberately plays down the divine elements associated with the Siwah story in the other sources. He rationalizes and is critical of both the oracle's answers and Alexander's pretensions, although the king is ultimately vindicated.

However, the historian does not minimize the thematic and political importance of Siwah for Alexander's relationship with his officers. Significantly, the last questions put to Ammon were from Alexander's *amici* (friends), asking if they were allowed to pay divine honors to their king, with affirmative answers. Historically, Macedonian kings had been awarded divine honors before, although usually by non-Macedonian cities. It is not known for certain how Philip's nobles would have viewed his theatrical gesture of placing a thirteenth statue of himself among the Olympians, but it is possible that the Macedonians had conceded him divine honors.[60]

Yet at Siwah, Curtius clearly sees a demarcation in position occurring between the king and his nobles. The historian's initial judgment (4.7.30)

---

60. For Philip's gesture, see Diod. 16.92.5; see also Welles, 101 n. 3. Interpretation of his action is controversial. On divine honors in general, see C. Habicht, *Gottmenschentum und griechische Städte* (Munich, 1970). More specifically, see E. Badian, "The Deification of Alexander the Great," 27–71, esp. 67 f.; E. Fredricksmeyer, "Divine Honors For Philip II," *TAPhA* 109 (1979): 39–61; N.G.L. Hammond, *Philip of Macedon* (London, 1994), 182–85.

164 *Alexander the Great*

is from the Macedonian officers' perspective, but his final assessment (4.7.31), although anticipatory as he admits, is revealing.

> And the Macedonians, indeed accustomed to royal rule, but in the shadow of a greater liberty [in maiore libertatis umbra] than other peoples, were more stubbornly [contumacius] opposed to the king's affectations to immortality than was expedient, either for themselves or for their king.

The concepts of *libertas* and *contumacia* are linked. The Macedonians exercise *libertas* in their resistance to Alexander's wishes, and at 6.9.18 and 6.11.22, Curtius indicates that Philotas and his associates were specifically opposed to Alexander's claims. However, as Curtius' use of the adverb *contumacius* emphasizes, such activity is dangerous. As someone who at least understood the conflict between an emperor and the Senate, Curtius would have recognized the Macedonian position only too well: his comment that their behavior was more stubborn than was expedient underlines his own stance. The theme of the aristocrats' resistance, with its underlying relevance to contemporary Roman politics, is brought out very clearly in the second pentad.

Chapter 6
Regnum in the Second Pentad: Alexander, King, General, and Tyrant

All five books of Curtius' second pentad are extant, although, as noted earlier, books 6 and 10 are considerably plagued by lacunae.[1] One of the historian's main thematic concerns is whether Alexander will prove worthy of his *fortuna*. Thus the contradictory pattern of Alexander's *virtus* and *vitia*, present in the first pentad and expressed through the development of the Alexander and Darius antithesis, becomes paramount in the remaining five books as it matches the scale of the king's power. Despite the occasional digression, as with books 3–5, into geographical, zoological, or ethnographical detail, the historian's narrative is concentrated on Alexander's conquests.

The second pentad develops the theme of Alexander's moral decline. As we saw in chapter 1, the king's *superbia* was a popular topic in the vast array of rhetorical literature; Curtius' audience almost certainly would have been acquainted with the gist of the well-known anecdotes and likely even expected an elaborate, showy treatment. It was a chance for the historian to shine.

In book 6 significant aspects of the theme include the king's adoption of Persian costume and protocol, the deterioration of his relationship with the Macedonian Companions, and the prominence of another evil of *regnum* (one that Curtius probably understood only too well), namely, flattery and rivalry for imperial favor. These issues culminate in Curtius' narrative of the arrest and trial of Philotas, to which Curtius, of all the extant Alexander historians, devotes the most emphasis.

Regardless of whether Philotas was guilty or innocent, his death threatens Alexander's position; in the opening part of book 7, the king must use *vis, dissimulatio,* and a measure of judicious *misericordia* (mercy) to support his *regnum*. The conflict between Alexander's king-

---

1. See chap. 2, 42.

ship (particularly as he aspires to godhead) and the *libertas* of the Macedonian and Greek entourage is continued in book 8, with episodes like the murder of Cleitus, Alexander's marriage to Roxane, the opposition of Callisthenes, and the conspiracy of the Pages. Apart from court politics, Curtius' other main focus is Alexander the *dux,* particularly his personal military *virtus,* his genius for leadership, and his insatiable desire for *gloria,* which causes him to push his conquests eastward through Bactria and Sogdiana and into India. The political side of Alexander's relationship to his followers is somewhat subordinate to the military narrative in book 9, but it surfaces in several important confrontations: the mutiny of the army on the Hyphasis (9.2.11 f.), the officers' concern over the king's rashness as a result of his wound at the Malli fortress (9.6.6–27), and the Dioxippus incident (9.7.16–26).

As in chapter 5, the discussion here must be selective. I shall examine those vivid episodes of challenge between the king and his followers that were obviously intended by Curtius as rhetorical showpieces. But unlike Arrian, who examined the issue of Alexander's *sophrosyne* (or lack of it) by a lengthy digression at 4.7.4–4.14.4,[2] Curtius distributed the incidents chronologically throughout the second pentad and made them a climactic focus of books 6, 7, and 8. However, they are also an integral part of the structure and thematically relate to other episodes. Agis' war and Curtius' digressions on Alexander's adoption of Persian customs may be taken as a case in point; each is historically significant yet is also used by the historian as complementary material to the more explosive incidents.

Agis' War: Its Implications for Alexander's Kingship

In its extant state, the text opens with a description of the battle between the Spartans and their allies, led by the Spartan king Agis III and the Macedonians under Alexander's regent, Antipater. It is likely that the lost section of book 6 contained an account of the early stages of the war, including Agis' negotiations, the upheaval in Thrace, and initial Spartan successes against Antipater's forces.[3] Curtius has thus fulfilled the autho-

---

2. See Stadter, *Arrian of Nicomedia,* 83 f.; Bosworth, *FAA,* 140–48, and *HCA,* 2:45 f.
3. For the early stages of the revolt, see Diod. 17.48.1, 17.62–63; Curt. 6.1.1–21 (cf. 5.1.1). Chronological problems and the date of the revolt have formed the main focus of most modern discussion; for references, see E.J. Baynham, "Antipater: Manager of Kings," in *Ventures into Greek History,* ed. Ian Worthington (Oxford, 1994), 339 n. 27. See also E. Badian's comprehensive analysis "Agis III: Revisions and Reflections," in the same volume, 258–92.

rial promises he made in books 4 and 5 to return to a report of the events in Europe, and as Badian observed, he used a "flashback" technique to narrate the battle; the historian himself comments that the conflict was over before Alexander had defeated Darius at Arbela.[4]

Agis' war, although largely ignored by Arrian, was given detailed treatment by Diodorus (17.62.6–17.63.4, 17.73.5–6) and evidently by Trogus (J. 12.1.4). Unlike these two authors, Curtius was not an exponent of universal history. Rather, he was more like Livy, who was concerned with the rise of Roman power, but who drew on events and situations elsewhere by way of developing his main theme. In Curtius' history, the narrative of Agis' war serves three purposes in relation to the central focus of *regnum*.

First, the military valor of Agis himself is notable (6.1.3); the Spartan king is conspicuous among his fellow Lacedaemonians, not only for his fine physique and armor, but for his greatness of spirit. Justin (12.1.10–11) has only a slightly different emphasis. Agis is inferior to Alexander in *felicitas* but not in *virtus,* and although overwhelmed by weight of numbers, he excels in *gloria*. It is possible that Curtius read Trogus (or his source) and adapted the sentiment to a different context. Agis' *virtus* is described in terms that deliberately recall that of Alexander—for instance, at Issus (3.11.7) and Arbela (4.16.30–33)—while at 10.5.32 Alexander's *magnitudo animi* is one of his virtues in the historian's necrology.

Second, Antipater's fear of Alexander's jealousy emphasizes imperial envy over subordinates winning military laurels. Hammond believes that this aspect of the episode is an addition of the historian himself, and he cites as an example Nero's jealousy of Corbulo.[5] The comparison may be valid enough, and certainly there is no lack of examples from the period of the principate. One could also name Marcus Licinius Crassus (cf. Dio Cass. 51.24), Germanicus (Tac. *Ann.* 2.26, 59; Suet. *Tib.* 25, 52), or Agricola (Tac. *Agr.* 41–42), all of whom, by their military achievements, caused some concern for their respective *principes*. However, even if Curtius has interpreted Antipater's motives for calling a council of the Greeks in terms of contemporary experience, he was probably not inaccurate. Antipater, as regent of Macedonia, was already in a position of considerable power, and important military victories may

---
4. E. Badian, *Hermes* 95 (1967): 191.
5. Hammond, *THA,* 134.

well have aroused the concern of the absent king about the security of his authority.

Yet the main purpose of the episode is to enforce the link with Alexander. Agis must be a worthy opponent to enhance Antipater's victory, while the battle itself was waged in the name of Alexander, as Curtius has already indicated at the beginning of book 5. Thus the background presence of the king provides an appropriate transition point for Curtius to introduce the theme of Alexander's moral decline at 6.2.1–4. This latter aspect was noted by Lock:[6] Curtius exploited the literary convenience of having the revolt over before the battle at Arbela and thus freeing Alexander from any immediate military worries, so that he might stress the paradox of the king conquering Persian arms only to fall victim to their vices.

The point can be taken further. Alexander's moral deterioration does not take place after Gaugamela, nor are all his military challenges over with the defeat of Darius. New challenges arise as soon as the old ones are overcome; for instance, Darius is replaced by Bessus, Bessus by the lure of India. More important is the threat of danger from within. Alexander adopts Persian *vitia*, which, in turn, cause discontent among his officers.

In general terms, Rome itself offers a parallel through the motif in Roman historiography of *metus externus* (fear of an outside influence) or the commonplace *metus hostilis* (fear of an enemy). A classic example of a *metus externus* interpretation is Tacitus' necrology on Tiberius (*Ann.* 6.5.1), where only fear of his family kept him to any semblance of decent behavior. Other Roman historians, such as Sallust or Velleius Paterculus (cf. Sall. *Bell. Cat.* 10 f., *Iug.* 41, *Hist.* 1.10–12; Vell. Pat. 2.1.1), perceived that external enemies were needed to keep the city morally upright but that victory also sowed the seeds of moral destruction through contact with the enemy's vices. Thus the paradox of Alexander's situation is rather that while conquering is his raison d'être, success brings potential danger from the internal level. Ironically, Antipater, a representative of Alexander, defeats one of his enemies, but the real threat to the king will come from among his own Companions. There is a connection between Agis' war, which is an external threat to Alexander's control of Greece, and Curtius' digression at 6.2.1–4, which stresses Alexander's moral

---

6. R.A. Lock, *Antichthon* 6 (1972): 22.

decline and its effect on his followers. It is no accident that such a linkage between external and internal challenge is repeated just before the Philotas affair, with Alexander's assault on Barzaentes, an accomplice of Bessus.

Curtius' Digressions on Alexander's Moral Decline

The context and location of Alexander's adoption of Persian costume and court ceremonial varies among the vulgate traditions.[7] At 6.2.1–4 in Curtius' text is the first of two authorial digressions on the deterioration of Alexander's character in book 6. The second one follows the visit of the Amazonian queen Thalestris, which is where Justin and Diodorus also choose to comment on a change in the king's behavior. The *Metz Epitome* (1–2) appears to place the king's orientalism in Parthia (cf. Plut. *Alex.* 45.1), certainly before Alexander reached the Arii. In general it corroborates the tradition followed by Curtius, Diodorus, and Justin, and despite its general lack of interest in political themes, it also probably intended a negative interpretation, as opposed to the idea of a deliberate policy of conciliation suggested by Plutarch and Arrian.[8]

In the first excursus, Curtius stresses that Alexander's spirit was better suited to the pressures of military life than to leisure, since as soon as he was free of immediate martial cares, he gave himself up to pleasure and fell victim to the vices of the Persians, namely, early banquets, heavy drinking, and *greges pelicum* (flocks of harlots). For an author who elsewhere displays knowledge of Macedonian customs, Curtius has apparently sacrificed accuracy for rhetoric, for, as I noted earlier, heavy drinking at banquets was already an established Macedonian practice.

The historian comments that there was a gradual decline into adopting foreign habits and, with this general explanation, outlines a sketch of future events; he says himself in summary, at 6.2.4, that Alexander's emulation of foreign customs will cause his own men, both officers and soldiers alike, to regard him as an enemy, out of resentment over the abandoning of their military discipline, so emphasized by Charidemus. Their discontent results in conspiracies against the king's life and in anger

---

7. See Atkinson, *Curtius* ii, 167–68.
8. Plut. *Mor.* 329F–330A and *Alex.* 45.2–3, 47.5; Arr. 7.29.4. See A.B. Bosworth, *JHS* 100 (1980): 4–8; Goukowsky, *Essai sur les origines du mythe d'Alexandre*, 1:30 ff.; Briant, *Rois, tributs et paysans*, 13 ff.

and suspicion on his own part. Curtius is thus projecting the Macedonian perspective of Alexander, a selective bias for literary effect. Moreover, similar sentiments are repeated at 6.6.1–11, prior to the arrest and trial of Philotas.

Curtius touches on Alexander's sexual peccadillos just before the second digression. The sexual practices of rulers had long been a favorite motif with Hellenistic historians; yet Curtius' exploitation of Alexander's habits is notably low-key, at least at this point. Among the gifts Nabarzanes brings Alexander is Bagoas, "a eunuch of remarkable beauty" who had already been the concubine of Darius and was soon to be Alexander's (6.5.23). The historian does not comment on this episode beyond stating that it was mainly through the eunuch's entreaties that Alexander pardoned Nabarzanes; he thus lays the foundation of Bagoas' baleful influence.

Likewise, the visit of the Amazonian queen Thalestris (6.5.24–32), a story that was widely distributed in the Alexander sources, [9] passes without authorial censure. The version that appears in Curtius and the vulgate is not corroborated by Arrian; instead, he relates a *logos* (7.13.2–6), which he claims to be of dubious historicity. In 324 B.C., Atropates, the satrap of the large and powerful province of Media, presented Alexander with a troop of one hundred women, whom he declared were Amazons, armed with little axes and light bucklers, and with the right breast bared. The description of the display suggests the decorative rather than the authentic, and the display was likely deliberately calculated for sexual titillation, as well as flattery. Alexander sent the women away in case they were molested by his army; the inference is that unlike true Amazons, they were not capable of looking after themselves. Also, the heart of the vulgate account, namely, Thalestris' initiative to procure a child by the most belligerent father available, has been reduced to a somewhat arrogant or playacting remark on Alexander's part; he said that he would visit the queen and impregnate her. However, Thalestris, like Bagoas, is a barbarian to Curtius; hence an account of Alexander's sexual activities with unusual foreign queens and Persian catamites, although sparingly treated by Curtius, nevertheless provides an appropriate background for the elaboration on Alexander's adoption of Persian customs and its effect on his followers.

---

9. See chap. 3, n. 79.

Curtius' description at 6.6.1–12 is close enough to the other vulgate accounts to suggest a common source.[10] Both Curtius and Justin stress that Alexander crossed over to the customs and dress of the people he had conquered, as well as stressing the paradox of the victors being overcome by the vanquished. Curtius' digression is naturally more elaborate and richly rhetorical. Alexander's former *continentia* and *moderatio*, which were outstanding virtues in the highest *fortuna*, change to *superbia* and *lascivia*. By using key words, such as *continentia* and *fortuna*, Curtius deliberately reminds us of and reverses the Alexander of 3.12.18–22. Yet his portrait is far more complex than a simple change from king to tyrant: as stated earlier, the inconsistencies of *regnum* form a major theme of the second pentad.

The dilemma of Alexander's situation is clear: by crossing over to Persian customs at all, he rouses the hostility of the Macedonians, but as Curtius also demonstrates, he needs to conciliate the Persians, since Bessus is a very real threat. Alexander's solution to the problem is to prepare for war, dispelling potential mutiny with activity. The subsequent campaigns against Satibarzanes, the rebel satrap of Area, provides an immediate focus (6.6.20 f.). But despite the surrender of the satrapy's capital, Artacana, Curtius deliberately finishes the narrative of the campaign on an ominous note: Alexander proceeds to the territory of the Drangae, where its satrap, Barzaentes, was one of Bessus' accomplices in Darius' murder (6.6.35–36). Thus the cue of the uncaptured assassins of Darius, the former Persian king, provides an appropriate setting for Curtius to introduce the most important section of the book—Alexander will now face conspiracy from among his own followers (6.7.1): ". . . . when the king, not only unconquered [invictus] from foreign threats [externa vi], but secure [tutus], was attacked by a crime from within his own household [intestino facinore]." The sense of inevitability of success against the Persian regicides implied in *invictus* contrasts with the danger to Alexander from the internal level.

Philotas

Curtius' opinion of the importance of Philotas' downfall is amply demonstrated by the sheer amount of space (an approximate third of the

---

10. Cf. Diod. 17.77.4–17.78.1; J. 12.3.8–12. See Hammond, *THA*, 136.

extant book) that he devotes to it.[11] By way of comparison, the account of Arrian, who gives what could be called the official version, is quite sparse. It should be noted that the term *official,* referring here to Arrian's use of Ptolemy alone for the actual arrest, trial, and execution of Philotas, does not mean that Ptolemy's version would necessarily have recounted the whole story. As one of Alexander's friends, Ptolemy gained considerably from the trial's aftermath (Arrian 3.27.5), and it would have been in his interest to have kept an account of the trial to a bare minimum. In his opening words, Arrian (3.26.1) clearly accepts the guilt of Philotas and, possibly because of his own imperial administrative and military experience (including a term as a provincial governor), recognizes that Philotas' execution and the killing of Parmenion were politically necessary, without explanation or censure. Justin (12.5) and Diodorus (17.79–80) are also brief, and only Plutarch (*Alex.* 47–49) approaches Curtius in terms of length of narrative and information.

In Curtius, the episode is a very coherent and carefully constructed narrative, which draws together the aspects of *regnum* already under exploration in book 6, such as the king's orientalizing and his arrogance. The Philotas incident also raises new issues, such as the evil of rivalry for imperial favor, *dissimulatio,* and the necessity of force to maintain power, all of which are further developed in later books.

The opening words of the narrative establish a sense of dire consequences resulting from apparently small events. Dymnus, the catalyst of the incident, is described by Curtius as a man of *modicae auctoritatis et gratiae* [moderate influence and favor] with Alexander (Curt. 6.7.2). Diodorus (17.79.1) describes Dymnus as one of the king's *philoi,* which does not necessarily mean he held any important position but, as with Curtius' description, simply suggests he was not in the first circle of courtiers. Dymnus is mentioned nowhere else in Diodorus' text.[12] Plutarch implies (*Alex.* 49.2) that he was unimportant, and Arrian does not mention him at all.

Interestingly, Curtius gives Dymnus no apparent motive for wanting Alexander killed but instead presents him as an enthusiastic, if imprudent, member of a conspiracy. Dymnus, by a pledge of *fides,* tries to make his lover, Nicomachus, party to regicide, but the youth steadfastly

---

11. On the historical worth of Curtius' account, see Bosworth, *HCA,* 1:359 f.; Heckel, *Phoenix* 31 (1977): 17 f. Cf. Z. Rubinsohn, "The 'Philotas Affair': A Reconsideration," 409–20.

12. Cf. the list in Berve, 1:31, 2: no. 269.

denies any religious obligation to keep the crime secret. In fact, despite a moral comment on the young man's chastity (6.7.13), Curtius repeatedly stresses Nicomachus' loyalty to Alexander. This stress is significant; on the Macedonian hierarchy, Nicomachus and his brother are unimportant figures, as Cebalinus' later difficulty in gaining access to Alexander shows. Yet their testimony as evidence of their loyalty will be used to bring down far more powerful men. Nicomachus finally deceives Dymnus by pretending to have been won over to his cause, and he thereby learns the names of the other conspirators, of whom only one, Demetrius (6.7.15), appears to have been of any importance.[13] Nicomachus informs his brother, Cebalinus, of the plot. Again, the minor status of the brothers—later a salient point in Philotas' speech—is prevalent. As Nicomachus did not normally have access to the king, approaching him now would make the conspirators suspicious, and even Cebalinus himself is allowed to go no further than the vestibule of the royal quarters but must wait for someone from the first rank of Alexander's friends. The ensuing narrative in which Cebalinus informs Philotas of the plot yet eventually suspects him is drawn subtly enough to enable the reader at once to see Philotas' later defense, as well as his indictment.

At the very start (6.7.18), Curtius introduces Philotas' role in the whole affair with the word *forte* (by chance). It was by pure luck that Philotas happened to be the last of Alexander's friends to leave, and as he shortly says himself in his speech (6.10.8), if Cebalinus had not come to him, he would not even be on trial, as he was not named among the conspirators. One of his other and later points of defense (6.10.16), that he believed he was listening to a quarrel between a lover and his boyfriend, is supported by his condescending behavior toward Cebalinus (6.7.33), which, since there is a real conspiracy afoot, causes Cebalinus to go elsewhere.

The revelation of the news is subtly exploited by the historian. Cebalinus informs Metron, a page who has the important charge of the armory. The young man rushes in on the king as he is taking a bath, naked and vulnerable, and the mixture of emotions the king must feel—fear, relief, anger at Cebalinus, and then dismay at Philotas' implication in the plot—adds to his sense of betrayal. Whether he has waited for a

---

13. Demetrius is described as a *custos corporis,* which corresponds with Arrian's *somatophylakos,* at 3.27.5. In Curtius, the other conspirators, Peucolaus, Nicanor, Aphobetus, Iolaus, Dioxenus, and Archepolis, are unknown outside of this incident; see Waldemar Heckel, *GRBS* 16 (1975): 398.

chance to remove Philotas or not, Alexander immediately believes in his guilt. He asks Dymnus, who has stabbed himself on arrest, why it should have seemed that Philotas was more worthy to rule than himself. Although he gives Philotas a chance to explain and appears to accept his account, the king's pledge of renewed *gratia* is at best ambivalent, at worst founded on outright *dissimulatio* (6.7.35).

At 6.8 a new, ugly aspect of Alexander's kingship is introduced: rivalry for royal favor. Curtius especially emphasizes the role of Alexander's *amici* in destroying Philotas. Given a chance to bring down an important general at a time when he is under suspicion and when his power base is at its weakest, they take it so that, by Philotas' fall, each may increase his own position. At the time of Philotas' arrest, he was quite isolated from family support; two brothers, Hector (Curt. 4.8.7–8) and Nicanor (Curt. 6.6.18–19; Arrian 3.25.4), were already dead, and his father, Parmenion, had been left behind in Media.[14]

Alexander shows he is either doubtful about Philotas' loyalty or wants his other generals to deliberately condemn the man, when he calls a council to which Philotas is not invited. Only Craterus is named at the first meeting. The group referred to by Curtius at 6.8.10 presumably includes Alexander's other friends Hephaestion and Erigyius. These men are present at Philotas' arrest, along with Perdiccas and Leonnatus. Erigyius, named by Plutarch (*Alex.* 10) and Arrian (3.6.5–6) as a member of the group of young nobles exiled by Philip, is presented as an older man in Curtius. A marshal who plays a significant role is Coenus (6.9.30–32). Although he was married to Philotas' sister, he clearly perceived that his brother-in-law was doomed and later made a savage speech against him (6.11.10–12). The spokesman for this group of rivals is Craterus, described by Curtius as closer to the king than most of his friends, a statement that is corroborated by the other sources.[15] According to Curtius (6.8.2–3), Craterus was hostile to Philotas, *ob aemulationem dignitatis* [on account of his rivalry for status], and realized that because of the

---

14. Cf. Curt. 5.6.12, 7.2.15; Diod. 17.80.3; Arrian 3.19.7, 3.26.3; Plut. *Alex.* 49.13. E. Badian, "Alexander the Great and the Loneliness of Power," in *Studies in Greek and Roman History*, 196 f., suggested that Nicanor's death was the catalyst for Alexander's plan to destroy Parmenion and his family; while this hypothesis might seem overly premature, the king's Companions certainly exploited Philotas' ambiguous behavior, and Alexander himself needed little convincing.

15. See Diod. 17.114.2; Arrian 7.12.3; Plut. *Alex.* 47.9. See also Hamilton, *Plutarch*, 131.

general's excessive boasting of his own valor and deeds, the king suspected him not of crime but of *contumacia*. Curtius' pointed use of this term, employed previously to describe Betis of Gaza and the Macedonian resentment at Alexander's claims at Siwah, implies not only "stubbornness" or "opposition" but arrogance or self-importance beyond prudence—or even *libertas* exercised without care. Similar phrasing is also used of Callisthenes (8.6.1).[16] Curtius does not name the Macedonians who opposed the king's aspirations at Siwah, but the use of *contumacia* provides the link between this episode and accusations later raised by Alexander himself, as well as Philotas' later defense and his confession under torture.

Thus aware that he has an opportune moment for ruining his enemy, Craterus, like a Tacitean *delator,* indicts Philotas, hiding his hatred under *species pietatis* [a facade of duty] (Curt. 6.8.4). His speech is given a distinct Roman coloring by its emphasis on *beneficia* and *gratia,* yet it embodies one of the central themes of book 6: Alexander's changing position in respect to his own *hetairoi*. In effect, Philotas has been tried in his absence and in secret, before an absolute king and rivals who are eager to ruin him; such a scene recalls the notorious trials *intra cubiculum* (cf. Tac. *Ann.* 11.2.1) under Claudius. Curtius has Craterus maintain the fiction that Alexander is primus inter pares by emphasizing Parmenion's *dignitas,* while the historian simultaneously underlines the reality of the situation. The arguments of the other generals are concerned more with Philotas' actual behavior and his inherent disloyalty in concealing information pertinent to the life of his king, whether he believed it false or not.

Events move swiftly following the council. Philotas' invitation to a last banquet with a friendly Alexander is possibly the historian's contribution (6.8.16). Emperors like Caligula and Domitian were infamous for inviting their intended victims to banquets, presumably to disarm suspicion. However, another example of such *dissimulatio* occurs at 9.10.21; Alexander suspected Astaspes, the satrap of Carmenia, of harboring treacherous designs during his Indian campaign, but he concealed his anger until he could make a thorough inquiry. It is equally likely that such details in the vulgate appealed to Curtius because of their Roman

---

16. Cf. Curt. 6.8.2–3, . . . *et ob ea quidem sceleris, sed contumaciae tamen esse suspectum,* and 8.6.1, *in Callisthenen olim contumacia suspectum pervicacioris irae fuit;* see also the discussion on the Pages' Conspiracy at a later section of this chapter.

echoes and relevance for the historian's audience.[17] Yet it is credible enough that Alexander ordered the roads blocked, lest word escape to Parmenion that a considerable armed guard was used to seize the other conspirators as well as Philotas himself, half-drunk and sleepy, and that his rivals were on hand to ensure his ruin.

Likewise credible, as well as thematically significant, is the trial of Philotas before the Macedonian rank and file. This trial is also in Arrian (3.26.2 f.) and Diodorus (17.79.6, 17.80.1); only Curtius, however, gives relevant detail on Macedonian court practices. With capital cases, the army conducted the trial and passed judgment, and significantly, as the historian points out (6.8.25), the power of the king counted for nothing unless his *auctoritas* was significant prior to the trial.[18] Thus, conducting a trial of a major Macedonian citizen and general in traditional Macedonian manner is politically crucial to Alexander.[19] The trial is not just a question of Philotas' guilt or innocence but a statement of confidence in Alexander's *regnum*. Livy (1.26.5) depicts a similar scenario at the public trial of Horatius, where Tullus Hostilius is anxious to avoid an unpopular crowd response; the methods and motives of Tarquinius Superbus (1.54) are somewhat different.

Alexander had already tried Philotas in secret but, for the sake of image, was compelled to get the verdict ratified in public. He deliberately conceals Philotas from view (8.8.24–26), lest the sight of a former commander in bonds rouses the sympathy of the crowd before he can be accused. The corpse of Dymnus is brought in for theatrical effect, and Alexander establishes his stance and expression before he speaks (6.9.1–2). He waits for the impact of Dymnus' corpse on the crowd, since they mostly do not know what he had done or how he had been killed.

Contrary to certain scholarly criticism of what appears to be rhetorical indulgence on the historian's part,[20] the major speeches of both plaintiff and defendant are essential to the development of the narrative. As well as allowing Curtius to present opposing points of view with equal skill, the effect of the words of each speaker on the audience enables the

---

17. Cf. Suet. *Gaius* 27.4 and *Dom.* 11. Lane Fox, *Alexander the Great*, 284, argues that the whole setting in 6.16–22 is pure invention for the benefit of a Roman audience. But see Green, *Alexander of Macedon*, 343.

18. Hedicke added *rex iudicabat* to Curt. 6.8.25, a supplement that was refuted by R.M. Errington, in *Chiron* 8 (1978): 86–91.

19. See Bosworth, *HCA*, 1:361 f.

20. See Heckel, *Phoenix* 31 (1977): 19.

exploitation of different levels of irony: the reaction of the audience is not always what the speaker wants.

Alexander's harangue begins in an emotionally provocative fashion. Yet, clearly and perhaps deliberately so in order to stress his outrage, he does not display the flowing oratory he has shown before. As the king, he is in the highest position and is accorded *fides* and *pietas*. The obligations of these values are a recurring theme throughout his speech. Moreover, instead of immediately accusing Philotas, he indicts Parmenion as the instigator of the plot, with his son as a mere tool. But in terms of actual evidence, Alexander's case is shaky. The testimonies of Nicomachus, Metron, and Cebalinus did not, at any time, designate Philotas as a participant of the crime, and the king's best proof against Parmenion is the ambiguous contents of an intercepted letter from the aged general to his sons (6.9.14–15).

Yet in terms of implication and potential for the crime, Philotas and his father are truly guilty. Philotas' silence pointed to hope of profit at the very least, and his father's powerful position in Media gave Philotas the means of aspiring to the throne. Alexander does not ignore Philotas' record of faction and *amicitia* with enemies and, more recently, the insult over the oracle of Jupiter Ammon. He makes Philotas the epitome of resistance to his claims. Finally, in a sense, the positions of both Parmenion and his son, given the commands and responsibilities of each, recalls Caesar's famous comment on his divorce of Pompeia.[21] In all practicality, Alexander cannot afford even the breath of suspicion about two such high-ranking officers, lest he undermine the very fabric of his power and hence the point of his plea from 6.9.21–24.

However, the assembly is still moved to sympathy for Philotas and his father. Two of Alexander's adherents, Amyntas and Coenus, try to rouse the army against Philotas, but because of the nature of the trial and the prevailing mood of the men, Philotas must be given his chance to defend himself. The king says himself that Philotas must speak, although he promptly walks off before the accused's defense, the significance of which Philotas (6.10.3) does not ignore. Alexander's question as to whether the general will use the Macedonian tongue in addressing the men appears insidious in that he himself preferred to employ the Greek *koine*. The king was attempting to manipulate the prejudice of the Macedonian soldiery. Moreover, the point is later seized (6.11.1–7) by Bolon,

---

21. Cf. Curt. 6.9.10–13, 17–20; Suet. *Div. Iul.* 74.2; Plut. *Caes.* 10.8. On the source traditions, see M. Gelzer, *Caesar: Politician and Statesman* (Oxford, 1968), 60 n. 3.

the dour old Macedonian, who succeeds in inflaming the army in what must surely be one of the most cynical descriptions of mob behavior.

Tarn described Philotas' speech as "rhetoric of the worst school type," an accusation that is hardly borne out by the devastating logic of the man's argument: he systematically answers the accusations leveled at him over his alleged part in Dymnus' conspiracy and indicts Alexander himself for inconsistency.[22] The final part of his speech, 6.10.23–37, answers Alexander's other accusations, which had challenged Philotas' *fides*. His emphasis on his loyalty to Amyntas, the king's relative, foreshadows a similar issue elaborated by the son of Andromenes in book 7—namely, the dangerous predicament in having been associated with former relatives or friends of the king, who had been eliminated. Also, Philotas' response to Alexander's accusations of insolence over his claim to be the son of Jupiter Ammon continues the conflict between *libertas* and the will of the king. The divinity issue, as an aspect of Alexander's moral deterioration, underscores one of the historian's most important concepts. Philotas emphasizes that his reservations were addressed to the king himself, to advise him, not to belittle him—in the same spirit that Charidemus' criticisms were intended for Darius. In a sense Philotas is right; it is indeed *fides amicitiae* [loyalty to friendship] and *veri consilii periculosa libertas* [dangerous freedom in giving honest advice] that have betrayed him (Curt. 6.10.26). Philotas' last point also serves to heighten the inconsistency of kingship by linking the earlier Alexander with the present one. He reminds his audience (6.10.34–35) that Parmenion's warning about the doctor Philip carried no weight with Alexander because, at that time, it was more expedient for the king to trust his family retainer than his most loyal courtier.

The narrative of the episode does not finish, as one might expect, with the condemnation and execution of Philotas: at least one scholar has accused Curtius of clumsiness by continuing on to include a second council, Philotas' torture, and his eventual confession before his death.[23] However, the aftermath of the trial, with its grim detail of torment and perceptive authorial comment on the implacability of Philotas' rivals, serves two purposes.

In the first place, the historian has never committed himself over whether Philotas was guilty or innocent, although his powerful speech

---

22. Curt. 6.10.1–37; Tarn, *Alexander the Great*, 2:94.
23. See Lane Fox, *Alexander the Great*, 352.

demolished the case of the prosecution. Curtius has demonstrated that factors arising from chance, foolish, or arrogant behavior on Philotas' part and the arguments of rivals who were eager to see him fall combined to destroy him. Above all, the king was forced to use force in the face of grumbling opposition to his new policies. Philotas' death was thus politically necessary, and unlike Justin, Curtius does not revile Alexander. His open-minded stance is clearly shown in the general's confession, which the historian introduces with the comment (6.11.21) that it is impossible to determine truth or falsity from any confession given under torture, as an individual will say anything to escape the pain.[24]

Whether Philotas' disclosure was true or not is irrelevant. He took the chance to say what disturbed him about Alexander's rule; while on the point of death, his confession is a last expression of *libertas*, like that of Hermolaus in book 8 or Subrius Flavus in Tacitus' *Annals* (15.67). The point in common for all three is the complaint that the king has changed for the worse and hence is not deserving of loyalty as each perceives it. Opposition has surfaced and will not yet die with its martyrs. Secondly, the subsequent ending of the book not only summarizes the immediate importance of the trial for the king's regime but raises questions for its future. As the historian comments, the king had been freed from not only danger but also ill will, since unless openly proved guilty, Philotas and his father could not be executed without angering the army. Yet the doubts remain.

Textual problems render establishing Curtius' final sentence difficult, as the context can favor two readings.[25] However, because it appears to suit the context, the Bardon version is probably closest to the original sense of the text.

Itaque anceps quaestio fuit: dum infitiatus est facinus, crudeliter torqueri videbatur, post confessionem Philotas ne amicorum quidem misericordiam meruit.

---

24. I am grateful to Professor Bosworth for pointing out that the remark is a rhetorical topos; cf. Cic. *Pro Mil.* 57–58. See also D. MacDowell's reference to Antiphon (*Herodes* 32) in *The Law in Classical Athens* (London, 1978), 245–46.

25. Rolfe, ad loc., following Hedicke's text, offers: *Itaque anceps quaestio fuit dum infitiatus est facinus; crudeliter torqueri videbatur post confessionem; et iam Philotas amicorum misericordiam meruit* [Thus the issue of the case was doubtful as long as he denied the crime; that his torture was continued after the confession was considered an act of cruelty; and now Philotas merited the compassion of his friends] (trans. Rolfe).

[Therefore the interrogation had fluctuating effects; while Philotas denied the crime, it seemed cruel to torture him; after his confession, he did not even win the compassion of his friends.]

Philotas' confession appears to condemn him, even to his friends, and so fits Curtius' statement about Alexander being freed from *invidia*. This reading favoring the *ne . . . quidem* clause over *et iam* also seems preferable in view of the beginning of book 7. After Philotas' death, the mood of the army changed to compassion. The irony is paramount: Alexander has appeared to remove one threat, but by using force—however necessary, however apparently legally—he changed his own position. The trappings of Persian habit are but the outward symbols of his new status. Having used *vis* once against his own men, he will now continue to do so.

The Execution of Alexander Lyncestes and the Trial of Amyntas and His Brothers

The first two chapters of book 7 treat the aftermath of the Philotas affair, including the murder of Parmenion. Both these episodes have implications for both king and followers in that with the shift in the army's mood, Alexander's *auctoritas* seemed somewhat tarnished. The king, apparently unworried, called another assembly in a further attempt to justify himself. The second assembly is not supported by the other accounts, but its events are—respectively, by Diodorus (17.80.2) and Arrian (3.27.1–3). Diodorus agrees with Curtius on the execution of Alexander of Lyncestes but omits the subsequent trial of Amyntas, while Arrian is silent on Alexander Lyncestes but narrates the trial of Amyntas, with some variations.[26] Arrian also mentions an additional fourth brother, one Attalus, whom Curtius omits. In Curtius, the third brother, Polemon, who is common to both accounts, merely flees at the news of Philotas' torture, but in Arrian he deserts to the enemy and is brought back by Amyntas after the brothers' acquittal. According to Curtius, Polemon is brought back by others during the trial.

The case of Alexander Lyncestes, who had been already under arrest for some time, is raised, according to Curtius, by a prearranged demand from the king *(haud dubie ex composito)*, through Atarrhias, the man who was sent to arrest Philotas. As Curtius reminds his audience (7.1.6),

---

26. On Arrian's omission of Alexander Lyncestes' trial, see Bosworth, *HCA*, 1:163–64.

the Lyncestian was already suspected of previous conspiracy against the king, as well as complicity in the murder of Philip, yet he had been kept alive. It would have been unlucky as well as inappropriate for Alexander to have killed the man who had first hailed him as king, as Justin explicitly states (11.2.2; cf. Arrian 1.25.2). Also, the entreaties of Alexander's regent, Antipater, the man's father-in- law, also had carried some influence.[27] It should be added that Alexander Lyncestes was possibly a member of the Argead royal house and, as a dynastic alternative, was clearly a rival and a threat.[28] Hence the opportunity for Alexander to remove him, afforded by association of the old danger with the new, is too good to miss.

Yet the historian is not sympathetic toward this man. He emphasizes (7.1.8) that although Lyncestes has had three whole years *(totum triennium)* in which to compose and practice a speech, he is totally at a loss when given a chance. This lack of eloquence was evidently in the original source, since Diodorus refers to it as well (17.80.2), but Curtius draws a literary contrast between his indistinct utterances and the lengthy and powerful speeches of Philotas and Amyntas. The accusation and defense of Amyntas is also used by the historian to project strikingly contemporary questions, and in this aspect, Curtius differs markedly from Arrian.[29] However, the issues raised in Amyntas' speech are relevant to any *regnum* and any emperor.

Since their brother Polemon had fled, which seemed to indicate guilt, Amyntas and Simmias are charged with complicity in Philotas' conspiracy on the grounds of their former *amicitia* with Philotas, the king's letters from his mother warning him against them, and the anecdotal evidence of Antiphanes, a petty clerk of the cavalry. With an eye for the importance of his image, Amyntas (Philotas' former close friend) deliberately asks that he be freed from fetters and that a lance, the symbol of his position, should be returned to him to emphasize his *libertas* (7.1.18). He also shuns the place where Lyncestes' body had lain, possibly to avoid the ill augury. His speech is similar to Philotas' in that it methodically

---

27. On the two traditions in the sources on Lyncestes' arrest, see Bosworth, *HCA*, 1:162–63. Diod. 17.32.1 alone places the arrest prior to Issus; Arrian 1.25.10 and J. 11.7.1 place it earlier. Curtius' account of the arrest, implied at 7.1.6, must have occurred in his lost book 2; see Atkinson, *Curtius* i, 186.

28. See Hammond, *CQ* 30 (1980): 457 f.; on the dynastic rivalry of the upper Macedonian royal houses, see A.B. Bosworth, *CQ* 21 (1971): 93–105.

29. Cf. Arrian 3.27.1–3; see Bosworth, *HCA*, 1:364. On contemporary issues, see chap. 2, 34, 59.

answers each of the accusations. However, the tone of the speech is respectful apart from some subtle barbs at 7.1.35–36, and it thus differs from the open contempt of Philotas. Amyntas emphasizes that he is a Macedonian soldier with a citizen's free spirit (7.1.35), a point that he uses to again stress the difference in status between himself and Antiphanes. Amyntas' main defense is a question of Alexander's consistency, a similar theme to Philotas' own speech. His argument underlines one salient issue for a king's subjects: as far as lesser subjects are concerned, any favorite of the king is a substitute for the king himself. Both Tacitus (*Ann.* 13.19) and Curtius (3.12.25) stress the instability of a favorite's position. Hence Amyntas stresses the obligations of the *sacramentum pietatis* [oath of loyalty] (7.1.29); to court the favorite's approval means advancement or even survival, until that favorite loses his or her position. If a previous friendship with the fallen favorite is considered a crime, all people of lesser status would be guilty, since they either were friends or desired friendship with the favorite. Amyntas goes on to argue that Antiphanes' attempt to cast suspicion on Amyntas for keeping his horses is based on circumstantial evidence and motivated by personal invective. Amyntas considers base this man whose only military duty is to distribute horses to those who are going to fight. He does not ignore the implication of shame on Alexander's part at having a Macedonian soldier excuse himself at once to his king and to such a commonplace man.

Overall, Amyntas' argument is unanswerable. Yet ironically, the army is won over by the forced return of the youngest brother, Polemon, during the trial. In Arrian (3.27.2–3), Amyntas secures his acquittal by fetching Polemon back, an event that is no more dramatic than Curtius' depiction. However, Curtius has again chosen to stress the irrationality of the mob, which responds more to emotive factors. The mob is roused first to anger but then to sympathy—the latter by the young man's looks and apparent fraternal devotion. The historian comments somewhat sourly (7.2.3) that when the crowd heard Polemon's speech, they were moved to tears and so suddenly changed to the opposite opinion; thus the very act of Polemon's flight and, paradoxically, the guarantee of his brothers' innocence became his salvation. Alexander is not slow to exploit the political expediency of the situation: called on by the army and *amici* to pardon the brothers, he appears to restore his damaged prestige by an act of *clementia,* as well as to celebrate renewed ties of *fides* and *gratia.* Yet apart from the two-edged nature of *clementia,* which, as we have seen, by its very nature emphasizes the power of the individual who exercises it, the act has an ominous undercurrent.[30] These men were clearly of a lesser status than Philotas and his father.

The Death of Parmenion

The realities of power are shown by Curtius' narrative of the king's assassination of Parmenion. Alexander cannot afford to allow Parmenion to survive, for reasons that were given at 6.8.7 (cf. 6.8.18, 6.9.11), namely, that the general commanded a large army of his own and that his prestige with the soldiers was second only to the king's. One act of *vis* needs another, and this time it was too dangerous for the king to bring Parmenion to trial. In effect, the old general had already been accused by Alexander (6.9.4–15), and 6.11.39 perhaps implies that he had been condemned by the army as well, although his condemnation is not made explicit. Certainly at the beginning of book 7, the army is sympathetic to him. Diodorus (17.80.1) suggests that Parmenion was condemned at the same time as Philotas, Justin (12.5.1–3) claims that he was put to death after *quaestiones* (interrogations under torture) had been held for both himself and Philotas, and Strabo (15.2.10 [724]) says that Alexander sent agents to kill Parmenion, since he was seen as party to the conspiracy. Arrian (3.26.3–4) implies no formal condemnation, but he, too, recognizes that the assassination of Parmenion was politically necessary. As in Curtius, Parmenion's popularity with the soldiers is noted by Arrian (following Ptolemy), as one reason why he was so dangerous.

In Curtius, Alexander, shortly after Amyntas' trial, exploits both fear and *pietas* through his commissioning of Polydamas to go secretly and swiftly on racing camels to the Macedonian forces in Media, bearing a letter from himself to Parmenion and one signed with Philotas' seal, along with other letters to his prefects. The latter contained an indictment of Parmenion and his son and Alexander's prayer for vengeance. Polydamas' fear is emphasized at the outset. Alexander reminds the man of his loyalty to himself, over his association with Parmenion. He uses Polydamas, a personal friend of Parmenion, on the grounds that because of the latter's crime, the trust of both had been violated. Yet the king also holds Polydamas' brothers as hostages, thus enforcing the moral obligation with open threat.

---

30. On *clementia*, see chap. 5, 134–35. Syme, *Tacitus*, 1:414, notes it is not an aristocrat's virtue, as it expresses the will of a master. However, Seneca takes it seriously; see *De. Clem.* 1.3.3.

Curtius appears to have admired Parmenion, or at least he seized the opportunity of Parmenion's death to make a political point. His necrology of the general, particularly his statement at 7.2.33 that Parmenion had gained many successes without Alexander, while Alexander had achieved nothing without him, is not, pace Rolfe, necessarily more rhetorical than historically accurate.[31] Curtius has merely emphasized Parmenion's prominence before and since Alexander was king. He does not credit Alexander's achievements to Parmenion but rather simply notes the man's continual presence in Alexander's career, whether he was directly involved or not. But the death of Parmenion and, indeed, Amyntas' speech have demonstrated the increasing absolutism of the king's regime.

Alexander the General: *Virtus* and *Magnitudo Animi*

After the death of Parmenion, the king's initial campaigns are against the Arii (because of Satibarzanes' incursion) and the Arachosii. However, he rewards the Euergetae (the so-called Benefactors) for their *fides* to Cyrus.[32] Alexander's own valor on the battlefield and his constant thirst for *gloria* are prominent in the historian's narrative. These characteristics also feature in the speeches of Alexander (7.7.10–20) and the Scythian envoys (7.8.12–30). In fact, the king's eagerness to be at the forefront of the fighting results in his being wounded twice during the course of events. His genius for leadership and care for his soldiers are illustrated by two episodes, at 7.3.12–18 and 7.5.2–16, of which the latter is given a deliberate political twist in Curtius' narrative.

In the first of these incidents, the men fall victim to hypothermia, as the army crosses the frozen country of the Parapanisadae. Alexander personally goes among his soldiers, bodily lifting them and helping them to safety—an action that he repeats, more heroically again, at 8.4.2–17.

The second episode of the king's self-denial in his concern for his men occurs during the pursuit of Bessus, across the desert regions of Sogdiana: Alexander denies water brought to him in advance, because his soldiers are suffering from thirst.[33] Arrian (6.26.1–3) and Plutarch (*Alex*. 42.3–6)

---

31. Rolfe, 1:140.
32. See Arrian 3.27.4; Diod. 17.81.2. Cf. J. 12.5.9; *Metz Epit*. 4. Alexander's respect for the first Achaemenid king is well known (see Arrian 6.29.4–11 and Strabo 15.3.7 [730] = *FGrH* 139.F.51b, on the restoration of Cyrus' tomb) as well as his desire to surpass his achievements (see Arrian 6.24.3, on the Gedrosia crossing).
33. For the traditions on this story, see chap. 3, 81–82.

depict a spontaneous act of leadership; in Curtius, Alexander had been previously reminded by his friends that his courage is very important for the morale of the army (7.5.9). The king stands in battle dress and unrefreshed until the entire army has passed him by on its way to the river Oxus. This action may be in keeping with Curtius' explanation for the soldiers' *flagrans caritas* (burning affection) for Alexander back at 3.6.17. Such emphasis on a commander's physical excellence as well as his readiness to share hardship would have been well known to a Roman audience. Yet, although Curtius does not specifically allude to it, the prompting of Alexander's friends may carry a subtle implication that Alexander has to show himself as something more than mortal; gods do not need water.

In fact, the motif of divinity and divine favor occurs in three other episodes during book 7. In the first, at 7.6.4–7, a Sogdianian tribe surrenders on hearing of Alexander's wound in the leg, because only "impious people fought against the gods."[34] The second occurrence is during the Scythian's speech, at 7.8.26. Ironically in these two incidents, the historian's emphasis is on the king's mortality. In the third episode, 7.10.14–15, the soldiers are digging for water in the silted Oxus, without success, until a spring is found in Alexander's tent. As the men had failed to notice it before, they say it had only suddenly appeared, and the king himself is not slow to realize its value as divine propaganda.[35] The issue of Alexander's godhead, already heralded in the Macedonian response at Siwah and in the Philotas incident, surfaces again in the powerful confrontation between the king and his commander Cleitus.

The Death of Cleitus

Following the capture of Ariamazes' Rock, the opening sentence of book 8 recalls the importance of *fama* and *gloria*. The beginning of the book quickly reestablishes Alexander as a man of *vis*, a trait that also characterized Alexander's treatment of Ariamazes and his nobles. This furnishes a crucial background for the murder of Cleitus. Curtius' account (8.1.20–8.2.12) is by far the longest in the extant Alexander historians, together with Plutarch (*Alex.* 50–52), who himself offers, for the most part, a credible and profoundly revealing narrative of the murder. The

---

34. Cf. Hammond, *THA*, 142, who believes this episode is a romantic addition.
35. Cf. Arrian 4.15.7–8, where the author mentions springs of oil and water; on the other traditions, see Bosworth, *HCA*, 2:110–11.

episode was infamous, and Curtius, like Arrian, would have felt obliged to give it serious treatment, as well as being well aware of its dramatic impact.[36]

Out of our four main accounts, only Curtius establishes clearly that the episode took place at Maracanda. The elderly Artabazus wished to retire from his governorship of Bactria, and the king appointed Cleitus in his place, a detail that is only given in Curtius. The historian, true to his set practice of giving background information to enforce a point, emphasizes at 8.1.20-21 the strong ties of *fides* and familial *pietas* between Alexander and Cleitus; Cleitus is not only *vetus Philippi miles* [an old soldier of Philip's], who is famous by many campaigns, but the savior of the king's life and hence deserving of his *gratia*. Moreover, Hellanice, Cleitus' sister, who had reared Alexander, was as dear to him as his own mother. Thus Curtius, contrary to Schachermeyr's interpretation, believes that the appointment was an important one: as the historian says himself at 8.1.21, Alexander was entrusting the strongest part of his empire to Cleitus' loyalty and protection. Historically, while Cleitus' appointment might not have been a demotion, it could well have been a convenient and honorable way of removing him from court, of which he was only too well aware.[37]

The narrative of the episode, 8.1.22-52, agrees with and varies from the other sources. However, both in its presentation and certain details, it is quite unique. As a preliminary to the quarrel, Curtius' emphasis is on the king's excessive behavior as expressed by not only his drinking (the effects of which had already been earlier deplored by the historian, at 6.2.2) but also his boasting (8.1.22). The king's boasting is supported solely by Justin (12.6.1-2). Arrian (4.8.2-3), while stressing drinking, depicts flattery of Alexander from some of his followers, whereas Plutarch (*Alex*. 50.5-6) attests that Cleitus' resentment was initiated by drinking and a satiric song.

From 8.1.23-27, Alexander's boasts, in which he belittles Philip's achievements while extolling his own, are given in *oratio obliqua*. In particular, the king sneers at Philip's initiation into the religious mysteries on

---

36. On Cleitus, cf. Arrian 4.8-9; J. 12.6.1-16. On the episode's infamy, see Stadter, 104 f. For modern discussions, see Seibert, 141-43; Schachermeyr, *Alexander der Grosse*, (1973) 362-70; E.D. Carney, *GRBS* 22 (1981): 149-60. The best analysis of the traditions is Bosworth, *HCA*, 2:51 f. He is equally worthwhile on the other episodes included in Arrian's digression, 4.7.4-4.14.4; see *HCA*, 2:45 f.

37. Schachermeyr, *Alexander der Grosse*, (1973) 363 f.; cf. Lane Fox, *Alexander the Great*, 311; see also Bosworth, *HCA*, 2:56.

Samothrace (8.1.26) when Philip should have been attacking Asia. This peculiar detail suggests some interesting underlying issues; the evidence is obscure on the reasons for Philip's initiation, but according to Diodorus (5.48.35–50), several divine and quasi-divine figures, including Orpheus, Jason, the Dioscuri, and Heracles, were initiated there and attained success in their campaigns as a result. Not all of these heroes were prominent in Macedonian cult practices; however, Alexander's implication is not only that he did not need such association but that by his own deeds, the size of which had surpassed belief, he was already worthy of divine recognition.[38]

Oratio obliqua is used to convey the tensions inherent between young and old at 8.1.27–32; Cleitus' response, as the spokesman for the older men, is also in reported speech. Plutarch emphasizes these tensions with the additional levels of conflict between Greeks and Persians and between Macedonians and Greeks (*Alex.* 51.4). However, Cleitus' quotation from Euripides, used in Plutarch as a fatal punch line (*Alex.* 51.8–9), appears in Curtius at the start of the quarrel, heralding the main thrust of his argument, at 8.1.30–34, which in turn culminates in an outburst in *oratio recta*. Cleitus is not entirely free from blame: Curtius' attitude toward Alexander at this point is somewhere between the outright hostility of Justin and the conciliatory tone of Arrian. The king, though at first tolerating Cleitus' words, is seized by *ingens ira* because Cleitus, carried away by wine and *prava contentio animi* [base perversity] (Curt. 8.1.33) does not modify his speech. Thus, he is also guilty of *immoderatio*—a point that is stressed at 8.1.38 and 8.2.2.

In certain aspects, Cleitus' complaints are very different from what he says in the other extant sources. The championship of Philip, the conflict between the young and old, the sneer at Ammon, and Cleitus' actions at the Granicus—all of which appear in varying degrees in the other accounts—are there and carefully placed. But only in Curtius does Cleitus depreciate the campaign against Persia in terms of the worthiness of its soldiers, which, as I noted in chapter 2, appears to have been a rhetorical topos.[39] Moreover, Cleitus explicitly defends Parmenion (which increases Alexander's anger), in addition to reproaching the king for the death of Attalus. The linking of Parmenion and Attalus, both of blue-blooded Macedonian nobility, not only emphasizes Cleitus' sympathies

---

38. The Dioscuri and Heracles are compared with Alexander at Arrian 4.8.2–3. See Bosworth, *HCA*, 2:52 f. and, on Samothrace, 56.
39. Curt. 8.1.37; see chap. 2.

but reminds Alexander (and the audience) of his political murders, however necessary they were.

The account at 8.1.43–52 is short but comprehensive. Cleitus is ordered to leave but, despite the efforts of others to move him, remains behind—in Aristobulus' version, Cleitus is taken outside but returns to have the last word. Curtius' focus is on Alexander's great *ira*, at 8.1.43 and again at 8.1.49. The narrative at 8.1.43–49 is mostly in agreement with Arrian and Plutarch, although with variations. Alexander tries to kill Cleitus but is prevented; his weapon is taken away, which in turn causes him to believe he has been betrayed. He calls out for armed assistance. But at 8.1.49–52 the text departs radically from the other accounts. The king breaks away from Ptolemy and Perdiccas, who are trying to hold him; rushes into the vestibule of the palace; snatches another spear from a sentinel; and deliberately lies in wait for Cleitus, who must pass him on his way out. Thus the murder, far from being the impulsive act of violence cited by Justin (12.6.3) and Arrian (in one version, at 4.8.9) or the result of Cleitus' own stupidity (Plut. *Alex.* 51.8), becomes an explicit, deliberate act in Curtius.

Alexander's extreme desire for vengeance led to his excessive response. Whether this aspect was originally in Curtius' source or the result of an adaptation on his part is hard to say. Diodorus' version may have provided some answers to this question, but his account has been lost. Curtius' emphasis is clear: the deed is *licentia regni*. The consequences of Alexander's actions go beyond the deed itself, lending significance to the sequel, at 8.2.1–12. Unlike that of Philotas and Parmenion, this murder is not judicial, though, ironically, it is made so, *post factum*.

Along with the problems offered by the eyewitness accounts, the story of the murder must have been complicated by the many variant sources. Curtius and the other Alexander historians evidently sifted through the same or similar material. In a manner not too unlike some modern scholars, Curtius' account was probably composite, although it is colored by his own literary emphasis. Drama is of paramount concern; the issues at foot—the king's *superbia*, the generation conflict, political murder, Alexander's godhead, *fides*, and *libertas*—are deliberately kept in *oratio obliqua*, apart from Cleitus' one direct speech, to enhance the impact of Alexander's own exclamation.

However, these themes are highlighted in the king's reaction to the event. This reaction in itself is historical: the other four accounts all comment on Alexander's response, from a king who first exalts over the corpse and then repents (Justin 12.6.5–9), to an Alexander who shuts himself away in remorse, for three days (Arrian 4.9.4) or one and a half (Plut. *Alex.* 52.1). Interestingly, the other traditions depict one of Alexander's first responses as attempted suicide, although the story is given as a *logos* in Arrian. The vulgate historians seem convinced the attempt was genuine; some modern scholars have been more skeptical.[40]

Curtius' account adds some unique details. Like Arrian, he introduces the sequel with an authorial, moral comment. However, whereas Arrian pities Alexander for his lack of *sophrosyne* and then commends his repentance, Curtius focuses on the somber implications of the offense: "A king had taken over the loathsome function of an executioner [carnificis] and had punished license of speech [verborum licentiam], which may have been blamed on the wine by an abominable murder [nefanda caede]" (8.2.2).[41] Seneca (*De ira* 3.13.5) noted that the deed could have been avoided. In Curtius, Alexander's action is *nefas,* a crime that has strong associations with the transgression of divine law. Alexander violated the *gratia* he owed to Cleitus as his host and the savior of his life, as well as *pietas* from his association with the man's sister. Moreover, Cleitus, however ill advisedly *(inconsulte)* or rashly he had spoken, was behaving as a Macedonian *hetairos* was accustomed to do at banquets, which were often noisy, drunken, and sometimes violent occasions. Cleitus had indeed immoderately abused *libertas;* but Alexander's obligations to an *egregius vir* should have outweighed the insult.[42]

This last fact is considered by the king from 8.2.7: thus the king's repentance appears to be more out of concern for his image. Similarly theatrical is his gesture of having Cleitus' body, all bloody as it was, brought to him. In Curtius, Alexander tells himself that his crime was the result of Father Liber's wrath, rather than of what he was told by others, and there is no mention of the counseling activities of the philosophers Callisthenes or Anaxarchus at that point; plausibly a deliberate suppres-

---

40. The suicide attempt may have derived from Cleitarchus; see Hammond, *THA,* 104. On the theatricality of the episode, see Green, *Alexander of Macedon,* 364.
41. Cf. 9.10.29, where Curtius' comment on the execution of Astaspes might be an echo.
42. Heavy drinking of undiluted wine was a regular feature of Macedonian court symposia. Cf., on Philip's reign, Athen. 10.435C (= *FGrH* 115.F.236; cf. 115.F.162, 225); on Alexander's continuation of the practice, see E.N. Borza, *In the Shadow of Olympus: The Emergence of Macedon,* 241–42. There are other examples of Macedonian nobles making provocative remarks within such a context; cf. Plut. *Alex.* 9.7–8. But on Cleitus' abuse of *parrhesia,* see Bosworth, *HCA,* 2:57 f.

sion, in view of the historian's summary after the death of Callisthenes. The reference to Father Liber is also significant. Unlike Aristobulus, whose comment on Alexander's drinking habits is a well-known apologia (Arrian 7.29.4), Curtius interprets the king's *cupido vini* as part of his *licentia*. Interestingly, the motif of blaming the incident on the wrath of Dionysus is historical (cf. Arrian 4.9.5) and, as Bosworth suggests, perhaps part of the deliberate propaganda created by the king's entourage in relation to his imitation of the god.[43]

In a detail unique to Curtius (8.2.12), the Macedonian army declares Cleitus to have been justly slain *(iure interfectus)*, to the extent of even wanting to deny him funeral rights.[44] Curtius has neatly demonstrated not only the king's supremacy and his mens' utter dependence on him but the servility of what should have been a freethinking body. The death of Cleitus is also a turning point in Alexander's relations with his officers; hence the historian comments at 8.4.30 on Alexander's marriage to Roxane, "but after the slaughter of Cleitus, with free speech [libertas] removed, they agreed, but only as far as their faces, the feature that most expresses subservience." One wonders if the historian was perhaps thinking of the Roman Senate as well, foreshadowing Tacitus. The servility of this body under the principate is a dominant theme of the *Annals*.[45]

Alexander's Marriage to Roxane

In view of the preceding quotation, it seems appropriate to discuss the king's famous marriage (8.4.21–30) here. In context, the incident takes place after the army has nearly been wiped out by a violent storm (8.4.1–17). The climax of this episode is an anecdote about Alexander giving his own seat by the fire to a Macedonian common soldier who, half-frozen, had reached camp. When the man realizes where he is and starts up in fright, Alexander's reply is to point out the difference between the Persian Great King and himself. By highlighting the king's sense of obligation to his subjects, albeit his more lowly subjects, this

---

43. Bosworth, *Alexander and the East*, 98–132, esp. 119–27.

44. In a political context, the Romans considered homicide justifiable particularly when an individual's behavior was perceived to threaten the state; see Cic. *De or*. 2.106 and *Pro Mil*. 8; Livy *Epit*. 59; Val Max. 6.2.3; Vell. Pat. 2.4.4. On the significance of the army's decree, see Badian, *Studies in Greek and Roman History*, 198; Errington, *Chiron* 8 (1978): 108.

45. See Syme, *Tacitus*, 1:474 f.; cf. Tac. *Ann*. 1.2, where the historian implies it was a gradual process. At Augustus' death, there were no challenges to Tiberius; cf. *Ann*. 1.11 f.

episode illustrates Alexander's paternalism and apparent equity—an ironic contrast with the suppression of *libertas* prevalent after the death of Cleitus.

At 8.4.21, Roxane's father, Oxyartes, described as a noble satrap, surrenders to the king. Although the name of this man is the same in Arrian 4.19.5, Curtius has not similarly associated this event with the taking of a mountain fortress. In fact, the ancient sources are all in conflict on when and how the marriage took place.[46] However, they do agree that Roxane was very beautiful and that the king fell in love with her.

Curtius, Arrian, and Plutarch differ in their attitude toward the match. Plutarch, while stressing the love element, also says the marriage was part of Alexander's policy of reconciliation. Arrian commends Alexander's decision to marry the girl instead of taking her as a prize of war, as an example of the king's self-control. Curtius presents the episode in another light. In the narrative of the marriage, he carefully introduces elements that are stressed in his own summary of its significance. Roxane is brought in at a banquet of barbarian magnificence, and Alexander's *cupido* for her is the result of the indulgence of *fortuna*. The historian draws a deft contrast between Alexander's *continentia* when he met the female members of Darius' family and his current, more degenerate character, carried away by *amor* for this "little maiden, of low birth in comparison to royal stock" (Curt. 8.4.25). The rather derogatory comment on Roxane's status, since she is, after all, only the daughter of a Bactrian baron, undermines Alexander's own justification for the marriage at 8.4.25–26.

There is an element of impulse or haste about the whole undertaking—the king, in the ardor of his passion *(in medio cupiditatis ardore)*, appears to marry Roxane on the spot. Curtius describes the simple Macedonian marriage ceremony—an ironic detail, because he is also emphatic that the Macedonian nobility did not favor the match. The summary, 8.4.29–30, especially the *ex captiva* clause, emphasizes the historian's interpretation of the Macedonian nobility's point of view: their thought was for a future ruler born from a captive. Again, another irony becomes apparent at 10.6, when Alexander's unborn child by Roxane becomes a focus of contention in the debate over the succession. Ptolemy (10.6.13 f.) raises similar objections over Roxane's or Barsine's offspring as suitable kings for the Macedonians.

---

46. Cf. Arrian 4.19.5–6; Plut. *Alex.* 47.4. See Hamilton, *Plutarch*, 129; A.B. Bosworth, *JHS* 101 (1981): 30–31 and n. 95.

As one may expect, Curtius' tone is highly rhetorical and moral. Historically, Macedonian kings sometimes married non-Macedonians, usually for political reasons. Philip II married no fewer than seven wives, and only one of these, Cleopatra, came from the Macedonian nobility.[47] According to Diodorus (17.16.2), Alexander was urged to marry before he left on his Asian expedition; however, the reason was to produce an heir, not necessarily to take a Macedonian bride. In any case, marrying into a Macedonian noble house carried its own dangers of factional or family strife, as Philip found out to his cost.[48]

Yet the historian deliberately avoids suggesting any political motives on Alexander's part—until later at 10.3.11, when the king addresses his foreign troops after the Macedonians mutiny. At the time of the marriage, though, Curtius presents the deed as being far from an episode of the king's self-control, but rather an act of whim; despite the obvious dynastic implications, Alexander did not consult his *amici,* who were ashamed that Alexander had chosen his father-in-law from a conquered nation and amid wine and feasting, but who were too afraid to say anything. This character is Alexander *tyrannus.* As with the murder of Cleitus, Alexander's action is *licentia regni* at the expense of *libertas.*

The Debate on Alexander's Divinity

The sequel to the marriage in terms of internal politics and *libertas* is Alexander's wish that he should receive divine honors in the form of prostration, which is met by the opposition of the court historian, Callisthenes (8.5.5–24). This episode is in turn connected to the Conspiracy of the Pages. It is not my purpose to discuss the historicity of the subsequent debate on *proskynesis* given in Arrian and Curtius, although it very likely occurred. But regardless of the traditions behind the debate, the accounts of both historians were colored by their own contemporary views.[49]

Curtius' attitude toward Alexander throughout the *proskynesis* affair is hard to determine. Initially the characterization appears negative: the king's plan to have such honor paid to him is base (*pravus,* Curt. 8.5.8)

---

47. See Athen. 13.557D; Plut. *Alex.* 9.7; J. 9.7.3. See also A. Tronson, "Satyrus the Peripatetic and the Marriages of Philip II," *JHS* 104 (1984): 116–26; J. Ellis, *Philip II and Macedonian Imperialism,* 211 f.

48. See E.J. Baynham, "Why Didn't Alexander Marry Before Leaving Macedonia?" *RhM* (forthcoming).

49. See Bosworth, *HCA,* 2:78, for a summary of modern opinion on the historicity of the debate; see also *FAA,* 116–17, on Curtius' contemporary interpretation in particular.

and solely because of his desire to be believed the son of Jupiter, not merely called so. In addition, Cleon the Sicilian (mentioned by no other source), who makes a speech in support of divine honors, is lumped together with such Greeks as Agis of Argos, who is described as *pessimorum carminum conditor* [a composer of the most wretched poems] (8.5.8). These men who flatter the king are termed a perpetual bane of royalty *(perpetuum malum regum,* 8.5.6), a very similar sentiment to one expressed by Arrian elsewhere. Agis also appears in Arrian as a flatterer and a sophist, along with Anaxarchus.[50]

Curtius' contemporary prejudices are evident, exhibited by not only a dislike of adulation but also a certain amount of racism. However, whatever he personally thinks of Alexander's wishes or his use of flatterers who are *purgamenta* (excrement) mixed in among his followers, Cleon's speech at 8.5.9–12, in *oratio obliqua,* is clearly political and serious in tone. It should be noted that although Cleon was a professional parasite, a species that had long been attached to the courts of kings or despots, Alexander intended to use him as a spokesman, just as Antony's later gesture of offering a crown to Caesar (Suet. *Div. Iul.* 79.2; Plut. *Caes.* 61.5–8; etc.) could be seen as a way of testing public opinion.[51]

Cleon's speech differs considerably from the equivalent oration of Anaxarchus in Arrian. To some extent, it is a deliberate reflection of Roman imperial divine policy, particularly with its emphasis on the majesty of empire as its safety and on *gratia* in the form of a pinch of incense as an easy return for the great *beneficia* provided by the king; in much the same way, the Roman emperor was a kind of superpatron for the Roman people. We might recall Augustus' celebration of his largesse and his restoration of the temples in the *Res gestae* (15–24).[52]

Callisthenes is described (Curt. 8.5.13) as a man of some dignity, if not austerity *(gravitas),* and his ready freedom of speech *(prompta libertas)* is hateful *(invisa)* to the king. His speech at 8.5.14–19, in *oratio recta,* is

---

50. On Cleon's identity, see Berve, 2: no. 437. Mützell (751) noted, "Sonst nicht gennant"; see also L. Edmunds, *GRBS* 12 (1971): 387. Cleon's existence is accepted by Bosworth, *HCA,* 2:78. For Arrian's views on flatterers, see chap. 5, 137.

51. On parasites, see Athen. 6.234D f. Curtius is not alone in disliking non-Romans; cf. his 4.1.30 with Atkinson, *Curtius* i, 285. The episode of Antony's gesture was notorious; on the traditions, see Gelzer (supra, n. 21), 321 n. 2.

52. The idea that the majesty of the empire and its ruler was the guardian of its safety developed in the Hellenistic period; see W.W. Tarn and G.T. Griffith, *Hellenistic Civilisation* (London, 1952), 52–55; F.W. Walbank, *The Hellenistic World* (London, 1981), 210–17.

glib and polished, as were the orations of Philotas and the Scythians. He succeeds in making Cleon look foolish, at the same time as appealing to the Macedonians, particularly the older men, like Cleitus had done. Yet he also deliberately avoids the issue of policy, except for a crafty twist at the end of his speech, where he says he does not wish to be told by the conquered how to honor his king and instead addresses himself to the question of consecration per se.

Curtius also omits the anecdotes that Plutarch and Arrian give on Callisthenes' intellectual vanity and lack of diplomacy: the tactless display of eristics on Callisthenes' part in the former (*Alex.* 53.3–6), and the story of the historian refusing to do obeisance to Alexander and so "going short of a kiss," which is common to both (Plut. *Alex.* 54.4–6; Arrian 4.12.4–5). It thus appears relatively easy to believe that Curtius is favorable toward this man.

Curtius' attitude toward Callisthenes soon becomes evident. His own comment at 8.5.19 is "Callisthenes was heard with approval as if a champion of the public freedom" [veluti vindex publicae libertatis].[53] However, the *vindex publicae libertatis* phrase has been carefully qualified by *veluti*, "as if." Callisthenes' *libertas* has been rash, if not downright ostentatious—hence Curtius' makes apposite use of *contumacia* in referring to Callisthenes at 8.6.1. Again the term implies a stubbornness of opposition beyond prudence. It is tempting to draw a parallel between Curtius' Callisthenes and the Thrasea Paetus of Tacitus' *Annals*. Both are brave men, and each speaks his mind against the ruler. The *libertas* of both on a personal level emphasizes the servility of their peers yet, in turn, provokes the wrath of the *princeps* or *rex*.[54]

In summary, an ambiguous current runs through the *proskynesis* episode. While Curtius may be critical of Alexander's desire to stress his divinity, he apparently does not admire the historian who opposes the policy of the king in the name of *libertas* and who merely makes himself vulnerable. Nor is his obituary of Callisthenes, 8.8.21–22, necessarily a contradiction of his reserved attitude. He acknowledges Callisthenes' virtues—that he had a character that was ill suited to court life and to

---

53. *Vindex publicae libertatis* is a peculiar expression, which is hardly used elsewhere. Curtius uses *vindices* of the Athenians (10.2.6); cf. Seneca *Contr.* 9.1.4, *adsertor publicae libertatis*, describing Miltiades, who was defending his country's *libertas* against the Persians. See Pliny *NH* 20.160 on Iulius Vindex.

54. For the *libertas* of Thrasea Paetus, see Tac. *Ann.* 13.49, 14.12, 14.49; cf. C.H. Wirzubski, *Libertas as a Political Idea at Rome during the Late Republic and Early Principate*, 129.

flatterers as well as that his death aroused great ill will among the Greeks—just as Tacitus recognizes Thrasea Paetus' qualities, in his comment that by eliminating him, Nero was murdering *virtus* itself (*Ann.* 16.21). Yet in the final analysis, each historian's attitude toward these outspoken men is ambivalent: certainly Tacitus tempered his admiration, and Curtius could not condone waste.[55]

The Conspiracy of Hermolaus and the Pages

The opposition of Callisthenes is intrinsically connected to the Conspiracy of the Pages in view of the alleged role that he was supposed to have had in its instigation. Of the four historians who narrate the conspiracy and Callisthenes' fall, only Arrian (4.13.1) and Curtius (8.6–8) give this episode much detailed treatment. Plutarch includes the conspiracy within his discussion on Callisthenes (*Alex.* 55), while Justin (12.7.1–3) sees Callisthenes' destruction, along with that of many leading Macedonians who were executed "on the pretext of conspiracy," as the result of opposition to Alexander's wish for prostration. Justin's blame is thus squarely on the king; it is *superbia regia* at work, Persian or not.

Plutarch, Arrian, and Curtius also do not believe that Callisthenes was actually guilty of an active role in the conspiracy; rather, his outspokenness, Alexander's dislike of him, and the fact that he was a tutor of the Pages led to his indictment. Although Aristobulus and Ptolemy apparently believed in his guilt as an easy and convenient solution, Arrian is aware that most sources contradict this conclusion (4.14.1), and Plutarch (*Alex.* 55.5) and Curtius say outright that the boys did not denounce Callisthenes.

As an appropriate context to the conspiracy, both Curtius (8.6.2–6; cf. 5.1.42) and Arrian (4.13.1) discuss the origins of the young attendants. Their importance lay not only in that they were the sons of Macedonian nobles and thus, as Curtius points out, a *seminarium* (using the metaphor of a plant nursery) for future generals and governors but that they lived very closely to the king (8.6.23).[56] This latter factor emphasizes the

---

55. Syme, *Tacitus,* 1:561, and Wirszubski, *Libertas as a Political Idea at Rome,* 138–43, argue that Tacitus admired Thrasea Paetus; cf. Tac. *Ann.* 16.25-27. Syme terms the historian's censure at 14.49 "mild," which is perhaps appropriate in view of 15.23. A better example of Tacitus' cynicism is *Ag.* 41–42; cf. his comment on Musonius Rufus' *intempestiva sapientia,* at *Hist.* 3.81.

56. On the institution of the Pages (a convenient misnomer), see N.G.L. Hammond, *Historia* 39 (1990): 261–90; Heckel, *Marshals,* 237 f.

double danger to Alexander from their plot; this very closeness gave them ready access to him, and moreover, they would be least suspected. The conspiracy initially arises out of the personal grievances of Hermolaus and Sostratus, fellow Pages and lovers. Hermolaus had speared a boar intended for the king (8.6.7), and Alexander ordered him flogged for this insolence, which was consistent with Macedonian customs (8.6.5; cf. Aelian *VH* 14.48).

However, a Macedonian custom was to be the catalyst of a protest against a perceived "non-Macedonian" king. This reason for the conspiracy forms the basis for Hermolaus' attack on Alexander's *regnum* and his own reply, in a brilliant display of eristics on Curtius' part. The picture is not a simple one of idealism striking a blow for *libertas* against *superbia regni,* as the events are shortly to reinforce. At 8.6.8–25, the theme of *fides* is prominent. The boys' plan is carefully thought out without youthful rashness *(nec puerili impetu rem exsecuti sunt),* and Hermolaus and Sostratus persuade nine other Pages to join them, which evidently stresses the extent of the ill feeling against the king. Paradoxically, the loyalty of the boys rests on their common *ira* with Alexander (8.6.12).

The danger to the king was very real, as the Pages, on guard duty, planned to kill him as he slept. But his omnipresent *fortuna* and the entertainments at the banquet cause him to prolong the festivities. Just as Alexander is going to bed, a woman with the gift of second sight, who had become something of a guardian to the king, warns him to go back to the banquet. This tale, deriving from Aristobulus (Arrian 4.13.5–6), appears to be a somewhat odd choice for Curtius, given his accustomed scorn of anything to do with divination. But he rationalizes her presence by the comment that she was thought to be of unsound mind; besides, on one level, she is simply part of Alexander's *fortuna.*

In an appalling state of anticlimax, the loyalty of the Pages toward each other proves to be of short duration: ironically, either the king's *benignitas* toward the boys (since they had stood watch all night) or belief in the apparent opposition of the gods causes one of the Pages, Epimenes, in a manner reminiscent of Nicomachus, to reveal the plot to his brother, who in turn takes him to Alexander's quarters.

Hermolaus' speech at his trial (8.7 f.) is an attack on Alexander's *superbia,* his *saevitia,* his *luxuria,* his Medizing, his supposed godhead and desire for *proskynesis,* his oppression of *libertas*—in short, almost every example of corrupt behavior toward his followers that he has hitherto displayed. It is a brief, scathing, and emotional oration.[57] Yet despite the chief strength of Hermolaus' argument that Alexander has changed from being a Macedonian king to a *rex Persarum* and so does not deserve loyalty, the *impium facinus* remains: as Alexander has survived, he is still the king. The youth's father tries twice to physically stop him from speaking and even draws his sword on his own son (8.7.7), an action that was perhaps not entirely out of fear of the king's reprisals but rather also out of humanity. When the boys are handed over to members of their own cohort for punishment, Curtius, in a perceptive, bleak comment, remarks that the others tortured the offenders before putting them to death, so that by their savage zeal, they might show their *fides* to Alexander (8.8.20).

Hermolaus' broken *fides* and *pietas* is stressed by the king in the opening lines of his speech (Curt. 8.8.1–3): the boy is a robber and hence is lawless and a would-be thief of the king's life (other equivalent terms are used throughout as reminders); his action in attempting to kill Alexander, whom he should have looked to as a father, is madness *(dementia)*. This last word was also used of Bessus: the king has not only reminded his audience of the familial *pietas* Hermolaus owed him, but has linked him with the regicide Bessus.

Alexander quickly destroys Hermolaus' credibility, since it cannot be said that he even had a case. However, the king, in an ironic reversal of the accusation/defense situation that we find in the Philotas and Amyntas trials, proceeds to answer each of Hermolaus' charges against his rule. One might compare Arrian's defense of Alexander in his eulogy of the king, toward the end of book 7.[58] The speech is one of the longest of Alexander's orations in the *Historiae,* and it is a tribute to Curtius' rhetorical skill and insight that he can present both an indictment and a defense of *regnum* that appear equally convincing. Alexander justifies himself in terms of *fides, clementia, vis,* and *fama*.

Yet the speech is also a compilation of clever, sophistic arguments. For instance, Alexander emphasizes that the Macedonians had demanded the death of Alexander Lyncestes. Moreover, he argues that Cleitus "forced" the king to be angry with him and that Alexander had been more toler-

---

57. On the parallels between Hermolaus' direct speech in Curtius and his reported one in Arrian, see chap. 2, 50–51.
58. Arrian 7.29–30; on the peroration, see Bosworth, *FAA,* 135 f.

ant of his rash tongue as he abused the king and the Macedonians than Cleitus himself would have been. Alexander has adroitly identified the audience's cause and his own as one, and the latter argument is unanswerable.

Clementia, although included in Augustus' *Res gestae* (34) as a virtue for a *princeps,* also carries, as we saw earlier, an inevitable sense of power. Alexander defines *clementia* in these terms.

> The clemency of kings and leaders depends not just on their own character but on the character of their subjects too. Rule is rendered less harsh by obedience; but when respect leaves men's minds and we mix the highest and lowest together without distinction, then we need force to repel force. (8.8.8)[59]

The argument is blatantly monarchical. Alexander ignores any allowance for the obligations of either *amicitia* as Philotas or the Scythians would see it or *libertas.* The bottom line is obedience to the *rex.* From that point on, the king proceeds smoothly along to each answer (Curt. 8.8.12, 8.8.14–16); greed *(avaritia)* is, in fact, generosity *(liberalitas);* since the whole army shares in the spoils of victory, honor for the defeated Persian nobility is necessary for *gratia,* and their *fides* is necessary to maintain *imperium.* Finally, both the king's claims to be son of Ammon and his recent adorning of the army, far from being personal desires, are justifiable from the considerations of *fama,* in view of the coming Indian campaigns. Alexander's claim of godhead would impress the native populations.

This explanation of the king's policy is important: in addition to showing Curtius' interpretation of Alexander's motives, it is significant that the king feels obliged to defend himself at all. The conspiracy was a very dangerous affair. It cannot be denied that Callisthenes' role is a significant motif in both speeches. At 8.7.3, Alexander asks Hermolaus to tell what he had learned from his teacher, Callisthenes, a point that he returns to in the first line of his own speech at 8.8. Thus, in keeping with his desire to destroy Callisthenes, he wishes to present the Pages as mere disciples. Hermolaus himself, although insisting that Callisthenes was innocent, stresses that he has been shut away because of his dangerous

---

59. Curt. 8.8.8: *Regum ducumque clementia non in ipsorum modo, sed etiam in illorum qui parent ingeniis sita est. Obsequio mitigantur imperia; ubi vero reverentia excessit animis et summa imis confunduntur, vi opus est, ut vim repellamus.*

eloquence. Alexander ends his oration with a shrewd and correct reply to this: Callisthenes, being Olynthian, did not have Macedonian citizenship rights.

Finally, Curtius' account of the episode finishes with his necrology of Callisthenes. On another level, the conspiracy goes beyond the allegation that a group of idealistic youths, urged on by their teacher, believed themselves to be tyrant slayers—the allegation that caused the king to defend his *regnum*. Curtius does not admire Hermolaus or even condone his action; hence he stresses the youth's personal motives and the attempted crime itself. However, the boys' status and the implication of their deed is significant. Curtius' first statement about this youth is that he is a *puer nobilis* [a well-born boy] (8.6.7). Previously, aspects of Alexander's rule had disturbed his older officers, represented by Philotas during his confession and, more recently, by Cleitus. Each exercised *libertas* in criticizing the king. But Alexander also affronted members of the young nobility, and whatever Hermolaus' motives, his speech is likewise an expression of *libertas,* a statement of grievances that pertain to the whole Macedonian hierarchy of officers. Yet like Cleitus, whom the Macedonian army declared to have been "justly slain," the Pages are put to death. Importantly, their conspiracy is the last example of opposition to the king from his nobility on any scale for the rest of the *Historiae;* from now on, apart from a sole, drunken rebuke from Meleager (8.12.17–18), any confrontation will come from the army, which to date has been essentially loyal on all occasions.

In his summary at 8.8.20–23, Curtius draws together the threads of the internal political narrative from books 6–8. Although there is considerable conflict among the sources on the manner of Callisthenes' death, Curtius opted for the statement that he died after torture (8.8.21). The reference to his former counseling of Alexander during the Cleitus affair (which he did not mention at the time) links that episode's implications to the recent events. Also, the historian's final statement of the chapter is an echo of his comment on Darius' reaction after his execution of Charidemus; Alexander regretted his deed when it was too late (8.8.23). The absolutism of Alexander's power is complete. Curtius' attitude toward Alexander's internal operation of his kingship, more complex than the simple statement would perhaps imply, is encapsulated in the opening line of 8.9: "But lest he nourish idleness, which sows rumor, [Alexander] set out for India, being always more distinguished in war than after a victory." The king needed the impetus of war to maintain his *fama* and to provide distraction from the less appealing aspects of his *regnum*.

We cannot know what sentiments Curtius Rufus expressed in his lost preface. However, he has much in common with more celebrated Roman historians: namely, an inherent didacticism, consistent authorial moral comment, political insight, and literary skill. The contemplation of history, says Livy (praef. 10), can teach one what to imitate and what to avoid. Such a principle would admirably apply to a study on Alexander.

Appendix: The Problem of Curtius' Date and Identity

The bulk of Curtian scholarship has long been concerned with the problems of trying to ascertain a date for his history and a possible identity of its author.[1] Since no ancient commentator that we know of refers to a full Latin work on Alexander that would fit the *Historiae* or connects a Curtius Rufus with such an account, and as the preface of the history has been lost, any attempt to establish a date of composition must be based on contemporary references within the work itself.[2] As these references are sparse and ambiguous and as even the most important clue, namely, the panegyric in book 10, has been used to support scholars' arguments for a variety of emperors, the problem remains impossible to solve. Similarly, any attempt to connect what is known of several Curtii Rufi in antiquity with a history on Alexander must rest on conjecture.

However, some discussion of the issue is necessary, to set an approximate chronological context. Despite certain claims to the contrary, recent analysis of Curtius' Latinity seems to place him in the first or second century A.D.; Sir Ronald Syme's summation of Curtius' style as "sub-Livian but pre-Tacitean" is probably an accurate, broad chronological fixation.[3] The question is whether we can be more precise in assigning a date to the work. This appendix surveys the other internal evidence in the *Historiae* that suggests an approximate date of composition, along with the famous digression on Rome's new *princeps*. Modern analysis will naturally be taken into account, but a full critique of scholarship on the problem over the last thirty years is not my purpose.[4]

---

1. See chap. 1. See also Fears, *Hermes* 102 (1974): 623 nn. 1–2, and *CPh* 71 (1976): 214–23, nn. 17–18.

2. See Hamilton, *Historia* 37 (1988): 445 n. 3.

3. R. Syme, "The Word *Opimus*—Not Tacitean," *Eranos* 85 (1987): 111; cf. Syme, *The Augustan Aristocracy* (Oxford, 1986), 438. Contra, see K. Bourazelis, *Ariadne* 4 (1988): 258–59.

4. For early discussion of the problem, see Dosson's bibliography, 18 f.; for a more

Various clues in the *Historiae* have been used as indications of a date, such as references to cataphract (or fully armoured) cavalry, the Parthians and their Eastern cities, and archery, as well as a digression on the contemporary prosperity of Tyre.[5] These references have been particularly used in support of a late date for Curtius.[6] Yet Atkinson rightly asserts that Curtius consistently refers to the Parthians as masters of the old Persian Empire during his own day.[7] That some late writers interchange terms is not enough in itself to justify that Curtius wrote in complete ignorance of the collapse of the Parthian Empire, and unlike Ammianus, Curtius clearly differentiates between Persians and Parthians. His description at 6.2.12 indicates that Curtius thought the heartland of Parthia, with its capital of Hecatompylus, was the governing center of the East. This scenario easily fits a date in the first century A.D. but does not accord with the Sassanid period. Also, if Curtius were a late writer, it would have been more likely for him to reflect what was known about the collapse of the Parthian Empire: indeed, Atkinson's argument is supported by Curtius' own tendency to display his knowledge of foreign peoples. It seems hardly probable that he would have continually confused the two dynasties, especially in view of his emphasis on *fortuna:* if he were late, the fall of one empire and the rise of another would have provided a literary opportunity too good to miss.

A.M. Devine and other scholars have also used the Parthian references in an attempt to rule out a post-Trajanic emperor as a possible contender

---

recent survey, see Korzeniewski, "Die Zeit des Quintus Curtius Rufus," 4–50. See also the critique of Rodriguez, *Aspectos de Q. Curtius Rufus*, 3–84; Atkinson, *Curtius* i, 19–73. For the most recent, bibliographical survey, see Atkinson, *ANRW* II.34.4 (1997): section 3.

5. See Atkinson, *Curtius* i, 20–25. On archery, see infra, n. 28. Curtius refers to the Parthians as being dominant in the East, at 4.12.11, 5.7.9, 5.8.1, and 6.2.12. Cf. Atkinson's discussion on the historian's references to Persepolis (5.7.9) and Ecbatana (5.8.1), at loc. cit., 23.

6. See Fears, *Hermes* 102 (1974): 624, and *CPh* 71 (1976): 223. Fears argued that Curtius' statements on the Parthians indicate that he must have written before the victory of the Sassanids over the Parthian king Artabanus and the establishment of a new dynasty in ca. 226/7 A.D. According to Fears, the terms *Parthi* and *Persae* are used interchangeably by writers of the third and fourth centuries A.D., such as Festus and Ammianus Marcellinus; therefore, Curtius might be referring to the period after the Persian resurgence, and the references to the Parthians in power are not especially convincing.

7. Atkinson, *Curtius* i, 20–23. Digressions on ethnology are common in Curtius; cf. 4.7.18–21, 5.6.17–19, 7.3.7–11, 8.9.20–37.

for Curtius' *princeps*.[8] Hadrian, Septimius Severus, Severus Alexander, Gordian III, and even very late emperors, such as Constantine and Theodosius, have all found support at one time.[9] At 6.2.12, Curtius comments on Alexander's advance into Parthiene: "From here they marched into Parthiene, land of a people little known at that time but now the most important of all regions situated beyond the Euphrates and Tigris and bounded by the Red Sea."[10] Thus the Tigris and Euphrates Rivers are clearly the boundaries between Parthian and Roman rule. According to Devine, even if it cannot be established whether Curtius conflated Parthians with Persian Sassanids, one would still expect Curtius to know the eastern limit of the Roman Empire—or at least official territorial claims. Trajan pursued an aggressive policy in the East to extend Roman dominion, and so did his successors, with the exception of Hadrian. Devine concludes that Curtius must have written before the Romans had established a permanent foothold on the eastern bank of the Euphrates and therefore that an early Trajanic date marks a *terminus post quem non*.[11]

But this argument is not especially helpful. Curtius' phraseology does not rule out a post-Trajanic emperor; Hecatompylus remained the capital of the regions east of the Tigris and Babylonia, and Roman possessions east of the Euphrates are not relevant. It is possible that Curtius may have been referring to the Parthian capital of Ctesiphon, the *caput* of Babylonia, which might contrast with Hecatompylus, the chief center in the Iranian plateau. However, Devine is right to stress that the implications of the passages on the Parthians indicate that in Curtius' time they were still a powerful imperial force and a counterpart to Roman power. Such a situation would seem more appropriately suited to a date prior to 114 A.D.

Therefore, on historical evidence alone, it seems highly probable that

---

8. Devine, *Phoenix* 33 (1979): 143–59. Cf. Sumner, *AUMLA* 15 (1961): 30.

9. For Hadrian, see A. von Domaszewski, *Die Phalangen Alexanders und Cäsars Legionem* (Heidelberg, 1926), 3–5. For Septimius Severus, see C.A. Robinson, review of *Die Zeit des Curtius Rufus*, by Dietmar Karzeniewski, *AJPh* 82 (1961): 316–19; K. Bourazelis, *Ariadne* 4 (1988): 244–64. For Severus Alexander, see E. Griset, "Per la interpretazione di Curzio Rufo x, 9.1–6 e la datazione dell' opera," *RSC* 12 (1964): 160–64; R.B. Steele, *AJPH* 36 (1915): 401–23. For Gordian III, see E. Gibbon, *Decline and Fall of the Roman Empire*, vol. 1, ed. J.B. Bury (London, 1909), 189 n. 59. For Constantine and Theodosius, see Dosson, 18 nn. 1–2.

10. *Hinc in Parthiene perventum est, tunc ignobilem gentem, nunc caput omnium, qui post Euphraten et Tigrim amnes siti Rubro mari terminantur.*

11. Devine, *Phoenix* 33 (1979): 144–47.

Curtius' date can be narrowed down to sometime between Augustus and Trajan. Aspects of the imperial panegyric in book 10 would seem to eliminate certain emperors immediately. The ascensions of Tiberius, Caligula, Nero, Titus, Domitian, and Nerva were too smooth, and the reigns of Otho and Vitellius were too short. The most likely candidates are Augustus, Claudius, Galba, Vespasian, and Trajan. Of these four, Galba can be excluded on the grounds of his short reign and the reference to *posteritas eiusdem domus,* or the emperor's dynasty. Milns' arguments to the contrary are ingenious but not really convincing.[12]

Before examining the problematic excursus on Rome's new emperor, Curtius' digression on Tyre also warrants consideration. The final statement in the historian's note on Tyre reads: "After experiencing many disasters and rising again after its destruction, now at last, with long peace completely restoring its prosperity, Tyre enjoys tranquility under the merciful protection of Rome" (4.4.21).[13] Various phrases from this passage have been used to suggest a date. For example, McQueen rejects a Severan date on the grounds that, as Severus granted colonial rights to Tyre, Tyre could no longer be described as being under Roman protection.[14] Similarly, the reference to the "long peace" has been used to question a Vespasianic date due to Tyre's proximity to the Jewish war, which caused some damage to the city (Jos. *Vit.* 44–45), and its prosperity probably suffered under Mucianus' extortionist methods of raising money, which continued even after the advent of peace (Tac. *Hist.* 2.48).[15] Severus can be eliminated because the city was sacked by Niger in 193 A.D.[16]

However, Fears is probably right to say that Curtian scholarship has placed too much emphasis on this passage. The reference to a "long peace" may be nothing more than a general reference to the Pax Romana.[17] The passage is deliberately nonspecific; one would imagine

---

12. See Atkinson, *Curtius* i, 25. For Galba, see R.D. Milns, *Latomus* 25 (1966): esp. 493–96. For the objections raised to Milns' hypothesis, see Rodriguez, *Aspectos de Q. Curtius Rufus,* 45–50; Atkinson, *Curtius* i, 34. Ultimately, Galba must be ruled out for the same reason Claudius and Trajan are eliminated: Curtius is talking about civil war.

13. *Multis ergo casibus defuncta, et post excidium renata, nunc tandem longa pace cuncta refovente sub tutela romanae mansuetudinis acquiescit.*

14. See Fears, *CPh* (1976): 220–21; McQueen, 25.

15. But see Milns, *Latomus* 25 (1966): 492–93, who argues that the Jewish war had little effect on the city.

16. See Bourazelis, *Ariadne* 4 (1988): 254 f.

17. On the Pax Romana, see Milns, *Latomus* 25 (1966): 493; Hamilton, *Historia* 37 (1988): 445 n. 6.

that if Curtius had a particular emperor in mind who was generous to Tyre, he would have said so: for instance, he might have mentioned Claudius' *benignitas* to the Tyrians, in allowing them to style themselves Claudiopolitans.[18] A Roman writer might not be expected to know the constitutional status of cities like Tyre, as Fears points out, but such a gesture on the part of an emperor would not pass unnoticed, especially if the historian wanted to flatter his *princeps*. What Curtius wants to do is contrast the checkered career of Tyre with its current happiness as a Roman possession. The context of the statement, within a notice on the city, is highly rhetorical; one might compare Curtius' obituary on Persepolis at 5.7.8–9.[19] Thus the statement on Tyre could simply be eloquent lip service for the sake of audience appeal, rather than a pointed political comment.

Curtius may be offhand about Tyre, but in book 10 his enthusiasm for the emperor, who has ended or averted civil turmoil, cannot be doubted. In his preface, Curtius almost certainly made some kind of dedicatory eulogy to his *princeps;* it was thus structurally appropriate that he reinforce his praise in the final book of the *Historiae,* and since he had already dedicated the work, there was no need to name the emperor again.[20] By a peculiar trick of fate, we have thus been left with a digression in which the highly rhetorical language would have made any one of a number of emperors a likely candidate, were it not for the evidence already offered by other references.

Since so much discussion has rested on the interpretation of 10.9.1–6, it is worthwhile to quote the Latin passage with a full translation.

> Sed iam fatis admovebantur Macedonum genti bella civilia; nam et insociabile est regnum et a pluribus expetebatur. Primum ergo collisere vires, deinde disperserunt; et cum pluribus corpus quam capiebat onerassent, cetera membra deficere coeperunt, quodque imperium sub uno stare potuisset, dum a pluribus sustinetur, ruit. Proinde iure meritoque populus Romanus salutem se principi suo debere profitetur, qui noctis quam paene supremam habuimus novum sidus illuxit. Huius, hercule, non solis, ortus lucem caliganti reddidit mundo, cum sine suo capite discordia membra trepidarent.

---
18. Fears, *CPh* (1976): 220–21. On Claudius' *benignitas,* see Atkinson, *Curtius* i, 24.
19. On the necrologies of cities, see Pomeroy, *Appropriate Comment,* 255 f.
20. The *dedicatio* became increasingly common in the imperial period. Cf. Val. Max. praef; Lucan *De bell. civ.* 1.33–66; Polyaen. pref. 1; Aelian *Tact.* praef. 7.

Quot ille tum exstinxit faces! quot condidit gladios! quantam tempestatem subita serenitate discussit! Non ergo revirescit solum, sed etiam floret imperium. Absit modo invidia, excipiet huius saeculi tempora eiusdem domus utinam perpetua, certe diuturna posteritas.

[But already civil wars were being forced on the Macedonian people by the Fates, for kingship [regnum] is indivisible and was sought by many. Therefore, at first they brought their forces into conflict and from that point dispersed them, and when they had burdened the body with more than it was capable of carrying, the limbs also began to fail, and an empire [imperium] that would have been able to stand under one man crashed into ruins, while it was being upheld by many. Therefore, the Roman people rightly and deservedly assert that it owes its safety to its own *princeps*, who blazed forth, a new star of the night that we thought of as almost our last. By heaven, the rising of this star, not of the sun, restored light to a darkened world, since without their head, the discordant limbs shook. How many torches did he put out! How many swords did he sheath! How great a storm did he dispel with a sudden, fair calm! Therefore empire not only lives again but even flourishes. Provided that divine envy be absent, the posterity of that same house will take up the opportunities of this age, would that forever, to be sure for a very long time.]

Since Julius Mützell's study in 1841, many scholars, including Dosson, Bardon, Badian, Errington, Sumner, Atkinson, Bödefeld, Syme, Martin, and Hamilton, have supported Claudius as the mysterious *princeps*.[21] The argument rests chiefly on interpreting the turmoil Curtius refers to as a crisis, the potential outbreak of civil war, rather than actual civil war, which was opportunely averted by the accession of a strong emperor. Thus the phrase "the night that we thought of as almost our last" refers to the night of 24/25 January 41 A.D., following Caligula's

---

21. See Mützell i, xlviif; Dosson, 18 f.; Bardon, *LEC* 15 (1947): 3–14; Sumner, *AUMLA* 15 (1961): 30–39; E. Badian, *Studies in Greek and Roman History*, 263, and "Alexander the Great, 1948–67," *CW* 65 (1971): 37–56, 77–83; Errington, *JHS* 90 (1970): 49–77; Atkinson, *Curtius* i, 25–34, and *Curtius* ii, 26. The most detailed discussion for a Claudian date is H.J. Bödefeld, *Untersuchungen zur Datierung der Alexandergeschichte des Q. Curtius Rufus*. See also R. Syme, *HSCP* 86 (1982): 197 f.; Thomas R. Martin, *AJAH* 8 (1983): 161–90; Hamilton, *Historia* 37 (1988): 445–56. And see McQueen, 23.

assassination, when some members of the Senate wanted to restore the Republic, while others, such as Valerius Asiaticus and Marcus Vinicius, hoped to become emperors themselves.[22]

The Senate lost control of the Praetorians, who forced them to accept the appointment of Claudius. Rather than meaning the provinces, the "discordant limbs" refer to the social and political units within Rome: hence the city is divided into the Praetorians and people, on one hand, and the Republican senators and those who desired monarchy, on the other. Similarly, the phrases "kingship is indivisable" and "its own *princeps*, who blazed forth, a new star," as well as the reference to "posterity," are all applicable to Claudius, while "the rising of this star . . . restored light to a darkened world [caliganti mundo]" has been interpreted as a pun on Caligula. Finally, many Claudian supporters have stressed that Curtius' language, particularly his use of *trepidare*, is far too mild for a piece of rhetoric that is talking about civil war.[23] In short, Atkinson concludes that "nothing in Curtius' eulogy of the new emperor could not apply to Claudius" and that "none of the relevant emperors fits Curtius' statement on every count."[24]

Some Claudian supporters have also looked for Curtius' date on grounds other than the panegyric, including literary parallels to other contemporary writers as well as passages in the *Historiae* that seem to suggest Tiberius, Caligula, and Claudius himself.[25] Certainly Curtius develops contemporary concerns—for instance, the conflict between *regnum* and *libertas*—particularly in his treatment of episodes dealing with confrontation between the king and an individual.

A Claudian date has a certain amount of appeal; as we have seen, Livy's influence on the *Historiae* is without doubt, and Claudius was himself a historian who admired Livy. Indeed, according to Suetonius (*Div. Claud.* 41.1), Livy encouraged the young Claudius in his historiographical pursuits. Recently, too, an argument by J.R. Hamilton put a strong case forward for a Claudian floruit. In addition to provocative discussion on the excursus, Hamilton compared Curtius' style and language in certain passages with those of Seneca the Younger. However, one

---

22. On the accession of Claudius and individual senatorial ambition, see B. Levick, *Claudius* (London, 1990) 29 f.; infra, n. 28.
23. On the "mild language," see Sumner, *AUMLA* 15 (1961) 32; Milns, *Latomus* 25 (1966): 491–92; Bosworth, *CPh* 78 (1983): 150–61.
24. Atkinson, *Curtius* i, 35.
25. See ibid., 37–49.

problem with this approach (of which Hamilton was well aware) is the general popularity of the topoi that both Seneca and Curtius drew on, and it is thus very difficult to prove one writer specifically used the other.[26]

The arguments of Devine, Atkinson, and Sumner that identify the author of the *Historiae* with the senator named by Tacitus and/or the rhetorician named by Suetonius fit a Claudian date very neatly. Certainly, if evidence turned up tomorrow that asserted a Claudian date for Curtius beyond a shadow of a doubt, it would be less of a surprise than if the case were proven for other emperors who have been seriously put forward.

However, there are some questions concerning the identification of Claudius as Curtius' *princeps*. For instance, the abortive revolt of L. Arruntius Camillus Scribonianus, the governor of Dalmatia in 42 A.D., raises some interesting issues. Although the uprising occurred in the second year of Claudius' reign, in many ways it was a part of manifest senatorial dissatisfaction and unrest due to Claudius' accession. When the Praetorians proclaimed Claudius emperor in 41 A.D., there were several powerful and aristocratic senators in command of provincial legions. Any one of these men, including Appius Silanus (Hispania Citerior), Aulus Plautius (Pannonia), Camillus Scribonianus, and Galba (Upper Germany), could have presented a viable alternative to Claudius. In the wake of C. Appius Iunius Silanus' execution, Scribonianus ordered Claudius to resign his powers; Scribonianus' legions remained loyal to Claudius, and the rebellion only lasted five days.[27] Yet it is described by Suetonius (*Div. Claud.* 13.2) as a "civil war" and represented a direct, military threat to the emperor and the state—potentially more destructive than the accession crisis following Caligula's assassination. Either Curtius' work was published the first year of Claudius' reign, or his digression is referring to Scribonianus' revolt. The events of 41 may fit the description of the emperor as *novum sidus* but make the *discordia membra* difficult. It is true that Caligula had left the empire in a troubled state, especially through his interference in Judaea, but there was no provincial upheaval. In 42 there were indeed *discordia membra*, but the

---

26. Hamilton, *Historia* 37 (1988): 445–56. See chap. 2, 27–30.
27. See Dio Cassius 60.15.1–16; Tac. *Ann.* 12.52 and *Hist.* 1.89; Pliny *Ep.* 3.16.7, 9. See also T.P. Wiseman, "Calpurnius Siculus and the Claudian War," *JRS* 72 (1982): 57–67; Levick (supra, n. 22), 59. I am grateful to Professor Bosworth for drawing my attention to the revolt.

emperor was then hardly a *novum sidus*. Moreover, in view of the forceful rhetoric of the passage, which does seem to suggest a prolonged period of civil upheaval (see following discussion), neither explanation seems very satisfactory.

Other problems with a Claudian attribution were noted by Bosworth, who himself suggested an early Trajanic date for Curtius. Bosworth argued that the language of Pliny's *Panegyricus* was very close to the digression in book 10.[28] According to Pliny the Younger, Rome was in a state of virtual civil war, due to a praetorian mutiny. The news of Nerva's adoption of Trajan, however, restored peace: thus Curtius' eulogy may have been written in a similar climate, and he could well have been directly influenced by the phraseology of such a public statement.

A Trajanic date is also not without a certain amount of plausibility. Toward the end of his life, Trajan campaigned in the East, and we know from Dio Cassius (68.29.1, 68.30–31) that the emperor wished to emulate Alexander. Bosworth's emphasis on Curtius' comments on archery and his description of the Nasamonians—a rather unpleasant people who feature in Lucan (*De Bell. Civ.* 9.439–44) and Silius Italicus (1.408, 13.480–81)—is provocative. Moreover, Bosworth draws attention to Domitian's campaign against these people and suggests that Curtius added a "note from his own experience." Yet the historian says nothing specific, and the Nasamonians point to, at most, a Neronian *terminus post quem*.[29]

However, despite the claims of those scholars who see the excursus in book 10 as low-key, its very nature appears to eliminate Claudius—or Trajan. One main objective of this current study has been to demonstrate Curtius' arrangement of his work and his careful placement of episodes; logically, the context and placement of such a politically weighted passage within book 10 should be considerably significant.

In terms of overall structure, Alexander dies about halfway through book 10, and the remaining narrative is concerned with the struggles of the generals in the first seven days or so following the king's death. The digression at 10.9 occurs between the false reconciliation of Meleager

---

28. Bosworth, *CPh* 78 (1983): 151–52. He says Atkinson has too readily dismissed Curtius' statement at 7.5.42; it is difficult to establish that archery was common for the Julio-Claudians but that the archery cohorts were supplemented through the Flavian and Trajanic periods.

29. Bosworth, *CPh* 78 (1983): 152. Cf. R.T. Bruère, "Silius Italicus *Punica* iii, 62–162 and iv, 763–822," *CPh* 67 (1952): 219 f., who argued Curtius influenced Silius; but see Fears, *CPh* (1976): 216–17.

and Perdiccas (10.8.20–23) and the latter's execution of thirty of Meleager's men, during a rite of purification (10.9.11–19). Curtius sees in this *fraus* (treachery) an omen and a beginning of civil war; it was an act symbolic of the years of bloodshed to come. His comment at 10.9.1 is likewise an authorial expression on what is in store for the Macedonians. Forward-looking observations from Curtius occur often in the latter part of book 10. In his statement that the generals *collisere vires* [brought their forces into conflict], the historian is probably referring to the early wars of the Successors, at least down to the Battles of Ipsus (301 B.C.) and Corupedion (281 B.C.), which led to the division of forces into the Successor kingdoms. This plethora of kingdoms resulted in mutual debilitation, proof that the empire was a unit that was best served by single rule (cf. Tac. *Ann.* 1.12.3), and hence Curtius' later stress on *discordia membra* is pertinent.[30]

The message is emphatic. Without a strong king—without a legitimate, acceptable heir—Alexander's empire, "which would have stood under one man," crashed in ruins. There was not one of Alexander's generals who was strong enough to take the *moles* (burden) of empire, a point Curtius emphasizes himself in his obituary on the king. Coalitions between powerful men, such as the abortive relationship between Perdiccas, Meleager, and Philip Arrhidaeus, are tricky and unstable, for *insociabile est regnum*. The inevitable result is civil war. Along with Curtius' emphasis on civil chaos throughout the final part of the book, 10.9.1–2 and 4–5 show a very real appreciation of the horror of civil war and an identification of the fate of Alexander's empire with the situation facing Rome. Although Curtius stresses the inevitability of collapse through his symbolic depiction of struggle and treachery in those first seven days following Alexander's death, he demonstrates in the excursus (10.9.2) that what is to come will be gradual: *et cum pluribus corpus quam capiebat onerassent, cetera membra deficere coeperunt* [and when they had burdened the body with more than it was capable of carrying, the limbs also began to fail]. The *membra* (limbs) refer to the component territorial parts of the empire of which the Macedonian people *(gentes)* are overlords.

Similarly, the Roman Empire's *discordia membra* (10.9.5; the use of the same words would surely indicate the same meaning), lacking a head,

---

30. For forward-looking comments, see Curt. 10.9.1–2, 10.9.20, 10.10.5–8. The MS reading is uncertain on *collisere vires;* other texts read *collegere vires* [they brought their forces together]. But the former phrase is relevant to civil war: cf. Vell. 2.52.3 on Pharsalus.

shook, presumably on the point of collapse, but were saved by the advent of the *princeps*. One can also note the apposition of *gentes Macedonum* and *populus Romanus*. The use of *trepidare*, far from being too mild, is actually appropriate; on a "last night," surely a general metaphor for the approaching destruction, Rome's empire was threatened with dissolution, but unlike Alexander's empire, a strong ruler emerged for Rome, a new star, a *princeps* who could do what Alexander's successors could not—hold the empire together. Of course, such an argument is also reconcilable with the mere threat of civil war; Curtius could be simply reminding the Romans that they ought to be all the more grateful to their *princeps* for preventing disaster.

But Curtius' rhetoric toward the end of the passage is hardly mild. The new emperor not only put a stop to carnage *(gladii)* and destruction *(faces)* but dispelled a "great storm" [quanta tempestas]. This might suggest the troubled state the empire was in at the time of Claudius' accession, due to, for example, the disarray of the German legions, turmoil in Judaea, and individual senatorial ambition.[31] Yet the historian's use of *reviresco* and *floreo* is interesting. Both verbs are used in a metaphoric sense to describe the empire flourishing anew. Literally, the image suggests vegetation growing green again and blossoming; this renewal would enforce the sense of actual destruction implied in *gladii, faces*, and *quanta tempestas*. Suetonius' description of Vespasian's renewal of imperial stability bears some similarities (*Vesp.* 8.1: . . . *rem p. stabilire primo, deinde ornare*). Therefore, if we conclude that Curtius is talking about civil war, only two *principes* are left as suitable candidates: Augustus and Vespasian. Tarn preferred the former, and in 1959 Dietmar Korzeniewski also presented a case for Augustus.[32]

Korzeniewski asserted that Curtius' style and content suited the early imperial period and that many parallels are to be found between the information in Curtius' text and the reign of Octavian. For example, Octavian was the "head" Rome found; the association in book 10 between Perdiccas, Meleager, and Philip is similar to the triumvirate of Antony, Octavian, and Lepidus. The "new star" refers to Octavian him-

---

31. See Josephus *AJ* 19.1.22 f.; Suet. *Gaius* 58 f. and *Div. Claud.* 10; Dio Cassius 59.30, 60.1 f. See also Hamilton, *Historia* 37 (1988): 448 n. 20.

32. See Milns' arguments against civil war, in *Latomus* 25 (1966): 492. But see Stroux, *Philologus* 84 (1928/29): 233–51, who interpreted *faces* as a reference to the burning of the Capitol in 69 A.D.; contra, see Atkinson, *Curtius* i, 33. On the metaphorical use of *fax*, cf. Pliny *Pan.* 8.5. For Tarn's discussion on an Augustan date, see *Alexander the Great*, 2:11–114.

self, from his association with Julius Caesar, the *sidus Iulium*. Korzeniewski placed the completion of the *Historiae* between 25 and 23 B.C.: the reference to the "long peace" in the Tyre passage indicated the closing of the temple of Janus by Augustus, while the *posteritas* in 10.9.6 meant Marcellus, the designated successor of Augustus.[33]

Certainly, the digression could be applicable to Augustus, if some of its phrases were taken in isolation. For instance, the *a pluribus* at 10.9.1 becomes analogous to the last years of the Republic, and Augustus was first called *princeps* in connection with *salus* and *pax*.[34] Similarly, no *nox* (night) could be darker than the period of civil wars, both before and after Caesar's assassination. Bruère added that 10.9.7 in Curtius, where the historian says he has been distracted by the contemplation of public *felicitas*, could well be an answer to Livy's praefatio 5: in other words Curtius has deliberately reversed the complaint of the earlier historian.[35] As for *posteritas* and *eiusdem domus*, Augustus had a successor in Marcellus, indicated earlier, and after 23 B.C., his grandsons, Gaius and Lucius Caesar, as well as his stepson, Tiberius, also provided dynastic alternatives.

However, serious objections can be raised to Korzeniewski's thesis and indeed to the argument that Augustus is a candidate for Curtius' emperor. In particular, Korzeniewski is wrong to dismiss Livy's influence, and the case for a parallel triumvirate is very tenuous.[36] If Octavian is meant to represent Philip, the depiction of the latter does not coincide with the strong ruler of the digression. Philip, for all his noble sentiments at 10.8.16–19, is really little more than a figurehead, as Curtius' comment at 10.9.19 demonstrates. Likewise, Meleager hardly corresponds to Lepidus. Also, contemporary overtones from the *Historiae* overall seem to indicate that Curtius is writing at a time when the principate has been established for a considerable period. Certain echoes of earlier Augustan authors, such as Vergil, and of other writers from the early imperial period are noticeable.[37] However, the most striking of contemporary issues occurs at 7.1.18–40, where, as noted previously, the speech of

---

33. Korzeniewski, "Die Zeit des Quintus Curtius Rufus," 51 f. and, on *longa pax*, 84 f.

34. On *pax* and *princeps*, see C.H.V. Sutherland, *Coinage in Roman Imperial Policy, 31 B.C.–A.D. 68* (London, 1951), 29.

35. R.T. Bruère, review of "Die Zeit des Quintus Curtius Rufus," by D. Korzeniewski, *CPh* 55 (1960): 266–68.

36. Korzenieski, "Die Zeit des Quintus Curtius Rufus," 80 f.; but see my chap. 2, 21.

37. See Hamilton, *Historia* 37 (1988): 446; Steele, *AJPH* 36 (1915): 409 f.

Amyntas corresponds in certain places to the defense of Marcus Terentius, a Roman knight.[38]

Thus, by process of elimination, we are left with Vespasian. It remains to be seen whether a Vespasianic date can fit the digression and any of the other clues Curtius has provided. Ironically, Vespasian's adherents have made as persuasive a case based on the panegyric as the Claudian camp, although most of their arguments can also be countered—such is the cyclic nature of the problem! In 1928 J. Stroux published a lengthy article favoring Vespasian, and his work has been elaborated by several other modern scholars, Instinsky, Vogel-Weidmann, Grassl, Breebaart, and Scheda.[39] Costas Rodriguez' doctoral dissertation (1975) argued for a Vespasianic date, based on the digression and a close lexicological study of Curtius' vocabulary. The Vespasianic case has also been forcefully argued by A. Barzano, Francesca Minissale, and, most recently, Joachim Fugmann. Fugmann concluded (with the others) that the digression fits Vespasian better than Claudius.[40]

The following list summarizes some salient points of the Vespasian argument.

(a) The *nox* is metaphorical: so argues Stroux, citing other metaphorical examples; Scheda argues against a literal interpretation of *nox*, because Curtius did not qualify *nox* with a demonstrative pronoun; cf. Livy 6.17.4.[41]

(b) Scheda compares the expression *supremam habuimus* to Tac-

---

38. See chap. 6.
39. See Stroux, "Die Zeit des Curtius," *Philologus* 84 (1928/29): 233–51; H.U. Instinsky, "Zur Kontroverse um die Datierung des Curtius Rufus," *Hermes* 90 (1962): 379–83; U. Vogel-Weidmann, "Bemerkungen zu den Curtii Rufi der frühen Principatzeit," *AClass* 13 (1970): 79–88 and *AClass* 17 (1974): 41–42; H. Grassl, "Zur Datierung des Curtius Rufus," *Philologus* 118 (1974): 160–63; A.B. Breebaart, review, of *Die Zeit des Quintus Curtius Rufus,* by D. Korzeniewski, *Mnemosyne* 17 (1964): 431–33; G. Scheda, "Zur Datierung des Curtius Rufus," *Historia* 18 (1969): 380–83.
40. Rodriguez, *Aspectos de Q. Curtius Rufus;* A. Barzano, *Curzio Rufo e la sua epoca,* Memorie dell' Istituto Lombardo, Accad. di Scienze e Lettere, Classe di Lettere-Scienze Morale e Storiche, 38, no. 2 (Milan, 1985), 71–165; Minissale, *Curzio Rufo: Un romanziere della storia;* J. Fugmann, "Zum Problem der Datierung der 'Historiae Alexandri Magni' des Curtius Rufus," *Hermes* 123 (1995): 233–43.
41. See Stroux, *Philologus* 84 (1928/29): 238–40; Scheda (supra, n. 39), 381–82 n. 1. But see Atkinson, *Curtius* i, 28. Livy 6.17.3–4 reads: *Iam ne nocte quidem turba ex eo loco dilabebatur.*

itus' use of *supremus* to characterize the year 69 A.D.; cf. *Historiae* 1.11 fin.[42]

(c) The *novum sidus* refers to the establishment of a new dynasty: the *sidus Iulium* was possibly adopted by Vespasian, although the star image was a standard feature of court panegyric. However, the emphasis is on "new"; Instinsky argued for a comparison with Pliny *Naturalis historia* 33.12.41. Similarly, Stroux emphasizes that *eiusdem domus* (9.6) refers to the establishment of a new dynasty, since Claudius always stressed his affiliation with the Julio-Claudians.[43]

(d) Based on the phrase *huius hercule, non solis, ortus lucem caliganti reddidit mundo,* Scheda argues for an identification of *sol* with Nero; similarly, Grassl points to the significance of *ortus* and the rise of Vespasian in the East, demonstrated by various portents. Objections to a pun on *caliganti* include the fact that *caligo* (all long syllables) has a different scansion from *Caligula* (wholly short). Also, Caligula was known as Gaius, and finally Curtius uses *caligo* frequently without special significance.[44]

(e) Grassl asserts that *discors* appears frequently in the description of civil wars, and in any case the *discordia membra* (discordant limbs) refer not so much to the Senate, people, and army as to the groups of people that constitute the empire. Similarly, *trepidare* usually describes revolts.[45]

(f) Instinsky linked the description of the empire's revival at the end of the passage with Flavian reconstruction: relevant is the legend on Vespasian's coinage at this time, *Roma resurgens.*[46]

---

42. Scheda (supra, n. 39), 382.

43. See Atkinson, *Curtius* i, 30; Instinsky (supra, n. 39), 382–83. On the star as a standard imperial image, see J.R. Fears, "The Solar Monarchy of Nero and the Imperial Panegyric of Q. Curtius Rufus," *Historia* 25 (1976): 494–96.

44. Scheda (supra, n. 39), 382–83; Grassl (supra, n. 39), 163. But see Atkinson, *Curtius* i, 30–31; Fears (supra, n. 43), 494–96. Fears argues that there is no tangible evidence to suggest Nero identified himself with Sol. In fact, Vespasian replaced Vitellius rather than Nero directly anyway; at best Curtius would be stretching a point, but his emphasis is on the *novum sidus*. On the case for and against a pun on *caliganti*, see Atkinson, loc. cit., 31; Milns, *Latomus* 25 (1966): 502; Hamilton, *Historia* 37 (1988): 450–51.

45. Grassl (supra, n. 39), 162; but see Atkinson, *Curtius* i, 32. On the discordant provinces, cf. the parallel of Tac. *Germ.* 33, *urgentibus imperii fatis;* this does not necessarily eliminate Claudius.

46. Instinsky (supra, n. 39), 382.

If one may apply Atkinson's own conclusion about Claudius to Vespasian, there is still nothing in the digression that can conclusively eliminate him. One area in determining a date for the work is left to consider: where Curtius seems to make contemporary allusions in his depiction of events in Alexander's career.

Devine, Atkinson, Sumner, Errington, and Martin have argued for parallels between Curtius' Alexander and the emperors Tiberius, Gaius, and Claudius. For example, Devine emphasizes the Amyntas and Terentius trial, the *dissimulatio* of Alexander and Tiberius, the virtues of Tiberius found on his coinage, and similar motifs in the *Historiae*. Sumner notes a general relation between Gaius and Alexander in that they both began well but deteriorated. Atkinson, in addition to specific Gaius parallels—like Alexander's *pietas* toward his sisters—equates Alexander's execution of Bessus with Claudius' removal of Cassius Chaerea. Errington and Martin find a striking correlation between the accession of Claudius and the situation following Alexander's death in book 10. The reluctance of Perdiccas to accept *summa imperii* recalled the hesitancy of Tiberius.[47] Similarly, Curtius was reluctant to emphasize Philip Arrhidaeus as a half-wit, because of the obvious temptation to equate him with Claudius. Yet despite some parallels between Philip's accession and Claudius', Curtius' picture of the former is not especially flattering. Also, Claudius may not necessarily have been as unlikely a candidate for emperor as certain hostile traditions have suggested.[48]

Hammond argued for Neronian coloring: an example he cited was the parallel between Alexander hiding behind a curtain at 8.5.21 and Agrippina concealing herself in a similar manner. But such a comparison is hardly conclusive; Plutarch (*Alex.* 49.11) also depicts the king hiding behind tapestries at a sensitive moment.[49]

A negative case has also been presented. Grassl argued that Curtius was not presenting an allegory of a Roman emperor in his characterization of Alexander; likewise, Milns pointed out that an allegory was not

---

47. Devine, *Phoenix* 33 (1979): 150 f.; Sumner, *AUMLA* 15 (1961): 33; Atkinson, *Curtius* i, 38 (the *pietas* parallel between Gaius and Alexander has been criticized; see Bosworth, *CPh* 78 [1983]: 153); Errington, *JHS* 90 (1970): 49–51; Martin, *AJAH* 8 (1983): 161 f. Martin (176 f.) also compares Josephus' account of Claudius' accession to Curtius' picture of Arrhidaeus.

48. See Levick (supra, n. 22), 33 f.; see also Wiseman (supra, n. 27).

49. Hammond, *THA*, 148; see also 117. Cf. R.G. Tanner, "Thought and Style in Tacitus," *ANRW* II.33.4 (1991): 2690–2781.

the usual way of upbraiding a *princeps*.⁵⁰ Citing Tacitus, he said the "normal way of attacking an emperor was to wait for his death and then write nasty things about him"; Suetonius tells of people writing what they thought about the emperor in their wills. Milns' conclusion was that the *Historiae* is far too elaborate a work for an allegory and ultimately that it is the work of Curtius the rhetorician, written simply for interest and the sake of rhetoric.⁵¹

However, I have argued at length that the *Historiae* is a serious study on the politics of power. It is thus erroneous to see the work as an allegory for any one emperor. Curtius' interest lies in *regnum* itself, in the concept of absolute power and its effect on the *rex* and followers. Thus it is possible to see echoes of many *principes* within the *Historiae*, without the work being confined to only one emperor. The historian is aware of kingship's potential for good and evil but seems convinced that any alternative to strong rule is worse. We see this hypothesis in the way Curtius presents kings and kingship. Although his focus is chiefly on Alexander's *regnum*, his characterization of other kings, such as Darius and Bessus, not only allows Curtius to balance their *fortunae* against Alexander's but enables him to explore kingship from different angles and perspectives.

The final problem remaining for consideration is the identity of Curtius himself. Some information exists about four Curtii, with or without the praenomen *Quintus* or the cognomen *Rufus*, from the period of the late Republic to the first century A.D. Contrary to Milns' assertion, Curtii Rufi are not uncommon during the imperial period; thus our historian could literally be any Curtius, and there is no hard evidence proving otherwise. However, the nature of the information on some of the known Curtii has made identification with the historian very attractive.

The earliest Curtii are described by Cicero and Macrobius. First, the Q. Curtius mentioned by Cicero in a letter circa 55 B.C. (*Ad Quint. frat.* 3.2) is described as a "good and eloquent young man" [bonus et eruditus adulescens]. Second, Macrobius tells an anecdote to the effect that a Curtius who was a Roman *eques* of luxurious habits was dining with Caesar when he was served with a rather skinny thrush; he asked "if he could let it go," and having obtained Augustus' consent, he promptly threw it out the window (Macrob. *Sat.* 2.4, anecdote 22). If Curtius were an Augustan writer, either of these two gentlemen would be possibilities, particularly the first, by being a young man in Cicero's time (and presumably of

---

50. Grassl (supra, n. 39), 160; Milns, *Latomus* 25 (1966): 501 f.
51. Milns, *Latomus* 25 (1966): 504. But see Fears, *Hermes* 102 (1974): 623 n. 2.

senatorial background as well as *eruditus*). The identification with the gourmet *eques* is more difficult, although one would like to think that such an act of perverse humor is not entirely out of keeping with the ironical cynicism the historian occasionally displays. However, the connection is tenuous to say the least, and for the reasons mentioned earlier, it is highly unlikely that Curtius wrote during the Age of Augustus.

The two Curtii who have found rather more scholarly support are a proconsul of Africa, Curtius Rufus, mentioned by Tacitus and Pliny; and a rhetorician, Q. Curtius Rufus, mentioned in Suetonius' index to *De rhetoribus et grammaticus*.[52] The former, a man of apparently lower-class origins, was a Tiberian nominee for the praetorship, was subsequently inactive for a while, but then became consul during Claudius' reign (45 A.D.) and finally proconsul of Africa, where he died, probably sometime early in Nero's reign. Although the emphasis in both Pliny and Tacitus is on the fulfillment of a prophecy, Tacitus describes the senator, as maintaining *adversus superiores tristi adulatione, adrogans minoribus, inter pares difficilis* [a surly fawning to his superiors, arrogance to his inferiors, and an intractable attitude among his equals] (Tac. *Ann.* 11–21). Such an account perhaps suggests a recipe for imperial survival, although Tacitus' tone seems to indicate that the man was an obnoxious creature who, in view of his lowly origins, was not subservient enough to his aristocratic betters. Why Claudius gave him a consulship at all probably needs more explanation than why he was inactive for a while under Tiberius. However, the dates for this particular Curtius span the reigns of Tiberius, Gaius, and Claudius. Hence the idea that a successful imperial senator and civil servant, under the guise of writing a history about Alexander the Great, should choose to express certain attitudes about the dynasty that made him has proved irresistible to certain scholars. Likewise, Sumner and Atkinson have argued that the senator and rhetorician Curtius were one and the same person, since the gap in the senator's political career can be explained by his activity as a rhetor. The fall of Sejanus is put forward as the reason why Curtius was forced to turn to rhetoric. Sumner says, "*Nihil obstat,* and the dates fit."[53]

---

52. Tac. *Ann.* 11.20–21; Pliny *Ep.* 7.27; Suetonius, *De Grammaticis et Rhetoribus,* trans. J.C. Rolfe (Cambridge, Mass., 1979), 2:395. Cf. *PIR*² C 1618, C 1619. Also, on the rhetor, see Vogel-Weidmann, "Bemerkungen zu den Curtii Rufi der frühen Principatzeit" (supra, n. 39). For a discussion of Tacitus' Curtius, see Milns, *Latomus* 25 (1966): 504; Atkinson, *Curtius* i, 50–57; Sumner, *AUMLA* 15 (1961): 35–37; Devine, *Phoenix* 33 (1979): 147–50.

53. Sumner, *AUMLA* 15 (1961): 36; on the case against Curtius being Tacitus' senator, see McQueen, 25–26.

If, as deduced earlier, the *Historiae* is indeed Vespasianic, Tacitus' senator is automatically ruled out. Furneaux proposes the interesting solution that the historian could well have been the son of this man; the same argument could be extended to a grandson or other male relative.[54] But assuming Curtius the rhetor is not the senator—and it is perhaps unlikely that he became a rhetor after being a praetor—he presents an alternative solution yet again. In Suetonius' list of grammarians and rhetoricians, a Q. Curtius Rufus is placed between M. Porcius Latro and L. Valerius Primanus. Latro died possibly in 4 B.C. Very little is known about Primanus, but he appears to have been active during Claudius' reign. The last two rhetoricians in the list belonged to Vespasian's time. One conclusion to draw is that Curtius the rhetorician was working during the reigns of either Tiberius or Claudius.[55]

Yet a Tiberian or Claudian floruit does not mean that the rhetorician did not survive the Julio-Claudian dynasty. Milns argued that he would have been in his seventies in 69 A.D., and thus, if his, the *Historiae* would be the work of an old man, a product of "retirement."[56] Age is no bar to literary productivity, and several men in antiquity were known to have been writing very late in life, for instance, Aristobulus, Ptolemy (according to some), Livy, and Augustus. To these one could also add that very active rhetorician Isocrates.[57]

That the *Historiae* must have been the result of many years' work is amply illustrated by indications of Curtius' wide reading and the care he gave to the composition of his history. Although there is nothing indicative in the *Historiae* of the author's age, a general impression of the work seems to suggest at least a mature mind.

Interpretation of political history did not have to be left to those historians who had been politicians themselves, such as Sallust and Tacitus:

---

54. Furneaux, *Tacitus*, 2:27 n. 1. He points out (as others have done) that had Curtius been the historian, Tacitus would have said so. But the latter may have considered such information irrelevant at that point.

55. See Milns *Latomus* 25 (1966): 503; Atkinson, *Curtius* i, 57.

56. Milns, *Latomus* 25 (1966): 505 nn. 3–4.

57. Aristobulus began writing at the age of eighty-four: cf. [Lucian] Macrobius 22 (= FGrH 39.T.2). The date of Ptolemy's composition is controversial; see chap. 3, 73 n. 57. Other authors who wrote in their mature years include Sallust, Asinius Pollio, and Silius Italicus. According to Syme, *Tacitus*, 2:466 f., the *Annals* were composed toward the end of Tacitus' life. Isocrates, aged ninety, was known to have published a letter to Philip II in 346. For further discussion of the aged and their productivity, see T.G. Parkin, *Demography and Roman Society* (Baltimore, 1992), 107 f.

Livy was proof enough of that.[58] Seneca the Elder, himself a rhetorician, also wrote history.[59] The rhetorical bent of Curtius' *Historiae* cannot be denied. Yet it is no cardboard exercise, built around a series of tired old topoi. A grammarian, a rhetorician, or a teacher did not have to write in isolation.

Writing contemporary Roman history or a history of the late Republic could be a risky business in the Rome of the Julio-Claudian and Flavian dynasties, and there are several noted instances where historians either voluntarily burned their books or were compelled to do so.[60] There is no reason why Curtius should not have seen lessons relevant to his own day in the political intricacies of Alexander's changing career. Although there is no proof for the identification of any of the Curtii of the first century A.D., Suetonius' rhetor is not an impossible candidate.

In summary, the *Historiae* was written by an unknown Curtius, perhaps the aforementioned rhetor. Whoever he was, he appreciated an emperor's achievement in stopping civil war and made sure he said so. That emperor was most likely Vespasian, but on the evidence we have, we cannot be certain of his identification. The nature of the history itself suggests the following conclusions; the work was written up after many years' research, by a well-educated scholar, who combined literary aspiration with political acumen. But Curtius did not restrict himself to a catalogue of moral exempla. He firmly believed himself to be a serious historian.

---

58. Cf. Tac. *Hist.* 1.1 on the suppression of truth in historical writing after Actium, which would include Livy. See Emilio Gabba, "The Historians and Augustus," in *Caesar Augustus,* ed. Fergus Millar and Erich Segal (Oxford, 1984), 76 n. 45.

59. On the fragments of Seneca's lost history and its problems, see Fairweather, *Seneca the Elder,* 15 f.; J. Wilkes, "Julio-Claudian Historians," *CW* 65 (1972): 177–92, 197–203.

60. On book burning and censorship of historical works, see F.H. Cramer, "Bookburning and censorship in Ancient Rome," *JHI* 6 (1945): 157–96.

Bibliography

This bibliography is meant only as a selection of monographs and articles of particular relevance to Quintus Curtius, Greco-Roman historiography, and Alexander studies and does not include all the literature used for this book; additional coverage of the literature is provided in the notes to the text, and see the list of abbreviations at the beginning of the book.

Adams, W.L., and E.N. Borza, eds. *Philip II, Alexander the Great, and the Macedonian Heritage*. Washington, 1982.
Atkinson, J.E. "Q. Curtius Rufus' 'Historiae Alexandri Magni.'" *ANRW* II.34.4 (1997): 3447–83.
Badian, E. "Alexander the Great and the Unity of Mankind."*Historia* 7 (1958): 425–44.
———. "The Eunuch Bagoas." *CQ* 8 (1958): 144–57.
———. "The Death of Parmenio." *TAPhA* 91 (1960): 324–38.
———. *Studies in Greek and Roman History*. Oxford, 1964.
———. "Agis III." *Hermes* 95 (1967): 170–92.
———. "A King's Notebooks." *HSCP* 72 (1968): 183–204.
———. "Nearchus the Cretan." *YCS* 24 (1975): 147–70.
———. "Some Recent Interpretations of Alexander." In *Alexandre le Grand, image et réalité,* Fondation Hardt, *Entretiens* 22, 289–94. Geneva, 1976.
———. "The Deification of Alexander the Great." In *Ancient Macedonian Studies in Honor of C.F. Edson,* ed. H.J. Dell, 27–71. Thessaloníki, 1981.
———. "Agis III: Revisions and Reflections." In *Ventures into Greek History,* ed. Ian Worthington, 258–92. Oxford, 1994.
Balsdon, J.P.V.D. "The 'Divinity' Of Alexander." *Historia* 1 (1950): 363–88.
Bardon, H. "Quinte-Curce Historien." *LEC* 15 (1947): 3–14.
Baynham, E.J. "An Introduction to the *Metz Epitome:* Its Traditions and Value." *Antichthon* 29 (1995): 60–77.
———. "Who Put the 'Romance' in the Alexander Romance? The Alexander Romances within Alexander Historiography." *AHB* 9, no. 1 (1995): 1–13.
Bödefeld, H.J. *Untersuchungen zur Datierung der Alexandergeschichte des Q. Curtius Rufus*. Düsseldorf, 1982.
Bonner, S.F. *Roman Declamation*. Liverpool, 1949.

Borza, E.N. "Cleitarchus and Diodorus' Account of Alexander."*PACA* 11 (1968): 25–45.
———. "Fire From Heaven: Alexander at Persepolis." *CPh* 67 (1972): 233–45.
———. *In the Shadow of Olympus: The Emergence of Macedon*. Princeton, 1990.
Bosworth, A.B. "Philip II and Upper Macedonia." *CQ* 21 (1971): 93–105.
———. "Arrian's Literary Development." *CQ* 22 (1972): 163–85.
———. "Arrian and the Alexander Vulgate." In *Alexandre le Grand, image et réalité*, Fondation Hardt, *Entretiens* 22, 1–46. Geneva, 1976.
———. "Alexander and Ammon." In *Greece and the Mediterranean in History and Pre-history*, ed. K. Kinzl, 51–75. Berlin, 1977.
———. "Alexander's Iranian Policy." *JHS* 100 (1980): 1–21.
———. "A Missing Year in the History of Alexander the Great." *JHS* 101 (1981): 17–39.
———. "History and Rhetoric in Curtius Rufus." *CPh* 78 (1983): 150–61.
———. "Arrian and Rome: The Minor Works." *ANRW* II.34.1 (1993): 226–75.
———. *Alexander and the East*. Oxford, 1996.
Bourazelis, K. "*Floret Imperium*: The Age of Septimius Severus and the Work of Q. Curtius Rufus." *Ariadne* 4 (1988): 244–64.
Briant, P. *Rois, Tributs et paysans*. Centre de Recherches d'Histoire Ancienne 43. Paris, 1982.
Brown, T.S. "Callisthenes and Alexander." *AJPH* 70 (1949): 225–48.
———. *Onesicritus: A Study in Hellenistic Historiography*. Berkeley, 1949.
Brunt, P.A. "From Epictetus to Arrian." *Athenaeum* 55 (1977): 19–48.
———. "On Historical Fragments and Epitomes." *CQ* 30 (1980): 477–94.
Carney, E.D. "Alexander the Great and the Macedonian Aristocracy." Ph.D. diss., Duke University, 1975.
———. "The Conspiracy of Hermolaus." *CJ* 76 (1980/81): 223–31.
———. "The Death of Cleitus." *GRBS* 22 (1981): 149–60.
———. "Regicide in Macedonia." *PP* 211 (1983): 260–72.
———. "Olympias." *Anc. Soc.* 18 (1987): 35–62.
Cary, G. *The Medieval Alexander*. Cambridge, 1956.
Currie, H. MacL. "Quintus Curtius Rufus: The Historian as Novelist?" In *Groningen Colloquia on the Novel*, 3:63–77. Groningen, 1990.
Devine, A.M. "The Parthi, the Tyranny of Tiberius, and the Date of Quintus Curtius Rufus." *Phoenix* 33 (1979): 142–59.
Dunkle, J.R. "The Greek Tyrant and Roman Political Invective of the Late Republic." *TAPhA* 98 (1967): 151–71.
Earl, D.C. *The Political Thought of Sallust*. Cambridge, 1961.
Edmunds, L. "The Religiosity of Alexander." *GRBS* 12 (1971): 363–91.
Egge, R. *Untersuchungen zur Primärtradition bei Q. Curtius Rufus*. Freiberg, 1978.
Ehrenberg, V. *Alexander and the Greeks*. Oxford, 1938.
Ellis, J. *Philip II and Macedonian Imperialism*. London, 1976.

Engels, D.W. *Alexander the Great and the Logistics of the Macedonian Army.* Berkeley, 1978.
Errington, R.M. "Bias in Ptolemy's History of Alexander." *CQ* 19 (1969): 233–42.
———. "From Babylon to Triparadeisos." *JHS* 90 (1970): 49–77.
———. "The Nature of the Macedonian State under the Monarchy." *Chiron* 8 (1978): 77–133.
———. *A History of Macedonia.* Trans. C. Errington. Berkeley, 1990.
Fairweather, J. *Seneca the Elder.* Cambridge, 1981.
Fears, J.R. "Parthi in Q. Curtius Rufus." *Hermes* 102 (1974): 623–25.
———. "The Stoic View of Alexander the Great." *Philologus* 118 (1974): 113–30.
———. "Silius Italicus, *Cataphracti,* and the Date of Q. Curtius Rufus." *CPh* 71 (1976): 214–23.
Ferguson, J. *The Religions of the Roman Empire.* London, 1970.
Flower, M. *Theopompus of Chios.* Oxford, 1994.
Fornara, C.W. *The Nature of History in Ancient Greece and Rome.* Berkeley, 1983.
Furneaux, H. *The Annals of Tacitus.* 2 vols. Oxford, 1896. Reprint, 1978.
Gill, C. "The Question of Character Development in Plutarch and Tacitus." *CQ* 33 (1983): 469–87.
Gill, C., and T.P. Wiseman, eds. *Lies and Fiction in the Ancient World.* Exeter, 1993.
Goukowsky, P. *Essai sur les origines du mythe d'Alexandre.* 2 vols. Nancy, 1978–81.
Green, Peter. *Alexander of Macedon.* Harmondsworth, 1974.
Hamilton, J.R. "Cleitarchus and Diodorus 17." In *Greece and the Mediterranean in History and Pre-history,* ed. K. Kinzl, 126–46. Berlin, 1977.
———. "The Date of Q. Curtius Rufus." *Historia* 37 (1988): 445–56.
Hammond, N.G.L. "Some Passages in Arrian Concerning Alexander." *CQ* 30 (1980): 455–76.
———. *Alexander the Great, King, Commander, and Statesman.* London, 1981.
———. *The Macedonian State.* Oxford, 1989.
———. "Royal Pages, Personal Pages, and Boys Trained in the Macedonian Manner during the Period of the Temenid Monarchy." *Historia* 39 (1990): 261–90.
Hammond, N.G.L., and G.T. Griffith. *A History of Macedonia.* Vol. 2. Oxford, 1979.
Hammond, N.G.L., and F.W. Walbank. *A History of Macedonia.* Vol. 3. Oxford, 1988.
Heckel, Waldemar. "Amyntas, Son of Andromenes." *GRBS* 16 (1975): 393–99.
———. "The Conspiracy against Philotas." *Phoenix* 31 (1977): 9–21.
———. *The Last Days and Testament of Alexander the Great: A Prosopographic Study.* Historia Einzelschriften. Vol. 56. Stuttgart, 1988.

———. "Q. Curtius Rufus and the Date of Cleander's Mission to the Peloponnese." *Hermes* 119 (1991): 124–25.
———. "Notes on Q. Curtius Rufus' History of Alexander." *AClass* 37 (1994): 67–78.
Holzberg, N. "Hellenistiches und Römisches in der Philippos Episode bei Curtius Rufus." *WJA* 14 (1988): 185–201.
Hornblower, Jane. *Hieronymus of Cardia.* Oxford, 1981.
Hornblower, Simon, ed. *Greek Historiography.* Oxford, 1994.
Kennedy, George. *The Art of Rhetoric in the Roman World.* Princeton, 1972.
Kornemann, E. *Die Alexandergeschichte des Königs Ptolemaios I von Aegypten.* Leipzig, 1935.
Korzeniewski, D. "Die Zeit des Quintus Curtius Rufus." Diss. Cologne, 1959.
Lane Fox, R. *Alexander the Great.* London, 1973.
Leeman, A.D. *Orationis Ratio.* 2 vols. Amsterdam, 1963.
Lock, R.A. "The Date of Agis' War in Greece." *Antichthon* 6 (1972): 10–27.
Luce, T.J. *Livy: The Composition of His History.* Princeton, 1977.
Marincola, J.M. "Some Suggestions on the Proem and "Second Preface" to Arrian's *Anabasis.*" *JHS* 109 (1989): 186–89.
Martin, Thomas R. "Quintus Curtius' Presentation of Philip Arrhidaeus and Josephus' Accounts of the Accession of Claudius." *AJAH* 8 (1983): 161–90.
Mederer, E. *Die Alexanderlegenden bei den ältesten Historikern.* Stuttgart, 1936.
Mensching, E. "Peripatetiker über Alexander." *Historia* 12 (1963): 274–82.
Merkelbach, R. *Die Quellen des griechischen Alexanderromans.* 2d ed. Zetemata 9. Munich, 1977.
Milns, R.D. "The Date of Curtius Rufus and the *Historiae Alexandri.*" *Latomus* 25 (1966): 490–507.
Minissale, Francesca. *Curzio Rufo: Un romanziere della storia.* Messina, 1983.
O'Brien, J.M. *Alexander the Great: The Invisible Enemy.* London, 1992.
Pédech, P. "Strabon historien d'Alexandre." *GB* 2 (1974): 129–45.
Robinson, C.A. *Alexander the Great.* 2 vols. Providence, R.I., 1953.
Roisman, J. "Why Arrian Wrote the *Anabasis.*" *RSA* 13–14 (1983– 84): 253–63.
———. "Ptolemy and His Rivals in His History of Alexander." *CQ* 34 (1984): 373–85.
Rubinsohn, Z. "The 'Philotas Affair': A Reconsideration." In *Ancient Macedonia,* 3:409–20. Thessaloníki, 1977.
Sacks, Kenneth S. *Diodorus Siculus and the First Century.* Princeton, 1990.
Samuel, A.E. "Alexander's Royal Journals." *Historia* 14 (1965): 1–12.
Schachermeyr, F. *Alexander der Grosse: Das Problem seiner Persönlichkeit und seines Wirkens.* Vienna, 1973.
Schepens, G. "Arrian's View of His Task as Alexander Historian." *Ancient Society* 2 (1971): 254–68.
Schroeder, S. "Zu Plutarchs Alexanderreden." *MH* 48 (1991): 151–57.
Shrimpton, G.S. *Theopompus the Historian.* Montreal, 1991.
Stadter, P.A. *Arrian of Nicomedia.* Chapel Hill, 1980.
Steele, R.B. "Quintus Curtius Rufus." *AJPH* 36 (1915): 401–23.

———. "Curtius and Arrian." *AJPh* 40 (1919): 43–46.
Stewart, Andrew. *Faces of Power: Alexander's Image and Hellenistic Politics.* Berkeley, 1993.
Strasburger, H. *Ptolemaios und Alexander.* Leipzig, 1934.
Stroux, J. "Die Zeit des Curtius." *Philologus* 84 (1928/29): 233–51.
Sumner, G.V. "Curtius Rufus and the *Historiae Alexandri.*" *AUMLA* 15 (1961): 30–39.
Swain, S. "Character Change in Plutarch." *Phoenix* 43 (1989): 62–68.
Syme, Ronald. *The Roman Revolution.* Oxford, 1939.
———. *Tacitus.* 2 vols. Oxford, 1958.
———. "The Career of Arrian." *HSCP* 86 (1982): 181–211.
———. "The Date of Justin and the Discovery of Trogus." *Historia* 37 (1988): 358–71.
Tarn, W.W. *Alexander the Great.* 2 vols. Cambridge, 1948.
Thomas, T.F. *Lands and Peoples in Roman Poetry.* Cambridge, 1982.
Walbank, F.W. *A Historical Commentary on Polybius.* 3 vols. Oxford, 1957–79.
———. *Polybius.* Berkeley, 1972.
Will, W. *Alexander der Grosse.* Geschichte Makedoniens, no. 2. Stuttgart, 1986.
Wirth, G. "Anmerkungen zur Arrianbiographie." *Historia* 13 (1964): 209–45.
Wirzubski, C.H. *Libertas as a Political Idea at Rome during the Late Republic and Early Principate.* Cambridge, 1950.
Wiseman, T.P. *Clio's Cosmetics.* Leicester, 1979.
Worthington, Ian, ed. *Ventures into Greek History.* Oxford, 1994.

Index

Abdalonymus (king of Sidon), 117, 127n. 85
Abii (Scythian tribe), 88n. 107
Abulites (Persian satrap), 120
Achilles, 159
L. Aelius Seianus, 217
Aeneas, 154
agathe tyche, 109–10n. 33
Agesilaus II (Spartan king), 70
Agis III (Spartan king), 37, 133, 135
 war against Macedonia, 166–69
Agis of Argos (court poet), 193
Agricola (Gnaeus Iulius), 158
Agrippina (mother of Nero), 215
Albinovanus Pedo (Roman officer and poet), 28–29, 30
Alexander ("the Lyncestian," son of Aeropus), 38, 40
 execution of, 180–81, 197
Alexander (tyrant of Pherae), 149
Alexander of Epirus, popularity of, in rhetorical tradition, 25
Alexander III of Macedon ("the Great")
 Balkan campaign, 39
 campaign against the Arii and Arachosii, 184
 care for soldiers, 190–91
 corrupted by success, 128
 cures Ptolemy, 77
 dissimulatio of, 215 (see also *dissimulatio*)
 divinity of, 162–63, 166, 178, 185, 187, 192–95, 198
 fortuna of, 118–31, 196
 heroism of, 130
 historical traditions regarding, 60–62
 illness at Tarsus, 26, 135, 141–44
 imitation of, by Romans, 10
 imitation of Achilles, 159
 leadership qualities of, 184–85
 Lycian campaign, 40
 marriage to Roxane, 190–92
 orientalism of, 51, 145, 165, 166, 169–71
 peace negotiations with Darius, 151–55
 popularity of, 2
 promulgates Exiles' Decree, 45
 as rhetorical topos, 9–11, 25–26
 self-restraint around women, 133
 sexual practices of, 170
 speeches of, in Curtius, 47–48, 147, 184
  at Hermolaus' trial, 197–98
  at Philotas' trial, 177
 strategy at Issus, 147
 superstition of, 114–15
 wounding at Malli town, 48, 74–75, 77, 166
 youth of, 39
Alexander Romance, 61–62
Alexander "Vulgate," 85
Alfonso V of Aragon, 3
Amazon queen, visit of, with Alexander, 79n. 79, 169–70
Amazons, 170
Ammianus Marcellinus (historian), affinity with Curtius, 15, 202

227

228 Index

Ammon (Libyan deity) as Zeus or
    Jupiter, 130, 161, 163, 177, 178,
    187, 198
Amyntas (officer of Alexander), 177
Amyntas (son of Andromenes), 38,
    52, 54, 156, 178, 180–83, 184,
    213
Amyntas (son of Antiochus), 139
Amyntas (son of Perdiccas III), 178
Anaxarchus of Abdera (philosopher),
    189, 193
Antiochus III, 106
Antipater (son of Iolaus), 181
    as regent of Macedonia, 166–68
Antiphanes (clerk of Alexander's cavalry), 181
Antony (Marcus Antonius), 193n. 51,
    211
Arbela (Gaugamela), battle of, 119,
    120, 122, 153, 167, 168
Archelaus (king of Cappadocia), 144
Area, 171
    Arii, 169
Ariamazes (Sogdianian dynast), 38,
    52, 92–95, 123, 129, 158, 161,
    185
Aristander of Telmessus (Alexander's
    seer), 114
Aristobulus of Cassandreia (historian)
    on Alexander's drinking habits, 190
    on Cleitus' death, 188
    on Gordian knot, 91
    history of Alexander, 69, 72–73,
        74, 83, 134
    longevity of, 218n. 57
    on Pages' Conspiracy, 51, 195
    on Philotas, 79
    on the Sogdianian Rock, 92
Aristogeiton (Athenian tyrannicide),
    51
Aristotle
    relationship to Callisthenes, 72
    on whales, 29
Aristus of Salamis (historian), 77n. 74
Arrian (L. Flavius Arrianus)
    on the burning of Persepolis, 97–99
    career of, 1–2
    on Callisthenes, 72
    digressions of, 68
    on flattery, 137
    literary ambitions of, 55–56, 68
    methodology of, 5, 13
    necrology of Darius, 122, 133
    peroratio of, 101–2, 128, 162,
        197n. 58
    speeches in, 47, 50–52
    on the Sogdianian Rock, 92–94
    use of sources, 39, 67–68, 74n. 63,
        77n. 74, 81–82
Arses (son of Artaxerxes Ochus), 41,
    152
Artabazus (son of Pharnabazus), 92,
    144, 146, 158, 186
Artacana (Artacoana), capital of Area,
    171
Artaxerxes Ochus (Persian king), 41
Artaxerxes II (Persian king), 149
Asclepiades (historian), 77n. 74
Astaspes (Persian satrap), 45, 175
Atarrhias (Macedonian officer), 180
Attalus (son of Andromenes), 180
Attalus (uncle of Cleopatra), 187
Atropates (Persian satrap), 170
Augustus (Octavian) 7, 10n. 37, 193,
    198, 204, 216, 218
    fortuna of, 110–11
    identification with Camillus, 23n.
        23
    inquiry into *ergastula*, 49
    possible identification as Curtius'
        princeps, 211–13

Babylon, 79, 83, 135, 136, 151
Bactria, 166, 186
Bagoas (Persian eunuch, chiliarch of
    Artaxerxes Ochus), 40, 152
Bagoas (Persian eunuch, favorite of
    Alexander), 6, 42, 158, 170
Bagodarus (Persian noble), 52–53
Barsine (mistress of Alexander), 191

Barzaentes (Barsaentes), Persian regicide, 169, 171
bematists (Alexander's surveyors), 61n. 14
Benzo of Alessandria (humanist), 3
Bessus (Persian noble and regicide), 52–54, 133, 156, 158, 168, 171, 184, 197, 215, 216
Betis (governor of Gaza), 95, 129, 136, 155–59, 175
Bolon (Macedonian officer), 177–78
Bucephalas (Alexander's horse), 39

M. Caelius Rufus, 102
C. Caesar and L. Caesar (grandsons of Augustus), 212
Caligula (Roman emperor), 75n. 65, 175, 204, 206, 207, 208, 214, 215, 217
   imitation of Alexander, 10n. 37
   view of Livy, 18
Callisthenes of Olynthus (historian)
   counsels Alexander, 189
   fame of, 71–72
   history of Alexander, 69
   libertas of, 54
   in Pages' Conspiracy, 51–52, 195, 198–99
   resistance to *proskynesis*, 47, 71, 140, 158, 166, 192, 193–94
Cambyses (Persian king), 62
Camillus, 23
Carmania, 25, 45, 122, 175
Cassius Chaerea (Roman centurion and assassin of Caligula), 215
cataphract cavalry, 202
Catiline (L. Sergius Catilina), 102, 103, 109, 120–21, 129, 141, 148
Cato. *See* M. Porcius Cato
Cebalinus (brother of Nicomachus), 173
Celaenae, siege of, 146, 150
Cephalus (metic at Athens), 103
Chares (historian), history of Alexander, 69, 73

Charidemus (Athenian general), 38, 52, 79, 117, 128, 137–40, 144, 145, 169, 178, 199
de Chatillon, Gauthier, 3
Chorienes (Sogdianian noble), 92
Cicero, M. Tullius
   on flattery, 136
   on *fortuna*, 108
   on historiography, 46
   linguistic affinities with Curtius, 20n. 22
   on qualities of military commanders, 122
   reference to a Q. Curtius, 216–17
   on *regnum*, 11n. 42
   on vulnerability of youth, 101
Claudius (Roman emperor), 7, 217
   admiration of Livy, 207
   affiliation with Julio-Claudians, 214
   generosity to Tyre, 205n. 18
   manipulation of, by freedmen, 129
   possible identification as Curtius' princeps, 204, 206n. 21, 207–9
   trials *intra cubiculum*, 175
M. Claudius Marcellus (Roman general), 115–16
M. Claudius Marcellus (son of Octavia), 212
Cleitarchus of Alexandria (historian)
   history of Alexander, 7, 58, 60, 69, 78–79, 95, 134
   date of composition of, 69n. 43
   proverbs of, 89
   as source of Curtius, 74–81, 139
Cleitus ("the Black," son of Dropides), murder of, 22, 51, 54, 126, 130, 166, 185–90, 192, 197, 199
clementia as a motif in Curtius, 13, 127, 134–35, 136, 143, 182–83n. 30, 197–98
Cleon (court flatterer), 47, 137, 193
Cleopatra (wife of Philip II), 192
Cobares (Gobares), Persian noble, 52–54, 140

Coenus (son of Polemocrates, phalanx commander), 174, 177
Constantine (Roman emperor), 203n. 9
contumacia as a motif in Curtius, 13, 95, 156, 158–59, 164, 175, 194
convivia (banquets), 96
Cophes (son of Artabazus), 92
Corbulo. See Cn. Domitius Corbulo
Coriolanus (Cn. Marcius), Roman general, 105
P. Cornelius Scipio Africanus
　imitation of Alexander, 10n. 37
　meeting with Hannibal at Ephesus, 19nn. 20–21
L. Cornelius Sulla, 110
Corupedion, battle of, 210
Crassus. See M. Licinius Crassus
Craterus (marshal, son of Alexander), 143, 158, 174–75
Critobulus of Cos (physician), 48, 142
Ctesiphon (Parthian capital of Babylonia), 203
Cunaxa, battle of, 149
cupido as a motif in Curtius, 90, 93, 160–62
Curtii, 216–17
Curtius (Quintus Curtius Rufus)
　attitude to *proskynesis*, 192–93
　date of, 7–8, 201–19
　digressions on Alexander's character, 96
　eulogy of new emperor, 54–55, 205–7, 209–11, 213–15
　faults of, 13
　identity of, 8, 208, 216–19
　literary background of, 15–30
　literary structure of, 5, 13, 35–46, 209–10
　modern views of, 5–6, 14
　necrology of Alexander, 45–46, 101, 103, 113, 126–31, 167, 210
　necrology of Callisthenes, 194–95, 199
　necrology of Persepolis, 205
　philosophical views of, 10, 111–16
　potential content of lost to books, 38–42
　principles of historical methodology, 5, 13, 85–90
　rationality of, 162–63
　rhetoric in, 9, 72
　stylistics aspects of, 23–24, 32–33, 207
　themes of, 12–13, 38
　transmission of, 1–5, 37
　use of sources, 7, 39, 59, 74–85, 90–100
　use of speeches, 46–54
　view of *fortuna*, 10, 103, 118, 202
　view of *regnum*, 12–13, 52, 80, 210
Curtius Rufus (proconsul of Africa), 8, 217
Q. Curtius Rufus (rhetorician in Suetonius), 8, 217–19
Cydnus R., 141
Cyrus the Great, 184
　death of, 113
　in Gedrosia, 82
　tomb of, 73n. 60
Cyrus II (the Younger), 149

Dalmatia, 208
Damascus, 83, 123
　sack of, 38, 40, 41
da Pastrengo, Guglielmo (humanist), 3
Darius I (Persian king), 152
Darius III (Persian king)
　accession of, 40–41
　attire of, 141
　characterization of, 132–64, 216
　cowardice of, 132, 148, 149
　family captured, 2, 117, 118, 129, 150, 191
　final days and death of, 42–44, 112–13, 134, 135
　fortuna of, 118–23
　　corrupted by *fortuna*, 137

speeches in Curtius, 47, 52
strategy at Issus, 147
treatment of Charidemus, 38, 128, 136–40
treatment of Greek mercenaries, 145–46
Decembrio, Angelo (editor of Curtius), 37
Decembrio, Pier Candido, 3
Demaratus (Spartan king), 139
Demetrius (bodyguard of Alexander), 173
Demetrius ("Poliorcetes," son of Antigonus), 73
Dido (Carthaginian queen), 110
Dinon of Colophon (historian), 80
Diodorus Siculus (historian)
  methodology of, 85n. 102
  popularity of, 1
  tyche in, 117–18
  use of Cleitarchus, 77–78
Dionysus. *See* Father Liber
Dionysius of Halicarnassus, speeches of, in *Roman Antiquities*, 46
Dioscuri, 187
Dioxippus (Athenian athlete), 79–80, 96, 166
dissimulatio as a motif in Curtius, 165, 172, 174, 175
Diyllus (historian), 58n. 4
dogs, fighting, of India, 86
Domitian (Roman emperor), 106, 158, 175, 204, 209
Cn. Domitius Corbulo (Roman general), 14n. 50, 167
  treatment of Paccius Orfitus, 34
Drangae, 171
Drusus (Nero Claudius) 45
Dymnus of Chalaestra (conspirator), 172–74, 176

Ecbatana, 43, 120
Egypt, 62, 159, 163
Ennius (Roman poet), 106
Ephemerides, 61, 72, 83

Ephippus (historian), 61n. 15
Ephorus (historian), 16–17
Epicureanism, 112, 114
Epicurus, 105
Epimenes (Macedonian Page and conspirator), 196
Eratosthenes (geographer), 60, 73, 74n. 63
ergastulum (slave prison), 49–50
Erigyius (son of Larichus), 149, 174
Ethiopians, 160, 161
Euctemon of Cyme, 49–50
Euergetae (Benefactors), 184
Euphrates River, 153, 154, 203
Euripides, 187

Father Liber (Dionysus/Bacchus) 38, 189–90
fatum as a motif in Curtius, 111–12
fides as a motif in Curtius, 13, 21, 22, 40, 88, 114, 118, 132, 134, 136, 137, 141–42, 145, 149, 152, 156, 159, 177–78, 182, 186, 188, 196–98
flattery
  at Alexander's court, 165, 193
  in Greco-Roman literature, 136–37
fortuna
  Curtius' concept of, 10, 103
  Fortuna Muliebris, 105
  in Greco-Roman art, 108
  in Greco-Roman traditions, 104–11
  temples to, 105–6
Freinsheim, Johannes Caspar (editor of Curtius), 4

Galba (Roman emperor), 7, 204n. 12, 208
  adoption of Piso, 103
Gaugamela, battle of, 38, 71n. 51
Gaza, Alexander's siege of, 39, 114, 126
Gedrosia, Alexander's crossing of, 38, 81–82

Germanicus Caesar
  achievements of, 167
  compared with Alexander, 11
Gilgamesh (Babylonian epic hero), 62
Glaucias (physician), 142
Gordian III (Roman emperor), 203n. 9
Gordian knot, Curtius' narrative of, 23–24, 90–92, 150, 161
Granicus, battle of, 38, 39

Hadrian (Roman emperor), 7, 203n. 9
Halicarnassus, 126
Halys River, 153
Hannibal (Carthaginian general)
  death of, 113
  self-abnegation of, 141
  See also P. Cornelius Scipio Africanus
Harmodius (Athenian tyrannicide), 51
Harpalus (son of Machatas), death of, 45
Hecatompylus (capital of Parthia), 202, 203
Hector (son of Parmenion), 174
Hector (son of Priam), 159
Hedicke, Edmund (editor of Curtius), 3, 4, 5
Hegesias of Magnesia (orator and historian), 60n. 12, 156, 157
Hegesimachus (Macedonian noble youth), 123
Hellanice (Alexander's nurse, sister of Cleitus "the Black"), 39, 186
Hellespont, 153
Hephaestion (son of Amyntor), 39, 80, 125, 142, 174
Heracles
  Arrian's digression on, 68
  journey of, to Siwah, 161
Hermolaus (son of Sopolis, conspirator), 50–52, 54, 179, 195–99
  speech of, 196–97
Herodotus of Halicarnassus
  interest in Scythians, 88
  statement of methodology, 86
Hieronymus of Cardia (historian), 60, 100
Horatius, 176
Tullus Hostilius (Roman king), 176
Hydaspes River, 38, 123
Hyphasis River, mutiny at, 48, 166
Hyrcania, 61

Ichthyophagi ("Fish-Eaters"), 81
Illyria, 39
India, 73, 166, 168
  Curtius' digression on, 10
Ipsus, battle of, 72, 210
Iskandarnamah (Persian medieval romance), 62n. 18, 124
Isocrates (rhetorician)
  influence of, 16–17
  longevity of, 218n. 57
Issus, battle of, 2, 38, 119, 120, 133, 136, 146–50, 167

Janus, 212
Jason, 187
Judaea, 208, 211
Jugurtha, 102
Julius Caesar (C. Iulius Caesar)
  clementia of, 143
  divorce of Pompeia, 177n. 21
  fortuna of, 110
  imitation of Alexander, 10n. 37
  offered crown by Antony, 193
  as the *sidus Iulium,* 212
Justin (epitomist)
  Epitome of Pompeius Trogus, 1n. 3
  date of, 30n. 1
  methodology of, 31–32

Le Brun, Charles (French artist), 2, 125
Leonnatus (bodyguard of Alexander), 174
Lepidus (M. Aemilius) Triumvir, 211, 212

libertas as a motif in Curtius, 12, 13, 21, 23, 54, 136, 137, 139, 140, 158, 164, 166, 175, 178–79, 188, 189, 192, 196–99
licentia as a motif in Curtius, 13, 21, 42, 96, 128, 136, 159, 188, 190, 192
M. Licinius Crassus (proconsul of Macedonia), 167
C. Licinius Mucianus, 204
Livy (Titus Livius)
 attitude to Augustus, 23n. 32
 digression on Alexander, 11
 fame of, 18–19, 54
 influence on Curtius, 20–25, 35, 75–76, 207
 longevity of, 218
 purpose of history, 200
 speeches in, 46–47, 48
 summary of Hannibal's character, 129
 theme of Roman power, 167
 use of pentads, 36
Lucan (Marcus Annaeus Lucanus), 160
 affinity with Curtius, 15
 on Julius Caesar's *fortuna,* 110
 negative view of Alexander, 11
Lycia, 40

Macrobius (Ambrosius Theodosius), literary critic, 216
Malli (Indian tribe), 48, 74–78, 122
Maracanda (Samarkand), 186
Marathus, 151, 153
Marcellus. *See* M. Claudius Marcellus
Mardi (in Persis), 135
Marsyas of Pella (historian), 134
Mazaces (Persian satrap), 159
Media, 43, 170, 174, 177, 183
Medius of Larissa (historian), 69, 73
Megasthenes (historian), 60, 73
Meleager (Macedonian phalanx commander), 199, 209–10, 211, 212

Memnon of Rhodes (Greek mercenary general), 138
Memphis, 160
Metron (Page of Alexander), 173
Musicani (Indian tribe), 129
Mützell, J. (editor of Curtius), 4, 206

Nabarzanes (Persian chiliarch), 41, 53–54, 121, 144, 146, 158, 170
Nasamones, 160, 209
Nearchus (son of Androtimus, admiral and historian)
 adviser to Demetrius, 72–73
 appointment as satrap of Lycia, 40
 history of Alexander, 69, 70, 72–74, 81–82
Nectanebo (Egyptian pharaoh), 62
Nepos, Cornelius, non-Roman biographies of, 55
Nero (Roman emperor), 7, 10n. 37, 75–76, 106, 140, 167, 195, 204, 215, 217
Nerva (Roman emperor), 204, 209
Nicanor (Macedonian noble youth), 123
Nicanor (son of Parmenion), 174
Nicholas of Cuse (cardinal), 3
Nicobule, 61n. 15
Nicomachus (lover of Dymnus), 172–73
Niger. *See* G. Pescennius Niger

Ochus (son of Darius III), 154
C. Octavius. *See* Augustus
Olympias (mother of Alexander), 130
Onesicritus of Astypalaea (historian)
 history of Alexander, 69, 72–73, 74, 81
 methods of, 70
Opis, 65, 156
Orpheus, 187
Orsines (Persian satrap), 42, 45, 112, 130
Otho (Roman emperor), 204

Oxathres, brother of Darius III, 148, 158
Oxus River, 92, 185
Oxyartes (Bactrian noble, father of Roxane), 92, 191

Pacuvius (Roman poet), 106–8
Paeonia, 39
Pages, Conspiracy of, 122, 135, 166, 192, 195–200
Pamphylia, 40, 71n. 51
Pannonia, 36
Parapanisadae, 184
Parmenion (son of Philotas, marshal), 51, 97–98, 126, 142–43, 146, 150, 187
  accused at Philotas' trial, 177
  advice of, as a literary motif, 146, 154–55
  death of, 172, 183–84
  necrology of, 184
Parthia, Parthians, 169, 202, 203n. 5
Patron (Greek mercenary commander), 112, 113
Paulus of Aegina (physician), 142
Pelopidas (Theban general), 149
Perdiccas (son of Orontes, bodyguard), 44, 83, 133, 174, 188, 210, 211
Peripatetics, attitude of, to Alexander, 71
  on *tyche*, 105
Persepolis, 42, 48, 50, 87, 95, 135. *See also* Alexander III of Macedon; Arrian; Curtius
Perseus, 161
G. Pescennius Niger, 204
Peucestas (bodyguard of Alexander) at Malli town, 77
Philip the Acarnanian (Alexander's physician), 26, 38, 39, 48, 141–43, 178
Philip II (king of Macedon, father of Alexander), 103, 130, 138, 144, 162, 181, 186

  divine honors for, 163n. 60
  initiation into mysteries at Samothrace, 186–87
  marriages of, 192n. 47
Philip III (Arrhidaeus, Alexander's brother), 44, 210, 212, 215
Philotas (son of Parmenion), 48, 51, 79, 126, 135, 143, 145, 158, 164, 165, 170, 181, 183, 194, 198, 199
  arrest and trial of, 171–80
  speech at trial, 178–79
Photius (historian), 100
Pindar
  on Odysseus, 109
  on *tyche*, 104, 110
Pisidia, 40
Plato
  on *tyche*, 104–5
  on tyranny, 136
Aulus Plautius, 208
Pliny the Elder (Gaius Plinius)
  on *fortuna*, 108
  on whales, 29
Pliny the Younger (Gaius Plinius Caecilius Secundus)
  advised by Trajan, 158
  affinity with Curtius, 15, 54
  enjoyment of Livy, 19
Plutarch of Chaeronea
  on Alexander's fortune, 11
  attitude to Callisthenes, 72
  on *parrhesia*, 140
  popularity of, 1
  on Rome's *fortuna*, 110
  on *tyche*, 105
Polemon (son of Andromenes), 180–82
Asinius Pollio (historian)
  evaluation of Cicero, 19
  imitation of Thucydides, 17
  view of Livy, 18
Polyaenus (historian), 92–94
Polybius (historian)
  influence on Livy, 48

pragmatic approach to historiography, 18n. 17
treatment of *tyche,* 105, 120
view of Ephorus and Theopompus, 17n. 9
Polyclitus (historian)
history of Alexander, 69, 73
Polydamas (Macedonian officer), 183
Polystratus (Macedonian soldier), 43
Pompeia. *See* Julius Caesar
Cn. Pompeius Magnus (Pompey the Great)
death of, 113
imitation of Alexander, 10n. 37
Pompeius Trogus
date of, 31
influence on Curtius, 20, 30–35
on kingship, 11–12
structure of history, 35
style of, 30, 31
transmission of, 1
on world empire, 55
M. Porcius Cato (Uticensis), 143
M. Porcius Latro (rhetorician), 218
Porus (Indian king), 38, 95, 123–24, 129, 133, 158
bravery of, 148
pothos, 90, 161
Praetorian guards, 207, 209
proskynesis, 192n. 49, 196
Pseudo-Callisthenes. *See* Alexander Romance
Ptolemy I (Soter)
Arrian's use of, 83–84
attitude to Philotas, 79
Curtius' use of, 74–76, 82, 84–85
on the Gordian knot, 91
history of Alexander, 7, 69, 71, 72–74, 134
kingship of, 134
on Pages' Conspiracy, 57, 195
seizure of Alexander's body, 45–46, 83–84
wounded in India, 77

Pyrrhus (Molossian king of Epirus), 113

Quintilian (Marcus Fabius Quintilianus), grammarian
list of historians, 17
list of imperial writers, 24
view of Livy, 18
view of writing history, 16

regnum
Curtius' concept of, 12–13
Livy's interest in, 21–23
positive aspects of, 134
as a theme in Greco-Roman literature, 11
themes of, in Curtius, 135–36
Romulus (legendary king of Rome)
killing of Remus, 21
wins the *spolia opima,* 149
Roxane (Bactrian princess, wife of Alexander), 86, 166
marriage to Alexander, 190–92

Sallust (C. Sallustius Crispus)
affinity of the *Jugurtha* with Curtius' *Historiae,* 20
career of, 218
description of Jugurtha, 102
on *fortuna,* 108–9
interest in character, 9
on *metus externus,* 168
on *regnum,* 11
speeches in, 48
Sambus (Indian king), 74
Samothrace, 187
Sassanids, 202, 203
Satibarzanes (Persian noble), 149, 171
Schachermeyr, Fritz, view of Alexander, 12, 63, 65–66
Scipio. *See* P. Cornelius Scipio Africanus
Scribonianus (L. Arruntius Camillus), 208

Scythians
    and dialogue in Curtius, 48, 79
    envoy's speech, 87–89, 123, 163, 184–85, 194, 198
Sejanus. See L. Aelius Seianus
Semiramis (Assyrian queen), 82
Seneca the Elder (L. Annaeus)
    affinity with Curtius, 15, 27–30
    composed history, 219
Seneca the Younger (L. Annaeus)
    affinity with Curtius, 15, 207
    on flattery, 137
    on *libertas,* 140
    negative view of Alexander, 11
Septimius Severus (Roman emperor), 7, 203n. 9, 204
Severus Alexander (Roman emperor), 7, 203n. 9
Servius Tullius (king of Rome), 23
    and *fortuna,* 105
Shakespeare, William, 138
Silanus (C. Appius Iunius), 208
Silius Italicus, affinity with Curtius, 15
Simmias (son of Andromenes), 181
Sisimithres (Sogdianian noble), 92
Sisines (Persian noble), 144–45, 146
Sisygambis (mother of Darius III)
    Curtius' portrayal of, 80–81
    death of, 101
    meeting with Alexander, 124–27
    treatment under Artaxerxes Ochus, 41
Siwah, Alexander's visit to, 72, 84, 126, 136, 155, 158, 159–64, 185
Socrates, 103
Sogdiana, 82, 92, 123, 166, 184
Soli, 146
Sophocles, 138
sophrosyne, 68, 94, 166, 189
Sostratus (Macedonian Page and conspirator), 196
Spirensis, Vindelinus (first editor of Curtius), 4
Spitamenes (Bactrian rebel), 122

spolia opima (Roman decoration), 149
Stateira (daughter of Darius), 153
Statius, affinity with Curtius, 15
Stoicism in Roman historiography, 111
Subrius Flavus, 179
Sudracae (Oxydrace), Indian tribe, 74n. 64
Suiones, islands of, 30
Sulla. See L. Cornelius Sulla
Susa, 120, 156

Tacfarinas, revolt of, 36
Tacitus, Cornelius (historian), 3, 218
    affinity with Curtius, 15, 35, 72, 75–76
    attitude to Thrasea Paetus, 194–95n. 55
    belief in astrology, 10n. 35, 114
    impact of, 54
    interest in character, 9
    on *libertas,* 158
    necrology of Tiberius, 168
    on the servility of the Roman Senate, 190n. 45
    speeches in, 48, 52
    use of hexads, 36
    view of Alexander, 9
Tarn, Sir William Woodthorpe
    criticism of Curtius' methodology, 86, 101
    view of Curtius, 5
    views of Alexander, 63–65
Tarquinius Superbus (last king of Rome), 21, 22, 176
Tarsus, 26, 115, 141, 145
temeritas as a motif in Curtius, 90, 108, 115–16, 157
M. Terentius (Roman *eques*), trial of, 34n. 59, 52, 213, 215
Thais (Athenian courtesan), 95, 97
Thalestris. See Amazon queen
Theaetetus of Athens, 49–50

Thebes, revolt of, 39n. 75, 68, 126, 159
Theodosius (Roman emperor), 203n. 9
Theopompus (historian), 16–17n. 9
  structure of history, 35
Thrace, 36, 166
Thrasea Paetus (P. Clodius Thrasea Paetus), 72, 140, 194n. 54, 195
Thucydides
  incompleteness of history, 35
  methodological principles of, 19
  on *tyche*, 104
Thymondas (son of Mentor), 139
Tiberius (Roman emperor), 106, 168, 204, 207, 212, 217
  dissimulatio of, 215
Tigris River, 116, 119, 203
Timagenes (historian), 16, 58, 74, 75–76n. 69
  career of, 76n. 69
  Curtius' view of, 7
  Livy's view of, 59n. 6
Titus (Roman emperor), 204
Trajan (Roman emperor), 7, 10n. 37, 158, 204
  foreign policy of, 203
  imitation of Alexander, 209
  possible identification as Curtius' *princeps*, 209
Trogodytes, 160
Trogus. See Pompeius Trogus
Tullia (wife of Tarquinius Superbus), 22–23
tyche. See *fortuna*
Tyche of Antioch, 109
Tyre
  Alexander's siege of, 39, 119, 126, 151, 153, 154, 155, 159
  prosperity of, 202, 204–5

Utica, 143

Valerius Asiaticus, 207
Valerius Maximus (rhetorician)
  affinity with Curtius, 15, 25–27
  treatment of Alexander as *exemplum*, 26
L. Valerius Primanus, 218
Varus (Publius Quinctilius) 155n. 45
Vegio, Maffeo (humanist), 35n. 63
Veii (Etruscan city), 36
Velleius Paterculus (historian), 168
  affinity with Curtius, 15, 25
Veronese, Paolo (artist), 2, 125
Vergil, affinity with Curtius, 212
Veturia (mother of Coriolanus), 105
Vespasian (Roman emperor), 7
  coinage of, 214
  possible identification as Curtius' *princeps*, 204, 211, 213–15, 219
M. Vinicius, 207
vis as a motif in Curtius, 21–22, 92, 132, 136, 144, 149, 155, 180, 183, 185, 197
Vitellius (Roman emperor), 204
Volumnia (wife of Coriolanus), 105
von Ems, Rudolph, 3

Walter, Philip (bishop), 3
whales, ancient views of, 29

Xerxes, 97, 139, 152

Zumpt, C.G. (editor of Curtius), 4